GARDENING *for the* BIRDS

Gardening FOR THE Birds

How to Create a Bird-Friendly Backyard

George Adams

TIMBER PRESS

PORTLAND • LONDON

Photo credits appear on pages 442–443.
"Bird Nest Box Shelf Dimensions" on page 28 adapted from Homes for Birds, Conservation Bulletin 14, U.S. Department of the Interior, 1969.

This revised, expanded work incorporates portions of the author's *Birdscaping Your Garden*, first published in 1994 by Rodale Press in association with Lansdowne Publishing Pty. Limited.

Published in 2013 by Timber Press, Inc.

The Haseltine Building
133 S.W. Second Avenue, Suite 450
Portland, Oregon 97204-3527
timberpress.com

2 The Quadrant
135 Salusbury Road
London NW6 6RJ
timberpress.co.uk

Printed in China
Designed by Union Page Works

Library of Congress Cataloging-in-Publication Data
Adams, George Martin.
Gardening for the birds : how to create a bird-friendly backyard / George Adams. -- Rev.
p. cm.
Includes bibliographical references and index.
ISBN 978-1-60469-409-3
1. Gardening to attract birds--North America. 2. Bird refuges--North America.
3. Birds--North America. 4. Plants, Ornamental--North America. I. Title. II. Title: How to create a
bird-friendly garden.
QL676.5.A28 2013
598.156'4--dc23

2012037562

To my wife, Dianne, who should be included as coauthor but who graciously declined, and to Corinne Mansell for her unstinting help and support in bringing this book to life.

CONTENTS

INTRODUCTION

Birds have inspired mankind through the ages, bringing joy, song, and color to our gardens while taking away only insect pests. You and your family can have countless hours of pleasure from birds, plants, and the natural environment when you create a bird-friendly garden as your own backyard sanctuary. Your garden will become a source of entertainment and a restful escape from the pressures of the outside world.

When you landscape your yard with carefully chosen regional native plants to provide food, shelter, and nesting sites for birds, you'll find that an increased variety of birds will visit—species that might not usually be regarded as garden birds or attracted to a bird feeder. You will be providing a variety of food niches in your garden, and you will also be creating an environment that will encourage biodiversity, from the tiny organisms we are barely aware of, to captivating butterflies, moths, and dragonflies. Even if you only have a small place for planting, choosing plants that are beneficial to birds will add to the overall availability of habitat for our local bird populations.

A great benefit of creating a bird-friendly landscape is enjoying your garden while watching a bluebird dropping in for a worm in a freshly dug patch, a phoebe snapping at insects, or a hummingbird probing nectar-rich flowers while robins sing in the trees. Simply put, when you create a garden with attracting birds in mind, you will be providing an open invitation for spectacular birds to make your garden their home.

To attract birds to your garden, the backbone of your landscaping plan should be local native plants. By putting in native plants and using an organic, sustainable approach to gardening, you establish a balanced ecosystem in your yard. A greater variety of birds and butterflies will visit and linger, insect pests will be kept under control by insect-eating birds (reducing the need for harmful insecticides), and the wonder of nature will be part of your everyday living environment.

The ultimate aim of this book is to give you the tools to set up a sustainable ecosystem in your

Ruby-throated hummingbird nectaring on trumpet vine (*Campsis radicans*).

Ash-throated flycatcher
near its nest hollow in
a Fremont cottonwood
(*Populus fremontii*).

own yard. There, the natural order of things can flourish and you can count the local birds among your companions.

• • •

It is easy to turn an ordinary landscape into an extraordinary backyard filled with lively, colorful birds. In this book, I explain how. First, I introduce you to the basics of planning and creating a bird-friendly garden. I discuss the elements that all birds need—food, water, shelter, and nesting sites—and give you plenty of practical suggestions for providing them in your yard. You'll find details on creating a hummingbird garden, and how to use wild-flowers to provide for butterflies and seed-eating birds. I've also included flowering and fruiting calendars to help you select plants for a continuous supply of nectar, fruit, and seeds. And I offer tips for the best native nesting and shelter plants and how to build nest boxes.

Next, in part 2, I guide you through under-standing how your yard fits into the larger envi-ronment of your region and what plants will grow well in your geographic area. I discuss the importance of native plants in attracting birds, and give you helpful information on planning and creating a garden that will be full of likely bird habitats. To help you get your garden up and growing, I include many how-to tips: on soil care, planting, plant care, and plant feeding. And to make this section even more useful, I clarify how to choose and use plants in the garden to attract the most diverse range of birds. You'll also find suggestions on working with small garden spaces, and how to protect your garden from pests and unwanted visitors.

The Plant Directory, part 3, is a detailed guide to important North American native plants that provide food, shelter, and nesting sites for local birds. The native trees, shrubs, vines, perennials, annuals, ground covers, and grasses I describe are all beautiful landscape plants that appeal to the gardener as much as to the birds. Many of them may already occur naturally in your area. Each plant is discussed and many are illustrated in a color photograph. You'll find a list of birds attracted to the plants. Then I give the best plant species for attracting birds, with descriptions, distribu-tion, cultivation information, and hardiness zones for each.

Part 4, the Bird Directory, provides discussion of many of the delightful birds you may want to attract to your backyard garden. I have featured a broad selection of the most beloved birds from coast to coast, from the eastern bluebird to Anna's hummingbird. Each entry has a photo of the bird and one of my original drawings of the bird with a favorite native plant. You'll find a description of the bird and its habits, what its song sounds like, plus its preferred habitat, breeding behavior, nesting style, and feeding habits. A range map is provided for each bird, along with its migration and winter range and its breeding range, so you can see if it lives or spends time in your area. A list of plants for food and shelter tells you good plant choices to attract each bird.

At the back of the book, I've also provided a metric conversion chart. And if you want to learn more about birding and gardening to attract birds, I have included a resources section as well as a reading list. Joining some of the organizations listed in the resources is not only a great way to learn more; it's a wonderful way to meet other native plant enthusiasts and fellow bird fans.

• • •

By establishing a bird-friendly ecosystem around your home, arresting color, birdsong, and the antics of our native birds will add to the splendor of native trees, shrubs, and wildflowers to create a spiritually uplifting garden environment. You will also be making an important contribution toward the preservation of North America's distinctive natural heritage.

Male northern cardinal feeding on winterberry (*Ilex verticillata*) fruits in winter.

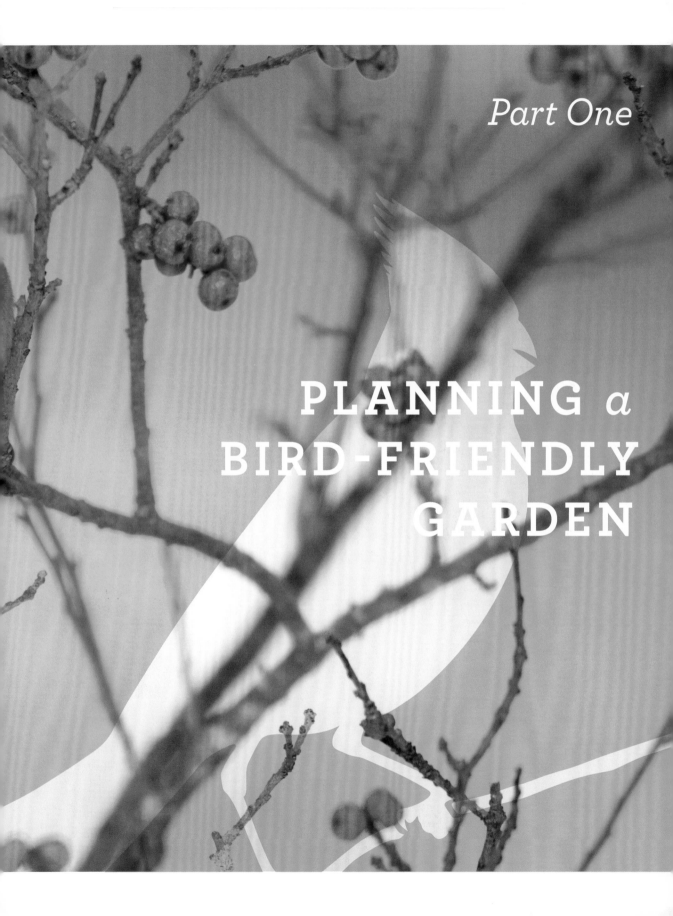

Part One

PLANNING *a* BIRD-FRIENDLY GARDEN

How do you turn your yard into an inviting sanctuary, where birds will come to nest, raise their families, and seek shelter for the winter? To start, look at your yard from a bird's-eye point of view. Find a vantage point where you can see the whole front yard or backyard at once (try the front steps or an upstairs window). Then ask yourself these questions:

➤ Are there places for birds to hide? Songbirds need protective cover from potential enemies, like cats.

➤ Are there places for birds to nest? Birds will be drawn to your yard during the breeding season if it offers inviting places for them to nest, such as suitable trees, shrubs, hedges, brambles, and vines.

➤ Are there sheltered areas where birds can protect themselves from the elements? Evergreens, shrubs planted against walls, and other sheltered areas will give birds a place out of the cold, wind, and rain.

➤ Is there food and water? It's important to provide natural food sources—flowers for nectar, grass seed heads, fruits, berries, and a diversity of plants to attract insects—since many songbirds are insectivores. You can garden with birds in mind for winter, for instance, by choosing plants that keep their berries or seeds well into the coldest months. A small pond or pool will attract thirsty birds and an interesting assortment of wildlife, including frogs, toads, butterflies, and dragonflies.

Now, take an inventory of your house and yard. Sketch a rough plan of your yard on graph paper. Draw in existing trees and shrubs you wish to keep, outline the house, and note the garage, doors, windows, pathways, and so on. Mark any pleasant views you wish to preserve or undesirable views you would like to screen out. Note any changes in elevation, soil differences, natural features like big rocks or trees, and shade patterns that could affect plantings. Consider sun-exposure/ weather and moisture issues: For example, a slope facing south will be warmer than one facing north, and a hillside will have better drainage than a level area.

Once you've sketched out and annotated your property plan, familiarize yourself with what grows well in your region. Visit local botanical gardens, arboretums, private gardens, and natural areas to see what's growing. If pine trees grow naturally in your neighborhood, then native plants that love shade and an acid soil (like pines) should thrive in your yard. If you find

ATTRACTING BIRDS *to* YOUR YARD

beech trees in local wooded areas, you'll know that plants thriving in semishade and in alkaline soil would be more appropriate. Maple trees indicate a more neutral soil.

If you're new to the idea of gardening with birds in mind, you'll usually get the best results if you stick to plants found growing naturally within a radius of 100 miles of your garden. In fact, I recommend using native plants in your landscape whether you're a beginning, intermediate, or advanced gardener and birder. I derive extra satisfaction from growing native plants that have evolved along with most of the birds in my area. Native plants can look attractive in both naturalistic or formal gardens, and you know they will be hardy when they are local. In part 3 of the book, Plant Directory, I list a wide range of native plants that are excellent ones for attracting birds.

A good way to find out about plants that are indigenous to your area is to contact your local native plant society. You can reach out to these organizations for guidance or, better still, you can join a group and help to preserve wild plants. These folks can also recommend reputable nurseries that sell a wide selection of nursery-propagated native plants. Other helpful resources are your local extension agent, state college of agriculture, and state forester.

You'll also want to become familiar with the U.S. Department of Agriculture (USDA) Plant Hardiness Zone Map, to learn which zone(s) you live in. On the Internet, you will find the updated, 2012 USDA Plant Hardiness Zone Map for the United States and the Plant Hardiness Zones of Canada Map. Each country is divided into plant hardiness zones that indicate the northern limit of a plant's natural distribution based on minimum average temperatures. In the book, you will find a zone range recommended for each plant discussed (Zones 5–9, for example).

Once you've discovered which plants grow well in your area, it's time to narrow the list for your particular landscaping plan. You'll want to put in a wide variety of plants, which will encourage a diversity of insects, fruits, and flowers, so that a range of bird species will be attracted to your garden. So select plants that will provide alternate layers of foliage. For example, grow tall trees with shorter trees, shrubs, wildflowers, and ground covers to create continuous layers of foliage from ground level to the tallest tree's foliage. Layered plants provide cover for many types of birds. If you choose plants that have a variety of shapes and foliage textures, you'll attract more birds.

You can plant your shrubs in natural-looking drifts, or for a more formal look, border your drifts of flowers with an evergreen, clipped hedge. The Calendar for Seasonal Fruiting (page 105) will help you select not only early fruiting shrubs but also shrubs that hold their fruits throughout the winter, to create a garden that's attractive for you as well as useful to birds throughout the year. Shrub borders are an excellent way to mark your property boundaries and provide for the birds. To give birds protective cover and a suitable nesting environment, the narrowest part of a shrub border between the property line and the lawn should be at least 8 feet wide. Allow some room for a colorful display of wildflowers, and a dense thicket of tangled vines and shrubs for small birds to hide and nest in.

Consider reclaiming the front yard for your private use by screening it with an evergreen hedge that's also useful to birds. Hedge plants like hemlocks, native roses, and hollies provide food and offer protection from predators. A group of evergreens, such as red cedars, spruces, or pines, will provide essential shelter for birds. If you have room, create a grove of evergreens in the backyard.

If you only have a small area for planting, be sure to learn the size plants reach at maturity. Try to select plants of a suitable size or alternatively look for compact forms. For example, blue spruce (*Picea pungens*) grows 65 to 115 feet tall in the wild, but several dwarf cultivars growing 5 to 10 feet tall are readily available. Some larger trees can be grown in containers to restrict their growth, and many are suitable for hedging. In a small area, consider many of the beautiful native vines that will grow well on a trellis or fence. You can also take advantage of the local trees that are not in your yard but are nearby and can be an extension of your garden plan.

Plan your lawn area with informal (or formal) borders, and break it up with gardens, shrubs, trees, and ground covers. Large lawns are useless to most birds except for American robins, northern flickers, and European starlings because birds usually need cover close by. Large lawn areas of traditional short-grass species are non-native and create a monoculture of little value in an ecosystem. They use excessive amounts

Layered New York garden with a birdbath placed near protective foliage, providing water, an essential element in a garden planted to attract birds and butterflies. Plants include black-eyed Susan (*Rudbeckia hirta*), purple coneflower (*Echinacea purpurea*), butterflyweed (*Asclepias tuberosa*), bee balm (*Monarda didyma*), and jewelweed (*Impatiens capensis*).

of water and need pesticides to keep weeds under control, an unhealthy environment for birds. So consider how much lawn area you actually need to satisfy your needs.

If you are delighted by the thought of attracting hummingbirds and butterflies to your garden, find which hummingbirds are likely to visit your area and when they are likely to be present. Then plant a variety of nectar-producing "hummingbird flowers" with a continuous sequence of flowering over the period that the birds are found in your locality.

You'll get the most pleasure from your landscape if you plan pathways through the garden so you can enjoy it close up. But don't forget to plan areas that can be left undisturbed, for nesting.

Before proceeding with planting, test your plan by marking the different garden areas with lengths of hose or string. To site major shrubs and trees, use filled plastic leaf bags or garbage cans to represent shrubs, and poles or stakes to indicate trees. Check the placement of your plants from several angles before you start planting, to double-check how they will all fit and grow together. To help you conceptualize your garden, I have included a typical landscape plan on page 166.

Native garden featuring Texas hill country wildflowers, which provide natural food, shelter, and nesting sites for a variety of birds.

PROVIDING FOOD, SHELTER, *and* NESTING SITES

If you want to attract a favorite bird to your garden, you'll want to first learn more about that bird. Find out where it lives, nests, or winters in your area, or whether it passes through during spring and fall migration. If the bird spends at least some time each year in your locale, you'll want to discover its favorite plants for food and shelter. (For more information, see part 4, the Bird Directory.)

Food

Many birds are closely associated with a particular plant species for food. Cedar waxwings, for example, are fond of the berries of eastern red cedar, and when the piñon seed crop is poor in one area, flocks of pinyon jays may fly hundreds of miles in search of a supply elsewhere. The yellow-rumped warbler was formerly known as the myrtle warbler, a name that reflects its taste for bayberry

Male American goldfinch feeds on the seeds of the cup plant (*Silphium perfoliatum*). At the junction of the stem and branches of this plant, the leaves form a cup where water collects, which becomes a source of drinking water for birds and insects.

Golden-crowned kinglet gathering insects from foliage.

Red-breasted nuthatch prizes insects from bark.

White-crowned sparrow feeding on seeds. A generous layer of mulch for foraging birds is considered the first layer in a bird-friendly garden.

House finch feeding on the seeds of a creosote bush (*Larrea tridentata*).

(also called wax myrtle). During migration, these tiny birds gather by the thousands along the Atlantic Coast to refuel on the waxy gray bayberry fruits. The cactus wren doesn't depend on its namesake plant for food, but it does rely on the thorns of cholla and other spiny plants to discourage predators from reaching its nest in cacti. The pine warbler usually builds its nest in pines, and often weaves pine needles into its nest. Many plants with tube-shaped flowers provide nectar for hummingbirds, which have long, thin bills adapted for these flowers.

Birds are attracted to the succulent fruits produced by many North American plants. These fruits, when immature, are usually green and hidden in the foliage. When the fruits ripen, they turn bright colors that attract birds to the tasty feast. The birds feed on the fruit and in turn spread the seeds, propagating the species and sometimes extending its range. Mistletoe relies totally on birds for colonization. When other food is scarce in winter months, mistletoe provides birds, including bluebirds and cedar waxwings, with its bite-sized berries, a major food for many birds. Jays play a role in reforesting, especially burned or logged land, when they bury acorns in good seasons and then do not come back for them.

You can lure a wide variety of birds to your backyard with a careful selection of garden plants that will provide a succession of flowering, fruiting, and seed set. The plants discussed in this book, with their long flowering time and abundant supply of fruit, nectar, and seeds, are ideal for welcoming birds to your yard throughout the year, even in winter. For example, many trees and shrubs will hold their fruits well into winter, and many ornamental grasses and wildflowers also keep their seed heads over winter. If you design your garden following the suggestions in this book, you can attract many species of birds to areas where they have not been seen for many years. Within the space of your yard, you may find hummingbirds sipping nectar from flowers, chickadees pecking insects from foliage, woodpeckers extracting insects from tree trunks, cedar waxwings feeding on fruits from branches, sparrows munching on grass seeds, wrens searching the understory for insects, and swallows flying overhead with mouths agape to take flying insects on the wing.

Shelter

Birds have many ways to regulate their body temperature to keep cool in summer and warm in winter. Feathers are amazing insulators, and when birds fluff out their feathers, they are creating small, insulated air pockets for warmth. Their legs and feet are covered with insulating scaly skin, and they can tuck their bills under their feathers for extra warmth. In autumn, they gorge on food to build up fat supplies to provide energy for winter survival or migration. But even the most hardy birds cannot survive without also seeking protective shelter, especially when weather conditions become extreme. Birds also use shelter for cover and protection from predators.

In natural areas, birds can count on evergreen trees and shrubs for shelter. Pines, hemlocks, and cedars provide them with protection from wind, snow, and rain. In your garden, you can provide shelter by planting a dense evergreen hedge or a dense stand of evergreen conifers. An overgrown thicket in a wild corner of the garden, densely planted with honeysuckle, native blackberry, raspberry, or rose will provide shelter and food to attract many birds including field and song sparrows, juncos, bobolinks, thrushes, and veeries.

Food Niches

By choosing a variety of tall, medium, and low-growing plants, you can create different food niches in your garden. The more food niches you provide, the more kinds of birds will be able to live and feed in the same area. In this one small section of the yard:

In the air:
Swallows catch flying insects in the air.

In the tree:
A Baltimore oriole feeds in the dense foliage at the top of the tree.
A chickadee looks for food in the outer foliage.
A woodpecker moves up the trunk searching for insects.
A nuthatch moves down the trunk looking for bugs that the woodpecker might miss.

In the shrubs and plants below the tree:
A cedar waxwing feeds on fruit at the top of the shrub.
A bluebird hovers nearby, catching insects the waxwing stirs up.
A wren searches for insects hiding lower in the shrub.
The towhee scratches for insects in leaf litter beneath the shrub.
A hummingbird hovers at a flower.
A bunting consumes grass seed.
The robin pulls worms out of the lawn.

All these birds can coexist within a few feet of each other when you provide layered vegetation.

Broad-leaved evergreen shrubs or vines may also be used to provide year-round shelter. Shrubs should be allowed to form dense clumps in some parts of the garden. While you are waiting for your garden to mature, you can create an instant shelter by building a brush pile ideally about 8 feet across and 4 feet tall, placed out of view but accessible to water. Build the brush pile out of branches from evergreen trees, leaving the foliage intact.

In summer, birds often need shelter from the hot sun. In regions where temperatures can soar, try to include at least one tree or thick hedge to provide deep shade, and make sure water is readily available. A brush pile will also be used if shade trees aren't available.

Bird Bills and Food

Each species of bird has its own food preferences, based on the bird's behavior and physical characteristics. And so different bird species can live in the same territory without competing for food. A bird's bill is its most important implement in gathering food, and the size and shape of a bird's bill is a good indication of the type of food fed on by that species. For example:

A. Hummingbirds have a needlelike bill and extendable tongue specialized for probing tubular flowers for nectar.

B. Jays are omnivorous birds equipped with a general-purpose bill and can consume many things, including acorns, fruits, seeds, eggs, and young birds.

C. Woodpeckers have specialized strong, sharp, pointed bills for excavating nest hollows and a long barbed tongue for extracting wood-boring insects.

D. Northern cardinals and finches have heavy, conical bills for cracking seeds and removing the kernel. The seed is held in the grooved upper bill and split by grinding the lower, sharply edged part of the bill.

E. Chickadees and wrens have small, sharp bills for pecking insects, such as aphids, from foliage.

F. Crossbills have distinctive crossed bills. The elongated upper and lower bill tips cross over each other like shears and are used to force pine cones apart while the tongue extracts the seed.

G. Swallows have small, weak bills that open wide to catch insects while they are flying.

Birds also need shelter for roosting. Roosting is the bird equivalent of getting a good night's sleep. Birds will roost anywhere they feel safe and can stay warm. Songbirds such as blue jays, cardinals, and finches prefer to roost in dense thickets of vegetation. Small garden birds favor the dense cover of evergreens, while cavity-nesters such as woodpeckers, titmice, nuthatches, and wrens will usually roost in tree cavities or nest boxes. Birds that perch in trees to roost will seek a sheltered position safe from predators. Roosting in groups provides additional warmth and protection from predation. Generally most trees that provide good shelter will also be used as roosting trees.

Nesting Sites

Many birds have distinctive coloration and subtle markings that give them a protective camouflage, allowing them to blend with the textures and colors of particular native plants.

Song sparrow in western hemlock (*Tsuga heterophylla*).

Plants for Shelter

These native trees and shrubs have dense foliage, providing shelter for many birds, and some also provide roosting, food, and nesting sites:

➤ firs (*Abies* spp.). The evergreen foliage is valuable for shelter and roosting.

➤ alders (*Alnus* spp.). Good shelter trees for many birds, including the blue jay.

➤ hollies (*Ilex* spp.). Dense, prickly foliage provides protective shelter.

➤ junipers (*Juniperus* spp.). Junipers offer valuable shelter and also provide berries for food. Junco, sparrow, and yellow-rumped warbler are among the birds that frequently roost in the foliage.

➤ mulberries (*Morus* spp.). Mulberries are useful for shelter, cover, and secure nesting sites, and are outstanding food trees.

➤ bayberries (*Myrica* spp.). Evergreen shrubs provide valuable shelter for many birds.

➤ spruces (*Picea* spp.). Spruces provide excellent year-round shelter for birds, as well as nesting and roosting sites.

➤ pines (*Pinus* spp.). Excellent shelter for many birds, larger pines are favored roosting sites for migrating robins and warblers.

➤ oaks (*Quercus* spp.). Oaks provide food (acorns), shelter, and nesting sites for many birds.

➤ rhododendrons and azaleas (*Rhododendron* spp.). These evergreen shrubs provide valuable shelter when planted in groupings.

➤ sumacs (*Rhus* spp.). Sumacs provide good summer shelter.

➤ roses (*Rosa* spp.). Rose thickets provide excellent shelter and protective cover.

➤ blackberry and raspberry shrubs (*Rubus* spp.). Prickly bramble shrubs provide shelter for towhees, native sparrows, warblers, thrushes, and buntings.

➤ hemlocks (*Tsuga* spp.). Excellent shelter trees, hemlocks also provide outstanding nesting opportunities. Chickadees, titmice, juncos, and cardinals are among the birds that shelter in the evergreen hemlock foliage.

The branching habit of red-osier dogwood (*Cornus sericea*) provides ideal support for crotch-nesting birds. Judicious pruning can increase the number of possible nest sites in your garden plants.

Birds that mainly live in the foliage of trees generally have olive or gray upper parts, like the arboreal wood warblers. Birds that are ground dwellers, such as quail and doves, often have earth-tone upper parts with patches of darker colors, enabling them to merge with stones, plant litter, or dappled woodland shadows. Birds that live in grasslands generally have streaked plumage, like the meadowlarks and bobolinks. Protective coloration is one reason certain plant species may be preferred nesting plants for specific birds.

The breeding season for many birds coincides with the peak flowering or fruiting period of their favorite food source. With abundant food within easy reach, the adults can feed quickly, allowing more time to attend to the needs of the nestlings. For example, the nesting period of the red crossbill is determined by the availability of ripe pine seeds, and the cedar waxwing also tends to coincide nesting with a plentiful supply of fruits.

Birds choose their nesting sites carefully. A breeding pair usually selects an area large enough to provide food, nest-building materials, and a good place to nest. The pair then defends their site against intruders of the same species. The territory is initially defended by the male, which is able to warn off members of his own species with his song, and thereby keeps the nest site and breeding territory off-limits to members of the same species competing for the same food.

Nesting sites must have some protective cover. The eggs and nestlings are most vulnerable to predators, and the degree of exposure often determines the nesting location. Songbirds usually seek protective shelter in dense foliage or prickly shrubs.

Many birds, including northern mockingbird, northern cardinal, gray catbird, thrashers, and towhees, choose to make their nests in dense, tangled thickets and shrubbery. You can create a "wild" or naturalistic corner of the garden by planting native roses, blackberry, raspberry, and honeysuckle together to make an ideal nesting environment. An effective nesting thicket should be ideally at least 8 feet wide and 3 to 15 feet tall. Other birds that may nest in garden thickets or hedge plants include the white-eyed vireo, yellow warbler, common yellowthroat, yellow-breasted chat, American goldfinch, chipping and song sparrows, and finches.

If you plant a dense evergreen hedge of conifers, such as hemlocks, spruces, or pines, you may attract many birds for nesting, including the mourning dove, blue jay, house finch, and chipping sparrow. Many more birds will gratefully use your evergreen hedge for shelter during the winter.

Tree-nesting birds usually build their nests in a crotch or fork of the tree or "saddled" on a limb, at heights from 3 to 50 feet above the ground. Crotch-nesters prefer wide angles (about 70 degrees), since this angle provides plenty of room and support for the nest. To increase the number of nest sites, try a little judicious pruning in early spring or autumn to create wider crotch angles at various heights.

Don't overlook the value to birds of a dead tree or limb. Throughout urban areas of North America, many hole-nesting birds have been deprived of a home because of the habit of

Rose-breasted grosbeaks nesting in Carolina cherry laurel (*Prunus caroliniana*). The male brings crushed insects to the nestlings. Insects make up 75 percent of the nestling's diet.

Female Costa's hummingbird at its nest in western hackberry (*Celtis reticulata*).

Mountain bluebird feeding its young in its nest built in a vacant woodpecker hole.

removing old, decayed, or dead trees or tree limbs; patching up cavities in established trees; and competition with introduced European starlings and sparrows. Starlings are extremely aggressive birds that will evict nesting native birds. In rural areas, a shortage of nesting sites has resulted from clearing of woodlands, removal of old orchard trees, and substitution of metal poles for timber fence posts. As long as dead limbs are not a safety issue, consider leaving them in place for the birds. If you have a dead tree or tree limbs, you can create or start holes for woodpeckers to finish. Some garden birds that nest in tree hollows include titmice, chickadees, nuthatches, house wrens, purple martins, and bluebirds.

Plants *for* Nesting

These plants are preferred by many birds for nesting and many also provide food and shelter. For best nesting success, plant in masses or clumps, preferably in quiet areas of the yard.

➤ firs (*Abies* spp.). Tanagers, grosbeaks, robins, and jays are among the many birds that nest in firs.

➤ hackberries (*Celtis* spp.). Many birds nest in hackberry foliage, including the indigo bunting, verdin, hummingbird, and white-winged dove.

➤ saguaro (*Carnegiea gigantea*). In the Southwest, the saguaro cactus is excavated for nesting by flickers and Gila woodpeckers. Their old nest holes provide nest sites for owls, martins, flycatchers, wrens, and kestrels.

➤ dogwoods (*Cornus* spp.). Bell's vireo and the summer tanager often nest in dogwoods.

➤ hawthorns (*Crataegus* spp.). The thorny branches provide abundant nesting sites for smaller birds, such as hummingbirds, cardinals, buntings, verdins, and wood thrushes. In the Southwest, roadrunners commonly nest in shrubby hawthorns.

➤ hollies (*Ilex* spp.). Dense, prickly holly foliage attracts towhees, thrashers, and mockingbirds.

➤ junipers (*Juniperus* spp.). Junipers are valuable nesting plants. The chipping sparrow, song sparrow, robin, and mockingbird are among the many birds that nest in these plants.

➤ prickly pears (*Opuntia* spp.). The spines of this cactus provide protective nesting sites for many birds, including the cactus wren, mourning dove, Inca dove, curve-billed thrasher, house sparrow, and roadrunner.

➤ spruces (*Picea* spp.). The white-crowned sparrow and warblers are among the birds that nest in the evergreen foliage of spruce.

➤ pines (*Pinus* spp.). The robin, purple finch, mourning dove, magnolia warbler, and white-crowned sparrow are among the many birds that nest in pines.

➤ oaks (*Quercus* spp.). Oaks are outstanding trees for nesting. The blue-gray gnatcatcher, orchard oriole, summer tanager, acorn woodpecker, and blue jay are some of the many birds that nest in oaks.

➤ roses (*Rosa* spp.). The dense, thorned stems of rose bushes provide excellent nesting sites for smaller birds, including indigo buntings, lazuli buntings, cardinals, yellow warblers, towhees, and sparrows.

➤ blackberries and raspberries (*Rubus* spp.). The spiny stems of berry bushes provide secure nesting sites for the indigo bunting, yellow warbler, cardinal, towhee, and sparrow.

➤ elderberries (*Sambucus* spp.). Warblers, grosbeak, and goldfinch nest in the foliage.

➤ hemlocks (*Tsuga* spp.). Hemlocks are outstanding nesting plants for many birds, including warblers, American robin, junco, veery, American goldfinch, and blue jay.

PROVIDING BIRD NEST BOXES *and* SHELVES

By building and setting out nest boxes, you can help redress the housing shortage for cavity-nesting birds. You can either obtain nest boxes commercially, or construct a simple nest box yourself.

Building a nest box is a great family activity. A nest box is easy to make and materials are readily sourced. Use untreated wood such as pine, cedar, or fir, and keep it rough internally so birds can easily climb out of the box. Galvanized, brass, or stainless-steel screws and hinges will not rust outdoors. Do not paint the interior of the nest box, because paints contain chemicals that can be detrimental to birds, especially birds that modify the nest box by chewing the timber and ingesting the paint. You can treat the exterior with a nontoxic wood preservative for durability and a natural finish. Make sure the roof has a slope and overhangs the box to keep water out, and provide drainage holes in the base to allow water to drain away if it enters the nest box. Provide a hinged roof or side panel so you can clean and inspect the box.

Decide what bird you are building the nest box for and make certain that the species is in your locality. The diameter of the entrance hole is critical to allow some birds entry while excluding other species and predators.

Typical nest box design

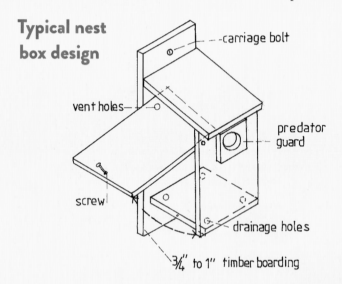

- carriage bolt
- vent holes
- predator guard
- screw
- drainage holes
- ¾" to 1" timber boarding

Eastern bluebird on its nest box at Tyler Arboretum's bluebird trail, Media, Pennsylvania.

Add a metal or thick timber predator guard around the entrance hole to deter predators from enlarging the hole and accessing the nest. Do not add a perch on the outside, since it is an aid for predators to access the birds. Position the entrance hole near the top of the nest box (leaving 2 inches between the hole and the roof for entry), to prevent predators, especially cats, from reaching in to get the nestlings.

Ensure that you have a suitable place to install the nest box, at the correct height and orientation. Learn to

Eastern bluebird at its nest box with predator guard.

Tree swallows at their nest box.

House wren bringing nesting material to its nest box.

identify the introduced European starling and house sparrows. These aggressive competitors for nest hollows kill occupants such as bluebirds or purple martins and should be evicted immediately and their nests destroyed.

You can make the nest box more appealing to birds by sprinkling the floor with moss and wood chips. For cross-ventilation, drill a few ¼-inch-diameter holes near the roof, and add a few drainage holes in the floor so that rain that enters can drain. Include a removable side or a hinged roof so you can clean the nest box. Many birds, like bluebirds and martins, prefer nest boxes mounted on poles.

Mount the nest box either on a pole or in a tree, and for added protection, wrap a 30-inch-wide metal sleeve around the pole or tree below the nest box, to protect the nest from cats and other predators. You should generally position the nest box in October or November to allow it to weather and to enable prospective tenants to become accustomed to it. Locate it facing south for the morning sun and for protection from prevailing winds, and tilt it forward to help protect the entrance hole from rain.

Tips *for* purple martin house success

➤ Choose an open location 30 to 120 feet from the house, with no trees higher than the height of the martin house within a radius of 40 to 60 feet, or less in the south of their range.

➤ The house should be 10 to 20 feet high.

➤ Install a predator guard on the support pole. Martins may abandon the nest if predation occurs.

➤ White painted houses seem to be most successful in attracting martins.

➤ Close up or store martin houses over winter for protection against unwanted occupants.

Most birds will desert their nest if they are disturbed, so inspect the nest box only when you know that the birds have completed their nesting and the young have fledged. When you are certain that the nesting period is finished and that the birds have left, you should clean the box. Burn old nest material, and sprinkle the interior with a safe, pyrethrum-based insecticide to destroy any insects and lice that might threaten future nestlings.

In colder climates, by leaving nest boxes up all year, you allow birds to use them for roosting as well as for nesting. These boxes can be supplemented with specially designed roosting boxes. Roosting boxes may be used by the screech owl, flicker, woodpecker, nuthatch, chickadee, wren, and bluebird.

The dimensions given in the chart Nest Boxes for Birds for the purple martin, for example, are for one compartment that is suitable for a nesting pair. Because martins are gregarious birds, eight compartments are usually constructed together to form a martin house.

Try building your own purple martin house, but be warned, a martin house also provides ideal conditions for house sparrows and European starlings. Make the house accessible for cleaning or purchase a house that can be lowered for inspection and for cleaning. You should locate the house in an open

Nuthatches, including pygmy nuthatches, will regularly use nest boxes.

Black-capped chickadee.

NEST BOXES FOR BIRDS

SPECIES	BOX FLOOR	BOX HEIGHT	ENTRANCE HEIGHT	ENTRANCE DIAMETER	HEIGHT ABOVE GROUND
bluebird: eastern, western, and mountain	5 × 5 in.	8–12 in.	6–10 in.	1½ in.	4–6 ft.
chickadee: black-capped and mountain	4 × 4 in.	8–10 in.	6–8 in.	1⅛ in.	4–15 ft.
titmouse: tufted and bridled	4 × 4 in.	8–12 in.	6–10 in.	1¼ in.	5–15 ft.
ash-throated flycatcher	6 × 6 in.	8–12 in.	6–10 in.	1½ in.	5–15 ft.
great crested flycatcher	6 × 6 in.	8–12 in.	6–10 in.	1¾ in.	5–15 ft.
nuthatch: brown-headed, pygmy, and red-breasted	4 × 4 in.	8–10 in.	6–8 in.	1¼ in.	5–15 ft.
white-breasted nuthatch	4 × 4 in.	8–10 in.	6–8 in.	1⅜ in.	5–15 ft.
prothonotary warbler	5 × 5 in.	6 in.	4–5 in.	1⅛ in.	4–8 ft.
purple martin	7 × 12 in.	5–7 in.	1 in.	2⅛ in.	10–20 ft.
swallow: tree and violet-green	5 × 5 in.	6–8 in.	4–6 in.	1½ in.	5–15 ft.
downy woodpecker	4 × 4 in.	8–10 in.	6–8 in.	1¼ in.	5–15 ft.

SPECIES	BOX FLOOR	BOX HEIGHT	ENTRANCE HEIGHT	ENTRANCE DIAMETER	HEIGHT ABOVE GROUND
hairy woodpecker	6 × 6 in.	12–15 in.	9–12 in.	1½ in.	8–20 ft.
Lewis's woodpecker	7 × 7 in.	16–18 in.	14–16 in.	2½ in.	12–20 ft.
northern flicker	7 × 7 in.	16–18 in.	14–16 in.	2½ in.	6–20 ft.
pileated woodpecker	8 × 8 in.	16–24 in.	12–20 in.	3–4 in.	15–25 ft.
red-headed woodpecker	6 × 6 in.	12–15 in.	9–12 in.	2 in.	10–20 ft.
red-bellied woodpecker	6 × 6 in.	12–15 in.	9–12 in.	2½ in.	12–20 ft.
yellow-bellied sapsucker	5 × 5 in.	12–15 in.	9–12 in.	1½ in.	10–20 ft.
wren: winter, Bewick's, and house	4 × 4 in.	6–8 in.	4–6 in.	1¼ in.	5–10 ft.
Carolina wren	4 × 4 in.	6–8 in.	4–6 in.	1½ in.	5–10 ft.
barn owl	10 × 18 in.	15–18 in.	4 in.	6 in.	12–18 ft.
screech owl; kestrel	8 × 8 in.	9–12 in.	3 in.	10–30 ft.	12–15 in.

BIRD NEST BOX SHELF DIMENSIONS

SPECIES	great horned owl	red-tailed hawk	American robin	phoebe	barn swallow	song sparrow
BOX FLOOR	platform 24 × 24 in.	platform 24 × 24 in.	7 × 8 in.	6 × 6 in.	6 × 6 in.	6 × 6 in.
HEIGHT OF TRAY SIDES	–	–	8 in.	6 in.	6 in.	6 in.
HEIGHT ABOVE GROUND	14 ft. min.	14 ft. min.	6–15 ft.	8–12 ft.	8–12 ft.	1– 3 ft.

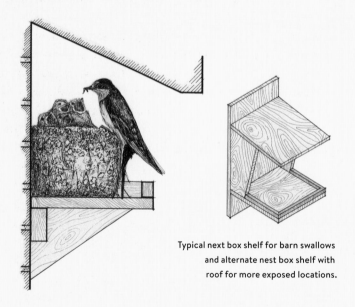

Typical next box shelf for barn swallows and alternate nest box shelf with roof for more exposed locations.

area, preferably with the entrance facing south, but away from prevailing springtime winds.

Bluebirds were once common throughout their range and their numbers collapsed because of overuse of pesticides, habitat loss, and competition for nest hollows. Bluebird trails have helped to reestablish populations in areas with suitable habitat. A bluebird trail is a series of nest boxes placed about 300 feet apart and may be as small as a few nest boxes placed in a large garden or a community project many miles long. Bluebirds are beneficial to the garden, because they feed almost exclusively on insect pests. The chart Nest Boxes for Birds gives you dimensions for building your own bird nest boxes.

PROVIDING *for* HUMMINGBIRDS

Hummingbirds are the exquisite jewels of the garden, and they are also major pollinators and insect predators. As the bird probes the long, tubular flowers with its long, thin bill, pollen is deposited on the bird's head and then transferred to the next bloom. The tubular flowers hold their nectar deep enough to deny less efficient pollinators, such as insects and butterflies, access to the nectar, but at a depth ideally suited to the hummingbird's bill that has evolved with the flower shape.

Because of their constant movement, with wings beating at up to 90 beats per second, the hummingbird needs to feed constantly, consuming up to one third to one half its body weight daily. In a study of Anna's hummingbird, it was estimated that each bird consumed nectar from 1,000 blossoms daily as well as numerous small insects for protein.

In a garden designed for hummingbirds, you should provide a continuous display of hummingbird flowers—tubular flowers of red, orange, or pink colors—from early spring to fall in the east and year-round in California and the Southwest. To learn which flowers to choose to provide a constant supply of nectar-rich flowers for the hummingbird season, see the Calendar for Hummingbird and Butterfly Flowers, page 43. If you plant the selected plants in massed clumps, in containers on your balcony or courtyard, or grouped in your garden, you will provide an attractive patch of color for you and the birds to enjoy.

If you don't have a lot of space, you can use a balcony planter or a fence or trellis to plant a trumpet creeper (*Campsis radicans*). The brilliant flame-colored flowers

Male ruby-throated hummingbird feeding in trumpet honeysuckle (*Lonicera sempervirens*).

Male Costa's hummingbird.

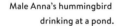

Male Anna's hummingbird
drinking at a pond.

of this vine have the highest volume of nectar per blossom of all the hummingbird flowers. When it is planted with the early flowering crossvine (*Bignonia capreolata*), you will have a powerful magnet for attracting hummingbirds from early spring throughout summer. Trim the vines back each fall to keep the flowers at viewing level.

Generally, arrange hummingbird plants from the lowest at the front, and grade the plants up to the taller species, so the hummingbirds can easily access the flowers and you can easily observe the birds. Hummingbirds prefer the same species of plants planted in clumps, rather than scattered throughout the garden. An island of hummingbird flowers surrounded by lawn is also an attractive arrangement for hummingbirds.

Hummingbirds enjoy water, especially from misters and dripping devices. They prefer to bathe by flying through a fine mist of water, rather than in a birdbath. Position the mist source near the flowerbed. Even an upward-pointing garden hose of mist spray will attract hummingbirds on a hot day and give them refreshing relief. You can purchase misting and dripping devices commercially to attach to birdbaths. If you are planning to install a garden pond, consider installing a spray feature that will be appealing to hummingbirds.

Hummingbirds often nest in suburban gardens, in tall trees like oak (*Quercus* spp.), alder (*Alnus* spp.), maple (*Acer* spp.), and hemlock (*Tsuga* spp.). The female builds a tiny, cup-shaped nest from collected plant down and lichen, which she binds with spider webs and fastens to a horizontal limb. She uses nesting material including the fuzz from young fronds of cinnamon ferns (*Osmunda cinnamonea*), American pussy willow catkins (*Salix discolor*), thistles (*Cirsium* spp.), and dandelions (*Taraxacum* spp.), and the cottonlike flower remnants (seeds) of bulrush or cattail (*Typha* spp.).

When active, hummingbirds need to feed almost continuously. When they roost at night, to conserve energy they go into torpor, a form of hibernation or deep sleep. In this state, their metabolism is lowered by 85 percent and their heart rate is markedly reduced, minimizing their energy needs. Hummingbirds roost anywhere they are warm and safe from predators.

Important: For the well-being of hummingbirds, avoid using pesticides and other harsh chemicals in your garden, because hummingbirds feed on large quantities of insects.

Hummingbirds will come to your garden if you provide a sequence of flowering plants attractive to them. In the Southwest, you can have hummingbirds year-round without the responsibility, constant maintenance, and the risk of harm associated with hummingbird feeders (see page 180).

Allen's hummingbird perched on an ocotillo branch (*Fouquieria* sp.).

Common Garden Hummingbirds

Of the 19 hummingbird species that migrate in North America, only 8 species travel considerably north of the Mexican border. In the Far West, 7 species nest, 4 species nest in Canada, and only 1 species, the ruby-throated hummingbird, regularly nests in the eastern half of North America. These are some of the hummingbirds most commonly seen in North American gardens:

Costa's hummingbird One of the smallest hummingbirds, the male is distinguished by its brilliant iridescent purple crown and throat. It is common in desert areas of southern California, Arizona, and Nevada. In midsummer, the birds migrate from the hot desert regions to scrublands and chaparral. They are resident in the far South and Southwest, extending their range in summer to include Utah and Nevada.

Ruby-throated hummingbird The only hummingbird regularly seen east of the Mississippi River. The male has a brilliant, iridescent metallic red throat. The birds arrive in coastal areas in late February or early March, and by mid-November their fall migration is completed.

Anna's hummingbird The only hummingbird to regularly winter in the United States, in California. The male has a brilliant pink-red iridescent crown and throat. Some birds migrate as far north as British Columbia and as far south as Arizona and Texas, returning to California in December. Common in open woodland, chaparral, scrubby areas, and gardens.

Black-chinned hummingbird feeding on Texas betony (*Stachys coccinea*).

Male broad-billed hummingbird feeding on autumn sage (*Salvia greggii*), a long-blooming hummingbird flower.

Allen's hummingbird A common, breeding bird in a narrow coastal strip of California. The male arrives in January and departs as early as mid-May, while the female is still raising young. The males arrive in their winter grounds in Mexico as early as August. The male Allen's hummingbird is similar in appearance to the rufous hummingbird.

Black-chinned hummingbird A summer visitor to British Columbia and south along the Pacific Coast, east to the Rocky Mountains, and south to Mexico and Texas. It is present in Arizona from March to September and in Texas from March to August.

Broad-billed hummingbird Summers in southern Arizona, southwestern New Mexico, and western Texas.

Broad-tailed hummingbird The common nesting hummingbird of the Rocky Mountains in Idaho, Montana, and Wyoming, and southward. Generally arrives in mid-May.

Calliope hummingbird The smallest North American hummingbird, it summers in the mountains of western North America. It nests from May to July in the Cascade Range, Sierra Nevada, and Rocky Mountains, and north into central British Columbia.

Rufous hummingbird The only hummingbird that summers in Alaska and the southern Yukon Territory, southward to northwestern California and southern Idaho, arriving in California between late February and early March.

Male rufous hummingbird feeding on the flowers of salmonberry (*Rubus spectabilis*).

PROVIDING *for* BUTTERFLIES

When you plan your garden to attract birds, an added bonus is that many of the plants recommended in this book for birds also attract butterflies. Butterflies provide food for birds and are colorful and diverse additions to your garden.

Butterflies go through four stages in their life cycle. The female butterfly lays her eggs on the underside of leaves of a suitable plant, known as a host plant. These leaves will later provide food for the caterpillar when it hatches from the egg. When fully grown, the caterpillar forms into a pupa, or chrysalis, where a remarkable transformation occurs—a butterfly emerges from the chrysalis, spreads its wings, and flies away to begin the life cycle again. Because butterflies are cold-blooded

Northeastern, wildlife-friendly summer garden, including sunflowers (*Helianthus* spp.), tansy (*Tanacetum* spp.), sage (*Salvia* spp.), and beeplant (*Cleome* spp.).

Juniper hairstreak butterfly laying her eggs on the host plant, eastern red cedar (*Juniperus virginiana*).

creatures, they cannot survive cold weather and need to migrate to a warm area. Several butterflies migrate great distances, including the monarch butterfly, which moves from the Great Lakes to the Gulf of Mexico, a distance of over 2,000 miles, flying at a maximum speed of 12 miles an hour, and returning the following spring. In tropical regions, butterflies migrate to form new colonies around a fresh group of host plants to ensure a plentiful food supply of leaves for their caterpillars.

If you plant a variety of nectar plants for adult butterflies and some host plants for caterpillars, butterflies will probably spend many generations in your garden. To attract a wide variety of butterflies to your yard or balcony container garden, select a variety of plants of varying height, color, blossom size, and depth from which the butterflies can obtain nectar continuously in the butterfly season, usually from early spring to late fall. You should group flowering plants that bloom at similar times to minimize the butterflies' movement and thereby decrease their exposure to predators. Whenever possible, leave

Pipevine swallowtail butterfly nectaring on Turk's cap lily (*Lilium superbum*). This butterfly has only one larval host plant, *Aristolochia* spp., which includes pipevines, Dutchman's pipes, and birthworts, and the butterfly is only found where these plants occur.

Checkerspot butterfly on its favored nectar plant, California buckwheat (*Eriogonum fasciculatum*).

Black swallowtail butterflies collecting
nectar on wild bergamot
(*Monarda fistulosa*).

dead flower heads so you do not accidentally remove eggs or pupating butterflies that can be concealed in them.

Locate your butterfly sanctuary in a sunny spot that is sheltered from prevailing winds. Butterflies need warmth in order to be active, and their delicate wings can be damaged by wind and rain.

A garden for birds will contain suitable plants for the butterflies to shelter in, such as firs, juniper, spruce, pines, and hemlocks (for specific plants, see Calendar for Hummingbird and Butterfly Flowers, page 43).

Large, flat rocks positioned in a sunny location should be incorporated in the garden so the butterflies can bask in the sun. Butterflies need to ingest salts from the soil, so include small puddles in the garden as well as a small, damp, sandy patch.

Keep the butterfly sanctuary free of pesticides and don't consider native caterpillars to be pests. Some introduced species, such as the caterpillar of the cabbage white butterfly (*Pieris rapae*), can become pests, so remove them by hand rather than spray.

If you meet all the butterflies' needs, you are likely to see them in your garden all season long. If you provide some potted nectaring plants on your balcony, butterflies will happily appear as casual visitors.

If you choose plants that thrive in your region and use this flowering calendar, your garden will have an abundant, continuous supply of nectar for hummingbirds. The plants listed are suggestions only, because other, similar plants in the same species may be available in your locality instead. Several of the plants will provide shelter and nesting sites, and many will also attract butterflies.

Hummingbirds are not found in all regions of North America. The plants in the calendar are grouped into three regional areas where hummingbirds occur: The Pacific Coast and the Mountains, where you will find Anna's, Costa's, rufous, Allen's, calliope, and black-chinned hummingbirds; the Southwest and the Plains and Prairies, where you will find the black-chinned, Costa's, broad-tailed, and ruby-throated hummingbirds, and the broad-billed hummingbird in desert areas; and the Northeast and Southeast, where the ruby-throated hummingbird is generally the only regular summer hummingbird visitor, although increasing numbers of rufous hummingbirds are overwintering in Florida.

The plants in the calendar are listed alphabetically by botanical name, with the widely used common name listed in the adjacent column. For each plant, you'll find information on flower color, the kind of light needed for successful cultivation, gardening and wildlife uses of the plant, flowering months, hardiness zones, and approximate mature height.

CALENDAR *for* HUMMINGBIRD *and* BUTTERFLY FLOWERS

KEY	
◯	full sun
◑	full sun to partial shade
●	light shade to shade
⊡	nesting plant
⬥	shelter plant
◢	roosting plant
🦋	nectar for butterflies
⊤	host plant for butterflies
❧	fall color
✹	showy flowers
⚹	nectar for hummingbirds

THE PACIFIC COAST *and the* MOUNTAINS

BOTANICAL NAME	COMMON NAME	FLOWER COLOR	LIGHT NEEDS	
Aquilegia formosa	crimson columbine	red and yellow	◐	
Arctostaphylos edmundsii	Little Sur manzanita	pink	◐	
Arctostaphylos uva-ursi	bearberry	white to purple	◐	
Campsis radicans	trumpet creeper	red or orange	○	
Castilleja foliolosa	Texas paintbrush	red, yellow	○	
Castilleja miniata	giant red paintbrush	red	○	
Cercis occidentalis	western redbud	magenta	◐	
Chilopsis linearis	desert willow	pink, white, lavender	○	
Crataegus douglasii	western hawthorn	creamy white	◐	
Delphinium cardinale	cardinal larkspur	red	○	
Epilobium canum	California fuchsia	red	○	
Fouquieria splendens	ocotillo	scarlet	○	
Heuchera maxima x H. sanguinea	'Santa Ana Cardinal' coral bells	rosy red	◐	
Ipomopsis aggregata	skyrocket gilia	bright red or deep pink	○	
Isomeris arborea	bladderpod	yellow	○	
Justicia californica	chuparosa	red, orange, or yellow	○	
Keckiella antirrhinoides	yellow bush snapdragon	yellow	●	

○ full sun   ◐ full sun to partial shade   ● light shade to shade   🐦 nesting plant   🦅 shelter plants   🐦 roosting plant

PLANT USES	APPROXIMATE FLOWERING MONTHS J F M A M J J A S O N D	HARDINESS ZONES	MATURE HEIGHT
🐦🦋✿	· · · · ◆◆◆◆◆ · · ·	3–7	2–4 ft.
🐦🦋T✿	◆◆◆◆ · · · · · · ◆◆	4	1–2 ft.
🐦🦋T✿	· ◆◆◆◆◆ · · · · ·	2–8	12 in.
🐦🦋T✿◻🐦	· · · · · ◆◆◆ · · ·	4–9	Vine
🐦🦋T✿	· · ◆◆◆◆ · · · ·	7–10	1–2 ft.
🐦🦋T✿	· · · · · ◆◆◆◆ · · ·	5	1–3 ft.
🐦✿🍃	· · · · · ◆◆◆ · · ·	7	15 ft.
🐦🦋✿◻🍃	· · · ◆◆◆◆◆◆ · · ·	7–9	10–20 ft.
🐦🦋T🍁✿◻	· · · · · ◆ · ◆ · · ·	4–6	5–20 ft.
🐦🦋✿	· · · ◆◆◆◆ · · · ·	7–8	3–7 ft.
🐦🦋✿	· · · · · · · ◆◆◆ · ·	8–10	1–3 ft.
🐦🦋T🍁✿◻	· · · · · ◆◆ · · · ·	8–10	8–20 ft.
🐦✿	◆◆◆◆◆◆◆◆◆◆◆◆	3–8	2–3 ft.
🐦✿	· · · · ◆◆◆◆◆ · · ·	5–8	6 in.
🐦🦋✿	◆◆◆◆◆◆◆◆◆◆◆◆	7–10	3–6 ft.
🐦🦋✿	· · ◆◆◆◆◆ · · · ·	8–10	3–5 ft.
🐦✿	· ◆◆◆◆◆◆◆◆ · · ·	7–9	3–4 ft.

🦋 nectar for butterflies   T host plant for butterflies   🍁 fall color   ✿ showy flowers   🐦 nectar for hummingbirds

THE PACIFIC COAST *and the* MOUNTAINS

BOTANICAL NAME	COMMON NAME	FLOWER COLOR	LIGHT NEEDS
Keckiella corymbosa (formerly *Penstemon corymbosus*)	red shrubby penstemon	red	○
Lobelia cardinalis	cardinal flower	red	●
Lonicera involucrata	twinberry honeysuckle	yellow	●
Lupinus sparsiflorus	Coulter's lupine	pale blue or bluish lilac	○
Malus fusca	Pacific crabapple	pinkish white	◑
Mimulus aurantiacus	sticky monkeyflower	yellow to orange	◑
Mimulus cardinalis	scarlet monkeyflower	scarlet	◑
Mimulus guttatus	common monkeyflower	yellow with brown spots	◑
Monarda citriodora	lemon bee balm	white, pink or purple	◑
Monardella macrantha	large-flower monardella	scarlet	●
Nicotiana trigonophylla	desert tobacco	cream	○
Penstemon centranthifolius	scarlet bugler	scarlet	○
Penstemon eatonii	firecracker plant	red	○
Penstemon pseudospectabilis	pink showy penstemon	rose purple	○
Rhododendron occidentale	western azalea	white to deep pink	●
Ribes sanguineum var. *glutinosum*	pink-flowering currant	pale to deep pink	●

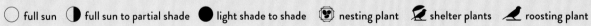

○ full sun   ◑ full sun to partial shade   ● light shade to shade   nesting plant   shelter plants   roosting plant

PLANT USES	APPROXIMATE FLOWERING MONTHS J F M A M J J A S O N D	HARDINESS ZONES	MATURE HEIGHT
hummingbird, butterfly, showy flowers	· · · · · ◆ ◆ ◆ ◆ ◆ · ·	7–9	12–20 in.
hummingbird, butterfly, host plant, showy flowers	· · · · · · ◆ ◆ ◆ · ·	2–9	2–3 ft.
hummingbird, butterfly, host plant, showy flowers, fall color	· ◆ ◆ ◆ ◆ ◆ ◆ · · · · ·	4–10	2–10 ft.
hummingbird, butterfly, host plant, showy flowers	◆ ◆ ◆ ◆ ◆ · · · · · · ·	8	8–16 in.
hummingbird, butterfly, fall color, showy flowers, +	· · ◆ ◆ ◆ · · · · · · ·	4–9	15–30 ft.
hummingbird, butterfly, showy flowers	· · ◆ ◆ ◆ ◆ ◆ ◆ ◆ · · ·	9–10	2–4 ft.
hummingbird, butterfly, showy flowers	· · · ◆ ◆ ◆ ◆ ◆ ◆ ◆ · ·	6–9	10–24 in.
hummingbird, butterfly, showy flowers	· ◆ ◆ ◆ ◆ ◆ ◆ ◆ ◆ · ·	6–9	7–36 in.
hummingbird, butterfly, showy flowers	· · · · ◆ ◆ ◆ · · · · ·	6–8	1–3 ft.
hummingbird, butterfly, showy flowers	· · · · · ◆ ◆ ◆ · · · ·	8–9	4–20 in.
hummingbird, butterfly, showy flowers	· · ◆ ◆ ◆ ◆ ◆ ◆ ◆ ◆ ◆ · ·	4	1–3 ft.
hummingbird, butterfly, showy flowers	· · · ◆ ◆ ◆ ◆ · · · ·	8–10	1–4 ft.
hummingbird, butterfly, showy flowers	· · · · ◆ ◆ ◆ ◆ · · ·	4–9	4 ft.
hummingbird, butterfly, showy flowers	· ◆ ◆ ◆ ◆ ◆ ◆ ◆ ◆ · · ·	5–10	3–4 ft.
hummingbird, butterfly, showy flowers, +	· · · ◆ ◆ ◆ ◆ ◆ ◆ · · ·	6–8	4–15 ft.
hummingbird, butterfly, fall color, showy flowers, +	◆ ◆ ◆ · · · · · · · · ·	6–8	3–10 ft.

Legend: 🦋 nectar for butterflies   T host plant for butterflies   🍁 fall color   ✿ showy flowers   🦅 nectar for hummingbirds

THE PACIFIC COAST *and the* MOUNTAINS

BOTANICAL NAME	COMMON NAME	FLOWER COLOR	LIGHT NEEDS
Ribes speciosum	fuchsia-flowered gooseberry	crimson	●
Salvia spathacea	hummingbird sage	magenta	◑
Satureja mimuloides	monkeyflowered savory	red to orange	○
Trichostema lanatum	woolly blue curls	bluish purple	○

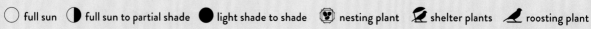

○ full sun   ◑ full sun to partial shade   ● light shade to shade   nesting plant   shelter plants   roosting plant

PLANT USES	APPROXIMATE FLOWERING MONTHS J F M A M J J A S O N D	HARDINESS ZONES	MATURE HEIGHT
🐦🦋❀🐾🐦	◆◆◆◆◆ · · · · · · ·	6–10	3–10 ft.
🐦🦋❀	· · · ◆◆◆◆ · · · · ·	9–11	18–3 ft.
🐦❀	· · · · · ◆◆◆◆◆ · ·	8–10	1–3 in.
🐦❀	· · · · · ◆◆◆ · · · ·	6–10	4 ft.

🦋 nectar for butterflies   🌱 host plant for butterflies   🍁 fall color   ❀ showy flowers   🐦 nectar for hummingbirds

THE SOUTHWEST *and the* PLAINS *and* PRAIRIES

BOTANICAL NAME	COMMON NAME	FLOWER COLOR	LIGHT NEEDS
Aquilegia elegantula	western red columbine	red and yellow	●
Bignonia capreolata	crossvine	orange	◐
Bouvardia ternifolia	scarlet bouvardia	scarlet	◐
Campsis radicans	trumpet vine	red or orange	○
Castilleja chromosa	desert paintbrush	red	○
Celtis reticulata	western hackberry	greenish	○
Chilopsis linearis	desert willow	pink, white or lavender	○
Delphinium parishii	desert larkspur	blue to purple	○
Delphinium parryi	San Bernardino larkspur	pink	○
Epilobium canum	California fuchsia	red	○
Erythrina herbacea	coral bean	red	◐
Fouquieria splendens	ocotillo	scarlet	◐
Heuchera maxima x H. sanguinea	'Santa Ana Cardinal' coral bells	rosy pink	●
Heuchera sanguinea	coral bells	red	○
Ipomopsis aggregata	skyrocket gilia	bright red or deep pink	◐
Justicia californica	chuparosa	red	○
Lobelia cardinalis	cardinal flower	red	●

 full sun   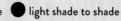 full sun to partial shade   light shade to shade   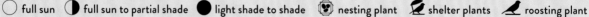 nesting plant   shelter plants   roosting plant

PLANT USES	APPROXIMATE FLOWERING MONTHS J F M A M J J A S O N D	HARDINESS ZONES	MATURE HEIGHT
🐦🦋✽	· · · · ◆◆◆◆◆ · · ·	3–7	6–12 in.
🐦🦋T✽✿🍃🐦	· ◆◆◆◆ · · · · · · ·	6–9	vine
🐦✽	· · · · ◆◆◆◆◆◆ ·	9–11	2–3 ft.
🐦🦋T✽⊡🍃🐦	· · · · · · ◆◆◆ · ·	4–9	vine
🐦🦋✽	· · · ◆◆◆◆◆ · · ·	4	1–2 ft.
🐦🦋T✽⊡🍃	· ◆◆◆ · · · · · · · ·	7–9	20–30 ft.
🐦🦋T✽⊡🍃	· · ◆◆◆◆◆◆◆ · ·	7–9	10–20 ft.
🐦🦋✽	· · · ◆◆◆ · · · · ·	3–8	1–2 ft.
🐦🦋✽	· · · ◆◆ · · · · · ·	3–8	2–3 ft.
🐦🦋✽	· · · · · · · ◆◆◆ · ·	8–10	1–3 ft.
🐦🦋✽	· · ◆◆◆◆◆◆◆◆ · ·	7–9	4–6 ft.
🐦🦋T🍁✽⊡	· · ◆◆◆◆ · · · · ·	8–10	8–20 ft.
🐦✽	· · · · · ◆◆◆ · · ·	3–8	2–3 ft.
🐦✽	· · ◆◆◆◆◆◆ · · ·	3–8	10–20 ft.
🐦✽	· · · ◆◆◆◆ · · · ·	5–8	6 in.
🐦🦋✽	· · ◆◆◆◆◆ · · · ·	8–10	3–5 ft.
🐦🦋T✽	· · · · · · ◆◆◆◆ · ·	2–9	2–3 ft.

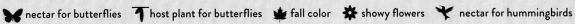
🦋 nectar for butterflies   T host plant for butterflies   🍁 fall color   ✽ showy flowers   🐦 nectar for hummingbirds

THE SOUTHWEST *and the* PLAINS *and* PRAIRIES

BOTANICAL NAME	COMMON NAME	FLOWER COLOR	LIGHT NEEDS	
Lonicera arizonica	Arizona honeysuckle	red or purple	○	
Lonicera involucrata	Twinberry honeysuckle	yellow	◐	
Lonicera sempervirens	trumpet honeysuckle	orange-red	○	
Lupinus sparsiflorus	Coulter's lupine	pale blue or bluish lilac	○	
Mimulus bigelovii	Bigelow's monkeyflower	pink to purple	○	
Mimulus guttatus	common monkeyflower	yellow and brown spots	◐	
Nicotiana trigonophylla	desert tobacco	cream	○	
Penstemon barbatus	common beardtongue	red	○	
Penstemon eatonii	firecracker plant	red	○	
Penstemon parryi	Parry's beardtongue	red or pink	○	
Penstemon strictus	Rocky Mountain penstemon	violet blue	○	
Salvia coccinea	scarlet sage	scarlet	●	
Salvia greggii	autumn sage	red, pink or white	○	
Salvia microphylla	little-leaf sage	red	◐	
Stachys coccinea	Texas betony	red	◐	

 full sun full sun to partial shade light shade to shade nesting plant shelter plants  roosting plant

PLANT USES	APPROXIMATE FLOWERING MONTHS (J F M A M J J A S O N D)	HARDINESS ZONES	MATURE HEIGHT
nectar for hummingbirds, nectar for butterflies, showy flowers, fall color, + additional icons	· · ◆ ◆ ◆ ◆ · · · · · ·	6–8	vine
nectar for hummingbirds, nectar for butterflies, host plant, showy flowers, fall color	◆ ◆ ◆ ◆ ◆ · · · · · · ·	4–10	2–10 ft.
nectar for hummingbirds, nectar for butterflies, host plant, showy flowers, fall color, + additional icons	· · ◆ ◆ ◆ ◆ ◆ ◆ · · · ·	4–9	vine
nectar for hummingbirds, nectar for butterflies, showy flowers	◆ ◆ ◆ ◆ ◆ · · · · · · ·	8	8–16 in.
nectar for hummingbirds, nectar for butterflies, showy flowers	· ◆ ◆ ◆ · · · · · · · ·	8–9	8 in.
nectar for hummingbirds, nectar for butterflies, showy flowers	· · ◆ ◆ ◆ ◆ ◆ · · · · ·	6–9	7–3 ft.
nectar for hummingbirds, nectar for butterflies, showy flowers	· · ◆ ◆ ◆ ◆ ◆ ◆ ◆ ◆ · ·	4	1–3 ft.
nectar for hummingbirds, nectar for butterflies, showy flowers	· · · · · ◆ ◆ ◆ ◆ · · ·	3–8	18–36 in.
nectar for hummingbirds, nectar for butterflies, showy flowers	· · · · ◆ ◆ ◆ ◆ · · · ·	7–9	4 ft.
nectar for hummingbirds, nectar for butterflies, showy flowers	· ◆ ◆ ◆ ◆ · · · · · · ·	8–11	2–3 ft.
nectar for hummingbirds, nectar for butterflies, showy flowers	· · · · ◆ ◆ ◆ ◆ · · · ·	4–9	2–3 ft.
nectar for hummingbirds, nectar for butterflies, showy flowers	· · · · · ◆ ◆ ◆ ◆ · · ·	4–9	2–3 ft.
nectar for hummingbirds, nectar for butterflies, showy flowers	· · ◆ ◆ ◆ ◆ ◆ ◆ · · · ·	7–9	1–4 ft.
nectar for hummingbirds, nectar for butterflies, showy flowers	· · · · · · · ◆ ◆ ◆ ◆ ·	7–9	1–3 ft.
nectar for hummingbirds, nectar for butterflies, showy flowers	· · ◆ ◆ ◆ ◆ ◆ ◆ ◆ · · ·	7–9	3 ft.

Legend:
✖ nectar for butterflies   ⊤ host plant for butterflies   ❧ fall color   ✲ showy flowers   ✦ nectar for hummingbirds

THE NORTHEAST *and the* SOUTHEAST

BOTANICAL NAME	COMMON NAME	FLOWER COLOR	LIGHT NEEDS	
Aesculus pavia	red buckeye	red	◐	
Aquilegia canadensis	wild columbine	light pink and yellow to red	◐	
Arctostaphylos uva-ursi	bearberry	white to purple	◐	
Bignonia capreolata	crossvine	orange	◐	
Campsis radicans	trumpet vine	red or orange	○	
Castilleja coccinea	paintbrush	red	○	
Chelone glabra	turtlehead	white	◐	
Crataegus crus-galli	cockspur hawthorn	white	◐	
Impatiens capensis	jewelweed	orange and spotted brown	◐	
Impatiens pallida	pale touch-me-not	yellow	◐	
Ipomopsis rubra	red gilia	red	◐	
Liatris squarrosa	button blazing star	purple	◐	
Lilium canadense	Canada lily	yellow, orange, or red	◐	
Lobelia cardinalis	cardinal flower	red	◐	
Lobelia siphilitica	great blue lobelia	blue or violet	◐ ●	
Lonicera sempervirens	trumpet honeysuckle	red	○	
Lupinus perennis	wild lupine	purple	○	

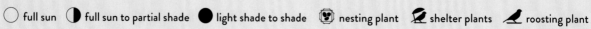
 full sun   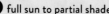 full sun to partial shade   ● light shade to shade   nesting plant   shelter plants   roosting plant

PLANT USES	APPROXIMATE FLOWERING MONTHS J F M A M J J A S O N D	HARDINESS ZONES	MATURE HEIGHT
hummingbird, butterfly, showy flowers	· · · ◆ ◆ ◆ · · · · · ·	6–9	15–25 ft.
hummingbird, butterfly, showy flowers	· · · ◆ ◆ ◆ · · · · · ·	3–8	1–3 ft.
hummingbird, butterfly, host plant, showy flowers	· · ◆ ◆ ◆ ◆ · · · · · ·	2–8	12 in.
hummingbird, butterfly, host plant, showy flowers, +	· ◆ ◆ ◆ ◆ · · · · · · ·	6–9	vine
hummingbird, butterfly, host plant, showy flowers, +	· · · · · · ◆ ◆ ◆ · · ·	4–9	vine
hummingbird, butterfly, showy flowers	· · · · ◆ ◆ ◆ · · · · ·	3–9	1–2 ft.
hummingbird, butterfly, host plant, showy flowers	· · · · ◆ ◆ ◆ ◆ · · · ·	3–8	2–6 ft.
hummingbird, butterfly, host plant, fall color, +	· · · ◆ ◆ ◆ · · · · · ·	4–6	30 ft.
hummingbird, butterfly, showy flowers	· · · · · ◆ ◆ ◆ ◆ · · ·	2	2–5 ft.
hummingbird, butterfly, showy flowers	· · · · · ◆ ◆ ◆ ◆ · · ·	2	2–5 ft.
hummingbird, showy flowers	· · · ◆ ◆ ◆ ◆ ◆ ◆ · · ·	4–10	2–6 ft.
hummingbird, butterfly, showy flowers	· · · · · ◆ ◆ ◆ ◆ · · ·	5–8	2–3 ft.
hummingbird, butterfly, showy flowers	· · · · ◆ ◆ · · · · · ·	3–8	2–4 ft.
hummingbird, butterfly, host plant, showy flowers	· · · · · · ◆ ◆ ◆ ◆ · ·	2–9	2–3 ft.
hummingbird, butterfly, showy flowers	· · · · · · · ◆ ◆ ◆ · ·	4–8	1–5 ft.
hummingbird, butterfly, showy flowers, +	· · · ◆ ◆ ◆ ◆ ◆ ◆ · · ·	4–9	vine
hummingbird, butterfly, host plant, showy flowers	· · · ◆ ◆ ◆ ◆ · · · · ·	4–9	8–24 in.

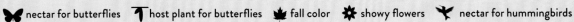

nectar for butterflies   host plant for butterflies   fall color   showy flowers   nectar for hummingbirds

THE NORTHEAST *and the* SOUTHEAST

BOTANICAL NAME	COMMON NAME	FLOWER COLOR	LIGHT NEEDS
Malus coronaria	wild sweet crabapple	pinkish white	◑
Mertensia virginica	Virginia bluebells	pink turning blue	●
Mimulus ringens	Allegheny monkeyflower	blue	◑
Monarda citriodora	lemon bee balm	white, pink, or purple	◑
Monarda didyma	bee balm	red	◑
Monarda fistulosa	wild bergamot	pink, lavender, or white	◑
Pedicularis canadensis	wood betony	yellowish or reddish	◑
Penstemon digitalis	foxglove beardtongue	white to purple	◑
Penstemon laevigatus	smooth beardtongue	purple	○ ●
Rhododendron calendulaceum	flame azalea	orange, red or yellow	◑
Rhododendron catawbiense	catawba	magenta	○ ●
Salvia coccinea	scarlet sage	scarlet	◑
Silene virginica	fire pink	red	●
Spigelia marilandica	Indian pink	red	◑
Verbena canadensis	rose verbena	purple	○

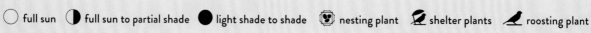

○ full sun ◑ full sun to partial shade ● light shade to shade   nesting plant   shelter plants   roosting plant

PLANT USES	APPROXIMATE FLOWERING MONTHS J F M A M J J A S O N D	HARDINESS ZONES	MATURE HEIGHT
hummingbird, butterfly, T, fall color, showy flowers, [face-in-box], [leaf-in-circle], [bird]	· · ◆ ◆ ◆ · · · · · · ·	5–7	30 ft.
hummingbird, butterfly, showy flowers	· · ◆ ◆ ◆ ◆ · · · · · ·	4–8	1–2½ ft.
hummingbird, butterfly, showy flowers	· · · · · ◆ ◆ ◆ ◆ · · ·	3–8	1–3 ft.
hummingbird, butterfly, showy flowers	· · · · ◆ ◆ ◆ ◆ · · · ·	6–8	1–3 ft.
hummingbird, butterfly, showy flowers	· · · · · ◆ ◆ ◆ ◆ · · ·	4–8	2–4 ft.
hummingbird, butterfly, showy flowers	· · · · · ◆ ◆ ◆ ◆ · · ·	3–9	2–4 ft.
hummingbird, butterfly, showy flowers	· · · · ◆ ◆ ◆ · · · · ·	3	6–18 in.
hummingbird, butterfly, showy flowers	· · · · · ◆ ◆ ◆ · · · ·	3–8	2–4 ft.
hummingbird, butterfly, T, showy flowers	· · · · · ◆ ◆ ◆ ◆ · · ·	3–10	1–3 ft.
hummingbird, butterfly, showy flowers, [face-in-box], [leaf-in-circle]	· · · · · ◆ ◆ · · · · ·	5–7	10–12 ft.
hummingbird, butterfly, showy flowers, [face-in-box], [leaf-in-circle]	· · · · · · ◆ ◆ ◆ · · ·	4–7	6–10 ft.
hummingbird, butterfly, showy flowers	· · · · · ◆ ◆ ◆ ◆ · · ·	4–9	2–4 ft.
hummingbird, butterfly, showy flowers	· · · ◆ ◆ ◆ ◆ ◆ ◆ · · ·	4–7	1–3 ft.
hummingbird, showy flowers	· · · · · ◆ ◆ ◆ ◆ · · ·	4–5	1–2 ft.
hummingbird, butterfly, T, showy flowers	· · · · ◆ ◆ ◆ ◆ ◆ ◆ · ·	6–10	6–18 in.

🦋 nectar for butterflies T host plant for butterflies 🍁 fall color ✿ showy flowers ✾ nectar for hummingbirds

GARDENING *with* WILDFLOWERS

Wildflowers are plants that grow naturally without cultivation. In North America, they were growing on the landscape before European settlement. They are a unique and integral part of the natural landscape, superbly adapted to their climate and geological regions. Growing local wildflowers in your garden promotes ecological diversity by creating a haven for insects that will in turn attract a greater variety of birds. Local plants, birds, and insects have evolved together and are part of the ecological web of your area. When you grow them, you will derive pleasure and satisfaction watching their subtle and beautiful changes through the seasons, with the added bonus of watching insectivorous birds feasting in summer and seed-eating birds taking sustenance in winter. The diversity and stunning beauty of wildflowers provides the gardener with endless design possibilities, and the Calendar for Wildflowers (page 69) will help you select plants for a year-round sequence of flowers and seeds.

Wildflowers will grow most successfully where they have grown historically before European settlement, where they have adapted to local conditions, including soil type, rainfall, temperature, and pests. They will need less maintenance and provide the most benefit for local birds.

Where coniferous forests once grew or still do grow, the soil will be acidic, and where deciduous forests once grew and still grow, the soil will be less acidic. The acidity of the soil affects which wildflower species will thrive in your locality. Wildflowers from prairie and semiarid grasslands will thrive in a neutral garden soil. Desert and seashore areas have an alkaline soil that is most suitable for the plants that occur there naturally.

Diverse wildflowers, planted along with cultivated varieties of native flowering plants,

Wildlife-friendly garden in New York containing cardinal flower (*Lobelia cardinalis*), wild bergamot (*Monarda fistulosa*), tall coneflowers (*Rudbeckia maxima*), jewelweed (*Impatiens capensis*), and American elderberry (*Sambucus canadensis*).

Cardinal flower (*Lobelia cardinalis*).

Orange jewelweed (*Impatiens capensis*).

Ragged coneflower (*Rudbeckia laciniata*).

Wild bergamot (*Monarda fistulosa*).

California meadow garden with poppy mallow (*Callirhoe involucrata*), blue thimble flower (*Gilia capitata*), and California poppy.

California brittlebush (*Encelia californica*).

Prairie garden including black-eyed Susan (*Rudbeckia hirta*), butterflyweed (*Asclepias tuberosa*), and pale purple coneflower (*Echinacea pallida*).

Blue thimble flower (*Gilia capitata*).

provide endless garden possibilities. As natural areas are cleared or compromised by development, many species have become threatened or endangered. Cultivating locally native wildflowers in your garden can help preserve them for the future.

More important than climate for successful wildflower gardening are soil composition and moisture content. Temperature is a less critical factor. Annual wildflowers are not often affected by winter freeze-ups. Perennial wildflowers are generally more sensitive to summer heat than to cold weather, and the primary effect of temperature is on their flowering times.

In an established garden, the existing trees will be the determinant of which wildflowers can survive best on your site. For example, if a group of conifers is growing on your property, around them you should choose to plant forest wildflowers that thrive in shade and acid soil. Under established deciduous trees, the soil will be less acid and will have lighter shade, and wildflowers from a deciduous woodland environment will thrive there. Where an unshaded lawn is now growing, a meadow garden that contains native ornamental grasses and prairie wildflowers will thrive. If you have surface water on your property in the form of a brook, pond, or swampy area, a wetland garden of native plants that love water will thrive there.

Birds that normally or occasionally feed on or near the ground, such as buntings, sparrows, and common yellowthroats, can become resident in a densely planted wildflower garden. Towhees and thrushes can become resident in the quieter, undisturbed corners of the wildflower garden. The masses of wildflowers attract many insects that will in turn attract a wide variety of insectivorous birds.

A densely planted wildflower garden will contain valuable shelter and nesting sites for birds that normally nest on or near the ground. These birds include the indigo bunting, common yellowthroat, song sparrow, red-winged blackbird, and white-crowned sparrow.

Establish your wildflower garden in a sunny, well-drained location that is sheltered from prevailing winds and free of weeds. To thrive, most wildflowers prefer 5 to 8 hours of sunshine a day. Most wildflowers will not grow well in compacted soil, so you should create paths or stepping-stones for foot-traffic movement through the garden area.

Consider replacing some or all of your lawn area with a meadow of wildflowers and native grasses. Grasses are an inte-

Blue-eyed grass (*Sisyrinchium bellum*).

California poppy (*Eschscholzia californica*) and Douglas iris (*Iris douglasiana*).

New York City's High Line linear park is an elevated garden with mainly native plants including sweet coneflower (*Rudbeckia subtomentosa*), bee balm (*Monarda fistulosa*) 'Claire Grace', and wild quinine (*Parthenium integrifolium*).

gral part of a bird-welcoming meadow garden. Sow seeds in early spring. Make sure the area you intend to plant is free of weeds, till the soil to a depth of 1 to 2 inches, spread the seeds generously, and gently tamp down the soil. In the first and second growing season, you can high-mow your meadow in the fall after the flowers have set seed, to distribute seeds on the ground before the snow arrives. Once the garden is established, discontinue mowing and leave the seeds for the birds to enjoy.

After a few seasons, the perennial wildflowers will outperform the annuals, so if there are particular annual plants that you wish to retain, consider planting these as a garden border where they can easily be replanted each season. Place the plants by height to create a multileveled garden for a variety of food niches.

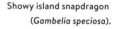

Showy island snapdragon (*Gambelia speciosa*).

California wildlife-friendly garden including Pacific coreopsis (*Coreopsis maritima*), California poppy, (*Eschscholzia californica*), native lilac (*Ceanothus concha*), the lavender-pink flowered, elegant clarkia (*Clarkia unguiculata*), and penstemons.

Santa Susana monkeyflower (*Diplacus rutilus*).

Matilija poppy
(*Romneya trichocalyx*).

Bladderpod (*Isomeris arborea*).

Poppy mallow (*Callirhoe involucrata*).

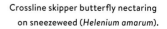

Streambank lupine (*Lupinus rivularis*).

Crossline skipper butterfly nectaring
on sneezeweed (*Helenium amarum*).

Providing Wild Food

Ralph Waldo Emerson once wrote, "What is a weed? A plant whose virtues have not yet been discovered."

Some native plants have a bad name among gardeners and are considered "weeds," which are pulled out so they don't contaminate our pristine gardens. Consider the lowly dandelion, whose many windborne seeds breed huge numbers of dreaded offspring in our lawns. But birds know the virtues of what we may call weeds. A weed patch in your yard will contain an enormous quantity of nutrient-rich seeds that will attract a variety of birds to the garden.

Many species that do not normally visit gardens or feeder stations will flock to a wild food patch, because these plants provide vast quantities of their staple wild foods. Weeds are also exceptionally good for attracting butterflies, and you won't be disturbed when the caterpillars eat their leaves. Many so-called weeds are in fact undervalued wildflowers, such as Joe-Pye weed, boneset, and goldenrod. Others include fleabane, chicory, asters, black-eyed Susans, yarrow, hawkweed, and sunflowers, which are widely considered beautiful garden plants and are beloved by garden birds.

Try establishing a wild food patch in a secluded, preferably sunny section of your backyard by simply exposing a patch of bare soil. Dormant seeds will soon result in a crop of self-seeding plants such as lamb's-quarter, ragweed, or foxtail—all excellent plants for attracting birds. To give the wild patch a somewhat controlled look, either make the area a regular shape or border it with a hedge. You will soon notice a marked increase in the number and variety of birds in your garden, and the birds will stay for an extended time. If you do not wish to have a wild food section in your garden, you could at least let a "weed" such as pokeweed grow in a corner of the garden and enjoy a large variety of birds that would not normally visit a garden environment.

Female ruby-crowned kinglet in goldenrod (*Solidago* sp).

Immature eastern bluebirds feeding on the fruits of pokeweed (*Phytolacca americana*), a weed worth cultivating.

Savannah sparrow feeding on the seeds of cow parsnip (*Heracleum maximum*).

In the winter months in cold climates, the seed heads that are left standing above the snow become an important food source when food is scarce. In summer months, when nestlings must be fed, your ready-made food patch will be an additional source of nutrient-rich food, which the birds constantly need.

Try stringing a wire across the wild-food patch, and a miniature hedgerow will be created by resting birds ejecting their favored seeds in a ready-made fertilizer onto the wild garden below.

If you leave a section of lawn unmown, many of these plants will appear from dormant seed. The plants in the wild food patch will generally self-sow and become a crop of seeds that the birds will harvest the following year.

SOME USEFUL WEEDS *and* WILD PLANTS

Monarch butterfly nectaring on
common milkweed (*Asclepias syriaca*).

Female Lawrence's goldfinch feeding in common fiddleneck
(*Amsinckia menziesii var. intermedia*). The seeds are the favored food of
Lawrence's goldfinch during the nesting season of spring and early summer.

The wild native plants described here, often considered weeds, are attractive to many bird species and can make useful additions to your garden. Many more examples can be found in part 3, Plant Directory.

➤ common fiddleneck (*Amsinckia menziesii* var. *intermedia*). An erect, bristly annual herb widespread and common, particularly in the west. Yellow-orange flowers are held in a terminal whorl. Flowers in February and March are followed by an enormous crop of seeds fed on by a wide variety of birds. Plants grow to 32 inches.

➤ common yarrow (*Achillea millefolium*). An attractive plant particularly useful for butterfly gardens. It is a drought-resistant perennial usually found growing in disturbed soil across most of temperate North America. Native species have white flower heads borne on a single upright stem up to 3 feet tall from May to June. In mountain regions, the flowers can be pink or light lavender. Several cavity-nesting birds use common yarrow for nest lining. Many birds feed on the seeds. Insects attracted to the flowers also attract many birds.

➤ milkweeds (*Asclepias* spp.). Many species of milkweed are excellent garden plants, flowering between May and September. Songbirds are attracted to the decorative seed heads, and hummingbirds and the hummingbird moth are attracted to the flowers. Milkweed plants grow to 4 feet tall, and are important nectaring and host plants for butterflies.

➤ lamb's-quarters (*Chenopodium berlandieri*). Annual weeds that produce an abundance of oily seed that garden birds favor. The plants are widespread across North America, from Alaska and northern Canada to Mexico. Scores of chickadees, siskins, buntings, white-crowned sparrows, and house finches will bypass feeder stations to flock to these plants. They are a host plant for butterflies. Plants grow 4 to 10 feet tall.

➤ doveweeds (*Croton* spp.). An important food source for birds in the southern and prairie states. Most species are annuals, but some are perennial. The seeds are favored by the mourning dove, white-winged dove, and common ground dove. Northern cardinals, bobwhites, and other ground feeders are attracted to the seeds. And butterflies use it as a host plant. Doveweeds grow 2 to 4 feet tall.

Blue grosbeak feeding on weed seeds.

➤ fleabanes (*Erigeron* spp.). Attractive plants to 2 feet tall, with numerous small, yellow-centered, daisylike flowers in a variety of colors. Flowers are followed by small, white-haired fruits that are consumed by many birds including native sparrows, goldfinches, house finches, and pine siskins. Many butterflies exclusively use fleabanes as host plants. Widespread, with 173 species found in North America, and most common in the west. It was once thought to repel fleas.

➤ California buckwheats (*Eriogonum* spp.). Drought tolerant, over 20 species in cultivation. The coastal species are salt-spray tolerant with a long flowering period of 6 months or more. Attractive to butterflies, especially coppers, blues, and hairstreaks, and predator insects. Provide good protective cover for small birds. California buckwheat (*E. fasciculatum*) grows 12 to 40 inches high and 30 to 50 inches wide. Pink flowers from May to October.

➤ Joe-Pye weeds (*Eupatorium* spp.). Many species are excellent garden plants. Songbirds are attracted to the nutritious seeds and to the insects attracted to the flowers. The plant is an important nectaring and host plant for butterflies, including the eastern tiger swallowtail, great spangled fritillary, pearl crescent, monarch, and the tawny-edged skipper. Flowers between July and October. Can be tall (2 to 12 feet) but dwarf varieties are available.

➤ cow parsnip (*Heracleum maximum*). A tall perennial (6 to 8 feet tall and 8 feet wide) that is the largest member of the carrot family. It provides shelter, and many birds are attracted to the large flower heads to forage for insects. Flowers appear from February to September. Butterflies go to it for nectar and use it as a host plant. (Caution: People with sensitive skin should avoid contact with this plant since it may cause a skin rash).

➤ sneezeweeds (*Helenium* spp.). Flowers from midsummer to well into fall. The plant produces nutritious seed at a time when other seed is scarce. Sneezeweed was once used to make snuff (its name is not derived from the effects of the pollen). It is an important host and nectar plant for butterflies. The plants grow from 1 to 3 feet tall. Many species are excellent garden plants, and many cultivars are available.

➤ native sunflowers (*Helianthus* spp.). One of the most important seed-producing plants for birds. At least 46 species of birds, including chickadees, nuthatches, and titmice, are known to feed on the seeds. Many species are attractive garden plants. The plants grow from 3 to 10 feet tall, and are important host and nectar plants for butterflies.

➤ witchgrass (*Panicum capillare*). An attractive grass species that is suitable for cultivation. Blue grosbeaks, native sparrows, larks, and bobwhites are among the at least 61 bird species that feed on the seeds.

➤ pokeweed (*Phytolacca americana*). A tall weed (to 10 feet tall) that is worth cultivating for birds. The black-purple berries are fed on by at least 52 species of birds. It is an excellent source of wild food for bluebirds, catbirds, thrushes, vireos, cardinals, and cedar waxwings. The plant is widespread, except for Alaska and the mountain states. It flowers in midsummer and dies back in winter. (Poisonous for humans unless cooked correctly.)

➤ goldenrods (*Solidago* spp.). Many species are excellent garden plants and grow well especially when local varieties are selected. Pine siskins, American tree sparrows, goldfinches, and juncos feed on the seed. The bright golden late-summer flowers attract substantial numbers of insects that pollinate the flowers and in turn attract insectivorous birds. Grow 2 to 6 feet tall; some compact cultivars are available.

➤ dandelions (*Taraxacum* spp.). Widespread across North America. An important plant for many birds, providing seed in all seasons. They will spring up naturally in your yard, and if you don't mind having them there, leave them for the birds. Sparrows, goldfinches, indigo buntings, and pine siskins are among the birds that feed on the dandelion seed, and the fluffy dandelion seed head provides nest-lining material. Grow to about 8 inches tall.

The wildflowers listed in this calendar include the wild grasses and plants with beautiful showy flowers that attract insects and have ornamental seed heads that produce nutritious seeds for seed-eating birds. Most of the flowers also attract butterflies, and several attract hummingbirds. The listed plants are suggestions only, because many other plants in the same species might be suitable for your locality. The list includes both annual and perennial plants. Annual plants live for 12 months or less, setting seed and then dying out. Perennials are hardier and live for many years, depending on the species, and include bulbs and rhizomes as well as woody plants. Biennials usually only survive for two years. Some plants may be perennial where they occur naturally, but if you are growing a warm-climate species in a cold zone, they may behave like annuals.

The plants in the calendar are listed alphabetically by botanical name, followed by the most widely used common name. For each plant, you'll find information on the flower color, the kind of light needed for successful cultivation, gardening and wildlife uses of the plant, flowering months, hardiness zones, and approximate mature height. The plants are grouped in four categories: annual wild plants for flowers and seeds, annual wild grasses, perennial wild plants for flowers and seeds, and perennial wild grasses.

CALENDAR *for* WILDFLOWERS

opposite, top: Desert garden, Boyce Thompson Arboretum, Arizona, containing many wildflower plants.

KEY	
○	full sun
◑	full sun to partial shade
●	light shade to shade
🐦	nesting plant
🦅	shelter plant
🐦	roosting plant
🦋	nectar for butterflies
⬮	host plant for butterflies
🍁	fall color
✳	showy flowers
🦅	nectar for hummingbirds

opposite, bottom: Plants in a northeastern wildlife-friendly native garden include goldenrods (*Solidago* spp.), cardinal flower (*Lobelia cardinalis*), white-flowered common yarrow (*Achillea millefolium*), and wild bergamot (*Monarda fistulosa*).

ANNUAL WILD PLANTS *for* FLOWERS *and* SEEDS

BOTANICAL NAME	COMMON NAME	FLOWER COLOR	LIGHT NEEDS	
Bidens spp.	beggartick, all species including:			
Bidens aristosa	tickseed sunflower	yellow	◯	
Centaurea spp.	knapweed, all species including:			
Centaurea americana	American basket flower	lavender to pink	◑	
Cleome spp.	cleome, all species including:			
Cleome serrulata	Rocky Mountain beeplant	pink to red	◑	
Coreopsis spp.	tickseed, all species including:			
Coreopsis bigelovii	Bigelow's tickseed	yellow	◯	
Coreopsis calliopsidea	leaf-stem tickseed	yellow	◯	
Helianthus spp.	sunflower, all species including:			
Helianthus annuus	common sunflower	yellow	◯	
Lupinus spp.	lupine, all species including:			
Lupinus bicolor	miniature lupine	violet to white	◯	
Lupinus concinnus	annual lupine	reddish purple	◯	
Lupinus texensis	Texas bluebonnet	blue	◯	

◯ full sun   ◑ full sun to partial shade   ● light shade to shade   🐣 nesting plant   🪶 shelter plants   🐦 roosting plant

PLANT USES	APPROXIMATE FLOWERING MONTHS J F M A M J J A S O N D	HARDINESS ZONES	MATURE HEIGHT
🦋 ✿	• • • • • • ◆◆ • • • •	6	3–6 ft.
🦋 ✿	• • • • ◆◆ • • • • • •	3–9	1½–5 ft.
🦋 ✿	• • • • • ◆◆◆◆ • • •	3–10	2–5 ft.
🦋 ✿	• ◆◆◆◆◆ • • • • • •	8	1–3 ft.
✿	• • ◆◆◆ • • • • • • •	8	1–3 ft.
🦋 ⊤ ✿	• • • • • ◆◆◆◆ • • •	4–8	6 ft.
🦋 ✿	• • • • ◆◆◆ • • • • •	4–9	1–3 ft.
🦋 ✿	• • ◆◆◆ • • • • • • •	3–8	1 ft.
✲ 🦋 ⊤ ✿	• • ◆◆◆ • • • • • • •	3–8	1–3 ft.

🦋 nectar for butterflies   ⊤ host plant for butterflies   🍁 fall color   ✿ showy flowers   ✲ nectar for hummingbirds

ANNUAL WILD PLANTS *for* FLOWERS *and* SEEDS

BOTANICAL NAME	COMMON NAME	FLOWER COLOR	LIGHT NEEDS	
Myosotis spp.	forget-me-not, all species including:			
Myosotis laxa	forget-me-not	blue	○	
Rudbeckia spp.	coneflower, all species including:			
Rudbeckia hirta 'Gloriosa'	'Gloriosa' black-eyed Susan	yellow	◑	
Symphyotrichum spp.	aster, all species including:			
Symphyotrichum ericoides	heath aster	white to pink	○	

 full sun 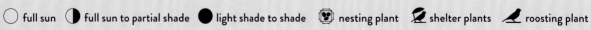 full sun to partial shade   light shade to shade   nesting plant   shelter plants roosting plant

PLANT USES	APPROXIMATE FLOWERING MONTHS J F M A M J J A S O N D	HARDINESS ZONES	MATURE HEIGHT
🦋 ✿	· · · · ◆◆◆◆ · · · ·	3–9	1 ft.
🦋 ✿	· · · · · ◆◆◆ · · · ·	3–9	1–3 ft.
🦋 T ✿	· · · · · · ◆◆◆◆ · ·	4–9	1½–3 ft.

 nectar for butterflies   T host plant for butterflies   🍁 fall color   ✿ showy flowers   nectar for hummingbirds

Huachuca agave (*Agave parryi* var. *huachucensis*).

Mojave pincushion (*Chaenactis xantiana*).

Copper Canyon daisy (*Tagetes lemmonii*).

Checkered white butterfly nectaring on blanketflower (*Gaillardia pulchella*).

Purple prairie clover (*Dalea purpurea*).

Costa's hummingbird in Texas betony (*Stachys coccinea*).

Violet prickly pear (*Opuntia gosseliniana*).

Parry's penstemon (*Penstemon parryi*).

Marsh marigold (*Caltha palustris*).

Monarch butterfly nectaring on pinxterbloom azalea (*Rhododendron periclymenoides*).

Common shooting star (Dodecatheon meadia).

Fire pink (*Silene virginica*).

Virginia bluebell (*Mertensia virginica*).

Dutchman's breeches (*Dicentra cucullaria*).

Canada lily (*Lilium canadense*).

Fruit of Jack-in-the-pulpit (*Arisaema triphyllum*).

ANNUAL WILD GRASSES

BOTANICAL NAME	COMMON NAME	FLOWER COLOR	LIGHT NEEDS	
Panicum capillare	witchgrass	green to purple	○	
Panicum clandestinum	deer-tongue grass	straw	●	
Panicum virgatum	switchgrass	gold	○	
Setaria spp.	bristlegrasses, all species including:			
Setaria macrostachya	plains bristlegrass	yellow	○	

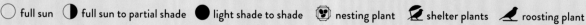 full sun   full sun to partial shade   light shade to shade   nesting plant   shelter plants   roosting plant

PLANT USES	APPROXIMATE FLOWERING MONTHS J F M A M J J A S O N D	HARDINESS ZONES	MATURE HEIGHT
🦋 ⊤	• • • • • • ◆◆◆ • • •	1–9	1–3 ft.
🦋 ⊤	• • • • ◆◆◆◆◆ • • •	5	1 ft.
🦋 ⊤	• • • • • • • ◆◆ • • •	3	4–6 ft.
🦋 ⊤	• • • • ◆◆◆ • • • •	4–8	3 ft.

🦋 nectar for butterflies   ⊤ host plant for butterflies   🍁 fall color   ✹ showy flowers   ⟡ nectar for hummingbirds

PERENNIAL WILD PLANTS *for* FLOWERS AND SEEDS

BOTANICAL NAME	COMMON NAME	FLOWER COLOR	LIGHT NEEDS
Aquilegia spp.	columbine, all species including:		
Aquilegia caerulea	Rocky Mountain columbine	blue and white	◑
Aquilegia canadensis	wild columbine	light pink and yellow to red	◑
Aquilegia chrysantha	golden columbine	yellow	◑
Aquilegia formosa	western columbine	red and yellow	◑
Arisaema spp.	Jack-in-the-pulpit, all species including:		
Arisaema triphyllum	Jack-in-the-pulpit	green and brown	●
Asclepias spp.	milkweed, all species, including:		
Asclepias purpurascens	purple milkweed	magenta red	◑
Asclepias speciosa	showy milkweed	rose	○
Asclepias syriaca	common milkweed	purple	◑
Asclepias tuberosa	butterfly weed	orange	◑
Baileya spp.	desert marigold, all species including:		
Baileya multiradiata	desert marigold	yellow	○

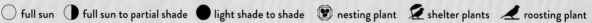

○ full sun   ◑ full sun to partial shade   ● light shade to shade   nesting plant   shelter plants   roosting plant

PLANT USES	APPROXIMATE FLOWERING MONTHS J F M A M J J A S O N D	HARDINESS ZONES	MATURE HEIGHT
hummingbird, showy flowers	· · · · · ◆ ◆ ◆ · · · ·	3–9	1–3 ft.
hummingbird, showy flowers	· · · ◆ ◆ ◆ · · · · · ·	3–8	1–3 ft.
hummingbird, showy flowers	· · · · · · ◆ ◆ · · · ·	3–9	2–3 ft.
hummingbird, showy flowers	· · · · ◆ ◆ ◆ ◆ · · · ·	3–7	2–4 ft.
showy flowers	· · ◆ ◆ ◆ ◆ · · · · · ·	4–9	1–3 ft.
hummingbird, nectar butterflies, host plant, showy flowers	· · · · ◆ ◆ ◆ ◆ ◆ · · ·	3–9	1–3 ft.
hummingbird, nectar butterflies, host plant, showy flowers	· · · · ◆ ◆ ◆ ◆ ◆ · · ·	3–9	2–4 ft.
nectar butterflies, host plant, showy flowers	· · · · ◆ ◆ ◆ ◆ ◆ · · ·	3–9	2–4 ft.
hummingbird, nectar butterflies, host plant, showy flowers	· · · · ◆ ◆ ◆ ◆ ◆ · · ·	3–10	1–2 ft.
nectar butterflies, showy flowers	· · ◆ ◆ ◆ ◆ ◆ ◆ ◆ ◆ ◆ ·	7–10	1–1½ ft.

nectar for butterflies   host plant for butterflies   fall color   showy flowers   nectar for hummingbirds

PERENNIAL WILD PLANTS *for* FLOWERS *and* SEEDS

BOTANICAL NAME	COMMON NAME	FLOWER COLOR	LIGHT NEEDS
Campanula spp.	bellflower, all species including:		
Campanula divaricata	southern harebell	white to pale lavender	◑
Campanula rotundifolia	bluebell bellflower	blue to violet	◑
Coreopsis spp.	tickseed, all species including:		
Coreopsis lanceolata	lance-leaf coreopsis	yellow	○
Coreopsis maritima	Pacific coreopsis	yellow	○
Coreopsis verticillata	thread-leaf coreopsis	yellow	○
Dalea spp.	prairie clover, all species including:		
Dalea purpurea	purple prairie clover	purple	○
Delphinium spp.	larkspur, all species including:		
Delphinium californicum	California larkspur	bluish purple	◑
Delphinium cardinale	cardinal larkspur	red	◑
Delphinium glaucum	Sierra larkspur	bluish purple	◑
Echinacea spp.	coneflower, all species including:		
Echinacea pallida	pale purple coneflower	lavender	◑

○ full sun   ◑ full sun to partial shade   ● light shade to shade   🐣 nesting plant   🪺 shelter plants   🐦 roosting plant

PLANT USES	APPROXIMATE FLOWERING MONTHS J F M A M J J A S O N D	HARDINESS ZONES	MATURE HEIGHT
nectar for butterflies, showy flowers	· · · · · · ◆ ◆ ◆ · · ·	3–8	2 ft.
nectar for butterflies, showy flowers	· · · · · · ◆ ◆ ◆ ◆ · ·	3–9	1 ft.
nectar for butterflies, showy flowers	· · · ◆ ◆ ◆ · · · · · ·	3–9	1–2 ft.
nectar for butterflies, showy flowers	· · ◆ ◆ ◆ · · · · · · ·	3–9	1–3 ft.
nectar for butterflies, showy flowers	· · · · · · ◆ ◆ · · · ·	3–9	1–3 ft.
nectar for hummingbirds, nectar for butterflies, showy flowers	· · · · · · ◆ ◆ ◆ ◆ · ·	3–9	1 ft.
nectar for hummingbirds, nectar for butterflies, showy flowers	· · · · · ◆ ◆ ◆ · · · ·	3–7	3–6 ft.
nectar for hummingbirds, nectar for butterflies, showy flowers	· · · · · ◆ ◆ ◆ ◆ · · ·	7–8	3–7 ft.
nectar for hummingbirds, nectar for butterflies, showy flowers	· · · · · · · ◆ ◆ ◆ · ·	3–7	3–6 ft.
nectar for butterflies, showy flowers	· · · · · ◆ ◆ ◆ · · · ·	3–7	3–6 ft.

nectar for butterflies   host plant for butterflies   fall color   showy flowers   nectar for hummingbirds

PERENNIAL WILD PLANTS *for* FLOWERS *and* SEEDS

BOTANICAL NAME	COMMON NAME	FLOWER COLOR	LIGHT NEEDS
Echinacea purpurea	purple coneflower	pink to purple, rarely white	◑
Encelia spp.	brittlebush, all species including:		
Encelia californica	California brittlebush	yellow	○
Encelia farinosa	brittlebush	yellow	○
Eschscholzia spp.	California poppy, all species including:		
Eschscholzia californica	California poppy	orange to yellow	○
Eupatorium spp.	Joe-Pye weed / boneset, all species including:		
Eupatorium fistulosum	Joe-Pye weed	pinkish purple	◑
Eupatorium perfoliatum	boneset	white	◑
Eupatorium purpureum	sweet-scented Joe-Pye weed	pinkish lavender	◑
Helenium spp.	sneezeweed, all species, including:		
Helenium amarum	bitterweed	yellow	○
Helenium autumnale	common sneezeweed	yellow	○

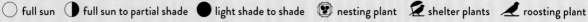

○ full sun   ◑ full sun to partial shade   ● light shade to shade   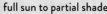 nesting plant   shelter plants   roosting plant

PLANT USES	APPROXIMATE FLOWERING MONTHS J F M A M J J A S O N D	HARDINESS ZONES	MATURE HEIGHT
🦋 ✿	· · · ◆◆◆◆◆◆ · · ·	3–9	2–5 ft.
✿	· ◆◆◆◆◆ · · · · ·	9	6–12 ft.
✿	· · ◆◆◆ · · · · · ·	9	1–3 ft.
✿	· ◆◆◆◆◆◆◆◆ · · ·	3–9	1–3 ft.
✖ 🦋 T ✿	· · · · · ◆◆◆◆ · ·	4–8	5–12 ft.
🦋 ✿	· · · · ◆◆◆◆◆ · ·	4–8	2–4 ft.
✖ 🦋 ✿	· · · · · · ◆◆◆ · ·	4–7	3–6 ft.
🦋 ✿	· · · ◆◆◆◆◆ · · ·	7–11	1–3 ft.
🦋 ✿	· · · · · ◆◆◆ · ·	3–8	1–3 ft.

🦋 nectar for butterflies   T host plant for butterflies   🍁 fall color   ✿ showy flowers   ✖ nectar for hummingbirds

PERENNIAL WILD PLANTS *for* FLOWERS *and* SEEDS

BOTANICAL NAME	COMMON NAME	FLOWER COLOR	LIGHT NEEDS
Helianthus spp.	sunflower, all species, including:		
Helianthus angustifolius	swamp sunflower	yellow	○
Helianthus californicus	California sunflower	yellow	○
Helianthus decapetalus	narrow-leaved sunflower	yellow	○
Helianthus tuberosus	Jerusalem artichoke	yellow	○
Liatris spp.	blazing star, all species including:		
Liatris pycnostachya	prairie blazing star	rose to purple	○
Liatris scariosa	large blazing star	purple	○
Liatris spicata	dense blazing star	rose to purple	○
Lobelia spp.	lobelia, all species including:		
Lobelia cardinalis	cardinal flower	scarlet	○
Lobelia puberula	blue lobelia	blue	○
Lupinus spp.	lupine, all species including:		
Lupinus palmeri	bluebonnet lupine	blue	○
Lupinus perennis	wild lupine	purple	○

 full sun 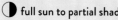 full sun to partial shade light shade to shade  nesting plant shelter plants 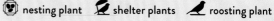 roosting plant

PLANT USES	APPROXIMATE FLOWERING MONTHS J F M A M J J A S O N D	HARDINESS ZONES	MATURE HEIGHT
🦋 host showy	· · · · · · ◆ ◆ ◆ ◆ · ·	6–9	4–8 ft.
🦋 host showy	· · · · · ◆ ◆ ◆ · · · ·	4–8	3–6 ft.
🦋 host showy	· · · · · · · ◆ ◆ ◆ · ·	3–9	2–5 ft.
🦋 host showy	· · · · · · · ◆ ◆ ◆ · ·	6–9	4–8 ft.
hummingbird 🦋 showy	· · · · · · ◆ ◆ ◆ ◆ ◆ ·	3–9	3–6 ft.
hummingbird 🦋 showy	· · · · · · · ◆ ◆ · · ·	4–8	2–4 ft.
hummingbird 🦋 showy	· · · · · · ◆ ◆ ◆ · · ·	3–10	3–4 ft.
hummingbird 🦋 host showy	· · · · · · ◆ ◆ ◆ ◆ · ·	2–9	1–4 ft.
hummingbird 🦋 host showy	· · · · · · · ◆ ◆ ◆ · ·	2–8	1–4 ft.
🦋 showy	· · · ◆ ◆ ◆ ◆ ◆ ◆ · · ·	8	1–3 ft.
host 🦋 showy	· · · · ◆ ◆ ◆ · · · · ·	4–9	1–3 ft.

🦋 nectar for butterflies   ⊤ host plant for butterflies   🍂 fall color   ✳ showy flowers   🐦 nectar for hummingbirds

PERENNIAL WILD PLANTS *for* FLOWERS *and* SEEDS

BOTANICAL NAME	COMMON NAME	FLOWER COLOR	LIGHT NEEDS
Lupinus villosus	lady lupine	blue to violet	○
Monarda spp.	bergamot, all species including:		
Monarda didyma	bee balm	red	◑
Monarda fistulosa	wild bergamot	pink, lavender or white	◑
Penstemon spp.	penstemon, all species including:		
Penstemon barbatus	common beardtongue	scarlet	○
Penstemon centranthifolius	scarlet bugler	scarlet	○
Penstemon eatonii	firecracker plant	red	○
Penstemon laevigatus	smooth beardtongue	purple	○
Phlox spp.	phlox, all species including:		
Phlox carolina	Carolina phlox	lavender to pink	●
Phlox divaricata	wild sweet William	light blue	●
Phlox paniculata	summer phlox	white to pink or lavender	●
Phlox stolonifera	creeping phlox	white, blue, or lavender	●
Rudbeckia spp.	coneflower/black-eyed Susan, all species including:		
Rudbeckia californica	California coneflower	yellow	◑

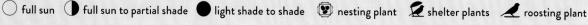

○ full sun   ◑ full sun to partial shade   ● light shade to shade   nesting plant   shelter plants   roosting plant

PLANT USES	APPROXIMATE FLOWERING MONTHS J F M A M J J A S O N D	HARDINESS ZONES	MATURE HEIGHT
🦋 ❋	· · · ◆◆◆◆ · · · ·	8	1–3 ft.
🐦 🦋 ❋	· · · · · ◆◆◆◆ · · ·	4–8	2–4 ft.
🐦 🦋 ❋	· · · · · · ◆◆◆ · · ·	3–9	2–4 ft.
🐦 🦋 ❋	· · · · · · ◆◆◆◆ · ·	3–8	1½–3 ft.
🐦 🦋 ❋	· · · · ◆◆◆◆ · · · ·	8–10	1–4 ft.
🐦 🦋 ❋	· · · ◆◆◆◆◆◆ · ·	7–9	4 ft.
🐦 🦋 ⊤ ❋	· · · · · ◆◆◆ · · · ·	3–10	3–4 ft.
🦋 ❋	· · · · ◆◆◆◆◆◆ · ·	5–8	1–3 ft.
🦋 ❋	· · ◆◆◆ · · · · · ·	3–8	8–18 in.
🦋 ❋	· · · · · ◆◆ · · · ·	4–8	3–6 ft.
🦋 ❋	· · · ◆◆ · · · · · ·	5–8	6–12 in.
🦋 ❋	· · · · · ◆◆◆◆◆ ·	3–9	2–3 ft.

🦋 nectar for butterflies   ⊤ host plant for butterflies   🍁 fall color   ❋ showy flowers   🐦 nectar for hummingbirds

PERENNIAL WILD PLANTS *for* FLOWERS *and* SEEDS

BOTANICAL NAME	COMMON NAME	FLOWER COLOR	LIGHT NEEDS
Rudbeckia fulgida	orange coneflower	orange to yellow	◑
Rudbeckia laciniata	tall coneflower	bright yellow and green	◑
Rudbeckia nitida	shining coneflower	yellow	◑
Salvia spp.	sage, all species including:		
Salvia azurea	blue sage	blue	○
Salvia clevelandii	Cleveland's sage	dark blue	○
Salvia coccinea	scarlet sage	red	○
Salvia greggii	autumn sage	red	○
Salvia spathacea	hummingbird sage	magenta	◑
Silene spp.	campion, all species including:		
Silene californica	Indian pink	red	◑
Silene hookeri	Hooker's silene	purple	◑
Silene virginica	fire pink	red	◑
Silphium spp.	silphium, all species including:		
Silphium laciniatum	compass plant	yellow	○
Silphium perfoliatum	cup plant	yellow	○

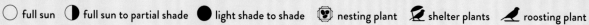

○ full sun   ◑ full sun to partial shade   ● light shade to shade   🐣 nesting plant   🍃 shelter plants   🐦 roosting plant

PLANT USES	APPROXIMATE FLOWERING MONTHS (J F M A M J J A S O N D)	HARDINESS ZONES	MATURE HEIGHT
🦋 ✿	· · · · · · ◆◆◆◆ · ·	3–9	1½–3 ft.
🦋 ✿	· · · · · · ◆◆◆ · ·	3–9	5–10 ft.
🦋 ✿	· · · ◆◆◆◆◆◆ · ·	4–9	3–4 ft.
🐦 🦋 ✿	· · · · · ◆◆◆ · · ·	5–9	3–4 ft.
🐦 🦋 ✿	· · · ◆◆◆◆◆ · · ·	8–11	3–6 ft.
🐦 🦋 ✿	· ◆◆◆◆◆◆◆◆◆ · ·	4–10	1–3 ft.
🐦 🦋 ✿	· · ◆◆◆◆◆◆◆ · ·	7–9	1–4 ft.
🐦 🦋 ✿	· · · ◆◆◆◆ · · ·	4–8	1½–3 ft.
🐦 ✿	· · ◆◆◆◆◆ · · · ·	3–10	1 ft.
🐦 ✿	· · · ◆◆◆ · · ·	5–8	1 ft.
🐦 🦋 ✿	· · ◆◆◆◆◆◆ · · ·	4–7	1–3 ft.
🦋 ✿	· · · · · · ◆◆◆ · ·	3–7	3–6 ft.
🐦 🦋 ✿	· · · · · · ◆◆◆ · ·	4–8	3–6 ft.

🦋 nectar for butterflies 🇹 host plant for butterflies 🍁 fall color ✿ showy flowers 🐦 nectar for hummingbirds

PERENNIAL WILD PLANTS *for* FLOWERS *and* SEEDS

BOTANICAL NAME	COMMON NAME	FLOWER COLOR	LIGHT NEEDS	
Silphium terebinthinaceum	prairie dock	yellow	○	
Solidago spp.	goldenrod, all species including:			
Solidago californica	California goldenrod	yellow	○	
Solidago canadensis	Canada goldenrod	yellow	○	
Solidago speciosa	showy goldenrod	yellow	○	
Symphyotrichum spp.	aster, all species including:			
Symphyotrichum novae-angliae	New England aster	lavender, violet, pink, or white	○	
Symphyotrichum novi-belgii	New York aster	white	○	
Tanacetum spp.	tansy, all species including:			
Tanacetum bipinnatum	Lake Huron tansy	yellow	○	
Viola spp.	violet, all species including:			
Viola blanda	sweet white violet	white	○	
Viola canadensis	Canadian white violet	white	●	

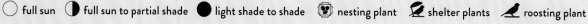

 full sun   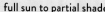 full sun to partial shade   light shade to shade   nesting plant   shelter plants   roosting plant

PLANT USES	APPROXIMATE FLOWERING MONTHS	HARDINESS ZONES	MATURE HEIGHT
	J F M A M J J A S O N D		
🦋 ✾	· · · · · · ◆◆◆ · · ·	4–8	3–6 ft.
🦋 ✾	· · · · · ◆◆◆◆ · ·	5–9	3–6 ft.
🦋 ✾	· · · · · · · ◆◆◆ ·	4–8	3–6 ft.
🦋 ✾	· · · · · · ◆◆ · · ·	4–8	3–6 ft.
🦋 T ✾	· · · · · · ◆◆◆ · ·	3–8	3–6 ft.
🦋 T ✾	· · · · · · ◆◆◆◆ · ·	3–8	1–6 ft.
✾	· · · · ◆◆◆◆◆ · ·	4	4–8 ft.
🦋 T ✾	· · · ◆◆ · · · · · ·	3–9	2–4 ft.
🦋 T ✾	· · · · ◆◆◆ · · · ·	3–8	1–3 ft.

🦋 nectar for butterflies   T host plant for butterflies   🍁 fall color   ✾ showy flowers   🕊 nectar for hummingbirds

PERENNIAL WILD GRASSES

BOTANICAL NAME	COMMON NAME	FLOWER COLOR	LIGHT NEEDS
Andropogon spp.	bluestem, all species including:		
Andropogon gerardii	big bluestem	blue	○
Andropogon scoparius	little bluestem	brown	○
Carex spp.	sedge, all species, including:		
Carex rosea	golden star sedge	green	●
Deschampsia spp.	hairgrass, all species including:		
Deschampsia flexuosa	wavy hairgrass	apricot	●
Elymus spp.	wild rye, all species including:		
Elymus canadensis	Canada wild rye	straw	◑
Elymus villosus	silky wild rye	straw	●
Hystrix patula	bottlebrush grass	straw	●
Schizachyrium scoparium	little bluestem	blue	◑
Sorghastrum nutans	Indian grass	gold	◑
Sporobolus heterolepis	prairie dropseed	gold	○

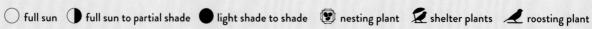

○ full sun ◑ full sun to partial shade ● light shade to shade 🐦 nesting plant 🦅 shelter plants 🐦 roosting plant

PLANT USES	APPROXIMATE FLOWERING MONTHS J F M A M J J A S O N D	HARDINESS ZONES	MATURE HEIGHT
🦋 T	• • • • • • • ◆ ◆ ◆ • •	4–8	5–8 ft.
🦋 T	• • • • • ◆ ◆ ◆ • • • •	4–9	1–3 ft.
🦋 T	• • • • ◆ ◆ • • • • •	4	1 ft.
🦋 T	• • • • ◆ ◆ • • • • •	4–9	3 ft.
🦋 T	• • • • • • ◆ ◆ • • • •	3	4–5 ft.
🦋 T	• • • • • • ◆ ◆ • • • •	3	4–6 ft.
🦋 T	• • • • • ◆ ◆ ◆ • • • •	3	2–5 ft.
🦋 T	• • • • • • • ◆ ◆ ◆ • •	2–7	2–3 ft.
🦋	• • • • • • ◆ ◆ • • • •	4	5–7 ft.
🦋	• • • • • • • ◆ ◆ • • •	3–8	2–4 ft.

🦋 nectar for butterflies   T host plant for butterflies   🍁 fall color   ✳ showy flowers   ✺ nectar for hummingbirds

Black-capped chickadee feeding on coreopsis. Spent flower heads left standing provide an excellent food source for seed-eating birds.

Mixed flock of mountain bluebirds and American goldfinches.

Columbia lily (*Lilium columbianum*).

Compass plant (*Silphium laciniatum*).

Damp area garden including white bog orchid (*Platanthera dilatata*), paintbrush (*Castilleja coccinea*), big-leaf lupine (*Lupinus polyphyllus*), and Columbia lily (*Lilium columbianum*)

Prairie blazing star (*Liatris pycnostachya*).

Downy paintbrush
(*Castilleja sessiliflora*).

Purple coneflower
(*Echinacea purpurea*).

Great spangled fritillary butterfly nectaring
on butterflyweed (*Asclepias tuberosa*).

White bog orchid (*Platanthera dilatata*).

Texas bluebonnet (*Lupinus texensis*).

PROVIDING WATER

A supply of fresh, clean water is an essential—and often overlooked—element for attracting birds to your garden. Throughout the year, birds need water for drinking and bathing. Unless you have a pond or stream on your property, the simplest way to provide water is to set out a birdbath.

Birds bathe and preen to keep their feathers in perfect condition for flying and to maintain the feathers' waterproofing and insulating properties. The individual feathers are made of keratin, the same substance as human fingernails, and become bent and disarranged with daily activity. So they must be repositioned and straightened by preening. The bird usually bathes and then passes the individual feathers through its bill, oiling them and snapping them back into position.

When bathing, birds scoop water up in their bills and splash it over their backs, flapping their wings and ruffling their feathers in a manner that could attract the attention of nearby cats. Wet feathers will hinder the birds' ability to fly and escape predators, including cats, so the placement and design of the birdbath is critical for the birds' safety.

Birdbaths

Birds will frequent a birdbath if you place one in your garden. Position the birdbath near protective shrubbery that is close enough to allow the birds to escape into it for safety, but not so close that a cat can pounce on the unwary birds. A pedestal

Marsh wren singing from a cattail flower spike.

Evening grosbeaks gather at a garden birdbath.

Rufous hummingbird collecting the cottonlike flower remnants from common cattail (*Typha latifolia*) for nest building.

birdbath is a good protection against cats and is available from garden supply stores. A wide, shallow bowl, preferably made from cast stone and mounted on a pedestal about 40 inches above the ground, is excellent. The birdbath should be shallow, because most birds dislike deep water. Ideal dimensions are ½ to 1 inch deep at the edges, sloping to a maximum of 2½ to 3 inches in the center. Choose a birdbath with a roughened bottom, allowing the birds to get a firm grip. Varying the depth of water in your birdbath will cater to the preferences of a greater variety of birds. Chickadees, goldfinches, and sparrows will bathe in the shallow section, while American robins, jays, and grackles will use the deeper water.

In the winter months, birds can have an especially hard time finding an adequate water source. You'll do birds a big favor by keeping the water in your birdbath unfrozen. It helps to locate the birdbath where it receives winter sunshine all day. But you'll get guaranteed results if you install a stock tank deicer or an electrical heating element designed for birdbaths. You will get a larger variety of birds attracted to your garden with a thawed water supply in winter. Make sure your power supply is safe, and consider having an outdoor power outlet installed close to the birdbath.

Eastern bluebird at a garden birdbath.

Garden Ponds

When you construct a garden pond, you can significantly increase the biodiversity in your yard. Frogs, toads, and salamanders can breed in a small pond, if it is 20 to 24 inches deep. Larger ponds can benefit swallows and purple martins, which feed on insects as they skim

Garden pond in Overland Park Arboretum and Botanical Gardens in Overland Park, Kansas, featuring blue pickerel plant (*Pontederia cordata*), white waterlily (*Nymphaea* spp.), and cordgrass (*Spartina* spp.).

SOME USEFUL NATIVE POND PLANTS

Pond plants provide food and shelter for aquatic critters, oxygenate the water, and are an essential ingredient when creating a successful garden pond. Plants should be grown in three zones: in the boggy zone around the perimeter of the pond, in the aquatic zone with plants floating on the water, and underwater in a submerged layer.

When you start your pond with a bucket of water from a successful pond, you will usually have collected some submerged plants, but they can also be purchased from aquarium suppliers or nurseries specializing in aquatic plants. These plants including coontail (*Ceratophyllum demersum*), American waterweed (*Elodea canadensis*), and white water-buttercup (*Ranunculus aquatilis*). There are many local varieties, but these examples are some found across North America.

Pond Edge or Shallow-Water Plants

Bulrushes and Cattails

Bulrushes and cattails provide food, shelter, and nesting sites for a wide variety of birds. They are important wetland plants for marsh and water birds. The seed is fed on by over 24 species of birds and the cottonlike fiber from old flower heads provides nest-building material for many birds. Some native bulrushes and cattails that grow in Zones 3–9 and are suitable for home ponds are:
➤small-fruited bulrush (*Scirpus microcarpus*). Grows 3 to 5 feet tall, 1 to 2 feet wide.
➤slender bulrush (*Schoenoplectus heterochaetus*). Grows 5 to 8 feet tall. Native to western North America from British Columbia to Texas.
➤common cattail (*Typha latifolia*). Up to 10 feet tall.
➤miniature cattail (*Typha minima*). Up to 5 feet tall.
➤narrow-leaf cattail (*Typha augustifolia*). Up to 5 feet tall.

Pickerel Weeds (*Pontederia* spp.)

These plants are widespread throughout North America in shallow water or bog areas. They produce large flower spikes in summer, attract hummingbirds, butterflies, and dragonflies, and provide protective cover.
➤blue pickerel plant (*P. cordata*). This plant at maturity is 18 to 24 inches tall and wide. The blue-violet flowers of this plant are borne on large spikes that appear from June to October and attract hummingbirds, butterflies, and dragonflies. Damselflies use the plant when shedding their larval stage, and several birds feed on the seed. The plant provides excellent shelter for wildlife when placed in clumps and shelter and food for fish and aquatic critters. Several cultivars are available. It has excellent filtration capabilities.

Marsh Marigolds (*Caltha* spp.)

These early spring-blooming pond plants have yellow to white flowers. They prefer cooler climates in part sun, in shallow water or moist edges. They attract butterflies, dragonflies, frogs, and birds. Zones 3–7.
➤marsh marigold (*C. palustris*). Grows 15 to 18 inches tall. Best in damp soil. Bright yellow flowers between March and July.

Monkeyflowers (*Mimulus* spp.)

A large and diverse group of plants, widespread in western North America, preferring constant moisture and full sun for best flowering. These are attractive pond edge or garden plants, attracting hummingbirds and butterflies. Numerous cultivars are available.
➤sticky monkeyflower (*M. aurantiacus*). Grows 2 to 4 feet tall. Zones 9–10. Yellow to orange flowers between March and August.

Rushes (*Juncus* spp.)

These useful background plants provide valuable shelter for aquatic life and nest building material for birds. Dragonfly larvae are often seen clinging to the stems, and several species of frogs and fish use rushes as a spawning ground. They grow in wet soil or water up to 6 inches deep.
➤California gray rush (*J. patens*). Grows 24 inches tall and 18 inches wide. Zones 6–10.
➤common rush (*J. effusus*). Grows 2 to 3 feet tall. Zones 4–10.

Sedges (*Carex* spp.)

Over 500 North American species of sedges provide food for over 50 species of birds. Clump-forming evergreen perennials with bladelike leaves, suitable for damp edges in full sun or part shade. Zones 6–9.
➤Payson's sedge (*C. paysonis*). Grows 1 to 2 feet tall. Zones 6–9.
➤tufted sedge (*C. elata*). Grows 10 to 15 inches tall. Zones 6–9.

Native Iris (*Iris* spp.)

Approximately 30 species are native to North America. They are perennial plants with swordlike leaves and showy flowers from May to August. They attract hummingbirds and butterflies. Suitable for planting along the pond edge or in shallow water.
➤northern blue flag (*I. versicolor*). Zones 2–9.
➤California iris (*I. tenuissima*). Grows 10 inches tall. Zones 7–8.
➤western blue flag (*I. missouriensis*). Grows 1 to 3 feet tall. Zones 3–9.

Other valuable pond edge plants that attract hummingbirds and butterflies include:
➤cardinal flower (*Lobelia cardinalis*).
➤great blue lobelia (*Lobelia siphilitica*).
➤bee balms (*Monarda* spp.).
➤milkweeds (*Asclepias* spp.).

Aquatic Plants

Watershield (*Brasenia schreberi*)

Widely distributed across North America. These floating plants are an alternative to waterlilies, with small dark purple flowers in midsummer. Bright green oval leaves are purple on the underside. The plant provides habitat and food for aquatic life. Zones 3–9.

Waterlilies

These floating aquatic plants, with showy, fragrant flowers and rounded, green, floating leaves, provide food and shelter for fish and other aquatic life. Several water birds feed on the seeds.
➤American white waterlily (*Nymphaea odorata*). Grows 0 to 12 inches tall. Zones 4–10. Suitable for large ponds. Large, fragrant pink or white flowers between March and October. Deciduous in winter.
➤small white waterlily (*Nymphaea tetragona*). Grows 18 to 24 inches tall. Zones 4–10. Suited to small, still ponds. Hardy. Small fragrant pink to mauve flowers in summer.
➤yellow pond lily (*Nuphar lutea*). Grows 0 to 12 inches tall. Zones 4–10. Prefers still water, but will tolerate slow-moving water. Bright yellow flowers from July to August.

A wildlife-friendly pond in Texas with Hill Country wildflowers, waterlilies (*Nymphaea* spp.), and sedges (*Carex* spp.).

the water's surface. Provide a bog garden with bog plantings alongside the pond for increased biodiversity and to make mud available for nest building material for swallows. Smaller pond inhabitants may include pond skaters, water beetles, damselflies, and dragonflies, just some of the small creatures crucial to the ecological balance of the pond.

Setting Up a Garden Pond

The best time to set up a garden pond is in late winter or early spring. Position your pond in a reasonably sunny spot where most aquatic plants will thrive. Important issues for creating the pond include:
➤ Preferably, allow rainwater to fill your pond, or if using tap water, allow it to stand for a week before adding fish.
➤ A small pond constructed for wildlife need not be more than 3 feet in diameter and 20 to 24 inches deep. However, varying the water

Common rush (*Juncus effusus*) flowers.

Payson's sedge (*Carex paysonis*) flower spike.

Northern blue flag (*Iris versicolor*).

depth will provide opportunities for a greater biodiversity to establish.

➤ Ideally, construct your pond with gradually sloping edges from ½ inch to 3 inches deep, with rough surfaces for secure footing for birds.

➤ Flat rocks positioned at the pond edge will provide a perch for birds and will attract butterflies and dragonflies to bask in the sun. Leave some of the rocks with a gap of ½ to 1 inch underneath for frogs to hide from predators such as raccoons and herons.

➤ Add dead leaves to the bottom of the pond for frogs to hide, and in fall, add a few extra handfuls of leaves to keep the deeper water warmer, helping frogs to overwinter.

➤ Only use organic gardening methods near your pond. The main food of frogs are mosquitoes, flies, and insects, and to control mosquitoes, only two or three fish are needed in a small pond. Select small native fish, such as minnows, which do not harm tadpoles. Avoid mosquito fish (*Gambusia affinis*), which feed on tadpoles and other aquatic life.

➤ As a rule of thumb, to control algae, floating plants should cover at least two-thirds of the surface area and underwater plants should cover one-third of the floor area of the pond.

➤ Consider installing a water feature. Soft drips or gurgling water sounds are effective in attracting birds.

➤ To quick-start a diversity of life in a new pond, add a bucket of water and mud from an established pond.

In no time at all, water beetles, damselflies, and dragonflies, along with frogs, toads, newts, salamanders, possibly aquatic turtles, and a variety of birds may appear at your pond, enriching a bird-friendly environment.

Small-fruited bulrush (*Scirpus microcarpus*).

Urban development has led to a reduction in the area available for planting. So when you are planning a garden to attract birds, it is important to choose plants that produce the greatest abundance of food for birds over a long period. The Calendar for Seasonal Fruiting lists a selection of plants, by region, known to be attractive to birds because they bear an abundant natural harvest of fruits.

By using the regional tables as a guide to choosing plants, you can provide birds with a sequence of berries, fruits, and seeds throughout the year, especially during the winter months. In the warmer months, insects are plentiful and fruits become a less important part of many birds' diet. When you are selecting plants, include in your choices plants for nesting, shelter, and roosting, and your yard will be a sanctuary for a wide variety of garden birds.

CALENDAR for SEASONAL FRUITING

NORTH AMERICAN REGIONS MAP

- Northeast Region
- Southeast Region
- Plains and Prairies Region
- Mountains and Deserts Region
- Pacific Coast Region

This map is divided into the five regions of the United States and Canada, broadly based on the map of the Level 1 Ecoregions of North America produced by the U.S. Environmental Protection Agency. The divisions contain areas of homogeneity, including soil, climate, geology, vegetation, physical geography, hydrology, and wildlife distribution.

The tables show fruiting plants for each of the five regions, arranged alphabetically by botanical name, followed by the most widely used common name. (Common names can differ from region to region.) For each plant, you'll find information on the kind of light needed for successful cultivation, other wildlife uses, fruiting months, hardiness zones, and approximate mature height. The approximate fruiting months for each plant are influenced by local climatic conditions, seasonal variations, and how quickly the birds devour the fruits. Several of the plants listed also attract hummingbirds or butterflies, provide nesting sites, shelter, or roosting sites, have showy flowers, and good fall color.

KEY	
○	full sun
◐	full sun to partial shade
●	light shade to shade
🕸	nesting plant
🐦	shelter plant
🐦	roosting plant
🦋	nectar for butterflies
⊤	host plant for butterflies
🍁	fall color
✳	showy flowers
🐦	nectar for hummingbirds

NORTHEAST REGION

BOTANICAL NAME	COMMON NAME	LIGHT NEEDS
Abies balsema	balsam fir	○
Acer negundo	box elder	◐
Acer rubrum	red maple	◐
Acer saccharum	sugar maple	◐
Alnus incana subsp. *rugosa*	speckled alder	○
Amelanchier arborea	shadblow	◐
Amelanchier laevis	Allegheny serviceberry	◐
Amelanchier stolonifera	running serviceberry	◐
Betula alleghaniensis	yellow birch	◐
Betula lenta	sweet birch	◐
Betula nigra	river birch	◐
Betula papyrifera	paper birch	○
Celtis occidentalis	common hackberry	◐
Celtis tenuifolia	Georgia hackberry	◐
Cornus alternifolia	pagoda dogwood	●
Cornus canadensis	bunchberry	●
Cornus florida	flowering dogwood	◐

  full sun   full sun to partial shade 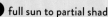 light shade to shade nesting plant shelter plants 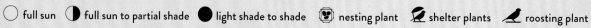 roosting plant

OTHER USES	APPROXIMATE FRUITING MONTHS J F M A M J J A S O N D	HARDINESS ZONES	MATURE HEIGHT
🦋 T ◉ 🍂 🐦	• • • ◆ ◆ ◆ • • • • • •	2–5	40–60 ft.
🦋 T ◉	◆ • • • • • ◆ ◆ ◆ ◆ ◆ ◆	2–8	50–70 ft.
🦋 🍁	• • • • • ◆ ◆ ◆ ◆ • • •	3–9	50–70 ft.
🦋 🍁	• • • • • ◆ ◆ ◆ • • • •	3–7	50–70 ft.
🦋 T 🍁 🐦	• • • • • • ◆ ◆ ◆ ◆ ◆ •	2–9	15–33 ft.
🦋 T 🍁 ✿	• • • • • • ◆ ◆ ◆ • • •	3–8	20–25 ft.
🦋 T 🍁 ✿	• • • • • • ◆ ◆ ◆ ◆ • •	3–8	40 ft.
🦋 🍁 ✿	• • • • • • • ◆ ◆ ◆ • •	5–8	1–4 ft.
🦋 T 🍁	• • • • • • ◆ ◆ ◆ • • •	3–6	60–75 ft.
🦋 T 🍁 ◉	• • • • • ◆ ◆ ◆ ◆ ◆ ◆ ◆	4–6	40–60 ft.
🦋 T 🍁 ◉	• • • • • • ◆ ◆ ◆ ◆ ◆ •	4–9	80 ft.
🦋 T 🍁 ◉	• • • • • • ◆ ◆ ◆ ◆ ◆ •	2–7	50–80 ft.
🦋 T 🍁 ◉ 🐦	◆ ◆ • • • • • • ◆ ◆ ◆ ◆	3–8	30–50
🦋 T 🍁 ◉ 🐦	◆ ◆ • • • • • • • ◆ ◆ ◆	6–9	6–25 ft.
🦋 T 🍁 ✿ ◉ 🐦	• • • • • • ◆ ◆ ◆ ◆ • •	4–7	15–25 ft.
🦋 T 🍁 ✿	• • • • • • ◆ ◆ ◆ ◆ ◆ ◆	2–5	8 in.
🦋 T 🍁 ✿ ◉ 🐦	• • • • • • • • ◆ ◆ ◆ ◆ •	5–8	15–40 ft.

NORTHEAST REGION

BOTANICAL NAME	COMMON NAME	LIGHT NEEDS
Cornus sericea	red-osier dogwood	◑
Crataegus crus-galli	cockspur hawthorn	◑
Crataegus phaenopyrum	Washington hawthorn	○
Empetrum nigrum	black crowberry	○
Fragaria chiloensis	beach strawberry	○
Fragaria virginiana	wild strawberry	○
Ilex decidua	possum haw	○
Ilex glabra	inkberry	◑
Ilex laevigata	smooth winterberry	◑
Ilex opaca	American holly	◑
Ilex verticillata	winterberry	◑
Juniperus virginiana	eastern red cedar	○
Larix laricina	tamarack	◑
Lonicera sempervirens	trumpet honeysuckle	○
Malus coronaria	wild sweet crabapple	◑
Morus rubra	red mulberry	○
Myrica cerifera	wax myrtle	◑

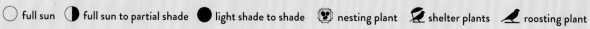 ○ full sun   ◑ full sun to partial shade   ● light shade to shade   nesting plant   shelter plants   roosting plant

OTHER USES	APPROXIMATE FRUITING MONTHS J F M A M J J A S O N D	HARDINESS ZONES	MATURE HEIGHT
🦋 🍁 ✿ 🙂 🐿	· · · · · · ◆◆◆◆ · ·	3–8	10 ft.
🐦 🦋 T 🍁 ✿ 🙂	◆◆◆ · · · · ◆◆◆◆◆	4–6	30 ft.
🦋 T 🍁 ✿ 🙂 🐿	◆◆ · · · · ◆◆◆◆◆ ◆	5–9	20–30 ft.
🦋 T 🙂 🐿	◆◆◆ · · · · ◆◆◆◆	2–6	10 in.
🦋 T ✿	· · · · · ◆◆◆ · · ·	5–10	6–12 in.
🦋 ✿	· · · · · ◆◆◆ · ·	4–9	6–8 in.
🦋 🍁 🙂 🐿	◆◆◆ · · · · · ◆◆◆	5–9	30 ft.
🦋 🍁 🙂 🐿	◆◆ · · · · · ◆◆◆◆	4–9	8 ft.
🦋 🍁 ✿ 🙂 🐿	◆◆◆ · · · ◆◆◆◆	5	10–20 ft.
🦋 T 🙂 🐦	◆◆ · · · · ◆◆◆◆	6–9	40 ft.
🦋 T 🙂 🐿 🐦	◆◆ · · · · · ◆◆◆◆	4–9	15 ft.
🦋 T 🙂 🐦 🐿	◆◆ · · · · · ◆◆◆◆	3–9	30–50 ft.
🦋 T 🍁 🙂	· · · · · · ◆◆◆ · ·	2–6	40–80 ft.
🐦 🦋 ✿ 🙂 🐿	· · · · · · ◆◆◆◆ ·	4–9	vine
🐦 🦋 T 🍁 ✿ 🙂 🐿 🐦	· · ◆◆◆ · · · ·	5–7	30 ft.
🦋 🍁 🙂 🐿	· · · · ◆◆◆◆◆ · ·	4–9	30–60 ft.
🦋 T 🐿	◆◆◆ · · · · · ◆◆◆◆	6–9	10 ft.–20 ft.

🦋 nectar for butterflies   T host plant for butterflies   🍁 fall color   ✿ showy flowers   🐦 nectar for hummingbirds

NORTHEAST REGION

BOTANICAL NAME	COMMON NAME	LIGHT NEEDS
Myrica pensylvanica	bayberry	◑
Picea rubens	yellow spruce	○
Pinus rigida	pitch pine	○
Pinus strobus	eastern white pine	○
Platanus occidentalis	sycamore	○
Populus deltoides	cottonwood	○
Prunus pensylvanica	pin cherry	○
Prunus virginiana	chokecherry	○
Quercus alba	white oak	○
Quercus coccinea	scarlet oak	○
Quercus laurifolia	laurel oak	○
Quercus palustris	pin oak	○
Quercus rubra	red oak	○
Rhus copallinum	winged sumac	○
Rhus glabra	smooth sumac	○
Rhus typhina	staghorn sumac	○
Rosa carolina	American wild rose	○

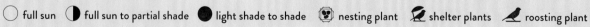

○ full sun   ◑ full sun to partial shade   ● light shade to shade   nesting plant   shelter plants   roosting plant

OTHER USES	APPROXIMATE FRUITING MONTHS J F M A M J J A S O N D	HARDINESS ZONES	MATURE HEIGHT
🦋 🌿	◆◆◆ · · ◆◆◆◆◆◆◆	4–9	6½ ft.
🐾 🌿 🐦	· · · · · · · ◆◆◆◆	3–6	70–80 ft.
🐾 🐦 🌿	· · · · · · · ◆ ◆◆	5	40–60 ft.
🦋 🌱 🐾 🌿 🐦	· · · · · · · · ◆◆◆◆	3–8	100 ft.
🐾 🌿 🌿	◆◆ · · · · · · ◆◆◆◆	5–9	115 ft.
🦋 🌱 🐾	· · · ◆◆◆◆◆◆ · · ·	3–9	70–100 ft.
🦋 🌱 🍁 ✽	· · · · · · · ◆◆◆◆ ·	3–7	30 ft.
🦋 🌱 🍁 ✽	· · · · · · · ◆◆◆◆◆	3–5	9–25 ft.
🦋 🌱 🍁 🐾 🌿 🐦 🌿	◆◆ · · · · · ◆◆◆◆◆	4–9	80–100 ft.
🍁 🐾 🌿 🐦	◆◆ · · · · · · ◆◆◆	5–9	65–100 ft.
🦋 🌱 🍁 🐾 🌿 🐦	◆◆◆ · · · · · ◆◆◆◆	6–9	60–70 ft.
🦋 🍁 🐾 🌿 🐦	◆◆◆ · · · · · ◆◆◆	3–8	60–75 ft.
🦋 🌱 🍁 🐾 🌿 🌿	◆◆◆ · · · · · ◆◆◆	3–9	60–80 ft.
🦋 🌱 🍁 ✽ 🌿	◆◆◆ · · · · ◆◆◆◆	4–9	10–18 ft.
🐦 🦋 🌱 🍁 🐾 🌿 🐦	· · · · · ◆◆◆◆◆ ◆◆	3–9	10–20 ft.
🦋 🌱 🍁 🌿	◆◆ · · · · ◆◆◆◆◆	3–8	10–15 ft.
🦋 🌱 🍁 ✽ 🐾 🌿	◆◆◆ · · ◆◆◆◆◆◆◆	5–8	4 ft.

🦋 nectar for butterflies　🌱 host plant for butterflies　🍁 fall color　✽ showy flowers　🐦 nectar for hummingbirds

NORTHEAST REGION

BOTANICAL NAME	COMMON NAME	LIGHT NEEDS
Rosa virginiana	Virginia rose	◯
Rubus alleghiensis	common blackberry	◯
Rubus idaeus	red raspberry	◯
Sambucus canadensis	American elder	◯
Sorbus americana	American mountain ash	◯
Sorbus decora	showy mountain ash	◑
Symphoricarpos albus	snowberry	◑
Tsuga canadensis	Canada hemlock	◑
Tsuga caroliniana	Carolina hemlock	◑
Vaccinium angustifolium	lowbush blueberry	◯
Vaccinium corymbosum	highbush blueberry	◯
Vaccinium vitis-idaea	mountain cranberry	◯
Viburnum cassinoides	Appalachian tea	◑
Viburnum dentatum	arrowwood viburnum	◯ ◑
Viburnum lentago	nannyberry viburnum	◑
Viburnum prunifolium	blackhaw viburnum	◑
Viburnum trilobum	American cranberry	◑
Vitis vulpina	frost grape	◑

 full sun   full sun to partial shade   ● light shade to shade   nesting plant   shelter plants   roosting plant

OTHER USES	APPROXIMATE FRUITING MONTHS J F M A M J J A S O N D	HARDINESS ZONES	MATURE HEIGHT
(icons)	◆·······◆◆◆◆	4–7	4–6 ft.
(icons)	····◆◆◆◆◆···	4–7	2–10 ft.
(icons)	·····◆◆◆◆···	5–8	3–9 ft.
(icons)	·····◆◆◆····	3–9	10–16 ft.
(icons)	◆◆◆·····◆◆◆◆	2–6	10–30 ft.
(icons)	◆◆◆·····◆◆◆◆	3–6	30–65 ft.
(icons)	◆◆······◆◆◆◆◆	4–7	4–6 ft.
(icons)	········◆◆◆◆	3–8	65–80 ft.
(icons)	········◆◆◆◆	5–7	40–60 ft.
(icons)	·······◆◆◆◆◆	2–8	6–8 in.
(icons)	··◆◆◆◆◆◆◆···	4–9	6–12 ft.
(icons)	◆◆······◆◆◆◆	5–6	8 in.
(icons)	◆◆◆·····◆◆◆◆	3–6	6 ft.
(icons)	·····◆◆◆◆◆··	4–9	15 ft.
(icons)	◆◆◆·····◆◆◆◆	2–7	30 ft.
(icons)	◆◆◆·····◆◆◆◆	3	8–15 ft.
(icons)	◆◆◆··◆◆◆◆◆◆◆	2–8	8–10 ft.
(icons)	········◆◆◆·	5–9	vine

 nectar for butterflies   host plant for butterflies   fall color   showy flowers   nectar for hummingbirds

SOUTHEAST REGION

BOTANICAL NAME	COMMON NAME	LIGHT NEEDS
Acer rubrum	red maple	◑
Acer saccharum	sugar maple	◑
Alnus incana subsp. *rugosa*	speckled alder	○
Amelanchier arborea	shadblow	◑
Betula nigra	river birch	◑
Callicarpa americana	American beautyberry	◑
Celtis laevigata	sugarberry	◑
Celtis occidentalis	common hackberry	◑
Cornus alternifolia	pagoda dogwood	●
Cornus florida	flowering dogwood	◑
Cornus racemosa	gray dogwood	◑
Cornus sericea	red-osier dogwood	◑
Crataegus crus-galli	cockspur hawthorn	◑
Crataegus marshallii	parsley hawthorn	○
Crataegus phaenopyrum	Washington hawthorn	○
Fragaria chiloensis	beach strawberry	○
Fragaria virginiana	wild strawberry	○

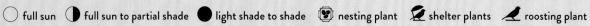 ○ full sun ◑ full sun to partial shade ● light shade to shade 🐾 nesting plant 🦇 shelter plants 🐦 roosting plant

OTHER USES	APPROXIMATE FRUITING MONTHS J F M A M J J A S O N D	HARDINESS ZONES	MATURE HEIGHT
butterfly, leaf	· · · · · · ◆ ◆ ◆ ◆ · ·	3–9	50–70 ft.
butterfly, leaf	· · · · · · ◆ ◆ ◆ ◆ · ·	3–7	50–70 ft.
butterfly, host, leaf, snail	· · · · · · ◆ ◆ ◆ ◆ ◆ ·	2–9	15–33 ft.
butterfly, host, leaf, flower	· · · · · · · ◆ ◆ ◆ · ·	3–8	20–25 ft.
butterfly, host, leaf, box	· · · · · · · ◆ ◆ ◆ ◆ ◆ ·	4–9	80 ft.
butterfly, host, leaf, flower	◆ ◆ · · · · · ◆ ◆ ◆ ◆ ◆	7–10	3–5 ft.
butterfly, host, box, snail	◆ ◆ ◆ · · · · ◆ ◆ ◆ ◆ ◆	6–9	70 ft.
butterfly, host, leaf, box, snail	◆ ◆ · · · · · · ◆ ◆ ◆ ◆	3–8	30–50 ft.
butterfly, host, leaf, flower, box, snail	· · · · · · ◆ ◆ ◆ ◆ ◆ ·	4–7	15–25 ft.
butterfly, host, leaf, flower, box, snail	· · · · · · · ◆ ◆ ◆ ◆ ·	5–8	15–40 ft.
butterfly, leaf, flower, box, snail	· · · · · · · · ◆ ◆ ◆ ◆ ◆	5	7–9 ft.
butterfly, leaf, flower, box, snail	· · · · · · · ◆ ◆ ◆ ◆ · ·	3–8	10 ft.
hummingbird, butterfly, host, leaf, box	◆ ◆ ◆ · · · · · ◆ ◆ ◆ ◆	4–6	30 ft.
butterfly, host, leaf, flower, box, snail	◆ ◆ ◆ ◆ · · · · ◆ ◆ ◆ ◆ ◆	6	5–25 ft.
butterfly, host, leaf, flower, box, snail	◆ ◆ · · · · · ◆ ◆ ◆ ◆ ◆	5–9	20–30 ft.
butterfly, host, flower	· · · · · · ◆ ◆ ◆ · · ·	5–10	6–12 in.
butterfly, flower	· · · · · · ◆ ◆ ◆ · · ·	4–9	6–8 in.

 nectar for butterflies   host plant for butterflies   fall color   showy flowers   nectar for hummingbirds

SOUTHEAST REGION

BOTANICAL NAME	COMMON NAME	LIGHT NEEDS
Ilex decidua	possum haw	◯
Ilex glabra	inkberry	◑
Ilex opaca	American holly	◑
Ilex verticillata	winterberry	◑
Ilex vomitoria	yaupon holly	◑
Juniperus virginiana	eastern red cedar	◯
Lindera benzoin	spicebush	◑
Lonicera sempervirens	trumpet honeysuckle	◯
Malus angustifolia	southern wild crabapple	◑
Morus rubra	red mulberry	◯
Myrica cerifera	wax myrtle	◑
Parthenocissus quinquefolia	Virginia creeper	◯ ●
Pinus strobus	eastern white pine	◯
Pinus taeda	loblolly pine	◯
Pinus virginiana	Virginia pine	◯
Platanus occidentalis	sycamore	◯
Populus deltoides	cottonwood	◯

 full sun   full sun to partial shade   light shade to shade    nesting plant   shelter plants   roosting plant

OTHER USES	APPROXIMATE FRUITING MONTHS J F M A M J J A S O N D		HARDINESS ZONES	MATURE HEIGHT
🦋 🍁 ▣ 🐦	◆◆◆ · · · · · · ◆◆◆		5–9	30 ft.
🦋 🍁 ▣ 🐦	◆◆ · · · · · ◆◆◆◆		4–9	8 ft.
🦋 T ▣ 🐦	◆◆ · · · · · · ◆◆◆◆		6–9	40 ft.
🦋 T ▣ 🐦	◆◆ · · · · · ◆◆◆◆		4–9	15 ft.
🦋 T 🍁 ✹ ▣ 🐦	◆◆◆ · · · · · ◆◆◆		7–9	15–25 ft.
🦋 T ▣ 🐦	◆◆ · · · · · ◆◆◆◆		3–9	30–50 ft.
🦋 T 🍁 ✹	· · · · · ◆◆◆◆ · ·		5–9	8–12 ft.
Y 🦋 ✹ ▣ 🐦	· · · · · · · ◆◆◆◆ ·		4–9	vine
🦋 T 🍁 ✹ ▣	◆◆ · · · · · ◆◆◆◆		4–9	25 ft.
🦋 🍁 ▣ 🐦	· · · ◆◆◆◆◆◆ ◆ · · ·		4–9	30–60 ft.
🦋 T 🐦	◆◆◆ · · · · ◆◆◆◆		6–9	10–20 ft.
🦋 🍁 ▣ 🐦	◆◆ · · · · · · ◆◆◆◆		3–9	vine
🦋 T ▣ 🐦 🐦	· · · · · · ◆◆◆◆		3–8	100 ft.
🦋 T ▣ 🐦 🐦	· · · · · · · ◆◆◆◆		7–9	80–100 ft.
🦋 T ▣ 🐦 🐦	· · · · · · ◆◆◆◆		5	40 ft.
▣ 🐦 🐦	◆◆ · · · · · ◆◆◆◆		5–9	115 ft.
🦋 T ▣	· · · ◆◆◆◆◆◆ · · · ·		3–9	70–100 ft.

🦋 nectar for butterflies　T host plant for butterflies　🍁 fall color　✹ showy flowers　 nectar for hummingbirds

SOUTHEAST REGION

BOTANICAL NAME	COMMON NAME	LIGHT NEEDS
Prunus americana	American plum	○
Prunus serotina	black cherry	○
Prunus virginiana	chokecherry	○
Quercus alba	white oak	○
Quercus coccinea	scarlet oak	○
Quercus falcata	southern red oak	◑
Quercus incana	bluejack oak	○
Quercus laurifolia	laurel oak	◑
Quercus palustris	pin oak	◑
Quercus rubra	red oak	◑
Quercus virginiana	live oak	◑
Rhus copallinum	winged sumac	○
Rhus glabra	smooth sumac	○
Rhus typhina	staghorn sumac	○
Rosa carolina	American wild rose	○
Rosa virginiana	Virginia rose	○
Rubus allegheniensis	common blackberry	○

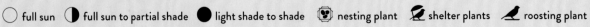
○ full sun ◑ full sun to partial shade ● light shade to shade   nesting plant   shelter plants   roosting plant

OTHER USES	APPROXIMATE FRUITING MONTHS J F M A M J J A S O N D	HARDINESS ZONES	MATURE HEIGHT
🦋 T 🍁 ✿	· · · · · · ◆ ◆ ◆ ◆ ◆ ·	3–9	20–30 ft.
🦋 T 🍁 ✿	· · · · · · ◆ ◆ ◆ ◆ · ·	4–9	30–50 ft.
🦋 T 🍁 ✿	· · · · · · · · ◆ ◆ ◆ ◆	3–5	9–25 ft.
🦋 T 🍁 ◉ 🍂 🐦	◆ ◆ · · · · · · ◆ ◆ ◆ ◆	4–9	80–100 ft.
🦋 T 🍁 ◉ 🍂 🐦	◆ ◆ ◆ · · · · · ◆ ◆ ◆ ◆	5–9	65–100 ft.
🦋 T ◉ 🍂 🐦	◆ ◆ ◆ · · · · · ◆ ◆ ◆ ◆	7	80 ft.
🦋 T ◉ 🍂 🐦	◆ ◆ ◆ · · · · · ◆ ◆ ◆ ◆	8	20 ft.
🦋 T 🍁 ◉ 🍂 🐦	◆ ◆ ◆ · · · · · ◆ ◆ ◆ ◆	6–9	60–70 ft.
🦋 🍁 ◉ 🍂 🐦	◆ ◆ ◆ · · · · · ◆ ◆ ◆ ◆	3–8	60–75 ft.
🦋 T 🍁 ◉ 🍂 🐦	◆ ◆ ◆ · · · · · ◆ ◆ ◆ ◆	3–9	60–80 ft.
🦋 T ◉ 🍂 🐦	◆ ◆ ◆ · · · · · ◆ ◆ ◆ ◆	8–9	40–50 ft.
🦋 T ✿ 🍂	◆ ◆ ◆ · · · · · ◆ ◆ ◆ ◆	4–9	10–18 ft.
🐦‍⬛ 🦋 T 🍁 ◉ 🍂 🐦	· · · · · · ◆ ◆ ◆ ◆ ◆ ◆	3–9	10–20 ft.
🦋 T 🍁 🍂	◆ ◆ · · · · · ◆ ◆ ◆ ◆ ◆	3–8	10–15 ft.
🦋 T 🍁 ✿ ◉ 🍂	◆ ◆ ◆ · · · ◆ ◆ ◆ ◆ ◆ ◆	5–8	4 ft.
🦋 T 🍁 ✿ ◉ 🍂	◆ · · · · · · · ◆ ◆ ◆ ◆	4–7	4–6 ft.
🦋 T 🍁 ✿ ◉ 🐦	· · · · · ◆ ◆ ◆ ◆ ◆ · ·	4–7	2–10 ft.

🦋 nectar for butterflies   T host plant for butterflies   🍁 fall color   ✿ showy flowers   🦅 nectar for hummingbirds

SOUTHEAST REGION

BOTANICAL NAME	COMMON NAME	LIGHT NEEDS
Rubus spectabilis	salmonberry	○
Rubus trivialis	southern dewberry	◐
Sambucus canadensis	American elder	○
Sorbus americana	American mountain ash	○
Sorbus decora	showy mountain ash	○
Tsuga canadensis	Canada hemlock	◐
Tsuga caroliniana	Carolina hemlock	◐
Vaccinium arboreum	farkleberry	◐
Vaccinium corymbosum	highbush blueberry	○
Viburnum cassinoides	Appalachian tea	◐
Viburnum dentatum	arrowwood viburnum	◐
Viburnum obovatum	Walter's viburnum	◐
Viburnum rufidulum	southern black haw	○
Vitis munsoniana	bird grape	○
Vitis riparia	riverbank grape	○
Vitis vulpina	frost grape	◐
Yucca filamentosa	Adam's needle	○

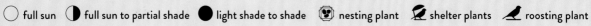

 full sun full sun to partial shade light shade to shade 🐦 nesting plant 🍂 shelter plants 🐦 roosting plant

OTHER USES	APPROXIMATE FRUITING MONTHS J F M A M J J A S O N D	HARDINESS ZONES	MATURE HEIGHT
butterfly, T, leaf, flower, face, berry	· · · · ◆ ◆ ◆ ◆ · · · ·	6–7	2–5 ft.
butterfly, flower, face, berry	· · · · · ◆ ◆ ◆ ◆ · · ·	6	vine
hummingbird, butterfly, T, leaf, flower, face, berry	· · · · · ◆ ◆ ◆ ◆ · · ·	3–9	10–16 ft.
butterfly, T, leaf, flower, face, berry, bird	◆ ◆ ◆ · · · · · ◆ ◆ ◆ ◆	2–6	10–30 ft.
butterfly, T, leaf, flower, face, berry, bird	◆ ◆ ◆ · · · · · ◆ ◆ ◆ ◆	3–6	30–65 ft.
butterfly, face, berry, bird	· · · · · · · · ◆ ◆ ◆ ◆	3–8	65–80 ft.
face, berry, bird	· · · · · · · · ◆ ◆ ◆ ◆	5–7	40–60 ft.
butterfly, T, leaf, flower, face, berry	· · · · · · · · ◆ ◆ ◆ ◆	7–9	10–26 ft.
butterfly, T, leaf, face, berry	· · · ◆ ◆ ◆ ◆ ◆ ◆ ◆ · ·	4–9	6–12 ft.
butterfly, leaf, flower	◆ ◆ ◆ · · · · · ◆ ◆ ◆ ◆	3–6	6 ft.
butterfly, leaf, flower	· · · · · · ◆ ◆ ◆ ◆ ◆ ·	4–9	15 ft.
flower, butterfly	◆ ◆ ◆ ◆ · · · · · ◆ ◆ ◆	9	9 ft.
butterfly, T, leaf, flower, berry	◆ · · · · ◆ ◆ ◆ ◆ ◆ ◆ ◆	5–9	15–25 ft.
leaf, face, berry	◆ ◆ · · · · ◆ ◆ ◆ ◆ ◆ ◆	6–9	vine
face, bird, bird	· · · · · ◆ ◆ ◆ ◆ ◆ ◆ ·	3–6	vine
face, berry	· · · · · · · · ◆ ◆ ◆ ·	5–9	vine
hummingbird, butterfly, T, flower, face	· · · · · · · ◆ ◆ ◆ · ·	7–10	5–15 ft.

🦋 nectar for butterflies   T host plant for butterflies   🍁 fall color   ✿ showy flowers   ✺ nectar for hummingbirds

PLAINS *and* PRAIRIE REGION

BOTANICAL NAME	COMMON NAME	LIGHT NEEDS
Acer negundo	box elder	◐
Amelanchier alnifolia	saskatoon serviceberry	○
Amelanchier arborea	shadblow	◐
Betula nigra	river birch	◐
Betula papyrifera	paper birch	●
Celtis laevigata	sugarberry	◐
Celtis occidentalis	common hackberry	◐
Celtis reticulata	western hackberry	○
Cornus amomum	silky dogwood	◐
Cornus canadensis	bunchberry	●
Cornus florida	flowering dogwood	◐
Cornus racemosa	gray dogwood	◐
Cornus sericea	red-osier dogwood	◐
Crataegus calpodendron	pear hawthorn	◐
Crataegus crus-galli	cockspur hawthorn	◐
Crataegus mollis	downy hawthorn	○
Crataegus succulenta	fleshy hawthorn	○

○ full sun   ◐ full sun to partial shade   ● light shade to shade   🐦 nesting plant   🍃 shelter plants   🐦 roosting plant

OTHER USES	APPROXIMATE FRUITING MONTHS J F M A M J J A S O N D	HARDINESS ZONES	MATURE HEIGHT
	◆ · · · · · ◆◆◆◆◆◆	2–8	50–70 ft.
	· · · · · · ◆◆◆◆ · ·	4–8	4–18 ft.
	· · · · · ◆◆◆ · · ·	3–8	20–25 ft.
	· · · · · · ◆◆◆◆◆ ·	4–9	80 ft.
	· · · · · · ◆◆◆◆◆ ·	2–7	50–80 ft.
	◆◆◆ · · · · ◆◆◆◆◆	6–9	70 ft.
	◆◆ · · · · · ◆◆◆◆	3–8	30–50 ft.
	· · · · · · · · ◆◆◆◆	7–9	20–30 ft.
	· · · · · ◆◆◆ · · ·	4	4–10 ft.
	· · · · · · ◆◆◆◆ ·	2–5	8 ft.
	· · · · · · ◆◆◆◆ ·	5–8	15–40 ft.
	· · · · · · · ◆◆◆◆◆	5	7–9 ft.
	· · · · · · ◆◆◆◆ · ·	3–8	10 ft.
	· · · · · ◆◆◆◆◆ · ·	6–9	15–20 ft.
	◆◆◆ · · · ◆◆◆◆◆	4–6	30 ft.
	· · · · · · · ◆◆◆◆◆	3–6	30–40 ft.
	◆◆◆◆ · · · · ◆◆◆◆	3–6	15–20 ft.

 nectar for butterflies　　host plant for butterflies　　fall color　　showy flowers　　nectar for hummingbirds

PLAINS *and* PRAIRIE REGION

BOTANICAL NAME	COMMON NAME	LIGHT NEEDS
Ilex decidua	possum haw	◯
Ilex opaca	American holly	◑
Ilex vomitoria	yaupon holly	◑
Juniperus ashei	Ashe juniper	◯
Juniperus deppeana	alligator juniper	◯
Juniperus monosperma	one-seed juniper	◯
Juniperus scopulorum	Rocky Mountain juniper	◯
Juniperus virginiana	eastern red cedar	◯
Lonicera sempervirens	trumpet honeysuckle	◯
Malus ioensis	prairie crabapple	◑
Morus microphylla	Texas mulberry	◯
Morus rubra	red mulberry	◯
Parthenocissus quinquefolia	Virginia creeper	◑
Picea pungens	Colorado spruce	◯
Pinus ponderosa	Ponderosa pine	◑
Populus tremuloides	quaking aspen	◑
Prunus americana	American plum	◯

 ◯ full sun ◑ full sun to partial shade ● light shade to shade   nesting plant   shelter plants   roosting plant

OTHER USES	APPROXIMATE FRUITING MONTHS J F M A M J J A S O N D	HARDINESS ZONES	MATURE HEIGHT
(icons)	◆◆◆ · · · · · · · ◆◆◆	5–9	30 ft.
(icons)	◆◆ · · · · · · · ◆◆◆	6–9	40 ft.
(icons)	◆◆◆ · · · · · · ◆◆◆	7–9	15–25 ft.
(icons)	◆◆◆◆◆◆◆◆◆◆◆◆	7	6–20 ft.
(icons)	◆◆◆◆◆◆◆◆◆◆◆◆	7–10	30–50 ft.
(icons)	◆◆◆◆◆◆◆◆◆◆◆◆	4–9	20–30 ft.
(icons)	◆◆◆◆◆◆◆◆◆◆◆◆	3–6	30–40 ft.
(icons)	◆◆ · · · · · · · ◆◆◆	3–9	30–50 ft.
(icons)	· · · · · · · ◆◆◆◆ ·	4–9	vine
(icons)	· · · · · · · · ◆◆◆ ·	4–7	10–30 ft.
(icons)	· · · · · ◆◆◆ · · · ·	7–9	20 ft.
(icons)	· · · · · ◆◆◆◆◆ · ·	4–9	30–60 ft.
(icons)	◆◆ · · · · · ◆◆◆ · ·	3–9	vine
(icons)	· · · · · · ◆◆◆◆◆◆	3–7	65–115 ft.
(icons)	· · · · · · · ◆◆◆◆	3–8	75–100 ft.
(icons)	· · · ◆◆◆◆ · · · · ·	2–6	30–60 ft.
(icons)	· · · · · · ◆◆◆◆◆ ·	3–9	20–30 ft.

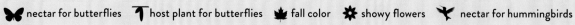

nectar for butterflies   host plant for butterflies   fall color   showy flowers   nectar for hummingbirds

PLAINS *and* PRAIRIE REGION

BOTANICAL NAME	COMMON NAME	LIGHT NEEDS
Prunus besseyi	western sand cherry	○
Prunus pensylvanica	pin cherry	○
Prunus serotina	black cherry	○
Prunus virginiana	chokecherry	○
Quercus gambelii	Gambel oak	○
Quercus virginiana	live oak	◑
Rhus copallinum	winged sumac	○
Rhus glabra	smooth sumac	○
Rhus trilobata	three-leaf sumac	○
Rhus typhina	staghorn sumac	○
Rosa arkansana	prairie wild rose	◑
Rubus allegheniensis	common blackberry	○
Rubus occidentalis	black raspberry	○
Rubus parviflorus	thimbleberry	◑
Sambucus canadensis	American elder	○
Sorbus decora	showy mountain ash	○
Tsuga heterophylla	western hemlock	○

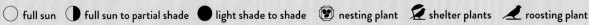 full sun   full sun to partial shade   light shade to shade   nesting plant   shelter plants   roosting plant

OTHER USES	APPROXIMATE FRUITING MONTHS J F M A M J J A S O N D	HARDINESS ZONES	MATURE HEIGHT
	• • • • • ◆ ◆ ◆ ◆ ◆ • •	3–6	3–5 ft.
	• • • • • • • ◆ ◆ ◆ ◆	3–7	30 ft.
	• • • • • • • ◆ ◆ ◆ ◆ •	4–9	30–50 ft.
	• • • • • • • • ◆ ◆ ◆ ◆	3–5	9–25 ft.
	• • • • • • • • ◆ ◆ ◆ •	6–9	20–30 ft.
	• • • • • • • • ◆ ◆ ◆ ◆	8–9	40–50 ft.
	◆ ◆ ◆ • • • • • ◆ ◆ ◆ ◆	4–9	10–18 ft.
	• • • • • • ◆ ◆ ◆ ◆ ◆ ◆	3–9	10–20 ft.
	• • • • • • • ◆ ◆ ◆ ◆ •	4–9	3–12 ft.
	◆ ◆ • • • • • • ◆ ◆ ◆ ◆	3–8	10–15 ft.
	◆ ◆ ◆ • • • ◆ ◆ ◆ ◆ ◆ ◆	2–5	2 ft.
	• • • • • ◆ ◆ ◆ ◆ ◆ ◆ •	4–7	2–10 ft.
	• • • • • • ◆ ◆ ◆ ◆ ◆ ◆	4	3–6 ft.
	• • • • • • ◆ ◆ ◆ ◆ ◆ ◆	4–7	3–6 ft.
	• • • • • • ◆ ◆ ◆ ◆ • •	3–9	10–16 ft.
	◆ ◆ ◆ • • • • • ◆ ◆ ◆ ◆	3–6	30–65 ft.
	• • • • • • • • ◆ ◆ ◆ ◆	5–9	130–200 ft.

PLAINS *and* PRAIRIE REGION

BOTANICAL NAME	COMMON NAME	LIGHT NEEDS
Vaccinium angustifolium	lowbush blueberry	◯
Vaccinium arboreum	sparkleberry	◑
Viburnum lentago	nannyberry viburnum	◑
Viburnum prunifolium	blackhaw viburnum	◑
Viburnum rufidulum	southern black haw	◯
Viburnum trilobum	American cranberry	◑
Vitis vulpina	frost grape	◑

 full sun   full sun to partial shade ● light shade to shade   nesting plant   shelter plants   roosting plant

OTHER USES	APPROXIMATE FRUITING MONTHS J F M A M J J A S O N D	HARDINESS ZONES	MATURE HEIGHT
🐦 🦋 🍁 ✿	· · · · · · · ◆◆◆◆◆	2–8	6–8 ft.
🦋 T 🍁 ✿ 🐵 🐌	· · · · · · · · ◆◆◆◆	7–9	10–26 ft.
🦋 🍁 ✿	◆◆◆ · · · · · ◆◆◆◆	2–7	30 ft.
🦋 T 🍁 ✿ 🐌	◆◆◆ · · · · · ◆◆◆◆	3	8–15 ft.
🦋 T 🍁 ✿ 🐌	◆ · · · · ◆◆◆◆◆◆◆	5–9	15–25 ft.
🦋 🍁 ✿ 🐌	◆◆◆ · · · · · ◆◆◆◆◆	2–8	8–10 ft.
🐵 🐌	· · · · · · · · · ◆◆◆ ·	5–9	vine

🦋 nectar for butterflies   T host plant for butterflies   🍁 fall color   ✿ showy flowers   🐦 nectar for hummingbirds

MOUNTAINS *and* DESERTS REGION

BOTANICAL NAME	COMMON NAME	LIGHT NEEDS
Abies grandis	grand fir	◑
Acer negundo	box elder	◑
Alnus rhombifolia	white alder	●
Amelanchier alnifolia	saskatoon serviceberry	○
Betula occidentalis	water birch	○
Betula papyrifera	paper birch	○
Carnegiea gigantea	saguaro	○
Celtis laevigata	sugarberry	◑
Celtis reticulata	western hackberry	○
Cornus canadensis	bunchberry	●
Cornus florida	flowering dogwood	◑
Cornus occidentalis	western dogwood	◑
Cornus sericea	red-osier dogwood	◑
Crataegus calpodendron	pear hawthorn	◑
Crataegus douglasii	western hawthorn	◑
Crataegus mollis	downy hawthorn	○
Cylindropuntia imbricata	tree cholla	○

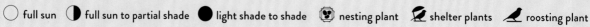 full sun   full sun to partial shade   light shade to shade   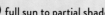 nesting plant   shelter plants   roosting plant

OTHER USES	APPROXIMATE FRUITING MONTHS (J F M A M J J A S O N D)	HARDINESS ZONES	MATURE HEIGHT
butterfly nectar, host plant, showy flowers, nectar, bird	· · · · · · · · ◆◆◆◆	6–9	100–200 ft.
butterfly nectar, host plant, showy flowers	◆ · · · · · ◆◆◆◆◆	2–8	50–70 ft.
butterfly nectar, host plant, showy flowers, nectar	◆◆◆◆◆ · · ◆◆◆◆	6–9	50–90 ft.
butterfly nectar, host plant, fall color, showy flowers, nectar	· · · · ◆◆◆◆ · ·	4–8	20–30 ft.
butterfly nectar, host plant, fall color, showy flowers, nectar	· · · · · · ◆◆◆◆	3–9	20–25 ft.
butterfly nectar, host plant, fall color, showy flowers	· · · · · ◆◆◆◆◆ ·	2–7	50–80 ft.
showy flowers, showy flowers	· · · · ◆◆◆◆ · ·	8–10	30–50 ft.
butterfly nectar, host plant, showy flowers, nectar	◆◆◆ · · · · ◆◆◆◆	6–9	70 ft.
hummingbird nectar, butterfly nectar, host plant, showy flowers, nectar	◆◆ · · · ◆◆◆◆	7–9	20–30 ft.
butterfly nectar, host plant, fall color, showy flowers	· · · · · ◆◆◆◆ ·	2–5	8 in.
butterfly nectar, host plant, fall color, showy flowers, nectar	· · · · · ◆◆◆◆ ·	5–8	15–40 ft.
fall color, showy flowers, showy flowers, nectar	· · · · · ◆◆◆◆ ·	6	15 ft.
butterfly nectar, fall color, showy flowers, showy flowers, nectar	· · · · · ◆◆◆◆ · ·	3–8	10 ft.
butterfly nectar, host plant, fall color, showy flowers, showy flowers	· · · · · ◆◆◆◆◆ ·	6–9	15–20 ft.
butterfly nectar, host plant, showy flowers, fall color, showy flowers	◆◆ · · · · · · ·	4–6	5–20 ft.
butterfly nectar, host plant, fall color, showy flowers, showy flowers, nectar	· · · · · ◆◆◆◆◆	3–6	30–40 ft.
butterfly nectar, showy flowers, showy flowers	◆◆ · · · · · ◆◆◆◆	7–9	3–7 ft.

nectar for butterflies   host plant for butterflies   fall color   showy flowers   nectar for hummingbirds

MOUNTAINS *and* DESERTS REGION

BOTANICAL NAME	COMMON NAME	LIGHT NEEDS
Empetrum nigrum	black crowberry	○
Fragaria californica	California wild strawberry	○
Ilex decidua	possum haw	○
Ilex opaca	American holly	◐
Ilex vomitoria	yaupon holly	◐
Juniperus californica	California juniper	○
Juniperus deppeana	alligator juniper	○
Juniperus monosperma	one-seed juniper	○
Juniperus occidentalis	western juniper	○
Juniperus scopulorum	Rocky Mountain juniper	○
Juniperus virginiana	eastern red cedar	○
Lonicera arizonica	Arizona honeysuckle	○
Lonicera hispidula	pink honeysuckle	○
Lonicera involucrata	twinberry	◐
Lonicera sempervirens	trumpet honeysuckle	○
Malus fusca	Pacific crabapple	◐
Morus microphylla	Texas mulberry	○

 full sun full sun to partial shade light shade to shade nesting plant shelter plants roosting plant

OTHER USES	APPROXIMATE FRUITING MONTHS J F M A M J J A S O N D	HARDINESS ZONES	MATURE HEIGHT
🦋 T ◉ 🌱	◆◆◆ · · · · · ◆◆◆◆◆	2–6	10 in.
🦋 T ✿	· · · · ◆◆◆◆ · · · ·	5–10	6–8 in.
🦋 🍁 ◉ 🌱	◆◆◆◆ · · · · · ◆◆◆	5–9	30 ft.
🦋 T ◉ 🌱 🐦	◆◆ · · · · · · ◆◆◆◆	6–9	40 ft.
🦋 T ✿ ◉ 🌱	◆◆◆ · · · · · · ◆◆◆	7–9	15–25 ft.
🦋 T ◉ 🌱 🐦	◆◆◆◆◆◆◆◆◆◆◆◆	8–10	10–35 ft.
🦋 T ◉ 🌱 🐦	◆◆◆◆◆◆◆◆◆◆◆◆	7–10	30–50 ft.
🦋 T ◉ 🌱 🐦	◆◆◆◆◆◆◆◆◆◆◆◆	4–9	20–30 ft.
🦋 T ◉ 🌱 🐦	◆◆◆◆◆◆◆◆◆◆◆◆	4–10	20–60 ft.
🦋 T ◉ 🌱 🐦	◆◆◆◆◆◆◆◆◆◆◆◆	3–6	30–40 ft.
🦋 T ◉ 🌱 🐦	◆◆ · · · · · · ◆◆◆◆	3–9	30–50 ft.
🐦‍⬛ 🦋 ✿ ◉ 🌱 🐦	· · · · · · · · ◆◆◆◆ ·	6–8	vine
🐦‍⬛ 🦋 ✿ ◉	◆ · · · · ◆◆◆◆◆◆◆	7	12 ft.
🐦‍⬛ 🦋 ✿ ◉	· · · · · · · ◆◆ · · ·	4–10	2–10 ft.
🐦‍⬛ 🦋 ✿ ◉ 🌱	· · · · · · ◆◆◆◆ · ·	4–9	vine
🐦‍⬛ 🍁 ✿ ◉ 🌱 🐦	· · ◆◆◆ · · · · · · ·	4–9	15–30 ft.
🦋 🍁 ◉ 🌱	· · · · ◆◆◆ · · · · ·	7–9	15–20 ft.

🦋 nectar for butterflies T host plant for butterflies 🍁 fall color ✿ showy flowers 🐦‍⬛ nectar for hummingbirds

MOUNTAINS *and* DESERTS REGION

BOTANICAL NAME	COMMON NAME	LIGHT NEEDS
Morus rubra	red mulberry	◯
Myrica californica	California wax myrtle	◯
Opuntia basilaris	beavertail cactus	◯
Opuntia phaeacantha	prickly pear cactus	◯
Parthenocissus quinquefolia	Virginia creeper	◐
Picea mariana	black spruce	◯
Picea pungens	Colorado spruce	◐
Pinus contorta	lodgepole pine	◯
Pinus edulis	piñon pine	◯
Pinus ponderosa	ponderosa pine	◐
Platanus racemosa	western sycamore	◯
Populas fremontii	fremont cottonwood	◯
Prunus pensylvanica	pin cherry	◯
Prunus virginiana	chokecherry	◯
Quercus emoryi	emory oak	◐
Quercus gambelii	Gambel oak	◯
Quercus kelloggii	California black oak	◐

 full sun   full sun to partial shade   light shade to shade   nesting plant   shelter plants   roosting plant

OTHER USES	APPROXIMATE FRUITING MONTHS J F M A M J J A S O N D	HARDINESS ZONES	MATURE HEIGHT
🦋 🍁 ◻ 🐿	· · · · ◆ ◆ ◆ ◆ ◆ · · ·	4–9	30–60 ft.
🦋 🐿	◆ ◆ ◆ · · · · · ◆ ◆ ◆ ◆	6–9	10–20 ft.
🦋 ✿ ◻ 🐿	· · · · · ◆ ◆ ◆ · ◆ · ·	8–10	6–24 in.
🦋 ✿ ◻ 🐿	· · · · · · ◆ ◆ ◆ ◆ · ·	6–8	3–6 ft.
🦋 T 🍁 ◻ 🐿	◆ ◆ · · · · · · ◆ ◆ ◆ ◆	3–9	vine
🦋 T ◻ 🐿 🐦	· · · · · · ◆ ◆ ◆ ◆ ◆ ·	1–6	16–60 ft.
◻ 🐿 🐦	· · · · · · · · · ◆ ◆ · ·	3–7	65–115 ft.
🦋 T ◻ 🐿 🐦	· · · · · · · ◆ ◆ ◆ ◆ ·	5–8	15–30 ft.
🦋 T ◻ 🐿 🐦	· · · · · · · · ◆ ◆ ◆ ◆	5–8	15–35 ft.
🦋 ◻ 🐿 🐦	· · · · · · · · ◆ ◆ ◆ ◆	3–8	75–100 ft.
🍁 ◻	◆ ◆ ◆ · · · · · ◆ ◆ ◆ ◆	7–10	40–90 ft.
🦋 T 🍁 ◻	· · ◆ ◆ ◆ ◆ ◆ ◆ ◆ · · ·	6–10	40–90 ft.
🦋 T 🍁 ✿	· · · · · · ◆ ◆ ◆ ◆ ◆ ·	3–7	20–30 ft.
🦋 T 🍁 ✿	· · · · · · · ◆ ◆ ◆ ◆ ◆	3–5	9–25 ft.
🦋 T ◻ 🐿 🐦	· · · · · · · ◆ ◆ ◆ ◆ ·	7–9	20–50 ft.
🦋 T 🍁 ◻ 🐿 🐿 🐦	· · · · · · · ◆ ◆ ◆ · ·	6–9	20–30 ft.
🦋 T 🍁 ◻ 🐿 🐿 🐦	· · · · · · · ◆ ◆ ◆ ◆ ◆	5–8	30–80 ft.

🦋 nectar for butterflies   T host plant for butterflies   🍁 fall color   ✿ showy flowers   ✦ nectar for hummingbirds

MOUNTAINS and DESERTS REGION

BOTANICAL NAME	COMMON NAME	LIGHT NEEDS
Quercus virginiana	live oak	◑
Rhus aromatica	fragrant sumac	○
Rhus copallinum	winged sumac	○
Rhus glabra	smooth sumac	○
Rhus integrifolia	lemonade berry	○
Rhus trilobata	three-leaf sumac	○
Rhus typhina	staghorn sumac	○
Rosa arkansana	prairie wild rose	◑
Rosa californica	California rose	○
Rosa nutkana	Nootka rose	◑
Rosa woodsii	Wood's rose	◑
Rubus arizonicus	Arizona dewberry	○
Rubus deliciosus	Rocky Mountain flowering raspberry	○
Rubus leucodermis	western raspberry	○
Rubus parviflorus	thimbleberry	◑
Rubus spectabilis	salmonberry	○
Sambucus caerulea	blue elderberry	○

 full sun   full sun to partial shade   light shade to shade   nesting plant   shelter plants   roosting plant

OTHER USES	APPROXIMATE FRUITING MONTHS J F M A M J J A S O N D	HARDINESS ZONES	MATURE HEIGHT
🦋 host 🌼 🐦 ...	· · · · · · · · ◆ ◆ ◆ ◆	8–9	40–50 ft.
🦋 leaf 🌼 ...	· · · · · ◆ ◆ ◆ ◆ ◆ ·	3–9	2–3½ ft.
🦋 host leaf 🌼 ...	◆ ◆ ◆ · · · · · ◆ ◆ ◆ ◆	4–9	10–18 ft.
🦋 host leaf 🐦 ...	· · · · · ◆ ◆ ◆ ◆ ◆ · ·	3–9	10–20 ft.
🦋 host leaf 🌼 ...	◆ ◆ · · · · ◆ ◆ ◆ ◆ ◆ ◆	9–10	4–25 ft.
leaf ...	· · · · · ◆ ◆ ◆ ◆ ◆ · ·	4–9	3–12 ft.
🦋 host leaf ...	◆ ◆ · · · · · ◆ ◆ ◆ ◆ ◆	3–8	10–15 ft.
🦋 leaf 🌼 ...	◆ ◆ ◆ · · · · ◆ ◆ ◆ ◆ ◆	2–5	2 ft.
🦋 leaf 🌼 ...	◆ ◆ ◆ ◆ · · · · ◆ ◆ ◆ ◆	6	10 ft.
🦋 leaf 🌼 ...	◆ ◆ ◆ ◆ ◆ · · · ◆ ◆ ◆ ◆	4–6	2–13 ft.
🦋 leaf 🌼 ...	◆ ◆ ◆ ◆ ◆ ◆ ◆ ◆ ◆ ◆ ◆ ◆	4	3 ft.
🦋 🌼 ...	· · · · · ◆ ◆ ◆ ◆ · · ·	4	3 ft.
🦋 leaf 🌼 ...	· · · · ◆ ◆ ◆ ◆ ◆ · · ·	6	4–6 ft.
🦋 leaf 🌼 ...	· · · · · ◆ ◆ ◆ ◆ · · ·	5–6	3–5 ft.
🦋 leaf 🌼 ...	· · · · ◆ ◆ ◆ ◆ ◆ ◆ · ·	4–7	3–6 ft.
🦋 leaf 🌼 ...	· · · · · · ◆ ◆ ◆ ◆ ◆ ◆	6–7	5 ft.
🦋 host leaf 🌼 🐦	· · · · · · · ◆ ◆ ◆ ◆ ◆ ·	6–9	15–30 ft.

🦋 nectar for butterflies　　T host plant for butterflies　　🍂 fall color　　🌼 showy flowers　　🐦 nectar for hummingbirds

MOUNTAINS *and* DESERTS REGION

BOTANICAL NAME	COMMON NAME	LIGHT NEEDS
Sambucus canadensis	American elder	○
Sambucus mexicana	Mexican elder	○
Sorbus americana	American mountain ash	○
Sorbus dumosa	Arizona mountain ash	◑
Tsuga mertensiana	mountain hemlock	○
Vaccinium arboreum	farkleberry	◑
Vaccinium ovatum	California huckleberry	◑
Vaccinium parvifolium	red huckleberry	◑
Viburnum lentago	nannyberry viburnum	◑
Viburnum rufidulum	southern black haw	○
Viburnum trilobum	American cranberry	◑
Vitis arizonica	canyon grape	○
Vitis californica	California wild grape	○
Vitis vulpina	frost grape	◑
Yucca elata	soaptree yucca	○

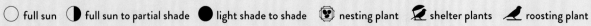 full sun   full sun to partial shade   light shade to shade   nesting plant   shelter plants   roosting plant

OTHER USES	APPROXIMATE FRUITING MONTHS J F M A M J J A S O N D	HARDINESS ZONES	MATURE HEIGHT
🐦🦋T✹⬛🍃	· · · · · · ◆◆◆◆ · ·	3–9	10–16 ft.
🦋🍁✹⬛🍃	◆◆ · · · · · ◆◆◆◆	8–10	20–30 ft.
🦋T✹⬛🐦	◆◆◆ · · · · ◆◆◆◆	2–6	10–30 ft.
🦋🍁✹	· · · · · · · ◆◆◆◆	6	8 ft.
⬛🍃🐦	· · · · · · · ◆◆◆ ·	5–8	80–115 ft.
🦋T🍁✹⬛🍃	· · · · · · · ◆◆◆◆	7–9	10–26 ft.
🦋✹⬛🍃	· · · · · · · ◆◆◆◆ ·	6–10	2–10 ft.
🦋🍁✹⬛🍃	· · · · · · · ◆◆◆◆ ·	5–8	4–12 ft.
🦋🍁✹	◆◆◆ · · · · · ◆◆◆◆	2–7	30 ft.
🦋T🍁✹🍃	◆ · · · · ◆◆◆◆◆◆	5–9	15–25 ft.
🦋🍁✹🍃	◆◆◆ · · · · ◆◆◆◆◆	2–8	8–10 ft.
🍁⬛🍃	· · · · · ◆◆◆◆◆◆ ·	7–9	vine
🍁⬛🍃	· · · · · · ◆◆◆◆◆ ·	7–9	vine
⬛🍃	· · · · · · · · ◆◆◆ ·	5–9	vine
🐦🦋T✹⬛🍃	· · · · · · ◆◆◆ · · ·	7–10	5–15 ft.

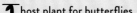

 nectar for butterflies T host plant for butterflies 🍁 fall color ✹ showy flowers 🐦 nectar for hummingbirds

PACIFIC COAST REGION

BOTANICAL NAME	COMMON NAME	LIGHT NEEDS
Abies concolor	white fir	◑
Abies grandis	grand fir	◑
Acer negundo var. *californicum*	California box elder	◑
Alnus rhombifolia	white alder	●
Alnus sinuata	Sitka alder	○
Amelanchier alnifolia	saskatoon serviceberry	○
Betula occidentalis	water birch	○
Celtis reticulata	western hackberry	○
Cornus canadensis	bunchberry	●
Cornus nuttalli	Pacific dogwood	◑
Cornus sericea	red-osier dogwood	◑
Crataegus douglasii	western hawthorn	◑
Fragaria californica	California wild strawberry	○
Fragaria chiloensis	beach strawberry	○
Juniperus californica	California juniper	○
Juniperus occidentalis	western juniper	○
Juniperus scopulorum	Rocky Mountain juniper	○

 full sun   full sun to partial shade 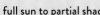 light shade to shade   nesting plant   shelter plants   roosting plant
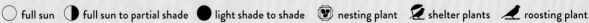

OTHER USES	APPROXIMATE FRUITING MONTHS J F M A M J J A S O N D	HARDINESS ZONES	MATURE HEIGHT
🦋🐦 (fruit, bird)	· · · · · · · · ◆ ◆ ◆ ◆	4–8	30–50 ft.
butterfly, host, fruit, bird	· · · · · · · · ◆ ◆ ◆ ◆	6–9	100–200 ft.
butterfly, host, fruit	◆ · · · · · ◆ ◆ ◆ ◆ ◆	3	20–40 ft.
butterfly, host, fruit	◆ ◆ ◆ ◆ ◆ · · · ◆ ◆ ◆ ◆	6–9	50–90 ft.
butterfly, host, fall color, fruit	· · · · · · ◆ ◆ ◆ · · ·	2–8	20–30 ft.
butterfly, host, fall color, flowers	· · · · · ◆ ◆ ◆ ◆ ◆ · ·	4–8	4–18 ft.
butterfly, host, fall color, fruit	· · · · · · · ◆ ◆ ◆ ◆ ·	3–9	20–25 ft.
hummingbird, butterfly, host, fruit	◆ ◆ · · · · · · ◆ ◆ ◆ ◆	7–9	20–30 ft.
butterfly, host, fall color, flowers	· · · · · · ◆ ◆ ◆ ◆ · ·	2–5	3–8 in.
fall color, flowers, fruit	· · · · · · · · ◆ ◆ ◆ ◆	9	20–30 ft.
butterfly, fall color, flowers, fruit, bird	· · · · · · ◆ ◆ ◆ ◆ · ·	3–8	10 ft.
hummingbird, butterfly, host, fall color, flowers, fruit	· · · · · · ◆ ◆ ◆ ◆ ◆ ·	4–6	5–20 ft.
butterfly, host, flowers	· · · · · ◆ ◆ ◆ · · · ·	5–10	6–8 ft.
butterfly, flowers	· · · · · ◆ ◆ ◆ · · · ·	5–10	6–12 ft.
butterfly, host, fruit, bird	◆ ◆ ◆ ◆ ◆ ◆ ◆ ◆ ◆ ◆ ◆ ◆	8–10	10–35 ft.
fruit, bird	◆ ◆ ◆ · · · · ◆ ◆ ◆ ◆ ◆	5–10	20–60 ft.
fruit, bird	◆ ◆ ◆ ◆ ◆ ◆ ◆ ◆ ◆ ◆ ◆ ◆	3–6	30–40 ft.

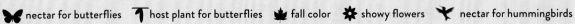

 nectar for butterflies   host plant for butterflies   fall color   showy flowers   nectar for hummingbirds

PACIFIC COAST REGION

BOTANICAL NAME	COMMON NAME	LIGHT NEEDS
Lonicera hispidula	pink honeysuckle	◯
Lonicera involucrata	twinberry honeysuckle	◑
Malus fusca	Pacific crabapple	◑
Myrica californica	California wax myrtle	◯
Picea mariana	black spruce	◯
Pinus contorta	lodgepole pine	◯
Pinus edulis	piñon pine	◯
Pinus ponderosa	ponderosa pine	◑
Pinus sabiniana	digger pine	◯
Pinus torreyana	Torrey pine	◯
Platanus racemosa	western sycamore	◯
Populas fremontii	Fremont cottonwood	◯
Populus tremuloides	quaking aspen	◑
Prunus emarginata	bitter cherry	◯
Prunus ilicifolia	hollyleaf cherry	◯
Prunus lyonii	Catalina cherry	◯
Prunus virginiana var. demissa	chokecherry	◯

 full sun   full sun to partial shade   light shade to shade   nesting plant   shelter plants   roosting plant

OTHER USES	APPROXIMATE FRUITING MONTHS J F M A M J J A S O N D		HARDINESS ZONES	MATURE HEIGHT
🐦 🦋 ❋	◆ · · · · ◆ ◆ ◆ ◆ ◆ ◆ ◆		7	12 ft.
🐦 🦋 ❋	· · · · · · · ◆ ◆ · · ·		4–10	2–10 ft.
🐦 🍁 ❋ 🐤	· · ◆ ◆ ◆ · · · · · · ·		4–9	15–30 ft.
🦋 🐤	◆ ◆ ◆ ◆ ◆ ◆ ◆ ◆ ◆ ◆ ◆ ◆		7–9	30 ft.
🦋 T 🐤 🐦	· · · · · · · ◆ ◆ ◆ ◆ ◆		1–6	16–60 ft.
🦋 T 🐤 🐦	· · · · · · ◆ ◆ ◆ ◆ ◆ ◆		5–8	15–30 ft.
🦋 T 🐤 🐦	· · · · · · · · ◆ ◆ ◆ ◆		5–8	15–35 ft.
🦋 🐤 🐦	· · · · · · · · ◆ ◆ ◆ ◆		3–8	75–100 ft.
🐤 🐦	◆ ◆ ◆ ◆ ◆ ◆ ◆ ◆ ◆ ◆ ◆ ◆		8	40–80 ft.
🐤 🐦	◆ ◆ ◆ ◆ ◆ ◆ ◆ ◆ ◆ ◆ ◆ ◆		7	20–40 ft.
🍁 🐤	◆ ◆ ◆ · · · · · ◆ ◆ ◆ ◆		7–10	40–90 ft.
🦋 T 🍁 🐤	· · ◆ ◆ ◆ ◆ ◆ · · · · ·		6–10	40–90 ft.
🦋 T 🐤	· · · ◆ ◆ ◆ ◆ · · · · ·		2–6	30–60 ft.
🦋 T 🍁 ❋	· · ◆ ◆ ◆ ◆ ◆ ◆ ◆ ◆ ·		7	30 ft.
🦋 T 🍁	◆ · · · ◆ ◆ ◆ ◆ ◆ ◆ ◆		7	6–25 ft.
🦋 🍁 ❋	· · · · · · ◆ ◆ ◆ ◆ ·		8	15–35 ft.
🦋 T 🍁 ❋	· · · · · · · · ◆ ◆ ◆ ◆		3–5	9–25 ft.

🦋 nectar for butterflies   T host plant for butterflies   🍁 fall color   ❋ showy flowers   🐦 nectar for hummingbirds

PACIFIC COAST REGION

BOTANICAL NAME	COMMON NAME	LIGHT NEEDS
Quercus agrifolia	coast live oak	○
Quercus douglasii	blue oak	○
Quercus engelmanni	Engelmann oak	○
Quercus garryana	Oregon oak	○
Quercus kelloggii	California black oak	○
Rhus glabra	smooth sumac	○
Rhus integrifolia	lemonade berry	○
Rhus ovata	sugar bush	◐
Rhus trilobata	three-leaf sumac	○
Rosa californica	California rose	○
Rosa nutkana	Nootka rose	◐
Rosa spithamea	Sonoma rose	○
Rubus leucodermis	western raspberry	○
Rubus parviflorus	thimbleberry	◐
Rubus spectabilis	salmonberry	○
Sambucus caerulea	blue elderberry	○
Sambucus callicarpa	Pacific coast red elderberry	◐

 full sun   full sun to partial shade   light shade to shade   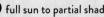 nesting plant   shelter plants   roosting plant

OTHER USES	APPROXIMATE FRUITING MONTHS J F M A M J J A S O N D	HARDINESS ZONES	MATURE HEIGHT
🦋 host-plant fruit bird	· · · · · · ◆◆◆◆◆ ·	9	15–50 ft.
🦋 host-plant fruit bird	◆◆◆◆◆◆◆◆◆◆◆◆	7	20–60 ft.
🦋 host-plant fruit bird	◆◆◆◆◆◆◆◆◆◆◆◆	7	20–50 ft.
🦋 host-plant fruit bird	◆◆◆◆◆◆◆◆◆◆◆◆	7	3–60 ft.
🦋 fall-color fruit bird	· · · · · · · ◆◆◆◆	5–8	30–80 ft.
hummingbird 🦋 host-plant fall-color fruit bird	· · · · · · ◆◆◆◆	3–9	10–20 ft.
🦋 host-plant fall-color showy fruit	◆◆ · · · · ◆◆◆◆◆◆	9–10	4–25 ft.
🦋 fall-color fruit	· · · · · ◆◆◆◆ ·	7–10	10 ft.
🦋 fall-color fruit	· · · · · ◆◆◆ ·	4–9	3–12 ft.
🦋 fall-color showy fruit	◆◆◆◆ · · · ◆◆◆◆	6	5–10 ft.
🦋 fall-color showy fruit	◆◆◆◆◆ · · ◆◆◆◆	4–6	2–13 ft.
🦋 fall-color showy fruit	◆◆◆◆◆◆◆◆◆◆◆◆	7	1 ft.
🦋 fall-color showy fruit	· · · · ◆◆◆ · · · ·	5–6	3–5 ft.
🦋 fall-color showy fruit	· · · · · · ◆◆◆◆◆	4–7	3–6 ft.
🦋 fall-color showy fruit bird	· · · ◆◆◆◆ · · ·	6–7	5 ft.
🦋 host-plant fall-color showy fruit	· · · · · ◆◆◆◆◆◆	6–9	15–30 ft.
🦋 fall-color showy fruit bird hummingbird	◆◆ · · · · · ◆◆◆◆◆	8	9 ft.

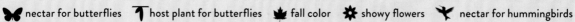

🦋 nectar for butterflies   host plant for butterflies   fall color   showy flowers   nectar for hummingbirds

PACIFIC COAST REGION

BOTANICAL NAME	COMMON NAME	LIGHT NEEDS
Sorbus dumosa	Arizona mountain ash	◯
Sorbus. sitchensis	Sitka mountain ash	◐
Vaccinium ovatum	California huckleberry	◐
Vaccinium parvifolium	red huckleberry	◐
Viburnum ellipticum	western viburnum	◐
Viburnum trilobum	American cranberry	◐
Vitis californica	California wild grape	◯

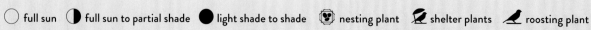
 full sun   full sun to partial shade   ● light shade to shade   nesting plant   shelter plants   roosting plant

OTHER USES	APPROXIMATE FRUITING MONTHS J F M A M J J A S O N D	HARDINESS ZONES	MATURE HEIGHT
🦋 🍁 ✿	• • • • • • • • ◆◆◆◆	6	8 ft.
🦋 🍁 ✿	• • • • • • • ◆◆◆ • •	5	3–15 ft.
🦋 ✿ ▣ 🐦	• • • • • • • ◆◆◆◆ •	6–10	2–10 ft.
🦋 🍁 ✿ ▣ 🐦	• • • • • • • ◆◆◆ •	5–8	4–12 ft.
🦋 🍁	• • • • • • ◆◆◆ •	6–9	8 ft.
🦋 🍁 ✿ 🐦	◆◆◆ • • • • ◆◆◆◆◆	2–8	8–10 ft.
🍁 ▣ 🐦	• • • • • • ◆◆◆◆◆ •	7–9	vine

Hugh Norris Trail, Tucson mountain district. Arizona's rich diversity of habitats supports more than 500 bird species including the vermillion flycatcher, elf owls, greater roadrunner, and gila woodpecker.

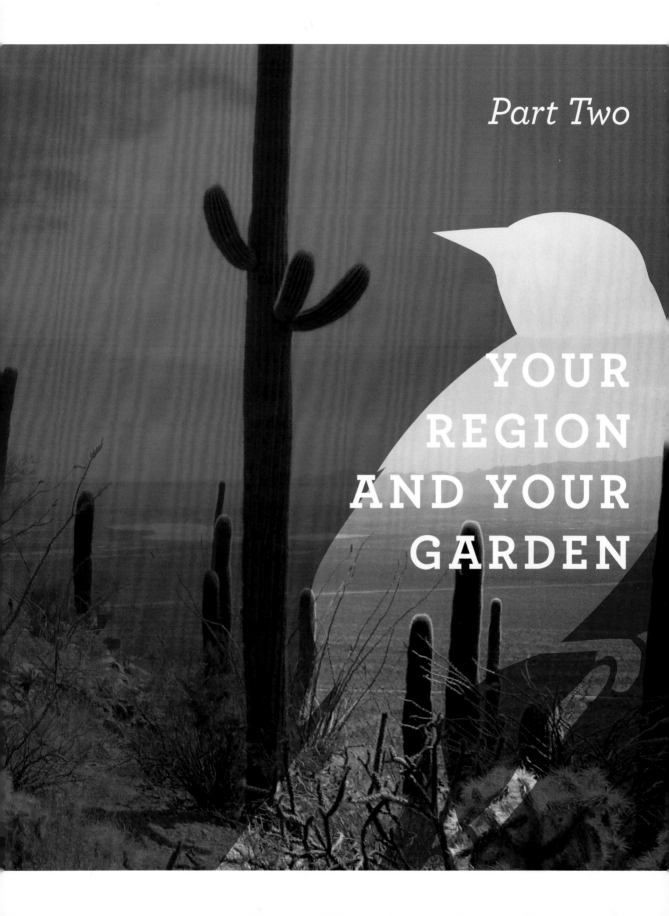

Part Two

YOUR
REGION
AND YOUR
GARDEN

In creating your garden to attract birds, first and foremost I recommend that you use plants that are native to your region, because those plants are most likely to meet the needs of your local bird species. Using the three flower and fruiting calendars in the book as a guide for selecting plants, you can help attract former resident birds back to your locality and maybe even get them to take up residence in your own backyard.

Native birds have coevolved with the plants of your region to provide themselves with both effective camouflage from predators and secure shelter from the elements. Many plants rely on birds to distribute their seed. The ripened fruit is a lure for the bird to feed on, and the seeds have evolved to pass through the bird unharmed and for the bird to eject them some distance from the parent plant.

Native plants are wonderfully adapted to their environment, and if you plant them to mimic their natural growing conditions, they will reward you with a beautiful garden that is wildlife friendly and environmentally sustainable. Native plants can require less maintenance, watering, fertilizing, and pest control than non-native species. By growing native plants and grasses, you can establish a healthy ecosystem in your backyard, which will help to preserve our natural heritage and biodiversity.

Native flowers often surpass non-native species for beauty and resistance to disease and drought conditions, and landscaping with native plants is just as easy as filling your yard with common introduced flowers, shrubs, trees, and lawns. When planting, mulching, or pruning, native plants need the same basic care that you give any landscape plant. Buying healthy plants that are adapted to your climate and preparing the soil well will help your garden get off to a great start. And then, a little routine care will keep your garden looking good for years to come.

Growing native trees, flowers, and grasses is a practical way to contribute to reducing pollution and improving the environment. By

WHY CHOOSE NATIVE PLANTS?

Northern cardinal feeding in wild bergamot (*Monarda fistulosa*).

minimizing the need for pesticides and fertilizers, you will help keep our waterways clean and healthy. Because of their more extensive root systems, perennials store more water and carbon from the atmosphere than traditional lawns, so consider replacing your lawn area with drifts of wildflowers or native grasses.

Nursery-grown native plants are selected by horticulturists and improved by selective breeding to increase the qualities that we find attractive in the garden. Because of the attention they receive in the garden, your plantings will have a lushness and a concentration of fruiting, seeding, and flowering not generally found in natural habitats.

This wildflower garden in Maine illustrates how beautiful native plants can be in a semiformal setting. Included are lupine (*Lupinus* spp.), wild bergamot (*Monarda fistulosa*), Canada lily (*Lilium canadense*), and asters (*Symphyotrichum* spp.), which attract birds including the ruby-throated hummingbird in summer and seed-eating chickadees and cardinals in winter. The trees on either side of the gate are well positioned to allow birds to dart quickly into cover.

GETTING *to* KNOW YOUR REGION

Generally, the historical composition of the soil is the determinant of what will grow most successfully in your locality. The determinant of the soil composition is what used to grow in it before European settlers began to dramatically change the landscape.

By observing the surrounding countryside in your region, birds present in remnant habitats, parks, and gardens, and researching the species that once lived in your area or passed through during migration, you can discover what species of birds are likely to be attracted to your garden. Then you can plan your garden to cater to their specific feeding, shelter, and nesting requirements.

North America can be broadly divided into five basic natural environmental regions—the northeast, southeast, plains and prairies, mountains and deserts, and Pacific Coast—each with its own growing conditions, including moisture, wind, minimum and maximum temperatures, depth of soil, and soil composition. By selecting plants that have adapted to these conditions, and keeping in mind the hardiness zones of your area, you can more easily establish a natural environment in your garden.

Northeastern coniferous woodlands are dominated by spruce, northern pines, hemlocks, and beeches. The soil is moist and acidic because of high rainfall, which leaches nutrients from the soil and leaf litter.

Northeast

The Great Lakes region and the northeast interior of North America (the northern forest region) once supported vast, moist, shady coniferous forests that were dominated by pines (*Pinus* spp.), spruces (*Picea* spp.), and hemlocks (*Tsuga* spp.),

Northeastern deciduous woodland, dominated by oak, beech, maple, and hickory trees. Dappled spring sunshine encourages a variety of forest flowers, followed by dense shade in summer. Deciduous leaves give a porous structure to the deep soil.

interspersed with smaller patches of deciduous beeches (*Fagus* spp.), birches (*Betula* spp.), and aspens and poplars (*Populus* spp.). The soil therefore has a relatively high acidity, of between pH4 and pH5.

One of the northern hemisphere's richest habitats is found south of the Great Lakes. The once continuous eastern temperate forest comprised deciduous woodlands: oaks (*Quercus* spp.), beeches (*Fagus* spp.), maples (*Acer* spp.), and hickories (*Carya* spp.) dominated the canopy. And the varied understory included dogwoods (*Cornus* spp.), hollies (*Ilex* spp.), redbud (*Cercis canadensis*), and witch hazel (*Hamamelis virginiana*). The region's humus-rich, porous soil therefore has a moderate acidity, of between pH 5.5 and pH 6.5.

This vast region is characterized by bitterly cold winters that feature heavy snowstorms and chilly winds. Birds' winter food supplies become scarce. Fallen seeds and berries are covered with ice or snow, and insects are difficult to find because they have either gone into hibernation or died from the cold. Deciduous trees have dropped their leaves, so less shelter is available for birds.

Notes regarding birds

In the northeast region, by planning your garden to attract and protect birds, you can improve the conditions and chances of survival of the birds that reside in your locality. Plant a variety of native trees and shrubs that produce a variety of fleshy fruit or seeds that persist throughout winter. Provide evergreen hedges or windbreaks to offer birds secure shelter from cold winds and snowstorms. Leave the seed heads on ornamental grasses and wildflowers, to provide birds with a nutritious supply of seed, a

A heated birdbath. Thawed water is often critical for winter survival for resident birds, including blue jays.

highly valuable winter food source that stands above the snow.

Water supplies will periodically freeze up, but birds still need to drink and bathe and preen throughout winter. When birds consume snow for moisture, they use up valuable energy in thawing it. Consider installing a birdbath heater to provide a permanent supply of fresh, unfrozen water throughout winter.

Vast numbers of birds appear during the migratory seasons of spring and fall, and many unusual or uncommon avian visitors may appear in your garden. Resident birds include the cardinal, red-bellied woodpecker, red-headed and downy woodpecker, chickadee, blue jay, tufted titmouse, white-breasted nuthatch, American robin, and cedar waxwing.

Southeast

The generally milder climate of the southeast region supported the vast, southeastern coniferous woodlands, which spread from New Jersey, across the coastal plains to Georgia and Florida and west to Louisiana and west Texas. The region's conifers, such as yellow pine (*Pinus echinata*) and loblolly pine (*Pinus taeda*), when compared to the conifers of the northeastern region, have foliage that is more open. Their branching begins higher up on the trunk so more sun can reach the ground, allowing the region's vast variety of understory plants to thrive. The well-drained, acid soil has a pH of less than 5.5. The region ranges from the mountainous areas of the Appalachians to the subtropical regions of Florida.

Southeastern coniferous woodland. More open branching of southern conifers allows more sun to reach the ground than northern conifers. Sandy subsoil offers good drainage and the soil is moderately acid.

Notes regarding birds

The generally milder climate of the southeast is attractive to many northern bird species, which migrate south for the winter months in search of fruiting trees and shrubs. If you select evergreen trees or shrubs that produce fruit or seed in winter, you will make your garden attractive to many of these migratory birds, as well as to resident birds.

Wetlands soils are water logged and very acid. Wetlands are scattered across the continent and are the result of glaciers that once covered much of North America. They are most common in the southeast, where they often contain cypress, sweetbay, and tupelo trees.

Tufted titmouse in the fall foliage of sugar maple (*Acer saccharum*).

Western prairie with wildflowers, including the blue camas (*Camassia* sp.) and buttercup (*Ranunculus* sp.).

When you are creating a garden in this region, you will want to provide birds with shelter from the extreme summer heat. In the hot, dry summer weather that typifies the region, water is especially important for birds to cool off in, as well as to drink and bathe in. (To stay cool, birds evaporate water in their mouths by panting.) Many plant species that are recommended for the northeast region will grow here, but you will have to water them regularly until they are established enough to survive the extreme summer heat.

Resident birds include the mourning dove, northern flicker, red-bellied and downy woodpecker, blue jay, tufted titmouse, white-breasted nuthatch, blue-gray gnatcatcher, brown thrasher, gray catbird, northern mockingbird, eastern bluebird, American robin, eastern meadowlark, cardinal, and eastern towhee.

Plains and Prairie

Prairie is a French word for meadow, a plant community of flowering perennials and grasses. The plains and prairie region is split on a line running through Bismarck, North Dakota, and Dodge City, Kansas. Both areas are too dry to support many tree species. The eastern zone annually has 20 inches or more of rainfall, has slightly acid soil, and supports tall grasses that grow up to 8 feet. The western zone, which extends to the foothills of the Rocky Mountains, has less rainfall, neutral soil, and supports shorter grasses. Prairie soils generally have a pH level of between 6 and 7.

As the grasslands were cleared during pioneer settlement of the prairie, the native bird populations became severely diminished. Today, only small remnant patches of grasslands remain, but they are an indication of how beautiful the grasslands once were. The region used to be dominated by beautiful grasses such as big bluestem (*Andropogon gerardii*), little bluestem (*Schizachyrium scoparium*), Indian grass (*Sorghastrum nutans*), switchgrass (*Panicum virgatum*), prairie drop seed (*Sporobolus heterolepis*), and side oats grama (*Bouteloua curtipendula*). All these species are highly adaptable, attractive plants that are suitable for cultivation. They not only produce highly nutritious seed for a wide range of songbirds but also serve as shelter and nesting sites for ground-nesting birds.

The grasslands of the region are studded with colorful flora that attract insects, butterflies, and hummingbirds. Coneflowers (*Echinacea* spp.), bergamots (*Monarda* spp.), blazing star (*Liatris spicata*), goldenrods (*Solidago* spp.), and purple prairie clover (*Dalea purpurea*) are among the plants that are both colorful features of the prairie environment and excellent garden plants. North of Kansas, the region is noted for its deep snowfalls, subzero winter temperatures, and howling winds.

Notes regarding birds

When you are planning your landscape, it is important to provide shelter for the resident birds. Evergreen windbreaks and hedges will enable birds to escape weather extremes. For a beautiful spring garden, reduce or replace your lawn area with prairie grasses and wildflowers. Leave the seed heads on the plants when they have finished flowering, so the seed heads in winter provide food for resident birds.

A supply of fresh water for birds is essential throughout the year. If it is frozen, you can thaw it by adding hot water to it, or you can purchase a commercially available birdbath heater to keep the water thawed. Consider wiring the switch to an indoor location for convenience, and watch the vast array of birds attracted to your permanent supply of scarce thawed water.

Resident birds include the mourning dove, greater roadrunner, northern flicker, American robin, meadowlarks, pine siskin, lark and Harris's sparrows, northern mockingbird, black-billed magpie, lazuli bunting, horned lark, black-capped chickadee, white-breasted nuthatch, house finch, American goldfinch, and the acorn, downy, hairy, and ladder-backed woodpeckers.

Tall grasses, including big bluestem (*Andropogon gerardii*), predominate in the eastern zone of the prairie, which has deep, slightly acid soil.

Harris's sparrow foraging for seeds.

High and windy Rocky Mountain woodland with a thin layer of slightly acid topsoil. Spruce, fir, and aspen trees dominate the landscape.

Mountains and Deserts

The mountains and deserts region is a vast area that encompasses several habitats. The northwestern forested mountain region includes the Rocky Mountain woodland that is dominated by aspens (*Populus* spp.), firs (*Abies* spp.), and spruces (*Picea* spp.), as well as frosty alpine meadows that support tough alpine wildflowers above the tree line. The thin, slightly acid soil has a pH of between 5.5 and 6.5. Farther south, the Colorado Plateau is dominated by piñon-juniper woodlands. East of the mountains in southeastern California, Arizona, New Mexico, and western Texas, the lowland deserts receive little rainfall because of the mountain ridges along the coast. The generally alkaline soil has a pH of 8 or higher. The hot, dry environment supports numerous plant species, including the saguaro (*Carnegiea gigantea*) and scores of flowering plants like brittlebush (*Encelia farinosa*), sunflowers (*Helianthus* spp.), and desert marigold (*Baileya multiradiata*), which produce vast amounts of seeds. The flowers attract many insects that in turn support a surprising number of bird species.

Notes regarding birds

In the northern sections of this region, choose plants that are hardy enough to survive the extremes of weather. Birds require evergreen windbreaks and hedges for protection from cold winds and snowstorms. Choose plants that will be year-round sources of fleshy fruits and seeds, especially in winter. Water supplies will periodically freeze, so you should regularly thaw the water for the birds or purchase a heater for your birdbath.

Although many bird species migrate from this region in winter, resident birds can include the mourning dove, northern flicker, Steller's jay, mountain chickadee, white-breasted, pygmy, and red-breasted nuthatches, American robin, meadowlark, red-winged blackbird, bohemian waxwing, and ladder-backed, hairy, and downy woodpeckers.

In the lowland desert areas of the southwest, choose plants that have adapted to the extremes of temperature and the arid conditions. Rather than a traditional lawn area, plant wildflower gardens and native ground covers that are drought tolerant and attract birds and butterflies.

Mountain chickadee. Dense shelter trees, such as pines, are critical for the survival of resident birds.

Of the 19 hummingbird species found in North America, 17 are found in this region and Anna's and Costa's hummingbird are resident species.

For birds in the southwest, a permanent supply of water can often be more difficult to find than food. A birdbath or garden pond will be visited

Desert landscape, with a surface of pebbles and sandy alkaline soil that mainly supports cactus, including teddy bear cholla (*Opuntia bigelovii*), ocotillo (*Fouquieria splendens*), and saguaro (*Carnegiea gigantea*).

Redwood (*Sequoia sempervirens*). Western coniferous woodland has slightly acid, shallow but rich topsoil and dense shade most of the year. The dominant trees include cedar, Douglas fir, hemlock, redwood, and sequoia.

regularly. In the Southwest, in any hardware store you can easily find the misters hummingbirds love to fly through, so you can install one in your desert garden.

The region's many resident birds include the verdin, cactus wren, Mexican jay, black-tailed gnatcatcher, bridled titmice, greater roadrunner, western meadowlark, and northern cardinals.

Pacific Coast

The Pacific Coast region of the Northwest, located north from northern California, encompasses the western coniferous woodland and is dominated by ponderosa pine (*Pinus ponderosa*), lodgepole pine (*Pinus contorta*), Sitka spruce (*Picea sitchensis*), Douglas fir (*Pseudotsuga menziesii*), and western hemlock (*Tsuga heterophylla*). In the California coastal ranges, giant redwood (*Sequoia sempervirens*) and red cedars (*Juniperus* spp.) dominate the landscape. The slightly acid soil has a pH level of between 5.5 and 6.5.

Farther south, the Mediterranean climate of southern coastal California is mostly chaparral habitat and contains low evergreen oaks, several pine species, and resinous woody shrubs, grass tussocks, and numerous wildflowers, such as manzanitas (*Arctostaphylos* spp.), buckthorns (*Rhamnus* spp.), and sumacs (*Rhus* spp.). The soil is generally neutral and has a pH of 7.

Notes regarding birds

Because of the wide range of habitats, a large variety of birds are resident in the Pacific Coast region, from woodland species to hummingbirds, including the Steller's jay, northern flicker, acorn and downy woodpeckers, black phoebe, black-capped and mountain chickadee, western bluebird, northern mockingbird, cedar waxwing, spotted and California towhees, dark-eyed junco, meadowlarks, rufous-crowned, sage, savannah, fox, song, and white-crowned sparrows, red-wing and tri-colored blackbirds, white-winged crossbill, pine and evening grosbeaks, American goldfinch and lesser goldfinch, and pine siskin. Anna's hummingbird is a popular resident throughout the region, and several other hummingbird species, including Allen's, calliope, rufous, Costa's, and black-chinned hummingbirds, appear in spring and summer.

More than 2,000 plant species are native to California, so you have a rich variety of native plants available for your garden. Plants native to this region are capable of surviving drought conditions and dry, coastal-soil conditions. Plan a garden for hummingbirds by providing year-round nectar-rich "hummingbird flowers." Include trees and shrubs that produce year-round fruit and seed for the birds, and rather than large lawn areas, use native wildflowers in your border planting or wildflower garden. Incorporate shelter, nesting trees, and shrubs, and a permanent supply of fresh water, so you encourage birds to take up residency in your garden.

Low-nutrient soil area, Sierra Nevada. The foreground includes common monkeyflower (*Mimulus guttatus*) growing in the damp soil along the creek, California poppy (*Eschscholzia californica*), and white brodiaea (*Triteleia hyacinthina*). Background plants include foothill pine (*Pinus sabiniana*) and buckbrush (*Ceanothus* spp.).

Female red-winged blackbird in a summer wildflower garden.

UNDERSTANDING YOUR YARD

Understanding how to make the best use of the conditions your garden site has to offer is a key part of creating a successful landscape plan. The many factors that will influence your plant selection include: landscape orientation, existing vegetation, sunny and shady areas, prevailing winds, views, climate, soil pH, fertility, and drainage. Let's consider a few of the most important issues in establishing your garden.

Orientation

Your garden design needs to consider the solar access to your house and the placement of outdoor living areas, because the orientation of your garden in relation to the sun's path will be a deciding factor in what you plant and where to plant it.

By observing the path of the sun, you can determine the warmest part of the garden area in winter. This will be a good area to locate an outdoor living area. Likewise, you can develop the shadier side of the house as a summer outdoor area. Ways to do this include a pergola covered with deciduous vines, or deciduous trees planted where they will shade your house in summer and allow the sun to penetrate and warm the house and outdoor living areas in winter. By observing the direction of prevailing winds in your location, you can plan the location of an evergreen hedge to provide wind protection. Such a hedge will provide shelter for birds and privacy, wind protection, and screening for the yard.

Existing Vegetation

If you have an established garden, consider "going native" over time. Choose native plants for infill planting or when existing plants need replacing, or choose a part of the yard in need of a makeover. Or perhaps start by installing a wildflower or hummingbird garden. For a dramatic change, remove the lawn and replace it with a meadow garden containing wildflowers and ornamental native grasses.

Take stock of what native trees and shrubs already exist in your yard. These trees will influence what and where to plant. Conifers will mean shade and acid soil; around deciduous trees the soil will be less acid and have lighter shade.

Climate

Temperature, rainfall, and other climate-related factors can have tremendous impact on which native plants will thrive for you. Native plants are ideally suited to the climatic conditions where they have grown and developed for thousands of years.

Winter cold is only one element of your climate. Parts of both Pennsylvania and Arizona are Zone 6, for instance, but the same plants don't grow equally well in both places. Much of the difference has to do with the amount of rainfall each area gets. Humidity and summer heat are other factors that affect how well a species will grow in a given area.

Soil pH

Your soil's pH is the measure of how acid or alkaline it is. The pH is normally expressed as a number somewhere between 1 and 14. A pH of 7 is said to be neutral. If the pH is less than 7, the soil is acid; if the pH is higher than 7, the soil is alkaline.

If the pH of your soil is between 6.5 and 7.2, you can grow a wide variety of native plants. Some natives, like highbush blueberry (*Vaccinium corymbosum*) and flame azalea (*Rhododendron calendulaceum*), are adapted to more acid conditions (pH lower than 6.5). Others, like hackberries (*Celtis* spp.), can tolerate a more alkaline soil (pH higher than 7.2). While it is possible to change the pH of your soil by adding compost, other organic matter, ground limestone (to make soil less acidic), or powdered sulfur (to make soil less alkaline), it's much less trouble to choose plants that are naturally adapted to your soil pH. Native plants that grow within a 100-mile radius of where you live will generally meet this criterion.

It's easy to find out the pH of your soil. You can get a rough idea by performing a simple home test with litmus paper (available from many garden centers and garden supply catalogs). Simply mix equal parts of soil and water, touch the paper to the resulting slurry, and match the color to the chart that comes with the litmus paper. Or, if you want more precise results, you can get your soil tested professionally. Your local Cooperative Extension Service and many garden centers sell soil-testing kits. All you have to do is collect a sample according to the directions in the kit, send it off for analysis, and wait 6 to 8 weeks for the test results.

Soil Fertility

To produce healthy, vigorous growth, your native plants need a balanced supply of soil nutrients. The most accurate way to find out about your soil's fertility is to have your soil tested professionally, as you would for pH. The test results will show you whether your soil is naturally low in nutrients (infertile or "poor") or if it has ample amounts of all the necessary nutrients (fertile or "rich"). Most soils will fall somewhere in between, with "average" fertility.

You may also be able to guess your soil's fertility level by taking a look at its texture. Texture refers to the balance of sand, silt, and clay particles in your soil. Take a grape-sized chunk of soil, put it in the palm of your hand, and add some water to make it soupy. Stir the mixture with your finger. If the mixture feels gritty, your soil is on the sandy side and probably tends to be infertile. If the mixture feels mostly smooth or sticky, your soil contains more silt or clay and likely has average to high fertility. If the mixture has some characteristics of each type, you probably have a loam, which tends to have average fertility.

You'll want to consider your soil's natural fertility level when choosing plants for your garden. Some plants are adapted to either poor or rich soil; otherwise, you can assume the plant grows best with average fertility. If you have naturally poor soil and want to grow a wider range of plants, work a 2- to 4-inch layer of compost or other organic matter into the planting area. As it breaks down into humus, the organic matter will release a small but balanced supply of nutrients to your plants.

Drainage

How quickly water drains from your soil is another important factor that affects which plants will thrive for you. Many natives grow well in moist but well-drained soil. That means that excess water will drain away but enough moisture will stay in the soil for roots to have a steady supply.

Your soil's texture influences its drainage. Sandy soils tend to be very well drained; in fact, the water may drain so quickly that the roots can't absorb it. Clay soils, on the other hand, often drain poorly; the tiny clay particles hold the water tightly and so roots can suffocate in the waterlogged soil. Silty soils also tend to hold lots of water. Loams, with a balance of sand, silt, and clay, are ideal for most plants. The sand particles allow excess water to drain freely, while the clay and silt particles hold enough water for good root growth. If your soil drains either too quickly or too slowly for good growth, you can improve drainage conditions and grow a wider range of plants by working in a 2- to 4-inch layer of compost, chopped leaves, or other organic matter.

DEVELOPING a LANDSCAPE PLAN

This landscape plan offers you some guidelines for grouping plants to create a diversity of habitats within an average-size yard.

To create a beautiful native garden and intensive habitat for birds, use the Calendars, the Plant Directory, and the Bird Directory to help you select suitable, productive plants for your locality.

Large Evergreen Trees	Deciduous Trees	Hedge	Tall Shrubs	Small Shrubs
Wildflowers	Brambles	Vines	Birdbath	Nestbox

Creating Edge Effects

The "edge effect" occurs where one vegetation zone merges into a different vegetation zone. The greater the diversity of plant species and food niches provided in this transitional area, the greater the variety of birds attracted. The sample landscape plan seeks to achieve this by creating several plant communities in one garden.

Each zone in the plan represents a different habitat, broadly mimicking the different habitats found in nature, which together with a vertical transition of plants from ground covers to trees and an equal balance between deciduous and evergreen plants, will provide a rich diversity of plant life to appeal to a large variety of garden birds.

Setting Out Nest Boxes

One advantage of creating a diversity of habitats in your garden is that when setting out nest boxes, you will be able to position them near or in each bird's preferred habitat, thereby increasing your chances of success. A surprising number of bird species will nest in close proximity, because each species has its own food and nesting niche. Each species defends an area around its nest against the same species, so it is usually a waste of resources to locate more than one nest box for each species in an average garden. An interesting exception is that providing four house wren nest boxes may increase your chances of success with this bird, because the male prefers to show the female several possible sites for her to choose from. Generally, the number of different nest box types that may be occupied in an area is about 10 per acre.

The Plan Habitats

The landscape plan offers you some guidelines for grouping plants in an average-size yard. The concept is to approximate the different habitats found in the natural world. Elements in the yard can be used to help create different habitats: the house can be treated as a rock outcrop, the roadway as a river or natural barrier, the lawn as a meadow or woodland clearing, and a thick dense hedge as an evergreen forest. Most birds are found in the transitional zone—the edge effect—where one habitat merges into a different habitat. The more edge effects you can create, the more bird species you are likely to attract. Other natural habitats to mimic in your garden design include a pond and bog garden, shady woodland, or a wild tangled, weedy environment.

In the landscape plan, I have suggested 7 different habitats that might be created in an average suburban garden.

It is not necessary to include all 7 zones for a successful garden. You should be guided by your natural surroundings in deciding what zones are most appropriate for your yard.

The Street Frontage

The roadway can be treated as if it were a natural barrier, like a river and an edge effect created by using lush planting and hedging in association with street trees. Birds such as orioles, titmice, flycatchers, gnatcatchers, hummingbirds, phoebes, and warblers will shelter in the foliage, darting out for insects in the open zone.

Suitable plants include juniper, holly, honeysuckle, spicebush, viburnum, blueberry, and mulberry.

Nesting Street trees can be suitable places to locate nest boxes: they need to be 15 to 20 feet above the ground for species such as woodpeckers or owls.

The House

When the house, patio, pergola, and paths are surrounded with shrubs, small trees, vines, and ground covers that merge them into the lawn area, birds such as hummingbirds, finches, and wrens will view the house as a natural feature in the landscape, like an rock outcrop.

Suitable plants include trumpet vine, Virginia creeper, grapes, honeysuckles, cherries, plums, wild strawberries, penstemons, roses, crabapples, and maples.

Nesting Sheltering vines on the side of the house provide a good location for a nesting shelf for the American robin. The rear of the house facing onto the garden is a good location for a nest box for flickers and a nesting shelf for phoebes or barn swallows.

The Hedgerow

A dense evergreen hedge or a hedgerow punctuated with small trees will provide shelter and nesting sites for birds, especially for winter residents, including jays, the northern cardinal, mourning dove, house finch, and chipping sparrow. A hedge will provide a transition zone from dense foliage to the more open foliage of deciduous trees and shrubs. Include plants that fruit at different times of the year.

Suitable plants include holly, juniper, honeysuckle, spruce, hemlock, blueberry, snowberry, arborvitae, and pine.

Nesting A house wren nest box is placed on the fence adjacent to shrubbery.

The Lawn and Wildflower Garden

An open sunny section of the garden planted with native grasses, abundant with seeds and insects, and fringed with wildflowers and hummingbird flowers is an attractive habitat for birds that prefer to feed in open fields, including buntings, sparrows, mockingbirds, and goldfinches.

Suitable plants include sedges, buffalo grass, blue grama grass, Indian grass, little bluestem, prairie dropseed, lupines, columbines, bergamots, sages, sunflowers, paintbrush, jewelweed, and asters.

Nesting A good location for another house wren box and boxes for chickadees and nuthatches is in a tree adjacent to the open lawn areas. Bluebirds prefer nest boxes located in open habitat.

The Pond Area

A pond ecology can be created with native aquatic plants and wetland edge planting that will provide habitat and a reliable source of water for birds and many other wildlife species.

Suitable plants include waterlilies, marsh marigolds, sedges, native iris, ferns, arrowwood viburnum, twinberry, and cranberry.

Nesting A good location for a tree swallow nest box is mounted on a pole, near water, in an open part of the garden.

The Woodland Area

Under tall evergreen trees, a dense planting of shade-tolerant understory small trees, shrubs, wildflowers, and ground covers creates a woodland environment. A small area of lawn extending into the shady section creates a mossy woodland edge effect attractive to ground-foraging forest dwellers like catbirds, wood thrushes, brown thrashers, cardinals, and mockingbirds.

Suitable plants include dogwood, holly, serviceberry, hemlock, sumac, elderberry, rhododendrons, spicebush, viburnums, fuchsias, flowered gooseberry, pink flowering currant, bunchberry, violets, cardinal flower, and columbines.

Nesting Titmice prefer a nest box in a woodland habitat.

The Wild Area

In an out-of-the-way area, allow some weeds to grow to attract a greater variety of birds, many of which would not normally visit a garden, such as bluebirds, thrushes, pine siskin, and blue grosbeak. A nearby bramble patch with leaf litter left on the ground will provide an ideal environment for ground-nesting and foraging birds.

Suitable plants include blackberry, raspberry, thimbleberry, and salmonberry.

Nesting A good location for house wren nest box.

CREATING YOUR GARDEN

Now that you have thought about what habitats to create in your garden, you should carefully consider what native plants will grow best there. Planning at this stage will ensure healthier plants and a garden that is easier to maintain. And it's exciting to realize that the most beautiful native plants attractive to the human eye are also irresistible to our native birds.

Choosing Plants

It's now time to decide which plants you really want to grow. The choices can be quite bewildering. Limiting your choices to plants that are naturally adapted to your climate and soil conditions will narrow the list. But you are still left with an exciting array of flowers, shrubs, vines, trees, ground covers, and grasses to choose from. To make sure you get the plants you really want, consider the following factors:

Spring blossoms of flowering dogwood (*Cornus florida*).

What birds can you attract?

If you live in an urban area on a migration flyway, you can try to attract migrating birds. Often habitat en-route for these species has been severely depleted by urban sprawl, and migrating birds such as yellow-rumped warblers will descend on your garden if you have some shelter and food available like ripe bayberries for them to gorge on. Find out what birds used to be in your area and include provision for them in your plant choices. It is possible to entice birds back into an area if there is sufficient food and shelter for them.

How much room do you have?

Always consider the ultimate height and spread of each plant before you decide to grow it. Don't be deceived by the small size of nursery plants, because when you give them the right conditions, they'll grow and spread quickly. Crowding plants together leads to more pruning later on and can also encourage plant diseases. If you have room for either one large tree or several smaller shrubs, remember that a variety of different plants will attract more birds than just one kind of plant.

What does the plant have to offer to your landscape?

While it's important to consider what the plant can offer birds, it's even better if you can enjoy the plant, too. If you like lots of color, consider showy flowering plants like columbines (*Aquilegia* spp.) and dogwoods (*Cornus* spp.). If you want to add winter interest, include evergreens like pine and spruce. Of course, you can also enjoy the berries of fruiting plants, at least until your feathered friends stop by!

Are pests and diseases a problem?

For the lowest maintenance and healthiest plants, look for natives that are naturally resistant to pest and disease problems. If you want to grow a species that can be disease-prone, like hawthorn (*Crataegus* spp.), make sure you give the plant the best possible growing conditions and be prepared to cope with the disease if it strikes. Your local Cooperative Extension Service can often recommend disease-resistant species and cultivars that are well suited to your area.

Sources of Native Plants

Once you've narrowed down your list of species, you're ready to get the plants for your garden. A growing number of nurseries sell native plant species. If you can't find what you're looking for, your local horticultural or native plant society may be able to recommend sources.

Whatever you do, don't be tempted to dig these plants up from the wild. Taking wild plants without a permit is prohibited in most states, but even more important, you can cause severe disruption to native plant and bird habitats that way. Also keep this issue in mind when you are buying your plants. Always ask if the plants you're buying are nursery-propagated. That means that the plants were grown from seed or divisions of existing plants in the nursery, and not procured from the wild.

Start your landscape with some locally native plants, or local subspecies of more widely available plants. For the best success rate in your garden, try to source locally propagated stock.

Preparing Soil and Landscape

Good soil preparation is perhaps the single most important thing you can do to ensure healthy, vigorous growth in your plants. So take a little extra care at planting time and you'll enjoy your beautiful garden for years to come.

Preparing the soil for native flowers and vines is really no different from starting a regular flower or vegetable garden. Strip off any existing lawn with a spade and dig out any remaining weed roots. Spread a 1- to 2-inch layer of compost, chopped leaves, or other organic material over the bed, and use a spade, shovel, digging fork, or rotary tiller to till the material into the soil while you are loosening the top 6 to 8 inches of soil. Rake the bed smooth and you're ready to plant.

For trees and shrubs, you have two options. If you're planting a few plants in different areas, you may just want to dig separate holes. If possible, though, consider grouping several plants in one large planting area you've dug up. The plants will thrive and it's really not much more work.

Preparing a planting area for trees and shrubs follows the same steps as for flowers and vines. If you're digging individual holes, make each hole just as deep as the plant's roots and twice as wide. Angle the sides of the planting hole inward so it's wider at the top than it is at the bottom, to encourage the roots to spread out into the surrounding soil.

Planting

The plants you buy for your garden may come in varying conditions. They can be bareroot, with just moist packaging around the base; container-grown; or (in the case of trees and large shrubs) balled and burlapped.

Bareroot plants arrive dormant (the plants are not in active growth and have no leaves), but they need prompt attention to get them settled in the ground as quickly as possible. Otherwise, the roots may dry out, become brittle, and break. Try to get bareroot stock planted within a day or two of receiving it. If you must wait, set the plants in a cool, dark place and keep the packing material moist. At planting time, leave a small cone of undisturbed soil in the center of the planting hole and spread the roots out evenly over the cone. Set the plant at the same depth it was growing at the nursery (look for a soil line at the base of the trunk). If you can't tell how deep it was planted before, set the crown (the point where the roots meet the stem) just even with the soil surface. Fill in with the soil you removed and water the plant well.

Container-grown stock can be planted any time of year that the ground isn't frozen. Slide the plant out or cut off the container. Snip off any dead or broken roots, as well as those that are circling around the outside of the root ball. Set the plant at the same depth as it grew in the container. Fill around the root ball with soil you removed from the hole and water the plant well.

Balled and burlapped trees and shrubs adapt best to planting when they are dormant, either in fall or early spring. Set the plant in the hole at the same depth it was growing and remove any binding rope or nails. If the roots are wrapped in natural burlap, simply peel it back from the top of the root ball and leave it in the hole to decompose. Remove synthetic wrapping without jarring the root ball. If the root ball is in a wire basket, cut off the top few wires. Fill in around the roots with soil from the hole, press the soil down so it secures and is in contact with the roots, and water well.

Watering

Keeping new plantings evenly moist is a critical step in getting them established. Even drought-tolerant species need some extra attention for the first year or two, until their roots start to spread out. Don't wait until your plants start to wilt; by that time, they're already quite stressed and can take longer to recover. Instead, check the soil in the root zone. Dig a small hole 4 to 6 inches deep and see how the soil there feels. If it is moist, wait a few days and check again; if it is dry, it's time to water. Check about once a week for the first year or two after planting and then occasionally during drought periods in following years.

For spot-watering small, individual plants, a watering can or a hose is fine. In larger yards, a drip irrigation system is a boon for time-pressured gardeners, and it will use 30 to 50 percent less water than a sprinkler system. Check the site after about an hour to see if the root zone is moist. If not yet moist, keep watering and checking the site at half-hour or hour intervals until the top 6 inches of soil becomes sufficiently moist. Once established, plants native to your locality will usually only need minimal watering.

Fertilizing

If you've chosen plants adapted to your soil's natural fertility and prepared the planting site well, the plants should be able to get all the nutrients they require from the soil. If you want to be sure they re getting what they need—especially for the first few years—apply a layer of compost about an inch thick under whatever mulch you use. Each spring or fall, pull back the top layer of mulch, top off the layer of compost, and replace the mulch.

Pruning

If you give each plant in your landscape enough room to develop without crowding, your pruning chores should be minimal. Each winter, while the plants are dormant, you may want to inspect the trees, shrubs, and vines, and prune out any dead, diseased, or damaged wood. Also remove any crossing or awkwardly directioned branches. Use a sharp pair of pruning shears (or a sharp pruning saw) to make a clean cut that will heal quickly. If you have a large tree that needs pruning, consult a local arborist, who will tell you whether the tree really does need work and who also can perform the necessary pruning safely. If your tree has dead limbs or snags, consider leaving them in place for the birds. You can create nest hollows in them by using a brace and bit. Existing holes can be enlarged and others started for woodpeckers to finish. Ensure that dead limbs are in a safe location and won't fall onto roads, walkways, power lines, or buildings.

Continuing Care for Herbaceous Plants

If you've prepared your soil well, chosen plants that are naturally adapted to your area, planted them carefully, and given them the attention they need to get established, the flowers, ground covers, and grasses in your garden will need minimal care.

One technique that will benefit many perennials, grasses, and ground covers is division. Division is simply the process of cutting apart plants to make several new plants. It's a great way to also revitalize old, overgrown clumps that have started dying out in the middle and stopped blooming well. And it's an easy way to propagate plants.

To divide a clump, cut around the plant with a trowel, spade, or garden fork. Lift the plant from its hole. If it's a small plant, cut sections off with a sharp knife or trowel, making sure each section has at least one healthy crown and plenty of roots. If the plant is large, you can cut off sections with a sharp spade. Or using two garden forks, plunge them into the middle of the clump back-to-back, and then press the handles together to divide the clump.

If the center of the plant you're dividing is woody or dead, discard or compost it, and replant sections from the outside of the clump. Whatever technique you use, the larger your divisions, the faster you'll have big, showy plants; the smaller your divisions, the more plants you'll have. Divide spring and early summer bloomers in late summer or early fall, and midsummer- and fall-blooming grasses and perennials in early spring. Replant your new divisions quickly in prepared soil, and water them well until they re established.

Mulching

Mulching will provide ideal growing conditions for most of your landscape plants. Mulch helps keep the soil cool and moist, reducing the need for frequent watering and encouraging good root growth. It suppresses weed growth by covering weed seeds, preventing them from sprouting. And as organic mulches (like chopped leaves or shredded bark) break down, they add humus and a small but steady supply of plant nutrients to the soil.

Exactly which mulch you'll use depends on your plants and what's most available in your area. If you're growing plants that thrive in acid soil, mulch with acidic materials like needles or leaves of spruce, fir, pine, hemlock, rhododendron, mountain laurel, oak, or beech. On soil that is neutral or near-neutral, use leaves of maples, ash, poplar, birch, dogwood, hickory, elm, and cedar. Compost makes a good all-around garden mulch, especially if you top the compost with a layer of wood chips or shredded bark to keep your mulch mixture from drying out.

Before applying organic mulch, make sure the area is free of weeds; the mulch won't control any weeds that are already growing on the site. Apply a 2- to 3-inch layer of a fine-textured mulch (like compost or chopped leaves) or 3 to 5 inches of coarser mulch (such as wood chips). Be sure to leave a mulch-free zone several inches wide around the base of each plant; moist mulch piled around stems has a tendency to promote rot and encourage pest damage. Top off the mulch once or twice a season as needed.

Mulching imitates the natural environment of most plants in your landscape: the forest floor, meadow, and prairie are naturally mulched with fallen leaves, branches, and dead grasses. Leaf litter left on the ground will provide habitat for ground-nesting birds and a place to scratch and forage for birds such as towhees and thrushes. The only place you may not want organic mulch is around plants that are naturally adapted to desert conditions, like ocotillo (*Fouquieria splendens*) and desert willow (*Chilopsis linearis*), which will thrive without mulch.

Controlling Pests and Diseases

There are times when, despite your best efforts and intentions, pests or diseases may appear in your yard. In most cases, the best approach—especially for insects—is to do nothing. One of the great things about landscaping for birds is that you're attracting some of nature's most effective pest controllers. If serious insect attacks occur, resist the urge to grab a chemical spray; it could contaminate your birds' food and water supply. Even strong organic controls, like rotenone, can harm wildlife. If pests are out of control, try a simple soap spray. Buy a commercial insecticidal soap or make your own spray by adding 1 to 3 teaspoons of liquid dish soap to a gallon of water. Spray plants thoroughly every 2 to 3 days for about 2 weeks. Your local garden center or Cooperative Extension Service should be able to help you identify and choose appropriate organic controls for other pests that are known to be particularly troublesome in your area.

Diseases are less often a problem than pests, but they are also more difficult to control when they do strike. On small plants, picking off and destroying spotted or discolored leaves as soon as you see them can often stop the disease cycle. If powdery mildew causes dusty white spots on leaves and stems, try a baking soda spray. Dissolve 1 teaspoon of baking soda and a few drops of liquid dish soap in 1 quart of warm water and spray infected plants thoroughly (including the undersides of the leaves). Fire blight can attack many plants in the rose family, including hawthorns (*Crataegus* spp.), apples and crabapples (*Malus* spp.), and mountain ashes (*Sorbus* spp.). Symptoms include shoot tips that turn black, wilt, and curl downward; dead leaves usually remain on the twigs. The best organic control is to prune out and destroy infected branches, cutting off 6 to 12 inches of healthy looking tissue along with the diseased part. Prune on a dry day to minimize the chance of spreading the disease, and disinfect your pruners after each cut with bleach.

UNWANTED VISITORS *and* OTHER PROBLEMS

Birds in our gardens warrant our protection, so before you set about inviting them into your yard, try to minimize or exclude any hazards that will affect their well-being.

Cats

The most dangerous visitor to the garden is the domestic cat. Hundreds of millions of birds, small mammals, and amphibians are killed by free-roaming and feral cats each year. The best way to protect wildlife, keep pet cats healthy, and protect human health is to keep cats indoors and encourage your neighbors to do the same. Outdoor cats and birds in your garden do not go together. A bird pecking the ground for seed is just unwitting catfood. For more information about protecting wild birds from cats, visit www.abcbirds.org/cats.

Nuisance Birds

House sparrows and European starlings are pests introduced from Europe, and will bully or kill native, cavity-nesting birds and compete with native species for limited tree hollows and nest boxes. In the west, the mountain bluebird is under threat because of competition for nest hollows, and the red-headed woodpecker no longer breeds in the northeast of its range, in part because of habitat loss and competition with European starlings for nest hollows. These birds will learn that they are not welcome when you discourage them by any means possible. Because they are not protected under the law, you should regularly remove and destroy their nests and eggs from nest boxes or tree hollows.

Permanent Feeder Stations

Feeder stations are not only attractive to birds; they will attract many unwelcome guests, including rats and mice. Rats will attack nests and eat the eggs or nestlings. You should remove rats and mice by using live box traps; avoid using poison baits because they can cause harm to pets and wildlife.

Bossy birds will often claim ownership of a permanent feeder station and exclude other species. For example, when crows, jays, ravens, blackbirds, northern mockingbirds, or introduced species take over a feeder station, they upset the natural balance of bird species in your garden and locality. Some of these birds will attack eggs, nestlings, and fledglings and will chase less aggressive birds away by raucously calling or by dive-bombing. A noisy chorus of squabbling birds at the permanent feeder station will be a lure for neighborhood cats.

If you set up permanent feeder stations, you could artificially increase bird numbers. However, if the birds grow to depend on the feeders and the food supply stops abruptly (for example, if you go away on holidays, become ill, or neglect to put food out), you could put the birds' well-being at risk. This will especially be the case if insufficient natural food is available or if the birds have delayed migrating because the permanent feeder stations contain a ready food source for them. These stations require constant vigilance, attention to the quality of food you provide, and attention to hygiene. Otherwise they can promote and spread often fatal diseases in bird populations.

You should treat artificial feeders as a supplement to your native garden, and they need only be stocked when the winter is harsh, the weather is unseasonal, a natural disaster is occurring, or when natural food is unusually lacking.

Hummingbird Feeders

Putting out a hummingbird feeder places a large responsibility on the gardener. Cleanliness is essential to ensure that it is safe for the birds to use. The solution needs to be changed every second day and more frequently when the weather is hot, even when it has not been used. This will prevent the solution from fermenting or going moldy.

At least once a week, the feeder needs to be disassembled and thoroughly washed using a bottle brush to reach all parts of the feeder. Soap or detergent should not be used according to most experts since it can be harmful to hummingbirds. Wash the feeder in warm water with a splash of vinegar or lemon juice to help remove any mold and bacteria. Rinse the feeder thoroughly to remove any residue. Clean the feeder until you would drink from it yourself.

Care must be taken when mixing up the feeding solution. Never use honey as it can cause a fatal fungal infection on the bird's tongue. Sugar mixtures should not exceed 1 part sugar to 4 parts water. The sugar mixture should be boiled (not using a microwave, as this will deplete the nutrient value of the sugar).

Hummingbird feeders also attract bees, wasps, and ants, so purchase one with a bee guard attached and use a coating of vasoline on the feeder support to deter ants.

The healthiest and most attractive way to attract hummingbirds is to plant your garden or balcony containers with flowers that hummingbirds love. Then you know your birds will be well fed and healthy, even when you are on vacation.

Glass Strikes

Birds, particularly hummingbirds, often die by flying at high speed into glass windows where the reflection of trees and sky in the glass give the illusion of being an extension of the yard. Fitting insect screens, awnings, beads, or stickers to the window to break up the reflected image can reduce glass strikes. If a bird is stunned, place it in a safe, shaded, quiet area to recover or contact your local wildlife rehabilitation center.

WORKING *with* SMALL GARDEN SPACES

Small gardens, balconies, courtyards, or rooftop gardens can contribute to the greening of our environment. A garden can start with a window box, or you can involve your neighbors and convert your apartment rooftop to a beautiful native garden space.

Your Small Garden

Any small urban garden space can be transformed into a valuable habitat, attracting birds such as swallows, house finches, American robins, and hummingbirds in summer in the east, or year-round in the west. During the migration season, many unusual visitors, including warblers and wrens, may drop in.

Small gardens or container gardens should try to mimic a small community of plants, with some taller trees, or vines for height and understory planting.

There are many small trees and shrubs suitable for small gardens or containers. Fruit-bearing plants can be espaliered to suit a small space, and many species grow well in a container, espaliered against a wall. Plants that have red berries or fruits that persist through winter are particularly valuable to birds. If you need privacy, you can use evergreens, such as red cedars (*Juniperus* spp.), to create a hedge and keep it clipped to satisfy your needs.

Try using vines in a creative way. Virginia creeper (*Parthenocissus quinquefolia*) will grow on a wall and other vines grown well on a trellis. The red flowers of trumpet honeysuckle (*Lonicera sempervirens*) will attract hummingbirds to its nectar, while birds including native sparrows and finches will feed on the red berries. Trumpet creeper (*Campsis radicans*) and cross-vine (*Bignonia capreolata*) planted together will provide nectar for hummingbirds from early spring through summer. In a small space, dense vines such as wild grape provide shelter and nesting sites for small birds. Deciduous vines will let you enjoy summer shade and winter sunshine.

Containers can be densely planted with smaller plants or wildflowers to provide an understory, and you can grow wildflowers cascading from hanging baskets.

Consider adding a water feature or birdbath into the mix for birds to drink and bathe in. The sound of moving water is a magnetic attraction for birds.

The variety of birds you are likely to bring to a small garden or balcony will depend on the number and variety present in your locality. In an urban environment, that will depend on the type of street planting and the proximity of parks and gardens.

Tips for Successful Container Gardening

Windowboxes or containers of any size are excellent ways to create bird-friendly gardens in small spaces.

Selecting containers

Select the container to allow for adequate root growth and stability. Choose pots that are approximately a third to half the size of the plant you wish to grow when it is mature or pruned to the size you want. Don't be deceived by the small size of nursery plants, always check what their size will be at maturity. Choose containers with adequate drainage holes and avoid containers with a narrow neck that will make repotting difficult. In hot climates, it is important to avoid overheating the root system. Therefore it is best to choose containers that are thick and light colored to reflect the heat, or use one container inside a slightly larger container for insulation. Care should be taken in selecting pots; in colder climates clay pots will crack in freezing conditions. Some potted plants may need to be sheltered during winter freeze-ups.

Potting mix

Select a potting mix that is quick draining, water retentive, and nutrient rich. Add water-retaining additives and environmentally friendly, organic fertilizers such as a commercially available mycorrhizal fungi or worm castings or blood and bone meal.

Keep the soil level 2 to 3 inches below the pot rim and add a layer of organic mulch to keep soil cooler, retain moisture, reduce weed growth, and improve soil fertility. Weeds compete with your plants for water and nutrients, so weed regularly.

Plant selection

Limiting your choices to plants that are naturally adapted to your local climatic conditions will simplify your list of what plants to pick. Orientation, the amount of sunshine or shade, radiated heat from nearby masonry walls, and prevailing winds will also influence your choice of plant material. Endemic plants are most likely to survive the extremes of weather in your locality, and to minimize problems with disease, choose plants that are naturally resistant to local pests.

Planting your containers

For best effect, plant low or cascading plants around the edge or front of the container and grade up to taller plants in the center or along the back edge.

Watering container plants

Container gardens sometimes fail when watering is interrupted or during high wind periods. Keep a watering can handy for spot watering individual plants until the top 6 inches of soil is sufficiently moist. An irrigation system with an automatic timer will make container gardening easier for busy gardeners.

Some Suitable Plants

Many native plants are suitable for containers or small gardens. The following selections are a starting point. The plants are generally drought resistant and will grow readily in containers when selected for your hardiness zone, with adequate sunshine or shade, nutritious soil mix, and water.

Shrubs

> beach plum (*Prunus maritima*), Zone 3
> black haw viburnum (*Viburnum prunifolium*), Zone 3
> California huckleberry (*Vaccinium ovatum*), Zones 7–9
> Colorado bristle cone Pine (*Pinus aristata*), Zone 4
> dwarf yaupon holly (*Ilex vomitoria* 'Nana'), Zones 7–9
> highbush blueberry (*Vaccinium corymbosum*), Zone 4
> inkberry (*Ilex glabra*), Zones 5–9
> junipers (*Juniperus* spp.), Zones 3–9
> maple-leafed viburnum (*Viburnum acerifolium*),
>   Zones 4–8
> red-osier dogwood (*Cornus sericea*), Zone 3
> winterberry (*Ilex verticillata*), Zones 4–9

Small trees

> Adam's needle (*Yucca filamentosa*), Zones 7–10
> American cranberrybush viburnum (*Viburnum trilobum*),
>   Zones 2–8

arrowwood viburnum (*Virburnum dentatum*), Zones 4–9

bayberry (*Myrica pensylvanica*), Zones 4–9

California wax myrtle (*Myrica californica*), Zones 7–9

flame azalea (*Rhododendron calendulaceum*), Zone 5

gray birch (*Betula populifolia*), Zones 4–7

nannyberry viburnum (*Viburnum lentago*), Zones 2–7

Schubert chokeberry (*Prunus virginiana* 'Shubert'), Zones 3–8

shadblow (*Amelanchier arborea*), Zones 3–8

smooth sumac (*Rhus glabra*), Zones 3–9

soaptree yucca (*Yucca elata*), Zones 7–10

staghorn sumac (*Rhus typhina*), Zones 3–8

Vines

Arizona honeysuckle (*Lonicera arizonica*), Zones 6–8

crossvine (*Bignonia capreolata*), Zones 4–9

grapes (*Vitis* spp.), Zones 3–9

trumpet honeysuckle (*Lonicera sempervirens*), Zones 4–9

trumpet vine (*Campsis radicans*), Zones 4–9

Virginia creeper (*Parthenocissus quinquefolia*), Zones 3–9

Ground covers

bearberry (*Arctostaphylos uva-ursi*), Zones 2–8

black crowberry (*Empetrum nigrum*), Zones 2–6

bunchberry (*Cornus canadensis*), Zones 2–5

creeping juniper (*Juniperis horizontalis*), Zones 3–10

Little Sur manzanita (*Arctostaphylos edmundsii*), Zones 7–10

prickly pears (*Opuntia* spp.), Zones 6–9

violets (*Viola* spp.), Zones 3–9

wild strawberry (*Fragaria virginiana*), Zones 4–9

Grasses

big bluestem (*Andropogen gerardii*), Zones 4–9

bottlebrush grass (*Hystrix patula*), Zone 3

hairgrasses (*Deschampsia* spp.), Zones 4–9

tufted fescue (*Festuca amethystina*), Zone 4

Wildflowers

asters (*Symphyotrichum* spp.), Zones 3–8

bee balms (*Monarda* spp.), Zones 3–9

black-eyed Susan (*Rudbeckia hirta*), Zones 3–9

blazing stars (*Liatris* spp.), Zones 3–10

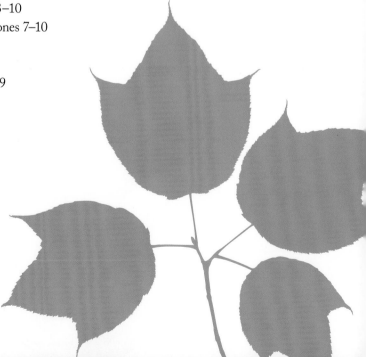

butterflyweed (*Asclepias tuberosa*), Zones 4–9
California fuchsia (*Epilobium canum*), Zones 8–10
columbines (*Aquilegia* spp.), Zones 3–9
coreopsis (*Coreopsis* spp.), Zones 3–9
goldenrods (*Solidago* spp.), Zones 4–9
hairbells (*Campanula* spp.), Zones 3–8
Indian pink (*Spigelia marilandica*), Zones 8–10
irises (*Iris* spp.), Zones 3–8
wild lupine (*Lupinus perennis*), Zones 4–9
monkeyflowers (*Mimulus* spp.), Zones 3–9
purple coneflower (*Echinacea purpurea*), Zones 3–9
sages (*Salvia* spp.), Zones 4–9
sunflowers (*Helianthus* spp.), Zones 3–9

BEYOND YOUR BACKYARD

Creating a bird-friendly backyard is only the first step in creating a more valuable bird habitat. There are many ways you can encourage birds back into your area. One way is to create a neighborhood landscape that welcomes birds. Think of how much more inviting to birds your neighborhood would be if everyone turned their yards into bird sanctuaries. Approach your neighbors and invite them to your garden. Once they've seen how attractive it is and how delightful it would be to have a riot of colorful birds in their own yards, they too may welcome this idea. You could even start a neighborhood birding association.

City parks are another place where landscaping with birds in mind could open up a whole area for environmental planning. Sections of these parks could be transformed into more natural and more easily maintained areas of native vegetation that birds would love. Other areas that are ripe for making birds feel at home include street plantings, freeway borders, and school grounds. You might also approach the owners of large industrial parks, and suggest the many benefits of creating a fashionable native landscape and wildlife habitat as a community service.

If you know local areas that shelter wildlife, you can work to have important areas preserved before they are threatened. Many state conservation agencies and national environmental organizations can offer valuable assistance. Reclamation of abandoned sites, such as mining pits and quarries, could provide valuable wildlife habitat when landscaped for birds, and they could make ideal sanctuaries for water birds.

Lincoln's sparrow feeding on the seeds of Engelmann spruce (*Picea engelmannii*).

Part Three

PLANT DIRECTORY

Plants have been selected for inclusion in the Plant Directory because of their long flowering or fruiting times as well as other essential attributes for bird habitat, such as dense or prickly foliage for nesting or shelter for roosting. The photographs have been selected to showcase the plant's usefulness and association with birds or other wildlife.

It is important in a bird-friendly garden to provide a variety of food niches. Often a simple way to do this is to have vegetation from ground level through varying layers to treetops. Don't forget the value of vines, and do seek out the shade-tolerant plants listed for those out-of-the-way corners.

Many plants have a specific relationship with specific birds: for example, the yellow-rumped warbler is also called the myrtle warbler in the north and southeast because of its preference for bayberry or wax myrtle fruits; the pine siskin, so named because of its close association with pines (*Pinus* spp.), feeds on pine cone seeds and nests and roosts in the foliage. The movements of the white-winged crossbill are largely determined by the ripening of spruce (*Picea* spp.) cone seeds, and the range of the evening grosbeak is determined by the availability of box elder (*Acer negundo*) seeds and buds, its preferred food source.

The directory plants are arranged alphabetically by botanical name, preceded by the common name, and followed by a general description of the plant and birds that are attracted to it. Then different species of that plant are listed, giving a specific description, native distribution, and cultivation tips. Many of these plants are also portrayed in part 4, Bird Directory.

The plant hardiness zones at the end of each plant listing indicate the northern limit of the plant's natural distribution, based on minimum average temperatures. Zones indicated are a general guide only, since microclimates can occur within a relatively small area.

ABOUT *the* PLANT DIRECTORY

KEY	
🐦	nesting plant
🌿	shelter plant
🐦	roosting plant
🦋	nectar for butterflies
🌱	host plant for butterflies
🐦	nectar for hummingbirds
🍁	fall color
✿	showy flowers

Balsam fir (*Abies balsamea*).

White fir (*Abies concolor*).

FIRS
Abies spp.

Tall symmetrical, cone- or pyramid-shaped, evergreen conifers with dense foliage, firs prefer cool, moist conditions and grow best in the northern states or in the higher mountains. In late fall, the upright cones mature and disintegrate, scattering their seed. There are about 40 species of true fir, 9 of which are native to North America.

Birds Attracted

The dense evergreen foliage provides valuable shelter for roosting and nesting, especially in winter. Fir needles are an important food for the blue grouse and sharp-tailed grouse. The scattered cone seeds are eaten by chickadees, crossbills, Clark's nutcracker, juncos, jays (including Steller's jay), towhees, finches, grosbeaks, and nuthatches (including the pygmy nuthatch). Tanagers, grosbeaks, and robins are among the birds that often nest in firs.

Abies balsamea
balsam fir

The only fir native to northeastern America, the balsam fir grows from 40 to 60 feet, in a symmetrical spire shape. Needles are 1 inch long, rounded, and very fragrant. Upright cylindrical cones disperse seed through autumn.

Native distribution Common over northeastern United States, in the Great Lakes states, and in Canada east of the Rocky Mountains.

Cultivation Performs best in moist, acid soils in cool northern areas or mountain areas farther south. Grows poorly in hot conditions; if you live in a warmer area (Zones 5–7), grow the similar Fraser fir (*A. fraseri*) instead. When grown in an open area, the lower branches remain alive and the foliage may touch the ground. The tree is shallow rooted, so it is susceptible to strong winds. Zones 2–5.

Abies grandis
grand fir, giant fir

A tall tree, growing to 200 feet in its native habitat with a relatively narrow, upright conical shape. Needles are long and flat, spreading in 2 irregular rows from opposite sides of the twig. Cones are borne at the top of the tree in small numbers. They disintegrate while still on the tree.

Native distribution Native to elevations below 3,000 feet in coastal British Columbia, the northwestern United States, on moist mountainsides, and in lowland valleys, especially along small streams.

Cultivation Shade tolerant. Prefers deep, moist, but well-drained, silty soils. Often planted in parks and gardens as an ornamental tree. Zones 6–9.

Abies lasiocarpa var. *arizonica*
Rocky Mountain fir

An evergreen conifer from 40 to 70 feet tall in cultivation, with a 15- to 20-foot spread. Single, stiff, needlelike foliage with rounded tips. Cones are purple, turning reddish brown and shattering in fall when ripe. Form and height are determined by environment. In sheltered areas, it is tall and steeple shaped with short branches; in open areas it can be shorter and more rounded in shape.

Native distribution Northern Canada along the Rocky Mountains to the Sierra Nevada.

Cultivation Prefers full sun in a cool, moist, deep, well-drained soil. Prune for size. A compact form is available (*A. lasiocarpa* 'Compacta'), from 12 to 15 feet tall and 6 feet wide. Zones 2–7.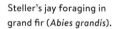

Other suitable species

white or Colorado fir (*A. concolor*), from 30 to 50 feet tall, Zones 4–8.

Rocky Mountain fir (*Abies lasiocarpa* var. *arizonica*) growing with quaking aspen (*Populus tremuloides*).

In summer the gray jay will cache food items, often gluing them with saliva among the needles of conifers, including noble fir (*Abies procera*).

Steller's jay foraging in grand fir (*Abies grandis*).

Wood thrush sheltering in box elder (*Acer negundo*).

Pine siskins feeding on the seeds of vine maple (*Acer circinatum*).

MAPLES
Acer spp.

Maples have distinctive winged seeds, called samaras, borne in pairs, and an opposite leaf arrangement. The exception is box elder (*Acer negundo*), which has compound leaves. Leaves of most species are palmate.

Maples are deciduous, and are among the most colorful of all trees in autumn, with brilliant red, yellow, and orange leaves, sometimes on the same tree. A variable group of trees, maples can be large shade trees, such as the red maple (*A. rubrum*), or shrubs and small trees, such as the mountain maple (*A. spicatum*). The bark is usually ridged or flaked. About 150 species of maple are native to the northern temperate regions, two-thirds of which are in China. There are 13 species native to North America.

Birds Attracted

Many birds feed on the ripe seeds in summer, including black-headed, evening, and pine grosbeaks, the purple finch, pine siskin, northern cardinal, and bobwhites. White-breasted nuthatches often nest in the cavities of mature trees. Chickadees, nuthatches, and brown creepers probe the rough bark for insects in winter. Insect-eating birds, such as orioles, wrens, and warblers, gather insects from the foliage.

Acer circinatum
vine maple

A large, multistemmed shrub with a gnarled appearance, from 15 to 24 feet tall and 20 feet wide. A desirable garden tree, it grows vinelike in shade. The palmate leaves with 7 to 9 lobes turn a showy red to orange in autumn. Flowers are umbels of reddish purple sepals and white petals, appearing in spring, followed by winged red fruits.

Native distribution Pacific Northwest, from south-west British Columbia south to northern California, within 200 miles from the coast.
Cultivation Prefers moist, humus-rich soil, in full sun to shade. Zones 6–9.

Acer macrophyllum
big-leaf maple
A deciduous tree from 30 to 50 feet tall. It has the largest leaves of all the maples, with good orange and yellow fall color. Spring flowers are greenish yellow in pendulous racemes, followed by winged fruits.
Native distribution Pacific Northwest from southern Alaska to southern California.
Cultivation Prefers a moist, well-drained soil in full sun to partial shade. Zones 5–9.

Acer negundo
box elder, ash-leaf maple
A small to medium-size tree growing from 50 to 70 feet tall. The leaves are opposite and compound. Plants have rounded crowns and often have multiple trunks. The tree produces abundant winged fruits, in late summer through fall, which self-sow liberally. The bark is deeply ridged on mature trees. One of the few maples with poor fall color.
Native distribution Streams, lakeshores, roadsides, and waste ground from southern Alberta, southern Ontario, and New York south to central Florida, and west to California. Box elder grows where many trees cannot.
Cultivation Ornamental, adaptable, and tolerant of poor conditions. Suitable for shelter belts, especially on the prairies. A fast-growing tree that grows well in poor soil. Mature trees are somewhat drought-resistant. A fast-growing screening plant. Zones 2–8.

Acer rubrum
red maple, swamp maple
A large, straight-trunked tree with an oval crown. Grows to 70 feet tall. Small but showy red flowers borne in clusters before trees leaf out in early spring. Trees have attractive silver-gray bark. Fall color can be yellow but is more often a brilliant red or scarlet.
Native distribution Native throughout the East, from Canada through Florida.

Southern sugar maple (*Acer barbatum*).

The autumn colors of sugar maple (*Acer saccharum* subsp. *leucoderme*).

Western tanager sheltering in big-leaf maple (*Acer macrophyllum*).

Cultivation A useful shade and street tree. It its very hardy with excellent red fall color. Can tolerate acidic, poorly drained to swampy soils. Prefers partial to full sun, but tolerates shade. Zones 3–9. 🦋 🍁

Acer saccharum
sugar maple, hard maple, rock maple
A large, straight-trunked tree with a dense, rounded crown. Grows from 50 to 70 feet tall. The bark on mature trees is dull gray, deeply furrowed, or somewhat scaly. Fall color can be brilliant orange, gold, and red, or a mix of these colors.
Native distribution Quebec to Texas.
Cultivation Commonly planted as a shade and ornamental tree. Prefers deep, fertile, well-drained soils with some moisture. It is shade-tolerant. Zones 3–7. 🦋 🍁

Other suitable species
southern sugar maple (*A. barbatum*), up to 20 to 25 feet, Zones 6–9. 🦋 🍁
striped maple, moosewood maple (*A. pensylvanicum*), from 15 to 30 feet, Zones 3–7. 🦋 🍁
mountain maple (*A. spicatum*), up to 25 feet, Zones 3–6. 🦋 🍁

ALDERS
Alnus spp.

Common plants along streams and damp areas. Alder flowers are hard, brown catkins that remain on the trees year-round; male and female catkins are separate. The female fruit looks like a small conifer cone. Fruits are small nutlets that release seeds when mature. The seeds have two floats; if they fall in a stream they stay on the surface, sprouting on damp soil where they land.

About 30 species of alder are distributed throughout the northern hemisphere in temperate and high-altitude regions. There are 8 species—6 trees and 2 shrubs—native to North America.

Birds Attracted

Many birds feed on alder seeds, including pine siskin, mourning dove, mallard, great blue heron, and goldfinches. Insects that are drawn to the foliage attract Blackburnian, Cape May, Tennessee, and palm warblers, vireos, goldfinches, and siskins. Scarlet tanager, indigo bunting, and rose-breasted grosbeak feed on the buds and the attracted insects. Alders are good shelter trees for many birds.

Alnus incana subsp. *rugosa*
speckled alder, hazel alder, tag alder

Usually a clump-forming shrub, but sometimes a small tree reaching 20 to 33 feet tall with a crooked trunk and irregular crown. The dark green leaves are egg shaped and wavy with a toothed margin; the undersides are paler.

Native distribution Across Canada from the Yukon Territory and British Columbia to Newfoundland, south to West Virginia, and west to Iowa and North Dakota. Speckled alders grow along streams and in swamps.

Cultivation Best results in damp soils in full sunshine. Plants grow rapidly. The speckled alder is particularly tolerant of cold climates. Zones 2–9. 🦋 🌱 🍁 🌿

Alnus serrulata
hazel alder

A thicket-forming shrub or small tree from 6 to 20 feet tall with large deciduous leaves. Flower catkins are red-green and open in March to April. Small reddish to brown conelike fruits mature in fall and are eaten by migrating songbirds.

Native distribution Widespread in eastern North America from Maine to northern Florida, west to Oklahoma, Missouri, and Illinois along streams and swampy areas.

Cultivation A hardy plant. Prefers moist soil in full sun or part shade. Zones 5–9. 🌿 🦋 🌱

....

Other suitable species

white alder (*A. rhombifolia*), from 50 to 90 feet tall, Zones 6–9. 🦋 🌱 🌿

Sitka alder (*A. viridis* subsp. *sinuata*), to 33 feet tall, Zones 2–8. 🌿

Long male catkins hanging from hazel alder (*Alnus serrulata*). The reddish female flowers point upward.

Female common redpoll feeding on the fruits of white alder (*Alnus rhombifolia*).

SERVICEBERRIES, JUNEBERRIES
Amelanchier spp.

Serviceberries are small trees or large shrubs usually growing to under 30 feet in height, with straight, slender trunks. Showy white flowers appear in early spring before the leaves have fully expanded. The leaves are finely sawtoothed and are alternate. Small edible purple-black fruits ripen between late July and early August. Serviceberry plants have attractive dark gold to red-orange foliage in autumn and an interesting branch structure that makes intriguing patterns in winter. There are 24 species widely distributed throughout temperate regions, and 18 of these are found in North America; 3 species grow to tree size, and the others are shrubs.

Birds Attracted

The fruits of serviceberries are eaten by at least 42 species of native birds, including the red-headed woodpecker, American robin, hermit thrush, waxwings, gray catbird, northern cardinal, blue jay, downy and hairy woodpeckers, wood thrush, mourning dove, American redstart, scarlet tanager, red-eyed vireo, kingbird, ruffed grouse, house finch, veery, junco, oriole, flicker, bluebird, towhee, chickadee, grosbeaks, phoebe, and thrasher.

Amelanchier alnifolia
Saskatoon serviceberry, juneberry, serviceberry, western shadbush

A shrub or small tree growing from 4 to 18 feet tall, usually with several trunks, often forming thickets. The gray or brown bark is smooth or slightly fissured. Fragrant white flowers in early summer. Leaves are almost round with orange-red fall color. Small purple fruits are borne in clusters.

Native distribution Central Alaska south along the coast to northern California and east to the upper Great Lakes area, western Minnesota and Colorado, along streams, at the edges of woods, and on dry mountain slopes.
Cultivation Grown for their early flowers and colorful foliage; new growth is bronzy, turning green in summer and yellow to reddish in fall. Plants prefer a sunny location in dry soil and grow well in rocky soil. Mature heights vary, with some plants only reaching 4 feet tall. Zones 4–8. 🦋 ⊤ 🍁 ❀

Amelanchier alnifolia var. *semi-integrifolia* (formerly *Amelanchier florida*)
Pacific serviceberry

An attractive spreading shrub from 3 to 20 feet tall. Bright green leaves and fragrant white flowers in showy clusters are followed by fleshy red fruits that ripen to a dark purple in late summer.
Native distribution Southern Alaska south to California, east to Alberta, through the Dakotas, Nebraska, Colorado, New Mexico, and Arizona.
Cultivation Prefers moist, well-drained soil in full sun. Requires watering in drought conditions. Zones 4–8. 🦋 ⊤ 🍁 ❀

Amelanchier arborea
shadblow, downy serviceberry, juneberry, shadbush

A small tree from 20 to 25 feet tall, with variable spread. Distinguished from other species of serviceberries by its pubescent emerging leaves, greenish yellowish buds, and pendulous fruit. The 1- to 3-inch ovate leaves are dark green, turning yellow to bronze-red in autumn. Profuse, pure white flowers in 2- to 4-inch-long pendulous racemes bloom in early spring to late summer. Reddish purple fruits appear in June.
Native distribution Often found growing along streams, from Ontario and Quebec, west to Minnesota, and south to Texas and Florida.
Cultivation Prefers well-drained, evenly moist soil in full sun or semishade. An ideal plant for shady yards. Zones 3–8. 🦋 ⊤ 🍁 ❀

Amelanchier laevis

Allegheny serviceberry, shadblow, shadbush, serviceberry

A tree growing to 40 feet tall, with small spreading branches forming a rounded crown. The bark is an attractive reddish brown color. Leaves are reddish when they emerge, maturing to dark green. In spring, fragrant white flowers are borne in long, drooping clusters, forming small red to dark purple fruits that ripen in summer.

Native distribution Cool ravines and hillsides from Newfoundland to Quebec and Ontario and south to northern Wisconsin, east through New England to Pennsylvania, and south along the Appalachian Mountains to northern Georgia.

Cultivation Provide evenly moist, well-drained soil in full sun or partial shade. Zones 3–8. 🦋 ⊤ 🍁 ❋

Other suitable species

Canadian serviceberry (*A. canadensis*), from 6 to 20 feet tall, Zones 4–8. 🍸 🦋 ⊤ 🍁 ❋

running serviceberry (*A. stolonifera*), from 1 to 4 feet, Zones 5–8. 🦋 🍁 ❋

Bohemian waxwing enjoying the fruits of Canadian serviceberry (*Amelanchier canadensis*).

Saskatoon serviceberry (*Amelanchier alnifolia*).

Bronze coloring of mature broomsedge flowers (*Andropogon virginicus*).

BLUESTEMS, BEARDGRASSES
Andropogon spp.

Species of these perennial grasses once covered the North American prairies. They are still found across the country, but, like the prairies themselves, they are no longer extensive. The common names bluestem and beardgrass refer to the plants' bluish flower stalks and fluffy flower heads. There are 32 native species in North America.

Birds Attracted

Bluestems are important winter plants for small seed-eating birds. Ground-nesting birds nest among the plant tussocks, and quail and other birds seek shelter among the clumps. Birds use dry blades of grass in nest building.

Purplish bloom clusters of big bluestem (*Andropogon gerardii*).

Andropogon gerardii
big bluestem, turkey foot

A deciduous perennial bunchgrass that grows in tufts from 4 to 7 feet tall. Foliage is blue-green to silver-blue. The grass flowers during fall, with purplish bloom clusters that rise on slender stems reaching 8 to 10 feet or more. Flowers mature to 3-branched seed heads shaped like turkey feet. Big bluestem turns tan or reddish during fall and winter.

Native distribution Quebec to Saskatchewan and south to Florida and Arizona, and especially in the Midwest states where the tall grass prairie once thrived.

Cultivation Prefers a deep, moist but well-drained soil and full sun. Water during summer droughts. Zones 4–10. 🦋 🌱 🐦 📷

Other suitable species

broomsedge (*A. virginicus*), from 2 to 5 feet tall, Zones 5–8. 🦋 🌱

COLUMBINES
Aquilegia spp.

Columbines are perennials found on woodland slopes and rocky outcrops, and in moist woods throughout North America except along the Gulf Coast. They are beautiful members of the buttercup family with large, showy, usually spurred, nodding flowers. There are about 6 native species, mostly in the mountain states. There is 1 native columbine in the east (*A. canadensis*), and from Europe there is a wild species (*A. vulgaris*) that is now well established here in the wild.

Birds Attracted

Hummingbirds are attracted to the nectar-rich flowers and are major pollinators, especially of the red-flowered species.

Aquilegia canadensis
wild columbine

Plants grow from 1 to 3 feet tall, with 1- to 2-inch-long nodding scarlet flowers with yellow centers and spurred petals. Flowers may vary in color from light pink and yellow to blood-red and appear between April and July.

Native distribution Rocky ledges in woodlands from Ontario to Quebec, south to Minnesota, and east to Georgia and Tennessee.

Cultivation Plant columbines in early spring, or in fall when the plants are dormant in moist, well-drained, slightly acid (pH 6.0 to 7.0) soil that's rich in organic matter. Prefers some morning sun and light overhead tree shade later in day. Often self-sows; flowers in the second year. Zones 3–8. ❦ 🦋 🍁

Aquilegia formosa
crimson columbine, western columbine

From 2 to 4 feet tall, with large 1½- to 2-inch-wide hanging red and yellow flowers, between May and August. Leaves are divided into numerous leaflets ¾ inch to 1½ inches long.

Crimson columbine
(*Aquilegia formosa*).

Sierra columbine
(*Aquilegia pubescens*).

Rocky Mountain columbine
(*Aquilegia caerulea*).

New growth, Little Sur manzanita
(*Arctostaphylos edmundsii*).

Blossoms of greenleaf manzanita
(*Arctostaphylos patula*).

Hermes copper butterfly
on big berry manzanita
(*Arctostaphylos glauca*).

Native distribution Open woods and woods' edges from southern Alaska to northern California and east to Utah and Montana.

Cultivation An adaptable native perennial, prefers a partially shaded, moist, well-drained site with early morning sun. Plants will also grow in almost full sunshine or shade. Zones 3–7. ❦ 🦋 ✿

Other suitable species

Rocky Mountain columbine (*A. caerulea*), from 1 to 2 feet tall, Zones 3–8. ❦ 🦋 ✿

golden columbine (*A. chrysantha*), from 2 to 3 feet tall, Zones 3–9. ❦ 🦋 ✿

Sierra columbine (*A. pubescens*), from 1 to 2 feet tall, Zones 7–10. ❦ 🦋 ✿

MANZANITAS
Arctostaphylos spp.

Members of the heath family (*Ericaceae*). Of the 50 known species, 43 are native to California. One species (*Arctostaphylos uva-ursi*) is circumpolar. In the western states, the species is commonly known as manzanita. It was widely used by Native Americans for traditional medicinal and ceremonial purposes.

Birds Attracted

Hummingbirds are attracted to the small flowers, and many bird species feed on the pea-sized red fruits.

Arctostaphylos edmundsii
Little Sur manzanita, Big Sur manzanita, Carmel Sur manzanita

A semiprostrate to mounded evergreen shrub, from 1 to 2 feet high and 6 feet across, with abundant pink flowers from January to December. Leaves are bright green with a red tinge.

Native distribution The Big Sur coastal region of California.

Cultivation Prefers full sun in moist well-drained soil. Zones 8–10. ❦ 🦋 🌾 ✿

Arctostaphylos glauca
big berry manzanita

Evergreen shrub or small, rounded tree from 7 to 10 feet tall with red bark that peels with age and gray to green foliage. White urn-shaped flowers in spring are followed by light red, edible berries in fall.

Native distribution Central coast of California south to Baja California in chaparral and woodlands.

Cultivation Plants are slow growing, and may live for 100 years. Prefers sunny well-drained location. Drought tolerant once established, it will grow in near-desert conditions, tolerates salty soil, and will also grow in snow-covered regions. Zones 6–10.

Arctostaphylos patula
greenleaf manzanita

An attractive, evergreen, mounding shrub 3 to 6 feet tall with smooth, bright red-brown bark and yellowish green leaves. Flowering from April to June, followed by smooth and chestnut-brown fruits.

Native distribution Widespread throughout the mountains of western North America and east to Colorado.

Cultivation Prefers well-drained acidic soils in an open, sunny area. Tolerates below-freezing winters and sandy soil. Zones 4–8.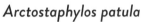

Arctostaphylos uva-ursi
bearberry, pine manzanita, kinnikinnick

An evergreen ground cover from 6 to 12 inches tall and spreading 3 to 5 feet in a dense mat. Small white to pink bell-shaped flowers appear in spring, followed by small red berries that persist in winter.

Native distribution Arctic areas and south to northern California and east to Virginia in open, sandy, or rocky soils.

Cultivation Slow growing, it prefers well-drained, acidic, sandy soil in full sun or light shade. Drought and salt tolerant, it is a good choice for coastal gardens. Requires no pruning or fertilizing. Zones 2–6.

Other suitable species

pointleaf manzanita (A. pungens), from 4 to 6 feet tall, Zones 7–8.

Pointleaf manzanita (*Arctostaphylos pungens*) in bloom.

Bearberry (*Arctostaphylos uva-ursi*) in bloom.

Bright red berries of bearberry (*Arctostaphylos uva-ursi*).

Big berry manzanita (*Arctostaphylos glauca*) flowers.

'Whitespire' gray birch (*Betula populifolia* 'Whitespire').

BIRCHES
Betula spp.

Birches are usually small, graceful, medium-sized trees that grow rapidly but are relatively short-lived. They have attractive bark, which is sometimes a showy white or salmon-pink. Birches bear male flowers in catkins and female flowers in conelike clusters. The triangular or oval, toothed deciduous foliage is yellow in fall. As many as 50 species of birch are found in the northern temperate and arctic regions of the world. Of those, 12 species are native to North America.

Birds Attracted

Birch seeds and flower buds are eaten by dark-eyed junco, blue jay, pine siskin, black-capped chickadee, cedar waxwing, purple finch, wood duck, American woodcock, titmice, goldfinches, towhees, and bobwhites. Insect-eating birds, including orioles, chickadees, vireos, warblers, and bushtits, are attracted to insects on the foliage. Sharp-tailed, ruffed, and spruce grouse feed on the catkins, buds, and seeds.

Betula lenta
sweet birch, cherry birch, black birch

A handsome tree with shiny red-brown bark, it may reach 60 feet in its native habitat, but is usually from 40 to 50 feet tall. The bark is smooth on young trees, but becomes broken into thick, irregular plates on mature trees. Oval, toothed leaves turn golden-yellow in fall.

Native distribution Rich uplands of southern Maine, and south in the mountains to northern Georgia.

Cultivation A fast-growing specimen tree that grows best in cooler gardens. It prefers moist, well-drained, humus-rich soil in full sun to light shade. Less prone to borers than white-barked birch. Zones 4–6.

Betula nigra
river birch

Reaching 80 feet in height with a broad, spreading crown. The light tan to reddish brown bark peels and curls attractively. The cultivar 'Heritage' has salmon-white bark. Leaves are finely toothed and oval, with yellowish fall color. Fruit appears in summer.

Native distribution Throughout the eastern United States and south to Florida, west to Kansas, and north to Minnesota.

Cultivation Plants prefer well-drained soil in full sun to light shade; they can tolerate acid soil. The species is resistant to borers. It is the best birch for the Midwest and South. Zones 4–9.

Betula occidentalis
water birch, black birch

Usually a small shrubby tree, growing from 20 to 25 feet tall. In the southern limits of its range, it often forms thickets 6 to 8 feet tall, especially along stream banks. Open, drooping branchlets form a broad, open crown. The bark is almost black on young trees, but turns reddish brown as the trees mature. Fine-toothed leaves are broad at the base, narrowing at the tip, with yellow fall color.

Native distribution Forested western Canada, Arizona, New Mexico, Colorado, Utah, Idaho, and California, mainly along streams banks and moist locations.

Cultivation Water birch will grow in dry soils, but prefers a sunny, moist location. Zones 3–9.

Other suitable species

yellow birch (*B. alleghaniensis*), 60 to 70 feet, Zones 2–7.

paper or canoe birch (*B. papyrifera*), to 80 feet tall, Zones 2–7.

gray birch (*B. populifolia*), to 30 feet tall, Zones 4–7.

Many woodpeckers, including the hairy woodpecker, prefer the soft wood of paper birch (*Betula papyrifera*) for excavating nest hollows.

Crossvine (*Bignonia capreolata*).

CROSSVINES
Bignonia spp.

The bignonia family is a large group of mainly tropical vines, trees, and shrubs with colorful, showy blossoms. It is one of the most floriferous native vines.

Birds Attracted

Hummingbirds are attracted to the nectar of the early spring-flowering vine. The dense foliage provides shelter and nesting opportunities for many smaller birds.

Bignonia capreolata
crossvine, trumpet flower

A climbing, evergreen, woody vine with showy orange-red tubular flowers 2 inches long that appear between late winter and early spring. The vine has tendrils, allowing it to climb fences and cling to walls. It is drought tolerant.
Native distribution Widespread from Maryland to Florida, and west to Missouri and Texas.
Cultivation Prefers moist, well-drained soil in full sun. Train over a trellis and cut back in spring to encourage flowering. An excellent hummingbird plant, particularly when planted with trumpet creeper (*Campsis radicans*). Zones 6–9.

TRUMPET VINES
Campsis spp.

Members of the bignonia family, these sturdy ornamental vines have beautiful trumpet flowers.

Birds Attracted
The trumpet-shaped flowers are attractive to hummingbirds.

Campsis radicans
trumpet vine, trumpet creeper

A vigorous, woody, deciduous climbing vine with red or orange flowers between July and September, followed by bean-shaped capsules. Large, dark green leaves are divided into 7 to 11 leaflets.

Native distribution Moist woods, thickets, and roadsides from New Jersey south to Florida, and west to Iowa, Missouri, and Texas.

Cultivation A vigorous plant, it prefers a sheltered, moist, but well-drained position in full sun. Grow on a sturdy support, away from buildings. It can become aggressive; prune rigorously to contain it. Zones 4–9.

Trumpet vine (*Campsis radicans*).

SAGUARO
Carnegiea spp.

A genus of one species, the saguaro (*Carnegiea gigantea*). Saguaros are slow-growing cacti of the Southwestern deserts. Their tall, high-branched columns dominate this arid region.

Birds Attracted

The Gila woodpecker and flickers excavate holes in the trunks for nesting. The many nesting holes are used by the elf owl, ferruginous owl, screech owl, American kestrel, crested and ash-throated flycatcher, cactus wren, Lucy's warbler, and western martin. In May, many birds feed on the large flowers, including ash-throated flycatcher and gilded flicker, while insect-eating birds consume insects attracted to the flowers. When the saguaro fruits ripen in July and August, many birds feast on them, including Gila woodpecker, curve-billed thrasher, mourning dove, cactus wren, white-winged dove, and gilded flicker. The mourning dove often nests in the fork of a branch.

Curved-billed thrasher among the flower buds of a saguaro (*Carnegiea gigantea*).

Common hackberry (*Celtis occidentalis*).

Sugarberry (*Celtis laevigata*).

Carnegiea gigantea
saguaro, giant cactus
Largest of the United States cacti, reaching up to 50 feet (usually 30 feet) and from 1 to 3 feet in diameter. It bears prominent vertical ridges on the thick trunk and branches. Thick spines are clustered on the ridges.

Native distribution Dry desert mesas and low rocky hills in southeastern California and southern Arizona, south to Sonora in Mexico.

Cultivation Slow-growing, usually less than 2 inches a year, though they often have a burst of growth when 3 to 4 feet tall. The plant may live up to 200 years. Suitable for dry, rocky, or gravelly soils in full sun. Be sure to buy nursery-propagated seedlings from a reputable cactus nursery, since wild collection has depleted the native population. Zones 8–10. ✹ ⬡

HACKBERRIES
Celtis spp.

Hackberries vary from shrubs to medium-size deciduous trees. They are members of the elm family and can be recognized by their gray to brown warty bark. Hackberries bear small, round, dark green fruits that ripen to dark red. The fruits mature in late summer or autumn, often continuing to hang on the tree in winter. Hackberries are widely distributed throughout the tropical and temperate regions of the world. There are 60 species, 6 of which are native to North America.

Birds Attracted
At least 48 species of birds feed on hackberry fruits, including the bluebird, northern cardinal, cedar waxwing, American robin, brown thrasher, hermit thrush, Townsend's solitaire, Gambel's and scaled quail, curve-billed thrasher, white-winged dove, evening grosbeak, greater roadrunner, band-tailed pigeon, pileated woodpecker, red-bellied woodpecker, oriole, phoebe, flicker, mockingbird, bobwhite, towhee, and titmouse. Verdin and white-

winged dove often nest in the foliage. Hackberries are host and nectaring plants for many butterfly species.

Celtis laevigata
sugarberry, hackberry

A deciduous tree to 70 feet tall and 40 feet wide with a light gray trunk and dark green foliage. Greenish yellow flowers in April and May are followed by small round fruits that mature between September and October and persist through winter.
Native distribution Virginia and southern Indiana, south to Texas and Florida.
Cultivation A hardy, fast-growing, pollution-tolerant tree. Prefers full sun in moist, rich soil, but will tolerate dry areas. An excellent bird-attracting, backyard, shade and street tree. Zones 6–9. 🦋 🌳 🐦 🍃

Celtis occidentalis
common hackberry, sugarberry

Growing 30 to 50 feet tall and nearly as wide, it may sometimes reach 100 feet, with a 1- to 2-foot-diameter trunk. It has a rounded top, arched branches, and slightly drooping branchlets. Dark brown to grayish brown bark is warty when mature. Leaves are deciduous, sharply oval, and toothed, with dull yellow fall color. Pea-size, round, dark green fruits ripen purple-black in autumn and persist through winter.
Native distribution Wooded slopes and bottomlands, rocky hills, and ridges from extreme southern Ontario and New England south to northern Georgia and west to Oklahoma, north to eastern North Dakota and southern Manitoba.
Cultivation A deep-rooted tree, it can withstand strong winds and tolerate dry periods when established. It is adaptable, will grow in alkaline soil but thrives in rich, moist situations. Plants withstand high heat, dry winds, and urban pollution. In the eastern states, the branches may be affected by "witch's brooms," caused by a mite, which makes twigs proliferate into a bushy tangle. Leaves may also be disfigured by nipple gall. Zones 3–8. 🦋 🌳 🍁 🐦 🍃

Celtis reticulata
western hackberry, netleaf hackberry, sugarberry

A large deciduous shrub or small tree with a short trunk and spreading crown, usually growing from 20 to 30 feet tall. The rough-surfaced leaves are oval, with a network of prominent veins on the underside. Small orange-red or brown, pea-sized fruits ripen in September. The fruits were a traditional food source for American Indians.
Native distribution River valleys, canyon slopes, and dry rocky ridges from western Texas, Oklahoma, and Kansas west to southern California and north to eastern Washington.
Cultivation Drought and wind resistant. Trees, suitable for desert plantings or limestone soils. Best growth occurs in rich, moist situations. Zones 7–9. 🌾 🦋 🌳 🐦 🍃

Celtis tenuifolia
Georgia hackberry, dwarf hackberry

Slow-growing shrub or small tree from 6 to 25 feet high and wide. Leaves are alternate and finely toothed. Inconspicuous greenish flowers appear in April and are pollinated by bees. Edible, purplish black berries ripen in October.
Native distribution Eastern North America in dry uplands and open woodlands and sandy shores. Uncommon north of the Ohio River.
Cultivation Intolerant of shade, it requires full sunshine. Prefers well-drained, dry to moist, sandy or loamy soil. It is drought tolerant once established. Zones 6–9. 🦋 🌳 🍁 🐦 🍃

Other suitable species
desert hackberry (*C. pallida*), from 10 to 20 feet tall, Zone 7. 🦋 🌳 🐦 🍃

Desert willow (*Chilopsis linearis*).

DESERT WILLOW
Chilopsis sp.

This genus has only one species, the desert willow (*Chilopsis linearis*).

Birds Attracted

The large, fragrant, nectar-rich flowers of the desert willow attract hummingbirds and verdins over the long flowering period between April and September. White-winged doves and other ground-feeding birds feed on the seeds.

Chilopsis linearis
desert willow, desert catalpa

A deciduous shrub or small tree with a spreading crown and narrow, willowlike foliage, from 10 to 20 feet tall with large, trumpet-shaped 1- to 2-inch-long flowers. The sweet blooms are pink, white, or lavender and mottled with brown and purple markings, followed by distinctive slender 6- to 12-inch-long seedpods.

Native distribution Washes and streambeds below 4,000 feet, across the desert from southern Texas to southern Utah, southern Nevada, and southern California, and south into Mexico.

Cultivation A beautiful ornamental tree, it thrives in warm, dry situations and moderately moist, heavy soils in full sun. It has been grown successfully in the San Francisco Bay Area of California in the warm East Bay hills. Suitable for desert gardens, it can be propagated from hardwood stem cuttings. Plants are fast-growing at first, growing as much as 3 feet in a season. The desert willow prefers occasional watering in midsummer. Zones 7–9.

DOGWOODS
Cornus spp.

Valued as ornamentals for their beautiful flowers and showy fruits, dogwoods were named in the Middle Ages for the use of their wood as skewers or "dogs." Comprising about 50 species, they are widely distributed in temperate

Bunchberry (*Cornus canadensis*) fruit.

regions of the Northern Hemisphere; the only species in the Southern Hemisphere is in Peru. There are 17 species native to North America, ranging from small herbaceous plants to trees.

Birds Attracted

Valuable trees for attracting birds, dogwoods provide secure nesting sites for smaller birds such as Bell's vireo. In northwestern Florida, the flowering dogwood is a favorite nest site for the summer tanager. Dogwood berries are eaten by at least 98 species of birds, including flickers, tanagers, downy and red-headed woodpeckers, gray catbird, eastern kingbird, brown thrasher, American robin, wood thrush, hermit and Swainson's thrush, veery, bluebirds, northern cardinal, waxwings, red-eyed and warbling vireos, grosbeaks, bobwhites, ruffed and sharp-tailed grouse, northern mockingbird, and sparrows.

Cornus canadensis
bunchberry, puddingberry

Deciduous herbaceous ground cover. Creeping roots send up 3- to 8-inch-tall stems with oval, whorled, deeply veined, pointed leaves. Leaves are red-tinged in fall. In late spring to early summer, white flowers crown the stems. The flowers are not made up of true petals, but of four white bracts surrounding the tiny yellowish green central flowers that become clusters of bright red berries in fall.

Native distribution Cool, wet northern woods across Canada to Labrador and south through the mountains to northern California, Idaho, and northern New Mexico. In the East, found as far south as the mountains of West Virginia.

Cultivation Bunchberry prefers a cool, boglike, acid soil in a shaded location with mulch of leaves or conifer needles. An excellent ground cover for moist woodland gardens. Grows best in cool regions. Zones 2–5. 🦋 🌳 🍁 ❀

Bunchberry in bloom in spring.

Male American goldfinch in a pink form of flowering dogwood (*Cornus florida*).

Brown thrasher feeding on the fruits of flowering dogwood (*Cornus florida*).

Cornus florida
flowering dogwood, eastern flowering dogwood, dogwood

A short-trunked tree with a rounded, wide-spreading crown. It grows from 15 to 40 feet tall, with graceful layered branching. The distinctive gray bark is segmented in coarse plates. Leaves are oval, pointed, and deeply ribbed. Leaves turn bright red in autumn. The tree has a magnificent display of white flowers in mid-spring, made up of tiny flowers surrounded by four showy white petal-like bracts, followed by shiny red berrylike fruits borne in upright clusters.

Native distribution Shaded locations in woodlands from southern Maine and Ontario south to northern Florida, west to central Texas, and north to southern Michigan.

Cultivation Grow in partial shade or full sun. Tolerant of most soils, it prefers a moist position and responds well to humus and a balanced organic fertilizer. Plants may be troubled by dogwood anthracnose disease, especially if trunks are injured by lawn mowers; check with your local extension agent for recommendations. Zones 5–8. 🦋 🍄 🍁 ❀ ☺ 🍃

Cornus nuttallii
Pacific dogwood

A small to medium-sized deciduous tree, usually from 20 to at least 30 feet tall and 25 feet wide. Dark green elliptical leaves turn deep pinkish red in fall. Greenish flowers tipped with purple with showy white bracts appear in spring and occasionally repeat in early fall. Bright red fruit clusters follow the flowers and ripen in autumn.

Native distribution Western North America from southern British Columbia to the mountains of southern California, and an inland population in central Idaho.

Cultivation Prefers full sun to light shade in well-drained, moist, deep, fertile soil. Zones 7–8 🦋 🍁 ☺ 🍃

Cornus sericea
red-osier dogwood

A deciduous shrub to 10 feet tall that spreads to a large clump. The dull green leaves turn red in fall. Branches are green in spring, turning yellow-green or reddish in late summer and bright green in winter. Clusters of small white flowers appear in May and are followed by white or bluish fruits that ripen in summer.

Native distribution Central Alaska east to Newfoundland, south to north Virginia and west to California.

Cultivation Spreading rapidly by underground stems to form a large clump, it is useful for naturalizing on slopes and as a screen. Prefers full sun and moist soil, but grows well in drier locations. Plants can tolerate acid soil. Prune heavily every 2 to 3 years because the reddest color is on the younger twigs. Zones 3–8

Other suitable species

pagoda dogwood (*C. alternifolia*), from 15 to 25 feet tall, Zones 4–7.

silky dogwood (*C. amomum*), from 4 to 10 feet, Zone 4.

pale dogwood (*C. amomum* subsp. *obliqua*), to 9 feet tall, Zones 5–8.

western dogwood (*C. occidentalis*), to 15 feet tall, Zone 6.

gray dogwood (*C. racemosa*), from 7 to 9 feet tall, Zone 5.

Hermit thrush feeding on the berries of red-osier dogwood (*Cornus sericea*).

Northern mockingbird feeding on the fruits of flowering dogwood (*Cornus florida* 'First Lady').

Pale dogwood (*Cornus amomum* subsp. *obliqua*).

Eastern kingbird in fleshy hawthorn (*Crataegus succulenta*).

Washington hawthorn (*Crataegus phaenopyrum*).

HAWTHORNS
Crataegus spp.

Hawthorns are small trees or shrubs with spines or thorns on their branches. Abundant flowers and colorful fruits make them popular garden plants. The fruits remain until late winter on many species. There are about 100 native species in North America.

Birds Attracted

The small applelike fruits are eaten by at least 39 species of birds, including the American robin, purple finch, pine grosbeak, cedar waxwing, blue jay, northern mockingbird, flicker, evening grosbeak, rose-breasted grosbeak, hermit thrush, and fox sparrow. Many birds find secure nesting sites in the protective foliage, including verdins, greater roadrunner, northern cardinal, and hummingbirds. Chickadees, warblers, and bushtits gather insects from the foliage.

Crataegus crus-galli
cockspur hawthorn

A small tree with a spreading, rounded crown, growing 30 feet tall. Spines are 3 to 4 inches long. In late spring or early summer, large clusters of white flowers appear. Leathery, glossy, oblong leaves are dark green, with little fall color. In autumn, the small, bright red fruits mature and persist through winter until spring.

Native distribution Low hill slopes in rich soils from Quebec to Michigan and south to North Carolina.

Cultivation Cockspur hawthorn is suitable for full sun or partial shade. It prefers a moist, loamy soil. This hawthorn is an excellent ornamental or hedge plant. May be afflicted with cedar-apple rust fungus, which particularly affects the fruit. Zones 4–6.

Crataegus douglasii
black hawthorn, western hawthorn, western black hawthorn

A small tree or deciduous shrub, from 5 to 20 feet tall with a long trunk and a compact, round-topped crown. Leaves are shiny, dark green, and shallow lobed. Small, fragrant, white flowers appear from May to June, and then it bears dark red fruits that blacken when ripe in August and September.

Native distribution Banks of streams, in meadows, and forests in British Columbia, Washington, Oregon, and California east through the Rockies into Wyoming at about 3,000 feet.

Cultivation In rich soil with ample water, it produces a mass of blooms. Full sun or partial shade. Zones 4–6. ❋ ❀ 🌿 🌼 ☀ 🐾

Crataegus phaenopyrum
Washington hawthorn

Dense, thorny, deciduous tree from 20 to 30 feet tall and wide, with white flowers in early summer, followed by clusters of orange berries in early fall that persist through winter. Green leaves turn orange to red in fall.

Native distribution Eastern and southern United States.

Cultivation Prefers full sun in well-drained soil. Zones 5–9. 🦋 🌿 🍁 🌼 ☀ 🐾

Crataegus succulenta
succulent hawthorn, fleshy hawthorn

A hardy, thorny deciduous tree from 12 to 20 tall and 15 feet wide. Showy white flower clusters appear in late spring through early summer, followed by small red fruits in early fall. Bright green leaves turn a showy bright red or orange in fall.

Native distribution The most widespread North American hawthorn, native to much of southern Canada, south to Arizona, New Mexico, Kansas, Missouri, North Carolina, and Tennessee.

Cultivation Prefers full sun in moist, well-drained soil. Will tolerate wet soils. Excellent border, hedge, or specimen tree. Prune to shape. Zones 3–6. 🦋 🌿 🍁 🌼 ☀ 🐾

Other suitable species

pear hawthorn (*C. calpodendron*), 15 to 20 feet, Zones 6–9. 🦋 🌿 🍁 🌼 🐾

Lavalle hawthorn (*C. ×lavallei*), 15 to 30 feet tall, Zones 4–9. 🦋 🌿 🍁 🌼 🐾 🌿

parsley hawthorn (*C. marshallii*), 5 to 25 feet, Zone 6. 🦋 🌿 🍁 🌼 🐾 🌿

downy hawthorn (*C. mollis*), 30 to 40 feet tall, Zones 3–6. 🦋 🌿 🍁 🌼 🐾 🌿

Cockspur hawthorn (*Crataegus crus-galli*) cultivar.

Black hawthorn (*Crataegus douglasii*).

Lavalle hawthorn (*Crataegus ×lavallei*).

Cactus wren in cane cholla (*Cylindropuntia spinosior*).

Cane cholla (*Cylindropuntia spinosior*) flowers.

Cactus wren at its nest in cane cholla (*Cylindropuntia spinosior*).

CHOLLA
Cylindropuntia spp.

A genus of approximately 50 species, usually small trees or shrubs. These cacti have stem joints that are cylindrical in shape. They are found in dry, arid regions.

Birds Attracted

An important nesting plant for many birds including the cactus wren, mourning dove, and Inca dove. Many birds feed on the fruit.

Cylindropuntia imbricata
tree cholla

A tall upright tree or bushy shrub, from 3 to 8 feet tall. The spiny stems are jointed and cylindrical. Reddish purple showy flowers from May to June are followed by yellow showy fruits.
Native distribution Arizona, east to Texas, Oklahoma, Kansas, Colorado, and Utah.
Cultivation Full sun or part shade with good drainage in sandy or gravelly soil. Zones 7–9. 🦋 ❀ 🐦

Other suitable species
cane cholla (*C. spinosior*), 5 to 10 feet tall. Zones 8–10. 🦋 ❀ 🐦

CROWBERRIES
Empetrum spp.

Crowberries are creeping shrubs with short, needlelike evergreen leaves like those of heaths. Flowers are inconspicuous, followed by round berries. There are several species in North America.

Birds Attracted

Berrylike fruits are eaten by golden-crowned sparrows, cedar waxwing, American robin, pine grosbeak, snow bunting, and at least 35 other species. The plant provides valuable winter food.

Empetrum nigrum
black crowberry

A low, straggling shrub or evergreen ground cover about 10 inches tall with a 2- to 3-foot spread. Plants have needlelike leaves. Tiny purplish flowers appear between July and August, followed by purple berry-like fruits that turn black and remain on the plants through winter.

Native distribution Arctic regions in North America, extending south to Newfoundland, New England, New York, northern Michigan, Minnesota, Alberta, and northern California.

Cultivation Suitable for colder areas, tolerating exposure and windy sites. Best results in an acid, sandy soil in a sunny, open location. Plants must have excellent drainage. Good rock garden plant. Zones 2–6. 🦋 ⱡ 🐾 🌿

Black crowberry
(*Empetrum nigrum*).

WILD FUCHSIAS
Epilobium spp.

Wild fuchsias are related to the ornamental fuchsias, which are native to South America. There are four species of wild fuchsia native to California. All are sprawling, carpetlike shrubs that produce masses of scarlet tubular flowers.

Birds Attracted

Hummingbirds are attracted to the colorful wild fuchsia blossoms and in return they act as their natural pollinators.

Epilobium canum
California fuchsia, hummingbird flower, hummingbird trumpet

A low, spreading, perennial shrub 1 to 3 feet tall with grayish green woolly leaves. Bright red, trumpet-shaped flowers 1½ to 2¼ inches in length, massed in terminal spikes, appear in August to October. This evergreen plant thrives in regions that enjoy mild winters.

Anna's hummingbird taking nectar from California fuchsia (*Epilobium canum*).

Verdin feeding from the flowers of an ocotillo (*Fouquieria splendens*).

Native distribution Dry slopes from sea level to high mountains ranging from Oregon to Mexico, east to southwestern New Mexico.

Cultivation An ideal ground cover or rock garden plant for the Southwest region. This drought-resistant fuchsia prefers light, well-drained, neutral to alkaline soil and grows best in full sun. Prune it to the ground in spring if necessary. Zones 8–10. ❧ 🦋 ✺

OCOTILLOS
Fouquieria spp.

Ocotillos are related to the olive and primrose families and are restricted to desert areas. The family consists of 1 or 2 genera and 11 species. One species, *Fouquieria splendens*, is native to the United States along the Mexican border.

Birds Attracted

The nectar-rich flowers attract hummingbirds, orioles, and verdins. The thorny shrubs provide protective cover for a variety of smaller birds. Verdins often nest in the plants.

Fouquieria splendens
ocotillo, coachwhip

A shrub of slender, upright, whiplike stems guarded by thorns, growing from 8 to 20 feet tall. After rain, the stems become covered with bright green leaves that shed during dry periods. Spectacular tubular red flowers appear in March and June.

Native distribution Open, dry, stony slopes and mesas from sea level to about 5,000 feet, from western Texas to southern California, south into Mexico.

Cultivation Spectacular plants that are suitable for warm, dry soils in full sun. They make a beautiful living hedge or fence that is both impenetrable and ornamental. Zones 8–10. ❧ 🦋 ⊤ 🍁 ✺ ⊕

WILD STRAWBERRIES
Fragaria spp.

Evergreen ground covers, strawberries are members of the rose family. Of about 12 species, 3 are native to North America.

Birds Attracted

The fruits attract at least 53 species of birds, including wood thrush, cedar waxwing, American robin, gray catbird, brown thrasher, ruffed grouse, towhees, flickers, quail, and grosbeaks.

Fragaria chiloensis
beach strawberry

Evergreen, spreading ground cover, from 6 to 12 inches tall, with reddish green foliage. White flowers are followed by red, edible fruits throughout spring and summer. The plants spread by runners.
Native distribution Pacific Coast of North America.
Cultivation Prefers a moist, well-drained, fertile soil in full sun. Zones 5–10. 🦋 🌱 ✳

Fragaria virginiana
Virginia strawberry, wild strawberry

A low perennial, from 6 to 8 inches tall, forming a matlike ground cover. The compound leaves have three shallow-lobed, deep-veined leaflets. Small white flowers appear in April and June, producing small, fleshy, red fruits.
Native distribution The edge of woods, meadows, and prairie grasslands from Labrador south to Georgia and from Alberta to Oklahoma.
Cultivation An open, sunny area with well-drained, humus-rich soil gives the best results. New plants, "daughter plants," are produced by runners in late summer and can be transplanted. Zones 4–9. 🦋 ✳

Other suitable species

California wild strawberry (*F. californica*), 6 to 8 inches, Zones 5–10. 🦋 🌱 ✳

Wild strawberry (*Fragaria virginiana*).

White ash (*Fraxinus americana*).

ASH
Fraxinus spp.

A genus of medium to large trees, containing 45 to 65 species, 22 of which are native to North America: 7 species are found in eastern North America and 15 species in the west and Southwest. The common name "ash" is derived from an old English word, referring to timber for spear making.

Birds Attracted

The trees produce a huge seed set every 2 to 3 years. The winged seeds are dispersed in winter and are relished by many birds, including the evening grosbeak and purple finch.

Fraxinus americana
white ash, American ash

A tall, oval-shaped, deciduous tree, growing to 50 to 80 feet tall. Fall color can be a showy yellow, turning to purple. Small purplish flowers appear in early spring, with male and female flowers on separate trees. Winged "helicopter" seeds appear in early fall and are dispersed by wind over winter.

Native distribution Nova Scotia, west to Minnesota, south to northern Florida and southwest to eastern Texas.

Cultivation Widely grown as an ornamental tree, the white ash can live up to 300 years. It prefers a sunny location, but will grow in half sun in a dry to moist soil. It is heat and disease resistant, and is often used as a residential street tree or for wide lawn planting. Zones 3–9.

Fraxinus pennsylvanica
green ash, red ash

Fast-growing deciduous tree from 30 to 50 feet tall, sometimes even 80 feet tall and 30 feet wide. Dark green leaves turn yellow in fall. Trees are covered in clusters of small flowers in spring followed by winged seeds in early fall.

Native distribution The most widespread of the American Ashes, from Nova Scotia, west to Alberta and eastern Colorado, south to Florida and eastern Texas.

Cultivation Adaptable to any soil, including alkaline soil. Prefers acid, moist, well-drained soil in full sun. Tolerant of urban conditions, it is an excellent specimen, shade, or street tree. Adaptable to hot, dry summers and cold winters, it is an excellent tree for the Midwest and Plains states. Drought tolerant once established. Prune in fall as required. Zone 3–9.

HUCKLEBERRIES
Gaylussacia spp.

A genus of about 50 species, with 8 occurring in North America. Huckleberries are closely related to *Vaccinium* spp.

Birds Attracted

At least 50 species of birds are known to feed on huckleberry fruits, including gray catbird, northern flicker, red-headed woodpecker, and blue jay. The plants also provide secure nesting sites.

Gaylussacia baccata
black huckleberry

A low, deciduous shrub from 3 to 4 feet tall and wide with small leaves that turn red in autumn. White, urn-shaped flowers appear from May to June, followed by blue-black berries between July and September.

Native distribution Eastern North America from Newfoundland to Georgia, Manitoba, Wisconsin, and Kentucky.

Cultivation An ornamental garden plant. Prefers full sun to partial shade in a well-drained rocky soil. Zone 2.

Gaylussacia brachycera
box huckleberry

A low, evergreen shrub 1 to 2 feet tall and 3 feet wide with small leathery leaves. Urn-shaped flowers are white, red striped, and appear in early summer, followed by blue-black berries in late summer.

Green ash (*Fraxinus pennsylvanica*).

Immature fruit of box huckleberry (*Gaylussacia brachycera*).

Native distribution Scattered colonies, mainly in the Appalachian Mountains.
Cultivation Prefers a sunny position in well-drained acid soil. Spreads from underground runners. Excellent accent or border plant. Zones 5–9. 🦋 🍁 🐦 🌿

Gaylussacia frondosa
dangleberry, blue huckleberry
A freely branched deciduous shrub 3 to 6 feet tall with bluish green elliptical leaves. Small, pinkish green, urn-shaped flowers are followed by dark blue berries in early summer to early autumn.
Native distribution Eastern North America.
Cultivation Prefers acid, well-drained soil in light shade, but will grow well in poor soil. Zone 5. 🦋 ⊤ 🍁 🐦 🌿

SUNFLOWERS
Helianthus spp.

Members of the sunflower family, about 50 species of annuals and perennials are native to the New World.

Birds Attracted
The nutritious seeds are eaten by a wide variety of birds, especially chickadees, nuthatches, and titmice.

Helianthus annuus

common sunflower
This plant is approximately 6 feet tall, with black-centered, golden daisy flowers 5 to 6 inches across. Each of the many branches and branchlets carries a flower. The wild plant is more daisylike, with longer petals and a much smaller central disk than cultivated varieties. Flowers appear between June and September, followed by black-shelled oval seeds.
Native distribution Common throughout much of North America, including Colorado, New Mexico, Texas, and the Plains states. American Indians ate the seeds and carried them throughout the country.

Jerusalem artichoke
(*Helianthus tuberosus*).

Song sparrow attracted to the seeds of common sunflower
(*Helianthus annuus*).

Cultivation Easily grown in a sunny location in average, well-drained soil. Stake them if they show a tendency to topple. Allow the plants to stand after frost to attract birds to the ripe seed heads. Zones 3–10.
🦋 🌱 ❀

Other suitable species
swamp sunflower (*H. angustifolius*), 4 to 8 feet tall, Zones 6–9. 🦋 ❀
woodland sunflower (*H. divaricatus*), 2 to 6 feet tall, Zones 3–8. 🦋 🌱 ❀
sawtooth sunflower (*H. grosse-serratus*), 6 to 8 feet tall, Zones 4–7. 🦋 ❀
willowleaf sunflower (*H. salicifolius*), 3 to 4 feet tall, Zones 4–8. 🦋 ❀
Jerusalem artichoke (*H. tuberosus*), 5 to 10 feet tall, Zones 4–8. 🦋 🦋 ❀

Black-capped chickadee feeding on sunflower seeds.

Red-breasted sapsucker drilling shallow holes to take sap from Christmas berry (*Heteromeles arbutifolia*).

Orange sulphur butterfly nectaring on sunflower (*Helianthus* sp.).

TOYAN
Heteromeles sp.

A sole *Heteromeles* species, native to California.

Birds Attracted
At least 20 species of birds feed on the berries including northern mockingbird, cedar waxwing, American robin, western bluebird, purple finches, towhees, and California quail.

Christmas berry (*Heteromeles arbutifolia*).

Heteromeles arbutifolia
Christmas berry, California holly
Perennial, evergreen shrub or small tree, usually 6 to 8 feet tall and 4 to 5 feet wide, but may reach 15 to 20 feet, with leathery, dark green leaves. Masses of small white flowers appear in early summer, followed by clusters of bright red berries that mature in fall and persist through winter.
Native distribution Southern California.
Cultivation Requires well-drained soil in full sun or part shade. Frost tolerant and drought tolerant once established. Zones 7–10. 🦋

American robin feeding on the fruits of 'Sparkleberry' winterberry holly (*Ilex verticillata* 'Sparkleberry').

Possum haw (*Ilex decidua*).

HOLLIES
Ilex spp.

Hollies are variable plants, with both shrubs and trees as well as both evergreen and deciduous species. Most hollies bear male and female flowers on separate plants. Grow plants of both sexes together to make sure your female plant sets berries. There are over 300 species of hollies, found in most tropical and temperate regions. There are 14 tree species and 2 shrub species native to North America.

Birds Attracted

Dense, prickly foliage provides excellent shelter and nesting sites for many birds. Fruits are eaten by at least 49 species, including flickers, northern mockingbird, gray catbird, brown thrasher, bluebirds, cedar waxwing, and American robin.

Ilex decidua
possum haw

A deciduous shrub or small tree growing to 30 feet tall with a spreading crown. Leaves are spoon-shaped with finely toothed margins. Small white flowers are followed by round, glossy, red or red-orange fruits on female plants, maturing in autumn and remaining attached in winter.
Native distribution Moist soils from Illinois to Florida and Texas.
Cultivation Possum haws grow best in a slightly acid, well-mulched, moist but well-drained soil in full sun. Zones 5–9. 🦋 🍁 ♥ 🐦

Ilex glabra
inkberry, gallberry

A hardy, evergreen shrub 6 to 10 feet tall and wide with glossy, leathery, oval leaves and small greenish white flowers from May to July. Flowers are followed by black berry fruits in September that persist through winter.
Native distribution Eastern and southcentral United States and southern Canada, in wet woods and coastal plains.

Cultivation An ornamental garden plant. Prefers full sun, but will tolerate some shade in moist, well-drained soils. Flood tolerant. Male and female shrubs produce berries on the female plant. Withstands heavy pruning. Zones 4–9. ✖ ❦ ▣ ▨

Ilex opaca
American holly

An evergreen tree from 40 to 50 feet tall with a pyramidal form. Leaves have spiny margins, and they may be dull or glossy green, depending on the cultivar. Bark is light gray. White flowers are followed by bright red fruits on female plants, maturing in autumn and remaining attached in winter.

Native distribution American holly grows in moist soils and on riverbanks from eastern Massachusetts south to central Florida, Missouri, and Texas.

Cultivation Prefers a moist but well-drained location in full sun to light shade with a slightly acid soil. Zones 6–9. ✖ ⊤ ▣ ▨ ⬗

Male varied thrush enjoying the berries of American holly (*Ilex opaca*).

Ilex verticillata
winterberry

A deciduous shrub that may reach 15 feet tall. The dark green leaves turn yellow in autumn. Inconspicuous flowers appear in June, followed by brilliant red berries that persist well into winter. The abundant red berries contrast beautifully with the bare, dark gray branches.

Native distribution Wetlands and along the banks of wooded streams from Newfoundland to Minnesota and south to Georgia and Texas.

Cultivation Winterberry grows well in most good garden soils in full sun to partial shade. The plant tolerates wet soils and prefers acid soils (pH 3.8 to 6.0). It is excellent for naturalizing and is especially attractive with a background of evergreens. Zones 4–9. ✖ ⊤ ▣ ▨ ⬗

Winterberry (*Ilex verticillata*)

Ilex vomitoria
yaupon holly

An evergreen, small, hardy tree 10 to 15 feet tall, with oval, glossy, green, leathery leaves with serrated edges. Inconspicuous white flowers in spring are followed in fall by an abundance of small red berries that persist through winter.

Native distribution Southeastern North America from Maryland, south to Florida, west to southeastern Oklahoma and Texas.

Eastern bluebird feeding on the fruits of yaupon holly (*Ilex vomitoria*).

Rocky Mountain juniper (*Juniperus scopulorum*).

Creeping juniper (*Juniperus horizontalis*).

Cultivation Prefers full sun for best fruiting, and thrives in an acid or alkaline soil. May be pruned for shape. An excellent wildlife-friendly plant, providing secure nesting sites and food for many bird species. A graceful weeping form, weeping yaupon holly (*I. vomitoria* 'Pendular'), is available. Zones 7–9.

🦋 🍁 👁 🐾

....

Other suitable species

large gallberry (*I. coriacea*), to 8 feet, Zone 7.
🦋 🌲 👁 🐾 🐦

smooth winterberry (*I. laevigata*), 10 to 20 feet, Zone 5. 🦋 🍁 ❋ 👁 🐾

myrtle dahoon (*I. myrtifolia*), to 23 feet, Zone 7.
🦋 🌲 👁 🐾 🐦

JUNIPERS, RED CEDARS
Juniperus spp.

Junipers are evergreen trees or shrubs found growing on poor, dry, stony or sandy soils. Most junipers have small, blunt, scaly leaves and berrylike succulent cones that are often called juniper berries. There are 15 species native to North America.

Birds Attracted

Junipers are important food trees for over 54 species of backyard birds. Juniper fruits are eaten by many native birds including the cedar waxwing, purple finch, American robin, evening grosbeak, yellow-rumped warbler, flickers, northern mockingbird, bluebirds, Swainson's thrush, tree swallow, cliff swallows, eastern kingbird, jays, bobwhites, wild turkeys, and others.

Junipers also provide valuable nesting and roosting sites for birds, including chipping sparrow, American robin, northern mockingbird, and song sparrow. Juncos, sparrows, and yellow-rumped warblers are among the birds that roost in the foliage.

Juniperus californica
California juniper

A dense evergreen shrub or small tree 10 to 25 feet tall with a wide-spreading irregular crown and bluish gray foliage. Blue-green berrylike cones appear throughout the year.

Native distribution California coastal ranges and the Sierra Nevada.

Cultivation Suitable for dry soils in full sun. It is alkaline tolerant and heat and drought tolerant once established. Zones 8–10.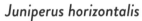

Juniperus deppeana
alligator juniper

An evergreen tree 30 to 50 feet tall with a wide crown and distinctive, hard, dark gray bark, cracked into square plates that resemble alligator skin. Leaves are scalelike. Blue-green berry cones appear all year.

Native distribution Western Texas to northwest New Mexico and northcentral Arizona to Mexico.

Cultivation A hardy tree. Prefers full sun, in a well-drained, rocky, sterile soil. An important food source to overwintering birds, including bluebirds, robins, and evening grosbeak. Zones 7–10.

Juniperus horizontalis
creeping juniper

A low-spreading or prostrate evergreen shrub, from 1 to 2 feet high and 4 to 8 feet across, with blue-green aromatic foliage and small blue fruits.

Native distribution Eastern Canada, Minnesota, Michigan, and Wisconsin, south to Pennsylvania and north West Virginia, and western North America, south to Arizona and New Mexico, usually in rocky soils.

Cultivation Prefers full sun in well-drained shallow soils. There are many cultivars, some of which do not produce fruits, so when selecting a plant, choose one that provides food for birds. Zones 3–9.

Juniperus monosperma
one-seed juniper, cherrystone juniper

A fast-growing juniper 20 to 25 feet tall with distinctive gray, shaggy bark that hangs in strips from the trunk. Leaves are tiny and scalelike, and the branches start from ground level. Blue berrylike cones appear all year on female trees.

Juniper titmouse, a resident of juniper woodlands.

Cedar waxwing feeding on the fruits of Rocky Mountain juniper (*Juniperus scopulorum*).

Northern mockingbird feeding on the fruits of eastern red cedar (*Juniperus virginiana*).

Eastern red cedar (*Juniperus virginiana*).

Native distribution Southwest North America along the Rocky Mountains.

Cultivation A hardy plant that is drought tolerant. Prefers well-drained sandy soil in full sun. Zone 5.

Juniperus occidentalis
Sierra juniper, western juniper

Slow-growing evergreen shrub or small tree with scaly leaves. Blue-green berrylike cones appear in fall. There are two varieties: *Juniperus occidentalis* var. *occidentalis*, in Southwest Oregon, Idaho, and northeast California, and Nevada, that grows 12 to 55 feet tall; and *J. occidentalis* var. *australis*, in California and western Nevada, that grows 35 to 70 feet tall.

Native distribution Western United States.

Cultivation Prefers well-drained, rocky soil in full sun. Drought resistant once established. Plant male and female trees to produce fruit. It is an excellent tree for sustaining wildlife. Zones 4–10.

Juniperus scopulorum
Rocky Mountain juniper

An evergreen tree, 30 to 40 feet tall. It has a short, thick trunk, which is often divided near the ground into several stems. The foliage is scaly, forming a dense, round-topped crown. The reddish, stringy bark is characteristic of the red cedars. The fruits are whitish blue with a waxy bloom.

Native distribution Alberta to South Dakota and northwestern Nebraska to western Texas, New Mexico, northern Arizona, Nevada, eastern Oregon, and British Columbia at elevations of 5,000 to 9,000 feet.

Cultivation An ornamental tree and excellent garden plant. It is fast growing and tolerates most soils. Prefers a well-drained, sunny site. Tolerant of dry climates and coastal areas at sea level. Zones 3–6.

Juniperus virginiana
eastern red cedar, red juniper

An evergreen pyramidal or columnar tree from 30 to 50 feet tall, with aromatic, scalelike, dark green leaves and reddish brown, fibrous, shredding bark. Its cones are small, circular, dark blue berries that ripen in early autumn and persist through winter.

Native distribution Dry rocky ridges and gravelly slopes to flood plains and swamps, from southern Ontario and Maine south to northern Florida, west to eastern Texas and north to eastern North Dakota.
Cultivation Best suited to east of the Rocky Mountains. It tolerates most soils. Prefers full sun in sandy, loamy soils of limestone origin. Plants are alternate hosts for the cedar-apple rust fungus. Bagworms can be a problem. Zones 3–9. 🦋🌱🐞🌿🐟

Other suitable species
Ashe juniper (*J. ashei*), 6 to 20 feet, Zone 7.
🦋🌱🐞🌿🐦

KECKIELLAS
Keckiella spp.

A recently new genus of shrubby plants closely related to penstemons. Some species are still referred to as beardtongues or penstemons because they once belonged to the genus *Penstemon*. Keckiellas are native to the Southwest, especially California.

Birds Attracted
The flowers of keckiella attract hummingbirds, which are their major pollinators. Seed-eating birds feed on the seeds.

Keckiella antirrhinoides
yellow bush snapdragon
A perennial shrub 3 to 4 feet tall with large, fragrant yellow flowers in late February to July. Foliage is deciduous during extended dry periods
Native distribution West of the mountains in southern California to Arizona.
Cultivation Prefers part shade or full sun when grown on the coast, in well-drained soil. Cold tolerant. Benefits from a small amount of watering in summer. Zones 7–9. 🐦🦋✿

Yellow bush snapdragon (*Keckiella antirrhinoides*).

Heartleaf penstemon (*Keckiella cordifolia*).

Keckiella cordifolia
heartleaf penstemon, climbing penstemon

A sprawling evergreen shrub that grows 3 to 6 feet tall in mild climates; it is deciduous in cold climates or during extended dry periods. Red, tubular flowers are 1 to 2 inches long and appear from May to July.

Native distribution Central and southern California.

Cultivation Prefers sun to part shade. It is cold and drought tolerant, but may require some water in summer. Exceptional plant for attracting hummingbirds. Zones 6–10.

Keckiella corymbosa
red shrubby penstemon, redwood penstemon

A low, dark green shrub, 12 to 20 inches tall, with leathery, oval leaves. Plants bear clusters of brick-red tubular flowers 1½ inches in length, usually between June and October.

Native distribution Open rocky slopes of Coast Ranges and the Sierra Nevada foothills of northern California.

Cultivation This penstemon is an excellent rock garden plant. It will be blooming when other flowers are scarce. It prefers to be in full sun in a well-drained location. Zones 7–9.

Other suitable species

yawning penstemon (*K. breviflora*), 2 to 5 feet tall, Zones 6–10.

Rothrock's keckiella (*K. rothrockii*), 1 to 2 feet, Zones 6–10.

scarlet penstemon (*K. ternata*), 2 to 3 feet, Zones 7–10.

LARCHES
Larix spp.

Larches (or tamaracks) are deciduous conifers: tall, slender trees with narrow, open crowns. Their slender, dark green needles turn golden-yellow in late autumn and are shed before winter. Small, scaly cones are carried on the dwarf twigs and stand upright, releasing winged seeds when mature. There are about 10 species of larch confined to the cooler parts of the Northern Hemisphere; 3 species are native to Canada and the northern United States.

White-winged crossbill feeding on the seeds of tamarack (*Larix laricina*).

Birds Attracted

Blue and spruce grouse consume the needles and buds. The ruffed grouse, pine siskin, red-breasted nuthatch, purple finch, red crossbill, and American goldfinch feed on the small seeds. The scarlet tanager sometimes nests in the tree.

Larix laricina
tamarack, American larch, eastern larch, Alaska larch

A deciduous pyramidal tree with a straight, tapering trunk, small horizontal branches, that grows 40 to 80 feet tall. Lacy needles turn bright yellow in fall. Cones are small, appearing in late summer and persisting to early fall.

Native distribution Tamaracks grow in poorly drained areas and cold, deep swamps. In the north, they are often found in drier uplands in rich, loamy soils. Tamaracks are native from Labrador to the Arctic Circle west to the Rocky Mountains, south through Canada to Pennsylvania and West Virginia, and west to Minnesota.

Cultivation Suitable for the coldest climates, it is a hardy tree. Plant in moist, acidic, humus-rich soil in full sun. Tamaracks thrive in wet soils. Zones 2–6.

Autumn foliage of tamarack.

Tiny flowers of common spicebush (*Lindera benzoin*) are a magnet for butterflies.

SPICEBUSHES
Lindera spp.

Member of the family Lauraceae, or laurel, flowering plants. Three species are native to eastern North America.

Birds Attracted

The fruits are high in fats and are an important food source for migrating birds, as well as resident birds, including northern flicker and northern bobwhite.

Lindera benzoin

common spicebush, northern spicebush
A rounded, deciduous shrub 8 to 12 feet tall, with fragrant green leaves that turn yellow to golden-yellow in fall. Small greenish yellow flowers appear in early spring, before the leaves appear. Red berries appear on the female plant from midsummer to mid-fall.
Native distribution Maine and Ontario, down through Florida, and west to Texas and Kansas.
Cultivation Prefers full sun or partial shade and moist, well-drained soil. It is an excellent hedge plant. Zones 5–9. 🦋 ⊤ ❀

Ruby-throated hummingbird taking nectar from cardinal flower (*Lobelia cardinalis*).

LOBELIAS
Lobelia spp.

Genus *Lobelia* is a widely distributed group: 29 species are native to North America. Plants have tubular flowers that add summer color to the landscape. Lobelias are members of the bellflower family.

Birds Attracted

Plants are pollinated mainly by hummingbirds attracted to the rich supply of nectar.

Lobelia cardinalis
cardinal flower, scarlet lobelia

A beautiful perennial wildflower, generally 2 to 3 feet tall, with numerous brilliant red 1½-inch-long tubular flower clusters on erect flower spikes between July and October. Leaves are alternate, toothed, and lance-shaped.

Native distribution Southern Ontario and Quebec south to Florida, and west to western Texas, southern California, and eastern Colorado on moist, shady slopes and stream banks.

Cultivation This plant does best in humus-rich soil in a well-drained, moist location with light to partial shade. Plants self-sow freely, producing seedlings in spring from seed dropped the previous fall and winter. Zones 2–9. 🦋 🐦 ⊤ ❀

Twinberry honeysuckle (*Lonicera involucrata*) berries.

HONEYSUCKLES
Lonicera spp.

Honeysuckles are shrubs or vines with showy and often highly fragrant tubular flowers. The tubular flowers are rich in nectar, giving the plants their common name. Of about 150 species, 24 are native to North America.

Birds Attracted

The flowers produce a rich supply of nectar favored by hummingbirds and orioles, and many birds feed on the berrylike fruits. Northern cardinal, gray catbird, northern mockingbird, and song sparrow often nest in shrubby honeysuckles.

Lonicera arizonica
Arizona honeysuckle

An erect or twining woody shrub or vine, growing 1 to 10 feet tall with small deciduous leaves. Clusters of slender, showy, orange-red, trumpet-shaped flowers appear between April and July, followed by red berries.

Native distribution Along streams and in open coniferous forests in Arizona, New Mexico, Utah, and western Texas at elevations of 3,500 to 11,000 feet.

Twinberry honeysuckle flowers.

Rufous hummingbird taking nectar from trumpet honeysuckle (*Lonicera sempervirens*).

Cultivation An attractive landscape plant that tolerates most soil types. It is easy to grow, preferring a well-drained, sunny location. Zones 6–8.

Lonicera involucrata
twinberry honeysuckle, bearberry honeysuckle

A shrub from 2 to 10 feet tall, with dark green deciduous leaves. The yellow tubular flowers of this plant are typically borne in pairs from early spring through to early summer, followed by paired purple-black berries in late summer.

Native distribution Arizona, New Mexico, Colorado, and Utah, west to California, and north to Quebec and British Columbia. Commonly found in moist areas in forests and beside streams from sea level to about 11,500 feet in elevation.

Cultivation Easy to grow and tolerant of most soils. Prefers a moist, well-drained location in full sun to light shade. Plants grow well in most areas of the United States. Zones 4–10.

Lonicera sempervirens
trumpet honeysuckle, coral honeysuckle

A semievergreen to evergreen vine, reaching 13 to 20 feet long. The showy, trumpet-shaped red flowers are yellow inside the tubes and 1 to 2 inches long. It flowers between April and September, followed by spherical scarlet berries through late summer and fall.

Native distribution Woods and thickets from Massachusetts and New York south to Florida and west to Texas.

Cultivation Requires some initial support to climb or it will become shrubby. Plants prefer a sunny location with well-drained, evenly moist soil. They will tolerate acid soil. Zones 4–9.

Other suitable species
pink honeysuckle (*Lonicera hispidula*), 12 feet, Zone 7.

MAHONIAS
Mahonia spp.

Mahonias are a widespread cosmopolitan genus of approximately 70 species, closely related to the genus *Berberis*, with approximately 8 species found in North America.

Birds Attracted

Hummingbirds are attracted to the flowers and many birds feed on the berries, including cedar waxwing, varied thrush, northern mockingbird, American robin, and hermit thrush.

Mahonia aquifolium
Oregon grape

An evergreen shrub 1 to 6 feet tall, with purple to bronze new growth, changing to dark green in summer and turning reddish in winter. Yellow flowers appear in spring, followed by dark blue fruits that ripen from early fall.
Native distribution West Coast of British Columbia, south to northern California.
Cultivation Prefers a well-drained, fertile soil in shade or part shade. Zones 6–9.

Mahonia pinnata
California barberry, Pacific mahonia

An evergreen shrub with dark green, spine-tipped leaves, 3 to 6 feet tall. Leaves are hollylike and new growth is an attractive bronze color. Spiky clusters of fragrant, yellow, bell-shaped flowers appear in spring, followed by edible purple berries.
Native distribution West Coast from British Columbia to Baja California.
Cultivation An ornamental, easily grown plant. Drought tolerant; prefers light shade in well-drained soil. Zone 7–11.

Mountain bluebird attracted to the flower buds of Oregon grape (*Mahonia aquifolium*).

California barberry (*Mahonia pinnata*).

Flowers of Oregon grape.

Eastern phoebe in wild sweet crabapple tree (*Malus coronaria*).

Cedar waxwings feeding on crabapple fruits.

APPLES, CRABAPPLES
Malus spp.

The genus *Malus* is made up of deciduous trees and shrubs. Of the 25 species found in temperate regions of the Northern Hemisphere, 9 are native to North America. The best-known species is the common domestic apple (*Malus pumila*), which is native to southeastern Europe and central Asia and from which most edible apples have been cultivated.

Birds Attracted

Many birds feed on the fruits, including American robins, northern mockingbirds, bobwhites, cedar waxwing, purple finch, house finch, red-headed woodpecker, common flicker, gray catbird, evening grosbeak, and pine grosbeak. The plants also provide secure nesting sites. Old trees provide valuable nest cavities for birds.

Malus coronaria
wild sweet crabapple, sweet crabapple, wild crabapple

A small, short-trunked tree to 30 feet tall. Fragrant, pinkish white flowers, 1½ inch in diameter, appear in spring, followed by yellow-green crabapple fruits about 1 inch in diameter. The leaves turn yellow in autumn.

Native distribution Southern Ontario east to New York, south to northern Georgia, west to Missouri and to elevations of 3,000 feet in the Appalachian Mountains. Found in moist soil in the deciduous forest region, usually in the shade of larger trees.

Cultivation Prefers evenly moist and well-drained loamy soil in full sun to light shade. It can tolerate acid soil. Susceptible to cedar-apple rust. Zones 5–7.

Malus fusca
Pacific crabapple, Oregon crabapple

A western species similar to wild sweet crabapple. It is a large shrub or small tree, 15 to 30 feet tall, and may have thorns. The flowers of the Pacific crabapple are pinkish white, appearing in spring; fruits are oblong, ½ inch long, ripening to purplish black.

Native distribution Damp coastal forests from Alaska south to central California.

Cultivation Pacific crabapple often grows as a thicket-forming shrub rather than as a tree. Prefers well-drained, loamy soil in full sun to light shade. Zones 4–9.

Malus ioensis
wild crabapple, prairie crabapple

A deciduous, broad, spreading tree with a rounded crown 18 feet tall and 12 feet wide. Deep green leaves are coarsely serrated and turn rich, dark red and orange in autumn. Fragrant white or pink blossoms appear in spring followed by small applelike fruits in summer.

Native distribution Upper Mississippi Valley from Minnesota and Wisconsin, south to Oklahoma, and southeast through Louisiana and Kentucky.

Cultivation Prefers full sun in a slightly acidic, moist, well-drained soil. Zones 4–7.

Other suitable species

southern wild crabapple or American crabapple (*M. angustifolia*), to 25 feet, Zones 4–9.

Wild crabapple (*Malus ioensis*) 'Plena'.

Crabapple trees and blossoms.

Wild bergamot (*Monarda fistulosa*).

Pipevine swallowtail butterfly nectaring in bee balm.

Ruby-throated hummingbird taking nectar from bee balm (*Monarda didyma*).

BEE BALMS
Monarda spp.

Bee balms are members of the mint family, and often have aromatic, minty leaves. They are flamboyant plants, with flowers borne in dense heads or whorls, often surrounded by colored bracts. There are 12 annual and perennial species native to North America.

Birds Attracted

Red-flowered species are particularly attractive to hummingbirds.

Monarda didyma
bee balm, Oswego tea, sweet bergamot

A perennial growing from 2 to 4 feet tall. Aromatic leaves are paired, dark green, and oval to lance-shaped. A round 4-inch terminal cluster of bright red tubular flowers and reddish bracts appears at the top of the square stems from July to September.

Native distribution Moist meadows and thickets throughout the eastern United States as far south as Georgia.

Cultivation Prefers moist, humus-rich, slightly acidic soil in full sun or partial shade. Plant in spring, 12 to 18 inches apart in clumps. Plants spread rapidly by underground stems, so plant them where they have room to spread or divide them regularly. Cutting back plants after flowering will encourage more flowers, but leave some for seed. Plants may get powdery mildew; thin the stems to increase air circulation. Zones 4–8. ❀ 🦋 ✿

Monarda fistulosa
wild bergamot

A fragrant, clump-forming perennial 2 to 3 feet tall with toothed, lance-shaped leaves 2 to 3 inches long. Lavender, white, or pink flowers appear from May to September followed by seed that is taken by seed-eating birds.

Native distribution Widespread from Quebec to Alberta, south to Texas.

Cultivation Best results are achieved in an average rich, moist, but well-drained soil in full sun to light shade. Zones 3–8. ❀ 🦋 ✿

MULBERRIES
Morus spp.

Mulberries are usually deciduous trees with many small branches and heart-shaped leaves. The fruits are a blackberrylike cluster of many fruitlets, each containing a seed within the red, pink, white, or purple pulp. The mulberry family has about 1,400 species, including figs, breadfruit, and rubber plants. The family is widespread in temperate and tropical regions of the world; 5 tree species are native to North America.

Birds Attracted

At least 59 species of birds feed on the ripe fruits, including the bluebird, cedar waxwing, orchard oriole, northern cardinal, blue jay, rose-breasted grosbeak, red-headed woodpecker, yellow-billed cuckoo, Baltimore oriole, wood thrush, red-bellied and downy woodpecker, eastern kingbird, northern mockingbird, scarlet tanager, red-eyed vireo, yellow warbler, American robin, gray catbird, titmouse and brown thrasher. In desert areas, the curve-billed thrasher, flickers, phainopepla, Gila woodpecker, and house finch feed on the fruits. The trees are also useful for shelter and cover, and provide secure nesting.

Morus microphylla
Texas mulberry, mountain mulberry

Mostly shrubby, but under ideal conditions may grow into small trees up to 20 feet tall. Leaves are small, toothed, and rounded to heart-shaped. The ½-inch-long cylindrical fruits are red, maturing to purple or black in late spring.
Native distribution Southern Oklahoma and Texas, west through New Mexico and Arizona, and south to Mexico, usually found along streams, grasslands,

and rocky slopes at elevations of 2,000 to 6,000 feet.
Cultivation As for red mulberry. Texas mulberry adapts to most conditions, but grows best in rich, moist soil in full sun. It is fairly drought resistant. Water regularly when young, and stake young trees to prevent losses from strong winds. Zones 7–9.

Morus rubra
red mulberry

Usually growing to about 30 feet tall, but may reach 60 feet with a 2-foot-diameter trunk. The variably lobed, deciduous leaves turn a clear yellow in autumn. Flowers are small, green, and inconspicuous, borne in separate male and female clusters. The red to dark purple fruits ripen in late spring.
Native distribution Moist, rich soils from southern Ontario south to southern Florida, west to central Texas, and north to southeastern Minnesota.
Cultivation A fast-growing tree adaptable to most conditions. Male and female trees may be required in order to produce a good fruit crop. Tolerant of coastal planting, it is somewhat drought resistant. Best results in rich, moist soils in full sun. Regular water and staking when young are advisable. Zones 4–9.

Curve-bill thrasher feeding on the fruits of red mulberry (*Morus rubra*).

The winter diet of berries, especially the high-fat berries of the evergreen bayberry (*Myrica pensylvanica*), enables yellow-rumped warblers to winter farther north than any other warbler.

BAYBERRIES, WAX MYRTLES
Myrica spp. (formerly *Morella* spp.)

Bayberries are deciduous or evergreen plants with inconspicuous flowers and small, waxy fruits. The common name wax myrtle comes from the early American colonists, who made candles from the waxy berries. They separated the wax by boiling the fruit, producing fragrant candles. *Myrica* species are widely distributed. There are about 50 species in the temperate and warmer regions of the world. North America has 5 native tree species and 3 shrub species.

Birds Attracted

The fruits are fed on by at least 86 bird species, including yellow-rumped warbler, tufted titmouse, common flicker, American robin, finches, white-eyed vireo, scarlet tanager, red-bellied and downy woodpeckers, black-capped chickadee, bluebird, gray catbird, brown thrasher, hermit thrush, scrub jay, tree swallow, meadowlark, bobwhite, and towhee. California wax myrtle is particularly attractive to the cedar waxwing, Baltimore oriole, yellow-rumped warbler, chickadee, flicker, tree swallow, wrentit, and towhee.

Myrica californica
California wax myrtle, Pacific wax myrtle, Pacific bayberry

A large evergreen shrub or small tree, growing from 10 to 30 feet tall and spreading 15 to 20 feet wide, with slender, ascending branches. Plants have narrow, toothed, oval leaves and small clusters of inconspicuous greenish flowers. Male and female flowers are borne separately on the same plant. Purplish

Yellow-rumped warbler in autumn plumage feeding on the fruits of California wax myrtle (*Myrica californica*).

¼-inch-diameter fruits are coated with a whitish wax. They are borne in clusters in summer and persist to the following summer.

Native distribution Santa Monica Mountains of southern California, north to Washington State, in canyons, on moist slopes, and along the ocean on sand dunes.

Cultivation It may reach tree size on the shores of San Francisco Bay; elsewhere it is normally a shrub. A particularly valuable plant for birds. Its evergreen, glossy foliage makes it an attractive screen, background, or specimen plant. It is suitable for coastal planting. It has a moderate growth rate, will grow in full sun or partial shade, and thrives with regular watering. It tolerates pruning and is often used as a hedge. Zones 6–9. 🦋 ⊤ ✿

Myrica cerifera
wax myrtle, southern bayberry

A large multistemmed evergreen shrub or small tree usually 10 to 20 feet tall, occasionally 30 to 40 feet. The yellowish green leaves are oval, slender, and toothed in shape. Male and female flowers are borne in catkins on separate plants. The round, light green fruits are covered with a bluish white wax. The fruits mature on female plants in fall and persist through winter.

Native distribution Pinelands, swamps, and moist sandy soils from New Jersey, south to the Florida Keys, through the Gulf states to southern Texas, and north to southeastern Oklahoma. The plant reaches its largest size in the south Atlantic and Gulf states, and forms great thickets in the Florida Everglades. In dry, arid situations, it often grows only a few inches tall.

Cultivation An attractive plant valuable for birds. Prefers a moist but well-drained site in full sun to partial shade. It is salt tolerant. Plant both sexes to ensure fruit set. Wax myrtles can be grown from seed. Useful screen or hedge plant. Zones 6–9. 🦋 ⊤ ✿

Myrica pensylvanica
bayberry, northern bayberry

A round, bushy, semievergreen to deciduous shrub, reaching 6½ feet tall, with slender, whitish gray branches. The aromatic leaves are oval and slender, remaining on the plants into winter. Male and female flowers are borne in catkins on separate plants. In summer, fragrant, round, gray fruits covered with a bluish white wax form thick clusters against the

Eastern bluebird feeding on bayberry fruits.

Wax myrtle (*Myrica cerifera*).

American robin feeding on the fruits of black tupelo (*Nyssa sylvatica*).

Black tupelo with fall foliage.

branches. Fruits persist through winter.

Native distribution Atlantic Coast from North Carolina through Maine, and west to Lake Erie, primarily in wet areas.

Cultivation Prefers a moist, well-drained site in full sun to partial shade. Plants tolerate acid soil and are salt tolerant; they also tolerate road salt and poor soil. Use for foundation or seaside plantings in naturalistic massing. Plant both sexes to ensure fruit set. Zones 4–9. 🦋 🍂

TUPELO
Nyssa spp.

A small genus of 9–11 species with five native to eastern North America.

Birds Attracted

An important food source for migratory and resident birds, including blue jay, American robin, hermit and wood thrush, northern mockingbird, eastern bluebird, scarlet tanager, gray catbird, eastern phoebe, and northern flicker, which are some of the 20 species recorded to feed on the fruits.

Nyssa sylvatica
black tupelo, sour gum, black gum

A slow-growing, deciduous, conical-shaped tree when young, spreading with age with flattened top. In cultivation, it grows to 40 feet tall and 30 feet wide. The glossy oval leaves have spectacular fall color, and branches are covered in small dark blue fruits by late summer or mid-fall.

Native distribution Widespread from Maine and Ontario to Michigan, Florida, and Texas, in wet flats or damp lowlands.

Cultivation Excellent specimen or shade tree. Best results achieved in full or partial sun in a moist, deep, acid soil. Zones 3–9. 🦋 🍁 🍂

OPUNTIA, PRICKLY PEAR
Opuntia spp.

Opuntia are the largest group of cacti in the United States. They form low, succulent, herbaceous plants, shrubs, or trees with jointed stems and spiny pads. Often referred to as "paddle cactus," the plant's pads are flattened in the prickly pear group. Some opuntias have very showy, large, luminous flowers of yellow, white, red, peach, orange, or pink. Fruits are edible and can be large and showy in some species, ripening to red or purple. There are about 60 species of *Opuntia* native to North America.

Birds Attracted

Opuntia are valuable nesting plants in desert areas, since their prickly spines give protective shelter. Cactus wren, mourning dove, Inca dove, curved-billed thrasher, greater roadrunner, and sparrows are among the birds that nest in the foliage. Many birds feed on the ripe fruit.

Opuntia basilaris
beavertail cactus, prickly pear cactus
A clump-forming succulent to 2 feet tall with a spread of 4 feet. It has flattened blue-gray pads and small, barbed bristles. Pink to rose colored flowers in March to April are followed by spineless fruits.
Native distribution Arizona, California, and Nevada at 200 to 3,000 feet elevation.
Cultivation Hardy; prefers full sun in a free-draining soil. Frost tolerant. Needs little to no water once established. Propagate from cuttings from cultivated plants. Zones 8–10. 🦋 ✿ 🐦

Opuntia polyacantha
plains prickly pear, many-spined opuntia
Plains prickly pear forms low clumps of spiny, flattened, oval pads. Flowers are yellow or occasionally

Flowers of beavertail cactus (*Opuntia basilaris*).

Western prickly pear in bloom (*Opuntia littoralis*).

Red-bellied woodpecker feeding on the fruit of Virginia creeper (*Parthenocissus quinquefolia*).

Crimson fall foliage of Virginia creeper.

Virginia creeper flowers.

magenta, and are borne on the edges of the upper pads between May and July, followed by egg-shaped, fleshy, tan fruits. This cactus usually only grows 6 inches tall, but may spread from 1 to 10 feet wide.

Native distribution Found on open plains from southern British Columbia, Oregon, and northern Arizona east to western Texas, Oklahoma, Missouri, and Iowa, and north to central Canada.

Cultivation Plains prickly pear needs full sun and poor, neutral, well-drained soil. Most prickly pears withstand a range of extremely hot and cold temperatures. They are suitable for desert or semiarid grassland areas and for xeriscaping. Prickly pear can be grown from seed or by planting a detached pad. Make sure you buy from a reputable cactus nursery that guarantees nursery-propagated stock. Zones 6–9. 🦋 ❋ 🐦

Other suitable species

pear or brittle cactus (*O. fragilis*), 8 to 10 inches tall by 1 to 3 feet wide, Zones 7–9. 🦋 ❋ 🐦

prickly pear (*O. humifusa*), East Coast species, to 1 foot tall, Zones 4–8. 🦋 ⊤ ❋ 🐦

western prickly pear (*O. littoralis*), 2 feet tall, Zone 9. 🦋 ❋ 🐦

tulip prickly pear (*O. woodsii*) 3 feet tall, Zones 7–9. 🦋 ❋ 🐦

WOODBINES
Parthenocissus spp.

These deciduous vines are members of the grape family, with brilliant orange to red autumn leaves. Virginia creeper is an excellent alternative to English ivy with the added benefit of gorgeous fall color.

Birds Attracted

Woodbines provide excellent shelter for smaller birds. House finches and bushtits often nest in the vines. Fruits are eaten by at least 39 species of birds, including the red-bellied and red-headed woodpecker, tufted titmouse, eastern bluebird, American robin, northern mockingbird, brown thrasher, black-capped chickadee, flicker, and thrush.

Parthenocissus quinquefolia
Virginia creeper, woodbine

May reach 50 feet. The leaves are 6 inches long and are divided into 5 coarsely toothed leaflets. Small whitish or greenish flowers are borne in early summer and followed by clusters of bluish black, grape-like berries in fall. Foliage turns brilliant crimson in fall.

Native distribution Widespread in open woodlands and roadsides from the Northeast to Florida, Texas, and Mexico.

Cultivation Plants are soil- and light-tolerant, growing in full sun to full shade. They grow best in moist, well-drained, lightly acid, humus-rich soil in partial shade. They will cling to almost anything with the disks on their tendrils. Disks will leave marks on wood, brick, or other house siding materials if the vine is removed. Zones 3–9. 🦋 🍁 🐾 🌿

Rock penstemon (*Penstemon rupicola*).

Palmer's penstemon (*Penstemon palmeri*).

PENSTEMONS, BEARDTONGUES
Penstemon spp.

Penstemon is a large genus with about 250 different species native to North America. Most penstemons grow in the western states. They may be perennials or shrubs, depending on the species. Called beardtongues because of the hairy stamens protruding from the showy tubular flowers, the flowers can vary considerably in color, from purple, red, to pink, yellow, or white.

Birds Attracted

The flowers, especially the red flowers, attract hummingbirds, the major pollinators.

Female calliope hummingbird sharing the nectar-rich flowers of Parry's beardtongue (*Penstemon parryi*) with a Mexican yellow butterfly.

Anna's hummingbird feeding on the flowers of common beardtongue (*Penstemon barbatus*).

Blacked-chinned hummingbird feeding on scarlet bugler (*Penstemon centranthifolius*).

Penstemon barbatus
common beardtongue, golden-beard penstemon

An upright perennial from 1½ to 3 feet tall. It has lance-shaped, gray-green leaves. Plants bear spikes of 1- to 1 ½-inch-long pink to carmine tubular flowers between June and September.

Native distribution Found on dry rocky slopes and open forests, from southern Colorado to Arizona, into Texas and south to Mexico.

Cultivation Prefers full sun and well-drained soil. Some watering helps plants get established; otherwise only water in drought conditions. Penstemons can be grown from transplants or seed sown in fall or early spring. The plants only flower on new growth. Prune them close to the ground in fall to encourage new shoots and more prolific flowering the following year. Zones 3–8. ❈ 🦋 ✳

Penstemon centranthifolius
scarlet bugler

A perennial 1 to 4 feet tall. Between April and July, the sparsely leafed stems bear clusters of brilliant red, tubular flowers, 1 to 1¼ inches in length. The leaves are 1¼ to 3 inches long, opposite, and spatula-shaped.

Native distribution Dry chaparral, in coastal ranges from central California to Baja California.

Cultivation Scarlet bugler prefers full sun and coarse, well-drained soil. It responds well to moderate watering. Zones 8–10. ❈ 🦋 ✳

Penstemon eatonii
firecracker plant, red bugler

Deciduous, perennial shrub up to 4 feet tall and wide, with deep green, leathery leaves arranged in pairs along purplish stems. Striking red, tubular flowers, 2 to 4 inches long, appear between May and August. An excellent plant for hummingbirds.

Native distribution Southern Utah and the mountainous west into California.

Cultivation Prefers a well-drained, low-fertility soil in full sun. Avoid organic mulch and fertilizer. Requires deep watering in the first year, but is drought tolerant once established. Zones 4–9. ❈ 🦋 ✳

Penstemon palmeri
Palmer's penstemon, balloon flower, pink wild snapdragon

An upright perennial, 2 feet tall, with 3-foot flower spikes. Pale pink flowers with a pleasant honey fragrance appear from late spring to early summer.
Native distribution In desert mountains from the eastern Mojave Desert to Utah and New Mexico.
Cultivation Prefers full sun in a well-drained soil. Drought tolerant. It will reseed under favorable conditions. Zones 2–10. ❀ 🦋 ❀

Other suitable species
Parry's beardtongue (*P. parryi*), 3 to 5 feet, Zones 9–10. ❀ 🦋 ❀

SPRUCES
Picea spp.

Spruces are pyramidal evergreen trees with long, straight trunks and solid, conical tops. Elegant trees with attractive dark green or blue needles, many species are grown as garden plants. Within their range, spruces often form pure forest stands. Of the almost 45 species of spruce, 7 are native to North America.

As is the case with other conifers, the male and female flowers are borne in separate cones on the same tree. Unlike pines and other conifers, spruce cones have brittle scales and mature in one season. The female cones contain winged seeds that detach when mature. The cones hang down from the branches rather than standing upright like fir (*Abies* spp.) cones.

Birds Attracted
The winged seeds of spruces are a food source sought after by the white-winged crossbill, chickadee, red-breasted nuthatch, cedar waxwing, pine siskin, American goldfinch, and evening grosbeak. Spruces provide excellent

Colorado spruce (*Picea pungens*) with black chokecherry (*Aronia melanocarpa*) in the foreground.

year-round nesting, roosting, and winter shelter for a great variety of birds. The spruce grouse and blue grouse feed on the spruce needles rather than the seeds.

Picea engelmannii
Englemann spruce

A tall evergreen tree usually 45 to 50 feet in cultivation (may reach 100 to 125 feet), with blue-green needles 1 inch long, and 3-inch elongated cones. Male flowers are purplish and hang from the lower crown; female flowers are reddish and are upright. Fruits appear in fall and ripen in September.

Native distribution Northwest from Central British Columbia and northwest Alberta, southwest to northern California, Arizona, and New Mexico, usually in wet and boggy areas.

Cultivation An adaptable, slow-growing conifer that can live to 300 years. Prefers a sunny location but will tolerate light shade, in a moist, acid, deep soil. An excellent specimen tree. Zones 3–7.

Picea glauca
white spruce

A dense, attractive, evergreen conifer up to 80 feet tall with purple-gray, scaly bark and blue-green needles. Pendulous cones appear in early fall.

Native distribution Northern regions of North America from central Alaska, east to Newfoundland and south to northern Montana and Maine.

Cultivation Prefers full sun to partial shade in a moist, well-drained soil. A slow-growing cultivar is available: dwarf Alberta spruce (*Picea glauca* var. *albertiana* 'Conica'), 10 feet tall and 3 feet wide, with a perfect conical shape. Zones 2–6.

Picea mariana
black spruce, bog spruce

A conical-shaped tree, growing 16 to 60 feet tall. This tree has short, pendulous branches that usually end in an upward-pointing curve. The gray-brown bark is thin and scaly. Light blue-green needles are short, dense, and four-sided. Ovoid cones often hang on

Gray jay feeding on the seeds of white spruce (*Picea glauca*).

the tree for many years and can appear when the trees are only 2 to 3 feet tall.

Native distribution One of the most widely distributed conifers in North America, the black spruce often forms pure forest stands from near the northern tree limit in Alaska, east to Labrador and south to British Columbia, Minnesota, and northern New Jersey.

Cultivation Prefers a cool climate and moist or boggy conditions in full sun and acid soil. But it will grow in well-drained soils. Plant in a sheltered position, because its shallow root system makes it susceptible to strong winds. Zones 1–6. 🦋 🌳 ☻ ☙ 🐦

Picea pungens
Colorado spruce, blue spruce

A tall, slender, pyramidal or conical shaped tree, growing 65 to 98 feet tall. It has short, spreading to slightly drooping branches that may end in an upward curve. The bark is pale gray to reddish brown and scaly or furrowed. Dull green, bluish gray or silver-blue needles are short, stiff, dense, and four-sided. The bluest needles are found on *Picea pungens* var. *glauca* and related selections. Cylindrical, leathery or woody cones are 2 to 4 inches long, green, ripening to shiny chestnut-brown, yielding a crop every 2 to 3 years. Several dwarf cultivars 5 to 10 feet tall are available.

Native distribution Colorado spruce is found from the higher elevations of the Rocky Mountains (at elevations of 5,750 to 11,000 feet) south to northern Mexico.

Cultivation Colorado spruce is most striking as a specimen plant, though it can also be grown as a screen. It grows best in full sun and rich, deep, well-drained, evenly moist soil. Plants can tolerate acid soil. Zones 3–7. ☻ ☙ 🐦

Picea rubens
red spruce, yellow spruce

A column-shaped tree growing to 90 feet tall, with a conical crown and light reddish brown, scaly bark. This tree has short, dense needles that are yellowish green and four-sided. Its cones are green and leathery, and measure 1 to 2 inches long. They turn brown at maturity.

Black spruce (*Picea mariana*) cone.

Lincoln's sparrow in Engelmann spruce (*Picea engelmannii*).

Pine siskin feeding on the immature cones of Colorado spruce (*Picea pungens*).

Lodgepole pine (*Pinus contorta*) flowers.

Native distribution The red spruce is the most southward-ranging eastern spruce. Plants are found from Ontario east to Nova Scotia and New England and south to the mountains of eastern Tennessee and North Carolina.

Cultivation Requires a cool climate. Plants grow best in moist soil and full sun. Zones 3–6.

Picea sitchensis
Sitka spruce

The largest of the spruce trees, 125 to 175 feet tall, with a straight trunk and thin, scaly bark. Needlelike leaves are blue-green; the cones are pendulous, maturing to a pale brown.

Native distribution Kodiak Island to northern California mostly in temperate rain forests.

Cultivation A hardy, fast-growing tree suitable for most soils and exposed positions. A long-lived plant. Usually too large for a garden, a dwarf variety (*Picea sitchensis* 'Papoose') is available, which is slow-growing to 6 feet tall and suitable for containers. Zones 7–8.

Other suitable species

Brewer's spruce (*P. breweriana*), slow-growing, 30 to 60 feet, Zones 3–7.

Black Hills spruce (*P. glauca* 'Densata'), to 65 feet, Zones 3–7.

PINES
Pinus spp.

Pines are evergreen trees or (rarely) shrubs with long needles and woody cone fruits maturing at the end of the second or third season. There are 80 or 90 species widely distributed throughout the Northern Hemisphere from the Arctic Circle to the West Indies, Central America, northern Africa, and the Philippines. About 35 species are native to North America.

Birds Attracted

More than 38 species of birds feed on pine cone seeds, including the red crossbill, Clark's nutcracker, and white-headed woodpecker, which rely on pine cone seeds for 50 percent of their diet. Other birds that feed on the seeds include chickadees, evening and pine grosbeaks, red-breasted, white-breasted, brown-headed, and pygmy nuthatches, blue, scrub, and Steller's jays, dark-eyed juncos, pine siskin, meadowlarks, red-cockaded, Lewis, and red-bellied woodpeckers, brown creepers, brown thrasher, and pine warblers.

Pine needles are consumed by the blue, spruce, and sharp-tailed grouse. Larger pines are favorite roosting sites for migrating American robins and are common nesting sites for mourning dove, purple finch, and magnolia warbler.

Female white-winged crossbill. Crossbills pry the cone scales apart with their bill and extract the pine seeds with their tongue.

Pinus contorta
lodgepole pine, shore pine

There are two distinct forms of lodgepole pine. On the Pacific Coast, shore pine (*Pinus contorta* var. *contorta*) is a short, scrubby tree that grows 15 to 30 feet tall. Lodgepole pine is the inland variety (*Pinus contorta* var. *latifolia*) and has a tall, slender, straight trunk, reaching 80 to 150 feet. Both varieties have 1- to 3-inch-long, dark to yellowish green needles borne in pairs. The 1- to 2-inch-long cones remain closed and attached to the trees for years. They open after a fire, reseeding burned areas. American Indians traditionally used these trees for lodge poles, and hence their common name.

Native distribution Coastal Alaska south through British Columbia, east to the eastern foothills of the Rocky Mountains, Montana, and Wyoming, south to southern Colorado and northern California, and south along the Sierra Nevada to southern California.

Cultivation Adaptable, but will not tolerate drought or high humidity. It grows best in well-drained, loamy soil in full sun, but is tolerant of most conditions. It is slow-growing in cultivation. This variety is a better choice for Midwestern and Eastern gardens than shore pine.

Red crossbill feeding on the seeds of ponderosa pine (*Pinus ponderosa*).

Monterey pine (*Pinus radiata*).

The shore pine variety is usually compact and irregularly pyramidal when bought as a nursery-grown tree. It does not thrive in hot, dry areas or in climates with humid summers. It will grow on coastal sand dunes or swampy areas. The shore pine is fairly fast-growing in cultivation. It makes a good windbreak or a plant for a small garden, container, or for screening. When exposed to coastal winds, plants acquire a dwarfed, interestingly contorted habit. Both varieties. Zones 5–8.

Pinus edulis
piñon pine, nut pine, Colorado piñon

An evergreen tree with a rounded crown, reaching 15 to 35 feet tall. Needles on young trees are a striking blue, but older trees have yellowish green foliage. Needles are borne in pairs and are ½ to 2 inches long. The egg-shaped cones are about 2 inches long, with large, spatula-shaped, chestnut-brown seeds. Generally found growing at elevations between 4,500 and 7,500 feet or to 9,000 feet on south-facing slopes.
Native distribution Northern Colorado, western Oklahoma, western Texas, west Wyoming, northern and central Arizona, southwest Utah, to southern California.
Cultivation Slow-growing piñon pines prefer a sunny, well-drained position. It is drought resistant and its slow growth makes it a useful rockery garden or container plant. Zones 5–8.

Pinus ponderosa
ponderosa pine, western yellow pine

A large evergreen tree that matures to develop a loose, spirelike crown. It is straight-trunked and bushy when young. Mature plants can be 75 to 100 feet tall. The bark on mature trees is distinctive in both color and texture. It is pinkish to orange-brown in hue and grows in broad, flaky plates. Dark green needles grow 4 to 10 inches long and are borne in clusters of 2 or 3. The lustrous, spined, red-brown cones grow 3 to 6 inches long.
Native distribution Nebraska and western Texas to coastal California, and from British Columbia south to lower California and northern Mexico, usually in forests at elevations of 5,500 to 8,500 feet.

Cultivation An excellent specimen, screen, or street tree, especially on the West Coast. It prefers a well-drained, sunny location. Plants are hardy, wind and drought tolerant, and tolerate the desert heat when grown at low altitudes. Zones 3–8. 🦋 🐝 🦋 🐦 ✿

Pinus radiata
Monterey pine, radiata pine
Grows up to 60 feet tall in cultivation, with shiny, bright green needles, upward-pointing branches, and a rounded crown. The cones form every 3 to 5 years and are 3 to 7 inches long, brown, and ovoid. The bark is dark gray to brown and fissured.
Native distribution Central and coastal California.
Cultivation A popular backyard tree in coastal California. Prefers full sun and a well-drained soil. Zones 8–10. 🐝 🦋 🐦 ✿

Pinus strobus
eastern white pine
The largest northeastern conifer growing to 100 feet or more. It has soft, blue-green needles to 5 inches long in bundles of 5. With age, the smooth, gray bark becomes rough and deeply furrowed into broad scaly ridges. Brown cylindrical cones are 3 to 8 inches long and remain on the tree for 2 years or more.
Native distribution Eastern North America, from sea level to elevations of 5,000 feet in the Appalachian Mountains.
Cultivation It is a useful tree for naturalizing or as a specimen. It prefers fertile, well-drained, slightly acid soils in full sun. Zones 3–8. 🦋 🌳 🐝 🦋 🐦 ✿

....

Other suitable species
pitch pine (*P. rigida*), 40 to 60 feet, Zone 5.
🐝 🦋 🐦

digger pine (*P. sabiniana*), 40 to 80 feet, Zone 8.
🐝 🦋 🐦

loblolly pine (*P. taeda*), 80 to 100 feet, Zones 7–9.
🦋 🌳 🐝 🦋 🐦 ✿

Torrey pine (*P. torreyana*), 20 to 40 feet, Zone 7.
🐝 🦋 🐦

Virginia pine (*P. virginiana*), 40 feet, Zone 5.
🦋 🌳 🐝 🦋 🐦 ✿

Red crossbill feeding on the seed of piñon pine (*Pinus edulis*).

Pine warblers prefer to nest in pine trees.

Autumn foliage of western sycamore (*Platanus racemosa*).

SYCAMORES, PLANE TREES
Platanus spp.

Sycamores, or plane trees, are large trees with large, deciduous maplelike leaves, mottled flaky bark, and hanging fruits about the size and shape of ping-pong balls. Of the 7 species, 3 are native to North America.

Birds Attracted

The fruits are packed with seeds, which are consumed by the oriole, cedar waxwing, chickadee, goldfinch, pine siskin, house finch, purple finch, and mallard duck. Sycamores are commonly used for nesting by orioles and the acorn woodpecker, which also uses the tree as a food larder. Hummingbirds use the flower down for nest construction. Flicker, chickadee, titmouse, bluebird, tree swallow, and the screech owl are among the many birds that occupy old woodpecker holes in sycamores.

Platanus occidentalis
sycamore, American sycamore, American plane tree

A large, conspicuous tree, 115 feet or more, with a broad, irregular crown. The showy bark exfoliates in large jigsaw-puzzle pieces, creating patterns of white, green, gray, and brown. The maplelike leaves have shallow lobes, and turn gold and brown in autumn before falling. Round, green, 1-inch-diameter fruits ripen to brown, remaining on the tree into early winter.

Native distribution Low-lying areas along streams and in abandoned meadows throughout the eastern United States, from New York and Massachusetts, south to northern Florida and west to eastern Texas and the Midwestern states.

Cultivation Grow sycamore as a shade tree and specimen plant. They shed twigs, leaves, bark, and fruits. Plants prefer full sun and rich, evenly moist soil. They are tolerant of acid and alkaline soils. Zones 5–9. 🐦 🦉 🐦 🪶

Platanus racemosa

western sycamore, California sycamore

A large (40 to 90 feet), conspicuous tree, spreading 50 to 70 feet. The bark near the base of the trunk is dark brown and often deeply furrowed, but higher and on the branches, it is ashy white. The deciduous leaves have 3 to 5 deep, maplelike lobes. The ball-like fruits hang in clusters of 3 to 7, each up to 1 inch in diameter.

Native distribution: Streams and in the coastal ranges of western California and northwest Mexico.

Cultivation: A large, rapidly growing, often multi-trunked tree. Prefers full sun and is heat and wind tolerant. It tolerates a wide range of soil conditions, but prefers deep, rich, moist soil. Useful for erosion control or as a shade tree. Zones 7–10. 🍁 🐦

Other suitable species

Arizona sycamore (*P. wrightii*), 90 to 100 feet. Zones 7–10. 🍁 🐦

POPLARS, ASPENS, COTTONWOODS
Populus spp.

Large, fast-growing trees with pale bark and coarsely toothed leaves. Of the approximately 35 species, 15 are native to North America. On some parts of the prairies, they are the only trees growing. Seed capsules mature in late spring and split into two parts, releasing numerous seeds. Each seed is carried on a tuft of white cottonlike hairs, giving the plants the common name cottonwood.

Birds Attracted

Goldfinch, pine and rose-breasted grosbeak, great blue heron, sharp-tailed and ruffed grouse, California quail, and northern shrike feed on the seeds and winter buds of these plants. Many birds nest in these trees. Cavity-nesters find the natural cavities in poplars especially well suited to their needs.

Male hooded oriole feeding on insects in western sycamore (*Plantanus racemosa*).

Red-naped sapsucker on quaking aspen (*Populus tremuloides*). Woodpeckers often excavate nest hollows in the soft wood of *Populus* spp.

Song sparrow feeding on the flowers of Fremont cottonwood (*Populous fremontii*).

Populus deltoides

cottonwood, eastern cottonwood

A large, open-crowned, deciduous tree 70 to 100 feet tall. The leaves are lustrous, bright green, and triangular toothed. Male and female flowers bloom in catkins and are borne on separate trees, in spring through early summer.

Native distribution New England south along the Atlantic Coast, west to Texas and north to Minnesota and central Canada, along streams, in swamps, and lowlands.

Cultivation A fast-growing plant often chosen as a shade tree. Cottonwood prefers moist to wet soil in full sun, and tolerates both acid and alkaline soils. Be sure to plant both a female and male tree to ensure seed production. Female trees produce masses of cottony seeds. Zones 3–9. 🦋 🌱 🐝

Populus fremontii

Fremont cottonwood, valley cottonwood

A deciduous tree with a broad, flat crown, growing 40 to 90 feet tall. It has yellowish green, triangular-toothed leaves that turn golden-yellow in fall. Male and female flowers bloom in catkins and are borne on separate trees. Female trees bear loose clusters of small, light brown seed capsules.

Native distribution Desert waterholes, on stream banks and moist desert slopes of southern California, coastal areas in central California, and east to south-western Nevada, southern Utah, southern Arizona, New Mexico, and Mexico.

Cultivation It prefers moist soil and a sunny site. Be sure to plant both female and male tree to ensure seed production. Female trees produce copious masses of seed-bearing cotton fluff. Zones 6–10. 🦋 🌱 🍁 🐝

Populus tremuloides

quaking aspen, American aspen

A deciduous tree 40 to 60 feet tall, with pale, smooth bark with black scar bands, and glossy green leaves that turn yellow in fall. Long catkin flowers appear in early spring and are fed on by many bird species. The flexible, flattened stalk that attaches the leaf blade to the stem allows the leaves to quiver in the slightest breeze, giving the tree its common name. Fruit capsules appear in late spring through to early summer.

Quaking aspen (*Populus tremuloides*) in fall.

Native distribution Across Alaska and Canada, south to north Nebraska and central Indiana, and in all western U.S. states except Oklahoma and Kansas.
Cultivation Thrives in cold climates and poor soils. Fast growing in full sun or part shade in well-drained moist soil. Propagate through root sprouts forming colonies. Zones 2–6. 🦋 ⊤ 🍁

....

Other suitable species
black cottonwood, California poplar (*P. trichocarpa*), 40 to 100 feet. Zones 3–8. 🦋 ⊤ 🍁

CHERRIES, PLUMS
Prunus spp.

The showy flowers, often edible fruit, glossy leaves, and lustrous bark of cherries and plums make them prized ornamental and food plants. About 200 species are widely distributed throughout the Northern Hemisphere, and 30 species are native to North America. The foliage of some species is poisonous to livestock.

Birds Attracted
The fruits are fed on by at least 84 bird species, including the pine grosbeak, cedar waxwing, house finch, Brewer's blackbird, western tanager, black-headed grosbeak, blue and Steller's jay, orioles, band-tailed pigeon, ruffed grouse, Townsend's solitaire, American robin, bluebirds, sharp-tailed grouse, Lewis's woodpecker, downy and hairy woodpeckers, gray catbird, song sparrow, northern mockingbird, white-crowned and white-throated sparrow, flickers, rose-breasted grosbeak, red-headed woodpecker, northern cardinal, and wood, hermit, and gray-cheeked thrush.

Prunus pumila var. *besseyi*
sand cherry, western sand cherry
A variable, deciduous shrub to 4 feet high, with gray-green leaves and attractive autumn color. Showy,

Male Baltimore oriole in Canada plum (*Prunus nigra*).

Rose-breasted grosbeak feeding on the flower buds of chokecherry (*Prunus virginiana*).

Male orchard oriole feeding on the ripe fruit of black cherry (*Prunus serotina*).

Chokecherry (*Prunus virginiana*) blossoms.

Sand cherry (*Prunus pumila* var. *besseyi*).

white flowers in April to May are followed by edible black fruit in July to August.

Native distribution Sand dunes, prairies, and grasslands from the Rocky Mountains and to the northeast United States.

Cultivation Hardy and adaptable to most soils, but prefers a moist, well-drained soil in full sun. Drought tolerant. Excellent for erosion control. Zones 3–12.

Prunus pensylvanica
pin cherry, bird cherry, fire cherry, wild red cherry

A large shrub or small tree, usually less than 30 feet tall (though it may reach 50 feet) with a rounded crown. Ornamental all year, the tree produces a mass of white blossoms in spring, followed by small red fruits that ripen in late summer. The shiny, yellowish green, lance-shaped leaves turn yellow-orange to bright red in autumn. The shiny bark is dark reddish brown.

Native distribution Most wooded parts of Canada from British Columbia to Newfoundland, south to northern Georgia and west to Colorado.

Cultivation Attractive in naturalistic plantings. In dry soils, they may only grow to shrub size. Pin cherries prefer a moist, rich soil in full sun, though they tolerate a wide range of conditions, including poor soil. Zones 3–7.

Prunus virginiana
chokecherry, common chokecherry

A variable plant, sometimes reaching 25 feet in height but often only 9 or 10 feet. These shrubs or small trees often develop in loose thickets, since they sucker freely. The finely toothed, oval leaves are dark green and shiny. The 5-petaled white flowers appear in spring in cylindrical clusters about 6 inches long. Small, dark red cherries ripen in late August or early September.

Native distribution Saskatchewan to Newfoundland and south to North Carolina, Missouri, and Kansas.

Cultivation Best for naturalized areas where there is room for it to spread. It prefers moist soil in an open, sunny situation. Relatively intolerant of shade. Chokecherries are plagued by eastern tent caterpillars, so be prepared to prune off infested parts. Zones 3–5.

Other suitable species

bitter cherry (*P. emarginata*), 30 feet, Zone 7.
🦋 🌱 🍁 ✿

hollyleaf cherry (*P. ilicifolia*), 6 to 25 feet, Zone 7.
🦋 🌱 🍁

Catalina cherry (*P. lyonii*), 15 to 35 feet, Zone 8.
🦋 🍁 ✿

Canada plum (*P. nigra*), 25 to 30 feet, Zones 3–6.
🦋 🌱 🍁 ✿

black cherry (*P. serotina*), 30 to 50 feet, Zones 4–9.
🦋 🌱 🍁 ✿

Bridled titmouse foraging for insects in Emory oak (*Quercus emoryi*).

OAKS
Quercus spp.

Oaks are among the most picturesque trees and shrubs in North America. Most oaks are deciduous, while others are evergreen and sometimes referred to as live oaks. Acorns are an important source of nourishment to wildlife. There are over 200 species widely distributed in the northern temperate regions, Central and South America, and southeast Asia. In all, 75 to 80 species are native to North America, 50 of which are trees.

Birds Attracted

Oaks provide food, shelter, and nesting sites. Acorn woodpeckers feed on acorns and store them for future use. Chickadees, titmice, northern cardinal, flickers, ruffed grouse, blue jay, meadowlarks, white-breasted nuthatch, mourning dove, hermit thrush, wood duck, mallard duck, bobwhites, California quail, evening grosbeaks, and downy, red-headed, and hairy woodpeckers feed on the acorns and insects attracted to the plants. Rose-breasted grosbeak feeds on the male flowers, and the scarlet tanager often nests in the trees.

Female acorn woodpecker in California black oak (*Quercus kelloggii*), storing acorns.

Song sparrow singing from the top of an Oregon oak (*Quercus garryana*).

Laurel oak (*Quercus laurifolia*).

The rough bark of blackjack oak (*Quercus marilandica*).

Quercus agrifolia
California live oak, coast live oak

Large, evergreen tree or medium shrub 15 to 50 feet and 15 to 30 feet wide. Leaves are glossy, deep green, rigid, and spiny toothed. It produces an acorn crop each year that attracts a wide variety of wildlife.

Native distribution West of the Sierra Nevada, it is the most common oak of the California coast and foothills, from Sonoma County south to Mexico.

Cultivation Adaptable to most garden conditions, it prefers a dry, free-draining soil in full sun or part shade. It is drought tolerant and is a host plant for several butterfly species. Zones 8–9.

Quercus alba
white oak

A large, deciduous tree that grows 80 to 100 feet tall. It has wide, spreading branches that become gnarled and twisted, giving the tree a rugged appearance. The bright green leaves have 7 to 9 lobes each, and they turn a deep, rich, red or brown-red in autumn. They often remain on the branches through the winter. The oval ½- to ¾ inch-long acorns are borne singly or in pairs and mature in only one season.

Native distribution Woodlands and woodlots from southern Maine to Quebec and southern Ontario south to northern Florida, west to eastern Texas and north to Minnesota.

Cultivation A slow-growing tree, it grows best in full sun in deep, moist soils with good drainage, but will grow well in most conditions. Zones 4–9.

Quercus emoryi
Emory oak, black oak, blackjack oak

A large shrub to medium-sized semievergreen tree, reaching 20 to 50 feet tall with a 2½-foot trunk diameter. The leathery, dark green, pointed leaves are 1 to 2½ inches long, remaining on the tree until spring, creating an evergreen effect. The acorns are oval and dark brown to nearly black; they are sweet and edible.

Native distribution In moist areas, especially in canyons where it forms dense forests. Native to the lower mountain slopes from western Texas, southern New Mexico, and Arizona south into northern Mexico.

Cultivation Emory oak reaches its greatest size and most beautiful form in deep, moist, well-drained soils in full sun. It will tolerate a variety of soils, but needs

regular deep watering in summer. It can be grown from acorns after removing the cup and inspecting for insects. Keep the nursery bed shaded and moist until top growth occurs. Growth rate is 1 to 2 feet per year. Zones 7–9. ✖ ⊤ 🐻 🐿 🕊).

Quercus falcata
southern red oak, Spanish oak

An excellent deciduous shade tree, growing 60 to 80 feet in height, with a large, rounded canopy, straight trunk, and dark brown to black bark that is ridged and furrowed. The leaves are shiny green, 5 to 9 inches long, and turn brown in fall. Acorns appear in fall. The tree is an important food tree for wildlife.
Native distribution Widespread in the southeast, south from New Jersey to Florida, and west to Texas.
Cultivation Grows well in full sun or part shade, in dry sandy or clay soils. Zones 7–9. ✖ ⊤ 🐻 🐿 🕊

Pin oak (*Quercus palustris*).

Red oak (*Quercus rubra*).

Quercus gambelii
Gambel oak, Utah oak, Rocky Mountain oak

A deciduous shrub or small tree growing 20 to 30 feet tall (rarely to 50 feet) with a rounded crown. Some plants may only grow to 6 feet and form thickets by creeping underground roots. Leaves are deeply lobed and turn yellow and reddish in autumn before dropping. Edible acorns may reach 1 inch long.
Native distribution Widespread in southwestern Texas west to southwestern Wyoming, Utah, and southern Nevada, and south to Arizona, New Mexico, and northern Mexico. Common in the foothills south of Denver. These trees grow at elevations of 5,000 to 8,000 feet.
Cultivation The mature size varies according to location; in dry soils, it is usually a dense-growing shrub or low tree. Plants reach their largest size in moist, sheltered positions in full sun. This plant is a slow grower. Zones 6–9. ✖ ⊤ 🍁 🐻 🐿 🕊

Quercus garryana
Oregon oak, Garry oak

An important tree for wildlife, it is deciduous, from 35 to 60 feet tall, or sometimes a shrub 3 to 15 feet tall. Green leaves have 3 to 7 deep lobes and turn yellow to coppery brown in fall. Catkin flowers are followed by small, reddish brown acorns that appear year-round.

White-breasted nuthatch foraging for insects in the rough bark of Arizona white oak (*Quercus arizonica*).

Blue jay feeding on the acorns of southern red oak (*Quercus falcata*).

A majestic oak, the intricate branching pattern gives the tree an intriguing sculptural form in winter.
Native distribution Southwestern British Columbia to southern California.
Cultivation A slow-growing tree, it prefers full sunshine in dry, well-drained soil with no summer watering. Drought tolerant. It grows larger and dense in fertile soils and smaller in infertile rocky conditions, but tends to stay shrubby in garden conditions.

Brewer's oak (*Quercus garryana* var. *breweri*) is a slow-growing dwarf form that grows 3 to 15 feet tall and 3 to 10 feet wide. Zone 7. 🦋 🌱 🐾 🍂 🐦 ✒

Quercus kelloggii
California black oak, Kellogg oak

A deciduous tree from 30 to 80 feet tall, with thick, spreading branches forming an open, rounded crown. New foliage is soft pink, maturing to glossy green, turning yellow or orange-yellow in autumn. Leaves are 1 to 1½ inches long with 7 sharply pointed lobes. Cylindrical acorns take 2 seasons to mature.
Native distribution Southern California, north to southwestern Oregon, in coastal ranges and in the Sierra Nevada.
Cultivation Suitable for large gardens or street planting. It prefers full sun and can tolerate clay or dry, gravelly soils. Plants have slow to moderate growth rate. Zones 5–8. 🦋 🌱 🍁 🐾 🍂 🐦 ✒

Quercus laurifolia
laurel oak, diamond-leaf oak

A deciduous shade tree, growing from 60 to 70 feet, with a large, rounded crown. Insignificant flowers in spring are followed by a frequently heavy acorn crop.
Native distribution Southeast from coastal Virginia to central Florida, west to southeastern Texas.
Cultivation A fast-growing tree, it prefers full sun to partial shade, in a deep, well-drained soil. It is frost hardy and an attractive specimen tree. Zones 6–9.
🦋 🌱 🍁 🐾 🍂 🐦 ✒

Quercus marilandica
blackjack oak

A small deciduous oak, 20 to 30 feet tall, with dark, glossy green, flared, 3-lobed leaves that turn red to brown in fall. The bark is dark and rough. Acorns appear in fall.

Native distribution In poor, thin soils in central and southeastern United States.

Cultivation Prefers full sun or part shade in dry, well-drained soil. Adaptable and hardy, will tolerate poor soils and is a valuable tree for growing in problem areas. Zones 5–9. 🦋 🌱 🍁 ☻ 🐿 🐦 🪶

Quercus palustris
pin oak

A medium-sized, attractive tree growing from 60 to 75 feet. Its lustrous dark green leaves turn deep red to bronze in autumn. Flower catkins in late winter are followed by acorns appearing throughout fall.

Native distribution Bottomlands and moist uplands in Ontario, south to Connecticut, west to Kansas, eastern Oklahoma, and south to Georgia.

Cultivation Fast-growing, it prefers moist, acidic soil in full sun or partial shade. Excellent street tree. Zones 3–8. 🦋 🌱 🍁 ☻ 🐿 🐦 🪶

Oak titmouse, a resident bird in West Coast oak woodland.

Live oak (*Quercus virginiana*).

Quercus rubra
red oak, northern red oak

A medium-size deciduous tree, from 60 to 80 feet tall, with a 3- to 5-foot-diameter trunk and a wide, rounded crown. The large leaves may reach almost 9 inches in length and have 7 to 9 sharply pointed lobes. Fall color is a deep to brilliant red. Acorns are large and cylindrical, taking 2 seasons to mature; plants bear enormous acorn crops every 2 to 5 years.

Native distribution Southeastern Canada and throughout the eastern United States, west to Kansas and Minnesota, and south to Georgia.

Cultivation It is the fastest growing oak, and is easier to transplant than other oaks. Plants prefer well-drained, evenly moist soil in full sun. Red oak tolerates acid soil. Zones 3–9. 🦋 🌱 🍁 ☻ 🐿 🐦 🪶

Quercus virginiana
live oak, southern live oak

A medium-size evergreen tree growing from 40 to 50 feet tall, with a 3- to 4-foot-diameter trunk and a wide-spreading and irregular crown. Foliage is shiny, dark green, and oval, usually with smooth edges. Slender oval acorns are about 1 inch long. This low, spreading tree, often covered with trailing Spanish moss, is a symbol of the South.

Native distribution The Gulf Coast from southeastern Virginia south to southern Florida and west to southern and central Texas, southwestern Oklahoma, and northeastern Mexico, in sandy soils, coastal dunes, and inland from 300 to 2,000 feet in elevation.

Cultivation Popular shade and ornamental tree in the southern United States, where it reaches its greatest size. The tree is often much smaller and occasionally only shrub size. Plants prefer deep, well-drained, evenly moist soil in a sunny location. They tolerate acid soil but can be damaged by drought. Best results achieved in the warmer parts of Zone 8 and in Zone 9; plants will grow in the colder parts of Zone 8 and the warmer parts of Zone 7, but they will not grow as tall.

🦋 🌱 👁 🌿 🗡

Southern red oak (*Quercus falcata*) in autumn.

Nuttal's oak (*Quercus nuttallii*).

Other suitable species

Arizona white oak (*Q. arizonica*), 60 feet, Zone 7. 🦋 🌱 👁 🌿 🐦

swamp white oak (*Q. bicolor*), 65 to 115 feet, Zones 4–8. 🦋 🌱 👁 🌿 🐦 🗡

canyon live oak (*Q. chrysolepis*), 25 to 100 feet, Zones 8–10. 🦋 🌱 👁 🌿 🐦

scarlet oak (*Q. coccinea*), 65 to 100 feet, Zones 5–9. 🍁 👁 🌿 🐦 🗡

blue oak (*Q. douglasii*), 20 to 60 feet, Zone 7. 🦋 🌱 👁 🌿 🐦

Engelmann Oak (*Q. engelmannii*), 20 to 50 feet, Zone 7. 🦋 🌱 👁 🌿 🐦 🗡

Nuttal's oak (*Q. nuttallii*), 40 to 60 feet, Zones 5–9. 🍁 👁 🌿 🐦 🗡

Shumard oak (*Q. shumardii*), 65 to 100 feet, Zones 6–9. 🍁 👁 🌿 🐦 🗡

AZALEAS, RHODODENDRONS
Rhododendron spp.

Rhododendron is an enormous genus of evergreen, semievergreen, and deciduous shrubs and some small trees. There are 800 species spread throughout Asia, central Europe, and North America, including some of our most colorful and beloved woodland plants. Some native species grow in swamps, clay, or sandy soils.

Pinxterbloom azalea (*Rhododendron periclymenoides*).

Birds Attracted

Rhododendrons provide food and shelter for many kinds of birds. In the mountains of northern Georgia and Virginia, rhododendron thickets are the most common nesting sites for the rose-breasted grosbeak. Hummingbirds visit the flowers for nectar, and warblers swarm over the flowers and foliage for insects. Ruffed grouse feeds on the buds.

Rhododendron calendulaceum
flame azalea

A deciduous shrub 10 to 12 feet tall, with a rounded shape and tiered branches. Foliage is oval and deep green. Plants bear showy clusters of tubular orange, red, or yellow flowers between May and June. Seed capsules are inconspicuous.

Native distribution Moist woods from southwestern Pennsylvania and southern Ohio south through the mountains to Georgia and Alabama.

Cultivation Plants prefer an evenly moist, well-drained, humus-rich soil, in partial to light shade in an acid soil. Zones 5–9. 🦋 ❀ 🐦 🍃

Pacific rhododendron (*Rhododendron macrophyllum*).

Rhododendron occidentale
western azalea

A deciduous shrub, 4 to 15 feet tall with egg-shaped, bright green leaves, and clusters of fragrant, white to deep pink flowers from April to August. Seed capsules are inconspicuous.

Native distribution Southwestern Oregon to southern California in partial shade along stream banks and other moist places.

Cultivation Prefers a moist, acid, humus-rich soil. Propagate plants by seed, cuttings, or layering. Suitable for shaded areas. Zones 7–9. 🦋 ❀ 🍃 🐦

Rhodora (*Rhododendron canadense*).

Other suitable species

Carolina rhododendron (*R. carolinianum*), to 6 feet, Zones 5–7. 🦋 ❀

catawba rhododendron (*R. catawbiense*), 6 to 10 feet, Zones 4–7. 🦋 ❀ 🐦 🍃

Pacific rhododendron (*R. macrophyllum*), 6 to 25 feet, Zones 7–9. 🦋 ❀

rosebay rhododendron (*R. maximum*), 10 to 15 feet, Zones 5–6. 🦋 ❀

pinxterbloom azalea (*R. periclymenoides*), to 9 feet, Zones 5–8. 🦋 ❀

The showy fruits of smooth sumac (*Rhus glabra*).

Lemonade berry (*Rhus integrifolia*) in bud.

SUMACS
Rhus spp.

Sumacs are colorful, familiar roadside plants with spectacular fall color and showy seed heads. There are 16 species native to North America, widely distributed from Canada to southern Mexico; 4 of these are trees.

Birds Attracted

Sumacs provide valuable winter food for a wide variety of birds. At least 98 species of birds are known to feed on the fruits, including flickers, red-headed and downy woodpecker, chickadees, American robins, bluebirds, tanagers, sparrow, bobwhites, wild turkey, phoebe, hermit and Swainson's thrush, white-eyed vireo, gray catbird, wood thrush, towhees, and white-crowned sparrow. The plants also provide valuable shelter for birds.

Rhus copallinum
winged sumac

Deciduous tree 10 to 18 feet tall and wide, with a rounded crown. Dark green foliage turns an attractive orange-red in fall. Small yellow flowers appear in summer, followed by small red clusters of berries that persist through winter.
Native distribution Widespread in eastern North America from Maine to eastern Texas and Florida.
Cultivation A hardy, drought-tolerant plant. Plant in full sun or part shade in most soils. Suitable for containers. Zones 4–9. 🦋 ⵣ 🍁 ❀ 🦎

Rhus glabra
smooth sumac

Growing 10 to 20 feet tall with smooth branches. Leaves are large, compound, and deciduous with good fall color. Female plants bear showy bright red fruits.
Native distribution Eastern Saskatchewan east to southern Ontario and Maine, south to Florida and central Texas, and from British Columbia south to the Mexican border at elevations of 7,000 feet.

Cultivation Extremely adaptable to soil type; prefers well-drained sites in full sun. Tends to form large colonies and may need containing. Zones 3–9.

Rhus integrifolia
lemonade berry, sourberry

An aromatic shrub 4 to 10 feet tall and 10 to 15 feet wide with simple, toothed, evergreen leaves that have a waxy appearance. Small, pinkish flowers appear from February to May, followed by clustered reddish fruits. Fruits are covered in down.
Native distribution Coastal southern California.
Cultivation Prefers well-drained soil in full sun with some summer watering. It is frost sensitive. Drought tolerant when established. Suitable for seaside planting and can be pruned for hedging or as required. A sour lemonadelike drink can be made by mixing the berries with water. Zones 9–10.

Rhus typhina
staghorn sumac

Very ornamental with spectacular autumn foliage and showy fruits. A large, flat-crowned, deciduous shrub, from 10 to 15 feet tall, but may reach 30 feet. Staghorn sumac produces numerous suckers, forming large clumps. The large, compound leaves are dull green, turning brilliant orange to scarlet in autumn. Dense clusters of yellowish green flowers appear in July, followed by cone-shaped clusters of red, hairy fruits on the female plants, which remain through most of winter. Male and female flowers are on separate plants.
Native distribution Southern Ontario east to Nova Scotia, south to South Carolina, west to Tennessee and Iowa, and north to Minnesota.
Cultivation Best results in evenly moist but well-drained soil in full sun. They will grow in poor or acid soil, are cold-tolerant, and spread rapidly. They require room to spread, or may need containment. Zones 3–8.

Other suitable species
fragrant sumac (*R. aromatica*), 2 to 3½ feet, Zones 3–9.
sugar bush (*R. ovata*), 10 feet, Zones 7–10.
three-leaf sumac (*R. trilobata*), 3 to 12 feet, Zones 4–9.

Sumacs are an excellent source of winter food for resident birds including the black-capped chickadees.

Fall foliage of staghorn sumac (*Rhus typhina*).

Female rufous hummingbird feeding in red-flowering currant (*Ribes sanguineum*).

Fuchsia-flowering gooseberry (*Ribes speciosum*).

CURRANTS, GOOSEBERRIES
Ribes spp.

A genus of about 180 species, common to the northern hemisphere. Widespread in North America, 31 species are found in California, 30 of which are deciduous. Gooseberries have spines or bristles, while currants are unarmed. Gooseberry flowers are singular; currant flowers are in racemes.

Birds Attracted

Many birds, including sparrows, bluebirds, northern flicker, and thrushes, enjoy the pulpy fruits. The prickly branches are excellent shelter and nesting habitat, and the tubular flowers attract hummingbirds.

Ribes sanguineum
pink-flowering currant, red-flowering currant

A drought-tolerant, deciduous shrub growing to 6 to 10 feet tall, with aromatic dark green leaves. As the leaves emerge in early spring, red to pink tubular flowers are produced on racemes of 5 to 30 flowers. Dark purple berries follow.

Native distribution Western North American coast and coastal ranges, from central British Columbia, south to central California.

Cultivation Prefers a sunny to partially shaded spot and well-drained fertile soil. There are several cultivars with flowers ranging from white to dark red. Suitable for formal gardens. Zones 6–8.

Ribes speciosum
fuchsia-flowering gooseberry

A low-growing, dense, evergreen shrub, with spiny stems and red tubular flowers that are followed by glossy red fruits. Growing 4 to 6 feet tall with a spread of 3 feet. The spiny stems make it an excellent barrier plant.

Native distribution Central and southern coastal California.

Cultivation Full sun or part shade, in most soils, but prefers a well-drained, humus-rich soil. Ideal for small garden spaces, it will thrive trained against a south- or west-facing wall. Flowers are showy cherry red blossoms, from mid to late spring. Zones 6–10.
✤ ✤ ✤ ✤

....

Other suitable species

golden currant (*R. aureum*), 3 to 8 feet tall, Zones 2–6. ✤ ✤ ✤ ✤ ✤

Missouri gooseberry (*R. missouriense*), 5 to 6 feet tall, Zones 3–5. ✤ ✤ ✤ ✤ ✤

ROSES
Rosa spp.

Roses are upright, trailing, or climbing shrubs with ornamental 5-petaled flowers and thorny stems. Their red fruits are known as rose hips. There are more than 100 native species of roses, many of which are widespread in North America.

Birds Attracted

Roses provide secure nesting sites for many birds, including the indigo bunting, northern cardinal, towhees, and sparrows. At least 42 species feed on the fruits, including the waxwings, wood thrush, northern cardinal, American robin, bluebirds, northern mockingbird, grosbeaks, ruffed and sharp-tailed grouse, bobwhites, goldfinches, vireos, and chickadees. The rose hips persist through the winter, making native roses a valuable cold-weather food source.

Rosa arkansana
prairie wild rose

A variable shrub 1 to 3 feet tall with prickly stems and fragrant pink or white flowers in mid-spring to early summer. In summer, red to purple berrylike fruits are fed on by at least 38 bird species.

Native distribution Central North America from Alberta to Texas and northeast to New York.

Golden currant (*Ribes aureum*) flowers.

Eastern bluebird feeding on rosehips (*Rosa* sp.).

Prairie rose (*Rosa arkansana*).

Northern cardinal feeding on rosehips of Carolina rose (*Rosa carolina*).

California rose (*Rosa californica*).

Thimbleberry (*Rubus parviflorus*).

Cultivation Prefers well-drained soil and full sun, but will tolerate light shade. It dies back to ground level each winter. Zones 2–5.

Rosa nutkana
Nootka rose
A thorny shrub 2 to 13 feet tall with toothed, deeply ribbed leaflets. Pink, single, 2- to 3-inch-wide flowers from May to July. Fruits are long, berrylike, reddish purple hips.

Native distribution Alaska to northern California, Utah, and Colorado, in woods, open mountain fields, and coastal areas.

Cultivation An excellent living hedge with attractive fruits, suitable for most situations. Plants prefer well-drained soil and full sun, but will tolerate light shade. Zones 4–6.

Rosa virginiana
Virginia rose
A low, thorny shrub, 4 to 6 feet tall. Compound leaves are glossy deep green, turning orange-red in fall. Plants bear single, 2- to 2 ½-inch-wide, purplish pink flowers in early summer, followed by showy rose hips from early fall to winter.

Native distribution Newfoundland south to Georgia and Alabama and west to Missouri.

Cultivation An attractive rose for massing, naturalizing, and border plantings. Plants prefer well-drained, evenly moist soil in full sun, and can tolerate acid soil. Zones 4–7.

Other suitable species
California rose (*R. californica*), 5 to 10 feet, Zone 6.

Carolina or American wild rose (*R. carolina*), to 4 feet, Zones 5–8.

Cherokee rose (*R. laevigata*), to 20 feet, Zones 8–9.

Sonoma ground rose (*R. spithamea*), 12 inches, Zone 7.

BRAMBLES
Rubus spp.

Brambles are a large genus of usually thorny shrubs. The fruit is produced as a cluster of fleshy drupelets, each with a seed inside. In raspberries, the berry slips off its receptacle (the stem end), while in blackberries, the berry remains attached to the receptacle.

Birds Attracted

Brambles are valuable plants for birds. They provide shelter, protection, food, and secure nesting sites for a great variety of birds, including northern cardinal, yellow warbler, buntings, and towhees. At least 149 species of birds feed on the fruits, including the tufted titmouse, red-headed woodpecker, American robin, wood thrush, bluebirds, cedar waxwing, orchard oriole, and Baltimore oriole, rose-breasted grosbeak, northern cardinal, flickers, and sparrows.

Rubus allegheniensis
common blackberry

A thicket-forming, deciduous shrub with prickly stems, 2 to 10 feet tall. Plants may remain low in open land, reaching only 1 to 2 feet in height. Leaves are compound, with 3 to 5 egg-shaped green leaflets. White flowers 1 inch wide are followed by sweet, succulent blackberries in summer.
Native distribution Common in clearings and dry meadows of northeastern and northcentral North America, from Nova Scotia south to Georgia, west to Oklahoma and Nebraska, and also from British Columbia south to California.
Cultivation A fast-growing and vigorous plant in most conditions. It prefers a rich, moist soil in an open sunny location. A corner position allowing ample room for growth is best. Zones 4–7. 🦋 🌱 🍁 ❀ 🐦 🌿

House finch feeding on the fruit of common blackberry (*Rubus allegheniensis*).

Kentucky warbler feeding its chicks. Ground-nesting birds often seek the protection of brambles.

Rufous hummingbird feeding on salmonberry (*Rubus spectabilis*) flowers.

Orange coneflower (*Rudbeckia fulgida*).

Rubus leucodermis
black raspberry, western raspberry

A prickly, thicket-forming shrub, 3 to 5 feet tall with yellowish canes. It is distinguished by its yellow-green, sharply toothed leaves, that are covered with whitish hairs on the undersides. Clusters of whitish flowers are followed by rounded, reddish or purple-black fruits in summer.

Native distribution Widespread, from British Columbia to California, east to Montana and Utah in canyons and on wooded slopes.

Cultivation Prefers a rich, moist soil in an open, sunny position. Suitable for naturalizing in wild gardens. Plant these spiny shrubs away from pedestrian areas. Zones 5–6. ❌ 🍁 ✿ 🐦 🍃

Rubus parviflorus
thimbleberry, white-flowering raspberry

A dense, evergreen bramble 3 to 6 feet high, differing from other brambles because it is without prickles. Large, fragrant flowers appear in early to midsummer, followed by edible fruits that ripen to a bright red in mid to late summer.

Native distribution Widespread in western North America from Alaska, east to Ontario and Michigan, south to northern Mexico.

Cultivation Prefers full sun to light shade in a dry-ish, well-drained soil. Grows 3 to 4 feet, Zones 4–7. 🦋 🍁 ✿ 🐦 🍃

Other suitable species

red raspberry (*R. idaeus*), 3 to 9 feet, Zones 5–8. 🦋 🍴 ✿ 🐦 🍃

salmonberry (*R. spectabilis*), prostrate to 5 feet, Zones 6–7. 🦋 🍁 ✿ 🐦 🍃

CONEFLOWERS
Rudbeckia spp.

Coneflowers, the beloved black-eyed Susan of roadsides, prairies, and meadows, are the quintessential American wildflowers. About 25 species of these annual, biennial, and perennial daisies are native to North America.

Birds Attracted

The seeds of coneflowers are favorites of finches, including house finch, purple finch, and gold-finches. Other birds that enjoy coneflower seeds include chickadees, northern cardinal, sparrows, nuthatches, towhees, and titmice.

Rudbeckia fulgida
orange coneflower

Perennial plants 1½ to 3 feet tall, with showy, yellow-orange daisy flowers, 2 to 2½ inches wide with dark brown cone-shaped centers. They flower in July through September. The oval leaves are true green, rough, and hairy. Seed heads remain on the plant over winter.

Native distribution Found along roadsides and in meadows and woods' edges from Connecticut to West Virginia, west to Michigan, Illinois, and Missouri, and south to Alabama.

Cultivation An excellent plant in a wildflower meadow or perennial border. Prefers moist, well-drained, average to rich soil, in full sun to light shade. Divide plants every 2 or 3 years. Grows readily from seed sown outdoors in spring or fall. Plants often self-sow. Zones 3–9. 🦋 ❀

Rudbeckia nitida
shining coneflower

A perennial plant 3 to 4 feet tall with yellow daisy flowers 2 to 3 inches wide with green to brown centers (cones). It blooms in July and August. Leaves are dark green, oval shaped, and sparsely toothed. The seed heads remain over winter and provide excellent food for birds.

Native distribution Meadows and woods' edges from Quebec to northern Florida and west to Texas and the Rocky Mountains.

Cultivation Thriving in moist soil, it is ideal for a damp meadow in average to rich soil, in full sun or light shade. Grows readily from seed sown outdoors in spring or fall. Plants often self-sow. Divide plants every 3 to 5 years. Plants may need staking. Zones 4–9. 🦋 ❀

Brown-eyed Susan (*Rudbeckia triloba*).

Great coneflower (*Rudbeckia maxima*).

Black-eyed Susan (*Rudbeckia hirta*).

Other suitable species

black-eyed Susan (*R. hirta*), 2 to 3 feet tall, Zones 3–10. 🦋 ⊤ ❋

ragged coneflower (*R. laciniata*), 2 ½ to 6 feet tall, Zones 3–9. 🦋 ❋

great coneflower (*R. maxima*), 5 to 6 feet tall, Zones 3–9. 🦋 ❋

brown-eyed Susan (*R. triloba*), 2 to 3 feet tall, Zones 3–10. 🦋 ❋

SAGES
Salvia spp.

Salvia is the largest genus of plants in the mint family, with over 900 species. There are 47 species native to North America. Mostly are woody subshrubs, with strongly scented opposite leaves of varying shapes and sizes and long-blooming flowers produced in tiered racemes.

Birds Attracted

The nectar-rich flowers are a magnet for hummingbirds and butterflies.

Salvia clevelandii
Cleveland sage

Perennial evergreen shrub 3 to 5 feet tall and wide, with fragrant, small, blue-green leaves and blue to lavender, trumpet-shaped flowers on 12-inch spikes between June and July.
Native distribution Southern California Coast south to Baja California.
Cultivation Prefers dry summers in well-drained soil in full sun. Several cultivars are available. Zones 8–11. 🐦 🦋 ❋

Salvia coccinea
scarlet sage, Texas sage

An annual wildflower in cold climates where the winter temperatures are below freezing, and a perennial subshrub in warmer climates. An ideal wildflower for a hummingbird garden, growing 2 to 4 feet tall, with 1- to 2-inch triangular leaves on long stems. The showy flowers are bright red and appear continuously from

Hummingbird sage (*Salvia spathacea*).

early summer until the first frost. Prefers full sun but will tolerate some shade.

Native distribution In dry soils from South Carolina, south to Florida, and west to Texas.

Cultivation Fast growing and drought tolerant. Prefers well-drained soil. There are several cultivars. Zones 4–9. ❧ 🦋 ✹

Salvia greggii
autumn sage, cherry sage, Mexican sage

A mounding evergreen shrub up to 4 feet tall and 2 feet wide. Flowers may be red, pink, or white. The leaves are small and leathery.

Native distribution Rocky soils in southwest Texas through the Chihuahuan Desert to Mexico.

Cultivation The plant will grow in full sun or part shade in well-drained soil. It is drought tolerant and will withstand extreme heat. Regular pruning is suggested, because the plants can become woody and spindly. Many cultivars are available with showy flowers. Flowers appear from March until frost. Zones 7–9. ❧ 🦋 ✹

Salvia spathacea
hummingbird sage

An evergreen perennial 1 to 2 feet tall and 4 to 5 feet wide. Leaves are arrow-shaped, light green, and approximately 6 inches long. Magenta flowers are tubular and 1 inch long, held on 30-inch-tall spikes from March to May.

Native distribution Coastal California from the Napa Valley to Orange County.

Cultivation Easy to grow, in cool sun or semishade, in well-drained soil, spreading by underground rhizomes. Drought and frost tolerant. Several cultivars are available.
Zones 9–11. ❧ 🦋 ✹

Other suitable species

blue sage (*S. azurea*), 3 to 4 feet, Zones 5–9.
❧ 🦋 ✹

black sage (*S. mellifera*), 3 to 6 feet, Zones 7–9.
❧ 🦋 ✹

little-leaf sage (*S. microphylla*), 1 to 3 feet, Zones 7–9.
❧ 🦋 ✹

Anna's hummingbird feeding in Cleveland's sage (*Salvia clevelandii*).

Black sage (*Salvia mellifera*).

Scarlet sage (*Salvia coccinea*).

The fruits of red elderberry (*Sambucus racemosa*) are eaten by many birds including the band-tailed pigeon (above) and the black-headed grosbeak (below).

ELDERBERRIES
Sambucus spp.

Elderberries are members of the honeysuckle family, and number about 20 species of shrubs and trees. The elderberry group is widely distributed throughout the temperate regions. Of the 9 or 10 species native to North America, 3 are trees. The deciduous leaves are large and pinnately divided. Flowers are borne in large, umbrella-shaped clusters, followed by hanging berries in loose clusters in autumn.

Birds Attracted

Elderberries are an important source of food for birds: at least 120 species feed on the fruits. American robins often begin feeding on the berries before they ripen. Other species include eastern and western bluebird, rose-breasted and black-headed grosbeak, towhees, white-crowned sparrow, red-headed wood-pecker, flickers, phainopepla, blue jay, red-eyed vireo, brown thrasher, gray catbird, northern mockingbird, cedar waxwing, white-breasted nuthatch, titmice, doves, and finches. The plants also provide nesting sites for many birds, including warblers, grosbeaks, and goldfinches.

Sambucus caerulea
blue elderberry

Blue elderberry is a shrub or a small tree growing about 15 to 30 feet tall, occasionally 50 feet. It has a spread of 15 to 30 feet and is variable in shape. Foliage has 5 to 7 oblong leaflets. The fragrant, creamy white flowers are borne in flat-topped clusters between April and August and are followed by clusters of blue-black fruits.

Native distribution Western Montana to New Mexico, west to southern California and north to coastal British Columbia.

Cultivation Blue elderberry is an excellent specimen, screening, or windbreak plant with a moderate to rapid growth rate. This elderberry prefers a moist, well-drained soil in full sun. Plants can be propagated from seed or cuttings and can be pruned during winter as required. Zones 6–9. 🐝 🍃

Sambucus canadensis
American elder, elderberry, common elderberry

American elderberry forms a deciduous shrub to 10 feet tall or a small tree to 16 feet. Compound leaves are gray-green and don't change color before they drop in fall. Fragrant white flowers are borne in 10-inch clusters in late spring and early summer and are followed by shiny black to purplish black berries from midsummer to early fall.

Native distribution The American elderberry is found from southeast Manitoba east to Nova Scotia, south to southern Florida, and west to western Texas. It grows at elevations up to 5,000 feet.

Cultivation Prefers evenly moist, well-drained soil in an open, sunny location, though plants are drought-tolerant. They will also grow in areas of wet soil, along stream banks or near ponds, and can tolerate acid soil. Zones 3–9. 🌾 🦋 ⊤ ❀ 🐝 🍃

Other suitable species
Mexican elderberry (*S. mexicana*), 20 to 30 feet, Zones 8–10. 🦋 🍁 ❀ 🐝 🍃

red elderberry (*S. racemosa*), 20 feet, Zones 4–7. 🦋 🍁 ❀ 🐝 🍃 🌾

Pacific Coast red elderberry (*S. racemosa* var. *callicarpa*), 9 feet, Zone 6. 🦋 🍁 ❀ 🐝 🍃 🌾

MOUNTAIN ASHES
Sorbus spp.

The mountain ashes are trees and shrubs with smooth, aromatic bark, deciduous leaves, and showy red or orange berries. Unrelated to ashes, they are members of the rose family. Of the more than 80 species widely distributed in cooler parts of the Northern Hemisphere, about 6 species are native to North America.

Blue elderberry (*Sambucus caerulea*) fruits.

Immature cedar waxwing feeding on showy mountain ash (*Sorbus decora*).

Showy mountain ash (Sorbus decora) fall color.

Showy mountain ash buds.

Birds Attracted

Mountain ash berries are a favorite winter food of song and game birds, including grouse, grosbeaks, cedar waxwing, eastern bluebird, gray catbird, orioles, red-headed woodpecker, brown thrashers, and American robin.

Sorbus americana
American mountain ash

A large deciduous shrub or small tree growing from 10 to 30 feet tall with a spreading crown. When grown in the open, this plant has a short trunk with spreading slender branches. Its leaves are pinnately compound, and are formed of 11 to 17 stalkless, lance-shaped leaflets. Leaves turn yellow in autumn. The bark of the American mountain ash is smooth and grayish green, becoming scaly with age. Numerous white flowers in flat-topped terminal clusters are followed by small, applelike, bright red or orange fruits that persist into winter.

Native distribution In moist soils on rocky hillsides from western Ontario to Newfoundland, south to northern North Carolina and Georgia, and northwest to northern Illinois.

Cultivation American mountain ash grows best in evenly moist, well-drained soil in full sun. It is tolerant of acid and alkaline soils. Plants may be stunted in dry soils. Borers and fire blight may attack these trees. Zones 2–6.

Sorbus decora
showy mountain ash

Similar to American mountain ash, but with larger, showier flowers and fruits. Trees reach 30 to 65 feet tall and develop a rounded crown. Leaves are divided into 11 to 15 sharp, pointed leaflets that turn orange in fall. Numerous white flowers in flat-topped terminal clusters appear about 1 ½ weeks later than those of American mountain ash. Glossy, scarlet, applelike fruits persist into winter.

Native distribution: In moist soils from western Ontario east to Newfoundland, south to Connecticut, and west to northeastern Iowa.

Cultivation: An attractive specimen tree. It prefers to be placed in a moist, well-drained site in full sun and tolerates acid soil. Zones 3–6.

Other suitable species

Arizona mountain ash (*S. dumosa*), 8 feet, Zone 6.
🦋 🍂 ✹

Sitka mountain ash (*S. sitchensis*), 3 to 15 feet, occasionally 30 feet, Zone 5. 🦋 🍂 ✹

Sitka mountain ash (*Sorbus sitchensis*) flowers and buds.

SNOWBERRIES
Symphoricarpos spp.

A small genus of 15 species of deciduous shrubs: 14 are native to North and Central America and 1 is found in China. Snowberries are in the honeysuckle family.

Birds Attracted

A valuable source of winter food for resident birds. Thrashers, cedar waxwing, pine grosbeak, and American robin feed on the fruits. Hummingbirds visit the flowers.

Symphoricarpos albus
common snowberry, upright snowberry

A deciduous, multistemmed, thicket-forming shrub, growing from 3 to 6 feet tall. Masses of small, pinkish, bell-shaped flowers appear in summer, followed by edible snow-white fruits in late summer, persisting through winter.

Native distribution Nova Scotia south to Kentucky, west to Alaska, and south to southern California.

Cultivation A hardy plant, it will grow in full sun or partial shade. It prefers a well-drained soil. A good hedge plant for shady gardens. Zones 4–7.

🌿 🦋 🍸 ✹ 🐞 🍃

Common snowberry (*Symphoricarpos albus*).

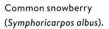

Coralberry (*Symphoricarpos orbiculatus*).

Common snowberry (*Symphoricarpos albus*) berries.

Symphoricarpos orbiculatus
coralberry

A deciduous, dense, mound-shaped shrub 2 to 5 feet tall with dark green, oval leaves and bell-shaped, pink-tinged white flowers. Flowers appear in late summer or early fall followed by coral-pink to purple berries that persist through winter.

Native distribution Widespread in eastern North America.

American goldfinch feeding in the prairie azure aster (*Symphyotrichum oolentangiense*).

Red-banded hairstreak butterfly nectaring on calico aster (*Symphyotrichum lateriflorum*).

Pacific aster (*Symphyotrichum chilense*)

Cultivation Easily grown. Prefers a well-drained, sandy loam or clay soil in full sun or shade. Zones 2–9.

Other suitable species
mountain snowberry (*S. oreophilus*), 3 to 5 feet, Zone 6.

ASTERS
Symphyotrichum spp.

About 200 species are commonly called asters. The largest group, of about 90 species, is included in the genus *Symphyotrichum*. Represented in all parts of North America, wild asters, with their multitude of starry flowers, are among the most beautiful wildflowers. Asters range from low-growing, single-stemmed plants to multistemmed, tall, shrubby plants that grow from desert regions to the cold western and northeastern coniferous woodlands.

Birds Attracted
When allowed to go to seed, asters attract seed-eating birds. Cardinals, goldfinches, sparrows, chickadees, nuthatches, titmice, towhees, and indigo bunting include aster seed in their diet.

Symphyotrichum chilense
Pacific aster
A common, clumped or spreading perennial growing 1 to 4 feet tall with variable, slightly hairy, lance-shaped, slightly toothed leaves 1 to 8 inches long. Flowers are violet to pink or white in open, branched clusters from June to October.
Native distribution Meadows, grasslands, and coastal sand from coastal British Columbia to southern California below 1,600 feet elevation.
Cultivation When cultivated in optimum conditions including full sun, in a moist and well-drained soil, it will spread vigorously, but it will also grow in partial shade in a fine to medium-textured soil with little water. It is relatively drought and salt tolerant. Zone 3.

Symphyotrichum novae-angliae
New England aster

An upright, multistemmed perennial with showy daisy flowers 1 to 2 inches wide, borne in clusters; flowers may be lavender, violet, pink, or white with yellow centers. Plants reach 3 to 6 feet, with 3- to 5-inch leaves.

Native distribution Meadows, thickets and damp areas from Newfoundland to Georgia and west to Wyoming and New Mexico.

Cultivation New England asters are hardy plants suited to most areas. They prefer full sun and evenly moist, well-drained garden soil, but will tolerate light shade. Set plants 2 to 3 feet apart. May need staking. Propagate by cuttings or division in spring. When making divisions, discard the woody centers before replanting clumps. Zones 3–8.

Many butterflies including the yellow sulphur and cabbage white are attracted to the smooth white oldfield aster (*Symphyotrichum racemosum*).

Other suitable species

western aster (*S. ascendens*), 6 inches, Zones 6–9.

heath aster (S. *ericoides*), shade tolerant, to 1 ½ to 3 feet, 4–9.

calico aster (S. *lateriflorum*), shade tolerant, to 1 to 3 feet, Zones 4–8.

New York aster (*S. novi-belgii*), 1 to 6 feet, Zones 3–8.

New York aster (*Symphyotrichum novi-belgii*) cultivar.

ARBORVITAES
Thuja spp.

Arborvitaes are in the family Cupressaceae, with 2 species native to North America. They are evergreen conifers with scalelike leaves, soft to the touch. They are not true cedars (*Cedrus* spp.), and are commonly referred to as arborvitaes from the Latin "tree of life," referring to a resin extract that reduces fever and blood pressure and increases blood flow.

Birds Attracted

Excellent nesting and roosting trees. Many birds including sparrows, juncos, crossbills, thrushes, and nuthatches feed on the enormous quantity of seed produced.

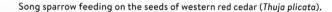

Song sparrow feeding on the seeds of western red cedar (*Thuja plicata*).

Dark-eyed junco feeding on the seeds of western hemlock (*Tsuga heterophylla*).

Canada hemlock (*Tsuga canadensis*).

Thuja occidentalis
eastern arborvitae, northern white cedar, American arborvitae

A small evergreen conifer 20 to 40 feet tall. Usually multitrunked with fanlike branches, small scalelike leaves, and dark reddish brown bark. The ripe cones are ½ inch long and pale cinnamon in color. The foliage turns a brownish color in winter. Numerous cultivars are available.

Native distribution Southeast Canada, from central Saskatchewan east to New Brunswick, and south to eastern Tennessee and the Appalachian Mountains, commonly in rich organic soils near streams.

Cultivation An excellent hedge or screening plant, preferring full sun in a moist, well-drained, loamy soil. Hardy, but susceptible to upper branches breaking under heavy ice or wet snow loads. Zones 2–8.

Thuja plicata
western red cedar, giant arborvitae

A broadly conical, evergreen, coniferous tree with aromatic deep green foliage to 50 to 70 feet in height.

Native distribution Southern Alaska and British Columbia, south to northwest California, inland to western Montana.

Cultivation A fast-growing hedge plant or living fence, growing to 15 feet in the first 10 years. The foliage will shoot out from old wood if the hedge is damaged. Prefers partial shade in well-drained soil. Zones 5–7.

HEMLOCKS
Tsuga spp.

Hemlocks are tall, graceful, straight-trunked evergreen trees. Unlike many pines, the cones of hemlocks mature in a single season. The cones hang from the ends of branchlets, and when mature release long winged seeds. Hemlocks often colonize areas that have been previously cleared. Four species are native to North America, mainly growing on moist, cool, northern slopes and high mountains.

Birds Attracted

Hemlocks provide favorite nesting sites for many birds, including Blackburnian warbler, American robin, black-throated blue warbler and green warbler, dark-eyed junco, veery, American goldfinch, and blue jay. Dense foliage also provides valuable shelter for many birds, including chickadees, titmice, juncos, and northern cardinal. Seeds are consumed by warblers, chickadees, pine siskins, crossbills, pine grosbeak, Swainson's thrush, and American robin.

Tsuga canadensis
Canada hemlock, eastern hemlock

An evergreen tree about 65 to 80 feet tall with dense, soft, fine-textured, flat needles, deep green above and whitish when viewed from below. The branches tend to droop downward. The bark is cinnamon-brown and deeply furrowed. Cones are less than 1 inch long, light brown and oval.

Native distribution Upland forests, rocky bluffs, and moist, cool valleys, from Nova Scotia to eastern Minnesota, south through Maryland to northern Alabama.

Cultivation A beautiful specimen, screen, or hedge plant. At maturity, the plants are smaller in the western states of its range than in the east. Prefers evenly moist, acid soil in a sheltered north-facing location in partial to light shade. (They can grow in full sun in northern gardens.) Best results in deep, organic, mulched soil. Plants are sensitive to polluted air, wind, and drought. Woolly adelgids may be a problem. Zones 3–8. 🦋 ⊛ 🐿 🐦 ✒

Canada hemlock (*Tsuga canadensis* 'Pendula').

Chestnut-backed chickadee sheltering in Carolina hemlock (*Tsuga caroliniana*).

The autumn colors of lowbush blueberry (*Vaccinium angustifolium*).

Lowbush blueberry fruits.

Savanna sparrow foraging among mountain cranberry (*Vaccinium vitis-idaea* subsp. *minus*) and black crowberry (*Empetrum nigrum*).

Tsuga caroliniana
Carolina hemlock

A more open tree than Canada hemlock and lacks the feathery foliage effect, since the needles of Carolina hemlock radiate around the stems in a bottle-brush effect as opposed to lying flat as do the needles of the Canada hemlock. Typically about 40 to 60 feet tall with a pyramidal habit and reddish brown bark. The cones are larger (to 1½ inches) and showier than those of Canada hemlocks, with an open, flaring, flowerlike shape.

Native distribution Rocky stream banks in the Appalachian Mountains from southwestern Virginia to northern Georgia.

Cultivation An attractive screen or hedge plant in a garden. This tree is more tolerant of city conditions than Canada hemlock. Prefers an evenly moist, well-drained, acid soil and should be positioned in partial to light shade. Zones 5–7. 🐾 🦋 🐦 🍂

Tsuga heterophylla
western hemlock

A large, slow growing, evergreen tree with dark blue-green needles that are aromatic when crushed and light attractive bark. The largest of the hemlocks, growing up to 200 feet in its natural range but usually 30 to 50 feet in cultivation. Fruit cones appear from summer to fall, with an abundant supply each 2 or 3 years.

Native distribution West Coast of North America, from southeast Alaska to Sonoma County in northern California.

Cultivation Prefers a moist, rich, acidic, well-drained soil with ample organic matter. An excellent plant for hedging. It prefers full sun but is shade tolerant. The seeds are the preferred food of chickadees and pine siskin. Zones 5–9. 🐾 🦋 🐦 🍂

Other suitable species
mountain hemlock (*T. mertensiana*), 80 to 115 feet, smaller in cultivation. Zones 5–8. 🐾 🦋 🐦 🍂

BLUEBERRIES
Vaccinium spp.

Blueberries are deciduous or evergreen shrubs that rarely grow to trees. They have succulent edible fruits attractive to numerous birds, and colorful fall foliage in the deciduous species. There are about 100 species widespread in the Northern Hemisphere, their region extending to tropical highlands south of the equator. Of the 25 to 30 North American native species, only 1 is of tree proportions.

Birds Attracted

Over 90 species of birds feed on the fruits of the blueberry plants, including the eastern bluebird, black-capped chickadee, American robin, orioles, tufted titmice, flickers, towhees, and kingbirds. This group of plants provides both cover and nesting sites for chipping and song sparrows.

Vaccinium corymbosum
highbush blueberry

A multistemmed, deciduous shrub about 6 to 12 feet tall. The oval-shaped leaves are lustrous dark green, changing to a brilliant red or orange in the autumn. Small clusters of bell-shaped white flowers appear in late winter, followed by sweet-tasting, blue-black berries with a whitish bloom in mid-spring to late summer. The berries of the highbush blueberry may be up to ½ inch in diameter.

Native distribution Wet woods, swamps, or upland woods in the east, ranging from Nova Scotia and Quebec to Minnesota and Wisconsin, south to Georgia and Florida and west to Alabama.

Cultivation Highbush blueberry is excellent for naturalizing, as a specimen shrub, and in mixed borders with perennials and other shrubs. Prefers an acid, evenly moist but well-drained, loose, or sandy soil in full sun. It will grow in shade, but under these conditions plants are rangier and produce less fruit. Zones 4–9. 🦋 🌱 🍁 💮 🌿

Mountain cranberry (*Vaccinium vitis-idaea* subsp. *minus*).

Urn-shaped flowers of California huckleberry (*Vaccinium ovatum*).

Highbush blueberry (*Vaccinium corymbosum*) flowers.

Juvenile tufted titmouse feeding on the fruits of southern mountain cranberry (*Vaccinium erythrocarpum*).

Vaccinium ovatum
California huckleberry, evergreen huckleberry

An evergreen shrub growing to 2 feet tall in sun and 10 feet in a shaded position. Deep green, glossy leaves with reddish new growth in spring. White to light pink urn-shaped flowers appear from March to May, followed by blue-black edible berries in late summer. The berries are fed on by at least 88 species of birds.

Native distribution Alaska to California.

Cultivation Prefers full sun to part shade in a moist well-drained, acidic soil. It tolerates sand or clay and withstands salt spray. It can be pruned to form a hedge. Zones 6–10. 🦋 ✺ 🐾 🌿

Vaccinium vitis-idaea subsp. *minus*
mountain cranberry, lingonberry

A dwarf evergreen, creeping, matlike shrub that produces terminal clusters of pink bell-shaped flowers, followed in the fall by dark red edible berries measuring about ¼ inch in diameter. The leaves are small, leathery, shiny, and very decorative.

Native distribution Northern Canada south to northern Minnesota and northern New England in bogs and rocky areas.

Cultivation An excellent ground cover and rock garden plant in evenly moist, well-drained, humus-rich acid soil in full sun. Propagate from fresh seed or division of root clumps. Plant grows to form a solid ornamental mat, but is slow growing. It will not tolerate hot, dry summers. Zones 2–4 as well as being suitable for mild summer areas of Zones 5–6. 🦋 ⊤ 🍁 ✺

Other suitable species

lowbush blueberry (*V. angustifolium*), 6 to 8 inches, Zones 2–8. ⊻ 🦋 ⊤ 🍁 ✺

farkleberry, tree huckleberry, sparkleberry (*V. arboreum*), 10 to 26 feet, Zones 7–9. 🦋 ⊤ 🍁 ✺ 🐾 🌿

southern mountain cranberry (*V. erythrocarpum*), 5 feet, Zone 6. ⊻ 🦋 ⊤ 🍁 ✺

red huckleberry (*V. parvifolium*), 4 to 12 feet, Zones 5–8. 🦋 🍁 ✺ 🐾 🌿

VIBURNUMS
Viburnum spp.

Viburnums are shrubs or small trees with very attractive foliage and showy flowers and fruits. This plant is a perfect ornamental and also often displays excellent fall color. The flower clusters can be mistaken for hydrangeas. Of the 15 species native to North America, most are deciduous shrubs; 4 species are small trees.

American cranberrybush viburnum (*Viburnum opulus* subsp. *trilobum*) in spring.

Birds Attracted

The berrylike fruits of most viburnum species attract many birds, including towhees, waxwings, eastern bluebird, rose-breasted grosbeak, American robin, flickers, brown thrasher, purple finch, gray catbird, hermit thrush, towhees, northern cardinal, ruffed and sharp-tailed grouse, and yellow-billed cuckoos.

American cranberrybush viburnum in summer.

Viburnum dentatum
arrowwood viburnum

A deciduous shrub or small tree, usually 15 feet tall and is at least as wide as it is tall, with multiple stems rising from its base. Fragrant, white, 3-inch flower clusters appear in late spring, followed by blue-black fruits in fall. The coarsely toothed, glossy, dark green leaves turn shiny red in autumn. The straight branches were reputedly used by the Indians to make arrows, giving the plant its name.
Native distribution New Brunswick west to Illinois and south to Florida and Texas.
Cultivation Best suited to loose, well-drained soils in full sun or partial shade. It can tolerate full shade and acid soil. It looks most attractive when naturalized or grown in a massed planting or as a background shrub. Zones 4–9. 🦋 🌿 ❀

American cranberrybush viburnum (*Viburnum opulus* subsp. *trilobum*) in fall.

Viburnum edule
squashberry

A variable shrub, erect to spreading and deciduous, 4 to 7 feet tall, with lobed or barely lobed leaves. White flowers appear in early summer, followed by orange-red berries that ripen in mid to late summer.

Nannyberry (*Viburnum lentago*).

Southern black haw
(*Viburnum rufidulum*) flowers.

Southern black haw fruits

Native distribution Alaska, across Canada to Newfoundland, New England, and west to the Great Lakes states, North and South Dakota, Wyoming and Colorado, and the Pacific Northwest, Idaho, and Montana. **Cultivation** Prefers an acidic, moist soil in full sun. Prefers some watering, but will not tolerate overwatering. Zone 3. 🦋 🍁 ☀

Viburnum lentago
nannyberry viburnum, black haw

A large shrub or a small bushy tree. It reaches about 30 feet tall with a compact, rounded crown and arching branches. The leaves are shiny, oval-shaped, and pointed, turning a purplish red color in autumn. Clusters of small white flowers are followed by small, bluish black, berrylike fruits that mature in autumn. The fruit remains on the shrub throughout winter.

Native distribution Saskatchewan east to Quebec and Maine, south to West Virginia and west to Wyoming and Nebraska, in moist soil, typically on the edge of forests or near streams and swamps.

Cultivation Nannyberry is a good plant for naturalizing and makes an effective, ornamental screen for your garden. It is attractive in all seasons. Prefers rich, evenly moist, well-drained soil in full sun to partial shade. It will tolerate both acid and alkaline soil conditions. It spreads by suckering from the roots. Zones 2–7. 🦋 🍁 ☀

Viburnum opulus var. americanum
American cranberrybush viburnum, highbush cranberry

A deciduous shrub growing to about 12 feet tall and 6 to 8 feet wide with glossy, maplelike leaves that turn a rich red in fall. Clusters of small white flowers appear in May, followed by brilliant scarlet, edible fruits in late summer and remain on the shrub all winter.

Native distribution Hedgerows, open woods, and the edges of woods throughout the northern United States and Canada.

Cultivation Prefers full sun or light shade and a well-drained, evenly moist, fertile soil. Grow it massed, as a specimen or in a border. Zones 2–8. 🦋 🍁 ☀ 🌿

....

Other suitable species

western viburnum (*V. ellipticum*), 8 feet, Zones 6–9.

Appalachian tea or withe rod (*V. nudum*), to 6 feet,
Zones 3–6.

Walter's viburnum (*V. obovatum*), semievergreen, 8
feet, Zone 9.

blackhaw viburnum (*V. prunifolium*), 8 to 15 feet,
Zone 3.

southern black haw (*V. rufidulum*), to 15 to 25 feet,
Zones 5–9.

Squashberry (*Viburnum edule*).

GRAPES
Vitis spp.

About 6 species of grape are native to North America. The plants are woody, deciduous vines with broad, heart-shaped leaves and long clusters of small flowers. The flowers are followed by round, juicy berries. The vines are a useful landscaping plant that can provide shade in summer and allow for sun penetration in winter when the leaves have fallen.

Birds Attracted

Wild grapes are fed on by almost 100 species of birds, including northern cardinal, house finch, American robin, blue jay, and towhees. If grown in a tangle, they provide effective shelter and nesting sites for many birds. Some birds use the bark for nest building.

Flock of cedar waxwings feeding on frost grape
(*Vitis vulpina*) entwined through hemlock (*Tsuga* sp).

Anna's hummingbird probing for insects among the grapes.

Vitis aestivalis
summer grape

A deciduous, vigorous vine to 65 feet, with variable leaves, lobed or unlobed. Sweetly scented flower panicles are followed by blue-black berries in fall.
Native distribution Ontario, east to Vermont, west to Oklahoma, and south to Florida and Texas.
Cultivation Prefers a warm, sunny position in well-drained moist soil. Prune in winter when plant is dormant. Zones 3–6.

California wild grape (*Vitis californica*).

Fall color of California wild grape (*Vitis californica* 'Roger's Red').

Vitis labrusca
fox grape
Fast growing, deciduous climber, growing to 50 feet and flowering in May to July. Flowers are followed by dark purplish fruits in late summer through fall. The source of many cultivars that are important to the wine industry, including 'Concord'.
Native distribution Eastern United States from Maine to South Carolina and Tennessee.
Cultivation Prefers full sun or part shade in a well-drained, deep, rich, moist soil. Zone 5. 🐦 🍂

Vitis vulpina
frost grape, winter grape, fox grape
A deciduous, high-climbing vine with heart-shaped leaves with coarse, sharp teeth. Small greenish flowers in late spring and early summer are followed by shiny black grapes, which become sweet after a frost.
Native distribution Banks of rivers and in bottomlands from southern New York to Kansas and south to Florida and Texas.
Cultivation Prefer a moist, well-drained location in sun or partial shade. They require a place to climb, so plant them at the foot of a tree or provide support. Zones 5–9. 🐦 🍂

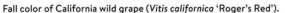

Other suitable species
canyon grape (*V. arizonica*), Zones 7–9. 🍁 🐦 🍂
California wild grape (*V. californica*), Zones 7–9.
🍁 🐦 🍂
riverbank grape (*V. riparia*), Zones 3–6. 🐦 🍂 🐦

FAN PALMS
Washingtonia spp.

A genus of palms native to southwestern United States and northwest Mexico. There are two species, both fan palms.

Birds Attracted
Many birds including the hooded oriole favor the fruit and disperse the seed.

Washingtonia filifera
California fan palm, desert fan palm, cotton palm

The only palm native to western North America, growing from 20 to 60 feet high, with a 2- to 3-foot-diameter gray trunk. Evergreen leaves, with cotton-like threads up to 6 feet long with a "fan" of leaflets. Dead leaf fronds remain attached and form a "petti-coat" around the trunk, forming a microclimate that provides habitat for birds and invertebrates. Numerous, branching, white and yellow flower clusters are followed by red-black fruits that mature in September.
Native distribution Southwestern California and Arizona in moist alkaline soils along streams, seeps, or springs.
Cultivation Prefers a sunny, well-drained position. Provides deep, cool shade when planted in clumps. Zones 8–10. 🐾 🦜 🐦 ✒️

Female hooded oriole constructing its nest in a California fan palm (*Washingtonia filifera*).

Acorn woodpecker nesting in fan palm.

YUCCAS
Yucca spp.

With their stiff, bayonetlike leaves, thick trunks, and large spikes of fleshy white flowers, yuccas are characteristic of arid regions. They are excellent plants for dryland gardens, but some species are also commonly grown in the northeastern states.

About 40 species of yucca are distributed from Oklahoma, the Gulf states, and Arkansas, and north to South Dakota, west to the Rocky Mountains and central California, south to Central America and Bermuda. Nine species grow to small tree size.

Birds Attracted

Various birds feed on the fruit of the yucca and many also find secure nesting sites in the protective foliage, including verdin, mourning dove, and house finch. Orioles probe the flowers for their nectar and insects the flowers attract. Hummingbirds also visit the flowers.

California fan palm.

Joshua tree (*Yucca brevifolia*).

Joshua tree provides shelter
and nesting sites for many birds
including Costa's hummingbird.

Yucca elata

soaptree yucca, soapweed, palmella

Palmlike shrub or small tree with slender leaves about 10 to 15 feet tall. Light green leaves are long and swordlike. Clusters of numerous, large, whitish flowers, typically up to 2 inches long. Flowers are moth-pollinated. Pods 3 inches long open to release winged seeds.

Native distribution Commonly found in desert grasslands from southern New Mexico, Arizona and western Texas south, to Mexico.

Cultivation These drought-tolerant plants are particularly suitable for desert gardens. Yuccas are often planted as ornamentals and can be seen along highways. These plants prefer to be planted in a dry situation that offers plenty of sunlight. Soaptree yucca is a slow-growing plant. Zones 7–10. ✱ 🦋 ⊤ ✿ 🐞 🍃

Flowers of Our Lord's candle (*Yucca whipplei*).

Yucca filamentosa

Adam's needle, needle palm

A herbaceous perennial that produces large, iris-like rosettes of upright, sword-shaped, blue-green leaves. Adam's needle grows about 5 to 15 feet tall, and the leaves of this plant may reach 2 ½ feet long. These plants bear enormous clusters of white, bell-shaped flowers that can measure up to 2 inches in length and mature to dry seedpods.

Native distribution Native to the East Coast from North Carolina south to Florida and Mississippi.

Cultivation This cold-hardy yucca makes a striking specimen in any garden and works well in a border with bold perennials and ornamental grasses. It is at its best when planted in a location with well-drained, sandy or average soil, and positioned in full sun to light shade. Propagate by dividing offsets in spring or fall. Zones 3–10. ✱ 🦋 ⊤ ✿ 🐞

Adam's needle (*Yucca filamentosa*).

Other suitable species

Joshua tree (*Y. brevifolia*), 25 feet, Zones 7–10.
✱ ✿ 🐞 🍃

Mojave yucca (*Y. schidigera*, formerly *Y. mohavensis*), 5 to 16 feet, Zones 7–10. ✱ ✿ 🐞 🍃

Our Lord's candle (*Y. whipplei*), 6 to 7 feet, Zones 8–12. ✱ 🦋 ⊤ ✿

Gray catbird feeding in
saskatoon serviceberry
(*Amelanchier alnifolia*).

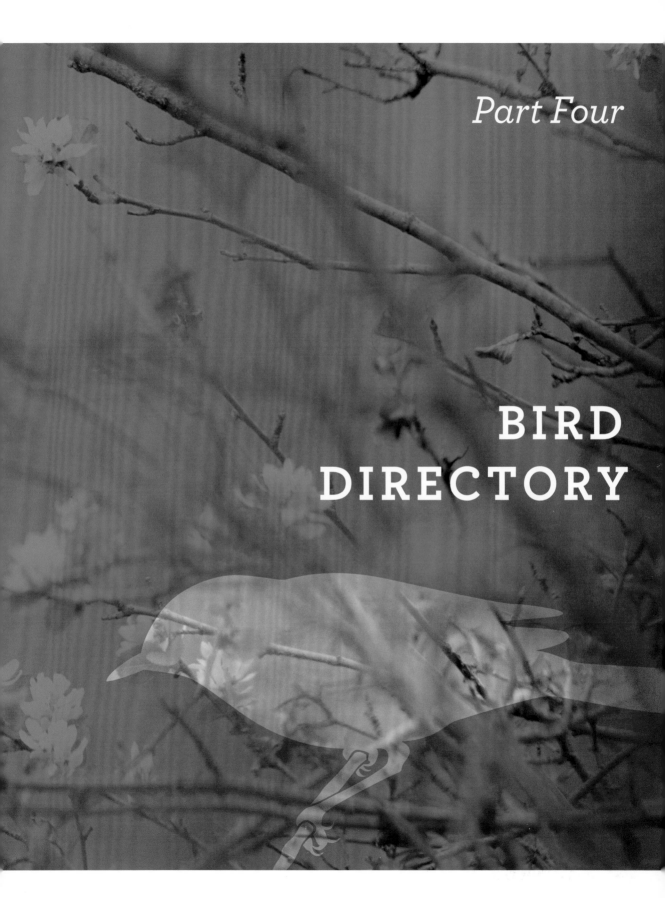

Part Four

BIRD
DIRECTORY

ABOUT *the* BIRD DIRECTORY

The Bird Directory includes many favorite and beloved North American garden birds. Their beauty, interesting life histories, and intimate connection to the natural world should inspire us to do what we can to preserve them and their habitat. In addition to photos, I've included my pen-and-ink illustration of each bird in its environment to show this connection.

These birds represent a cross-section of common family groups most likely to visit gardens throughout the various regions of North America. Individual species within those families have been selected to represent different regions across North America. The bird species are included in the directory by family groups, arranged in accordance with the current American Ornithologists' Union Check-list of North American Birds. To help you find birds in the Directory, see the list, Birds in the Directory by Common Name, on page 299.

Each bird entry includes the bird's scientific family name and common family name, the bird's individual scientific name and common name, as well as an introduction to the bird, a range map, and information on habitat, migration and winter range, breeding range, breeding behavior, nesting, and feeding habits, and some plants that the bird uses for food and shelter.

Bird Habitats and Behavior

By understanding the life history, nesting habits, food preferences, and other bird behaviors, you will be better equipped to plan your garden to cater to different birds from various bird families. Plus, birds are fascinating and you will enjoy them all the more knowing a bit about them. By finding out why birds do certain things, you'll be able to tell what they're up to in your yard. For example, you can recognize courtship behavior, or guess that a bird is migrating through your area.

All birds have a preferred habitat. Some, including the mourning dove and American robin, are widespread and may be found in diverse habitats. Other birds, however, have defined habitats and live only where species of particular plants grow. For example, Kirtland's warbler is only found in large tracts of Jack-pines.

Migration

One of the primary bird behaviors is migration: some birds migrate and others do not. Migration is an evolutionary adaption that allows birds to escape unfavorable conditions, like the lack of food or cold winter weather, in an area by moving to a more favorable area during part of the year. Some migration may consist of mountain species moving to the lowlands for winter, while some species, such as the evening grosbeak, will move east or west across the United States to winter.

Many birds breed in northern areas in spring and summer, then retreat to warmer southern climates for fall and winter. For example, of the 215 bird species known to breed in Michigan, less than 20 of these species remain there year-round. Migrating birds have regular migration patterns, usually returning to the same breeding area each spring, returning to the same wintering area each year, and probably following the same migration route each year.

For some birds, migration is a long and wearying journey. It has been estimated that approximately 100 species of birds that spend the summer in the United States will winter in the West Indies or Central and South America, with the greatest winter concentration of birds in Mexico and over a range south to Panama. But other birds only migrate slightly south of their summer range. Northern species that winter in the southern United States include American goldfinch, dark-eyed (slate-colored) junco, eastern bluebird, yellow-rumped warbler, chipping sparrow, house wren, and some American robins and meadowlarks. Some species that may remain resident in their territories year-round are the house sparrow, red-bellied woodpecker, downy woodpecker, pileated woodpecker, white-breasted nuthatch, tufted titmouse, and cardinal.

Although the concept of flyways (or migratory "highways") that birds follow during migration is a well-established and long-standing theory, it is now thought that most species of nocturnally migrating songbirds spread out over a broad front while they travel. The birds may follow a path marked by specific geographic features, such as a mountain ridge or a river, or may range widely across the countryside. However, waterfowl, shorebirds, and some raptors (birds of prey) are known to follow three main north-south flyways: the Pacific flyway, the Mississippi flyway, and the Atlantic flyway, with some intermediate routes. During their migration period, great concentrations of birds can be found along their flyways. This makes the migration period a particularly exciting and rewarding time of the year for bird fans.

Range Map

breeding range
(generally spring
and summer)

winter range

year-round range

Birds in the Directory by Common Name

acorn woodpecker
American goldfinch
American redstart
American robin
Anna's hummingbird
ash-throated flycatcher
Baltimore oriole
black-and-white warbler
Blackburnian warbler
black-capped chickadee
black phoebe
black-tailed gnatcatcher
blue-gray gnatcatcher
blue jay
Brewer's blackbird
bridled titmouse
brown thrasher
cactus wren
California towhee
Cape May warbler
cedar waxwing
Costa's hummingbird
dark-eyed junco
downy woodpecker
eastern bluebird
eastern meadowlark
eastern towhee
gray catbird
greater roadrunner
hooded oriole
house finch
house wren

Inca dove
indigo bunting
lark bunting
lazuli bunting
Mexican jay
mountain chickadee
mourning dove
northern cardinal
northern flicker
northern mockingbird
orchard oriole
pine siskin
purple martin
pygmy nuthatch
red-bellied woodpecker
red-breasted nuthatch
red crossbill
red-headed woodpecker
rose-breasted grosbeak
ruby-throated hummingbird
scarlet tanager
song sparrow
Steller's jay
summer tanager
tufted titmouse
verdin
white-breasted nuthatch
white-throated sparrow
wood thrush
wrentit
yellow-rumped warbler
yellow warbler

mourning dove / *Zenaida macroura*

Mourning dove feeding on the seeds of yellow wood sorrel (*Oxalis stricta*).

The mourning dove takes its evocative name from its common call: a low-toned series of soft coos. The notes are uttered slowly and have a melancholy quality. The bird has a long, pointed tail and slim 12-inch body with gray-brown plumage. Because of the arrangement of the stiff wing feathers, the wings make a whistling sound when the bird is in rapid flight.

Habitat

The mourning dove is widely adapted to varying habitats, including open fields, open deciduous and coniferous woods and windbreak trees on the Great Plains. The bird also inhabits both arid plains and mountains in the West. The mourning dove is the most common native dove of parks and gardens in suburban areas throughout its range.

Migration and Winter Range

The birds reach their breeding grounds in the north between March and April. The northernmost populations drift farther south to winter, with some remaining in the north, but the greatest concentration winters from southern California east through Nebraska to New Jersey.

Breeding Range

Breeding in all continental United States and also British Columbia, Alberta, Saskatchewan, and Manitoba to southern Ontario, southern Quebec, and southern New Brunswick.

Breeding Behavior

During the nesting season the birds are found in pairs. The birds indulge in an aerial courtship flight. After climbing steeply from a perch with vigorous wing flapping, the wings clapping together with each downbeat, the birds sail with stiffly held wings like a small hawk and then glide back to their perch. Mourning doves mate for life and, in the nesting season, become particularly devoted couples.

Nesting

Mourning doves primarily nest at the edge of woodland or grassland and usually choose a horizontal branch of an evergreen tree from 15 to 25 feet above the ground. Occasionally the nest is built on another species' old nest, or on the ground. The male brings building material to the site and the female constructs a loose, bulky platform of twigs; the female lays 2 (in rare cases, 3 or 4) white eggs. Both sexes share in the 14- to 15-day incubation. The female usually sits from dusk to dawn. The male sits through the day. Both birds care for the young.

The young birds are fed on "pigeon milk" (regurgitated food taken from the parents' crop), followed later by weed seeds and insects. The young fly from the nest 14 or 15 days after hatching. A pair may raise 2 to 5 broods in one year.

Feeding Habits

Foraging on the ground, they usually feed in pairs during the breeding season. In summer to late autumn, they feed in large flocks. Adult birds feed almost totally on seeds. Year-round, their principal food is weed seeds: 7,500 seeds of yellow wood sorrel were found in one bird's stomach, and 6,400 seeds of foxtail grasses were found in another. Spilled grain, pine seeds, and pokeberries are also fed on.

Plants *for* food *and* shelter include:

grasses (*Andropogon* spp.)
sunflowers (*Helianthus* spp.)
spruces (*Picea* spp.)
pines (*Pinus* spp.)
cottonwoods (*Populus* spp.)

Mourning dove on its nest in the protective spines of a tree cholla (*Cylindropuntia imbricata*).

Inca dove / *Columbina inca*

The Inca dove is a familiar bird that is often sighted in parks and gardens of the west. It is easily identified when in flight, because of the chestnut flash on the outer part of the wings that may be revealed and the distinctive white margin of the long, square-ended gray tail, helping to distinguish the 8¼-inch Inca dove from the similar ground dove. The dove's wings often make a twittering sound in flight. The song of the Inca dove is a repeated, melodious *coo-hoo*.

Habitat
An extremely tame bird, preferring areas of human settlement. The bird is extending its range north into settled areas, including suburban parks and gardens as well as ranches and fields.

Migration and Winter Range
The Inca dove is resident year-round within its range.

Breeding Range
Arizona, New Mexico, southeastern California, and Texas, south to Costa Rica.

Breeding Behavior
When courting, the male Inca dove struts around the female, cooing, with its tail raised almost vertically. If another male intrudes, the dove becomes pugnacious and a fierce fight may result, with savage buffeting of wings, and the birds also use their bills to peck each other on the head, often drawing blood. The mated pair show great affection, often indulging in mutual preening or caressing.

Nesting
The Inca dove prefers to nest near houses or barns close to human habitation. A horizontal fork or flattened tree limb is usually selected 4 to 25 feet above the ground. A variety of trees are used for nest sites, including cottonwoods, sycamores, elms, live oaks, mesquites, and fruit trees. The birds will also nest in opuntia cacti. They will sometimes use the nests of other birds, including the cactus wren, mourning dove, and mockingbird, after they do repair and relining work.

Inca doves feed on the fruits of prickly pear cacti, including the plains prickly pear (*Opuntia polyacantha*).

The nest is a small, compact platform 2 to 5 inches wide with a cavity about 1 inch deep, constructed of twigs, small rootlets, plant stems, grass, and feathers. When building the nest, the male brings material to the female, then alights on her back and passes it down to her while she sits on the platform.

The female lays 2 whitish eggs. Both sexes incubate for about 2 weeks. In Arizona, the Inca dove has the longest breeding season of any bird, often having 4 or 5 broods between January and November. Elsewhere, 2 or more broods are common, and the birds often use the same nest twice. The previous year's nest is sometimes relined and used again.

The young birds fledge after 2 weeks, but return and huddle between the parents to roost at night.

Feeding Habits

Weed seeds form the bulk of the Inca dove's diet. Because of their dry seed diet, water is very important to the birds. In times of drought, they extend their range in search of it, often staying in built-up areas.

Plants *for* food *and* shelter include:

opuntia cacti (*Opuntia* spp.)
western sycamore (*Platanus racemosa*)
Fremont cottonwood (*Populus fremontii*)
live oak (*Quercus virginiana*)

Inca dove with its young at the nest in a cane cholla (*Cylindropuntia spinosior*).

greater roadrunner / *Geococcyx californianus*

Greater roadrunner often nests in hawthorns, including the cockspur hawthorn (*Crataegus crus-galli*).

The greater roadrunner is a large (23-inch), streaky, brown and white bird with a long pointed tail and powerful, pale blue legs. A patch of bare skin behind the eye ends in an orange-red spot. At close range, the plumage displays a variety of iridescent colors. The bird's short, rounded wings make flying an effort, but the roadrunner lives mostly on the ground, where it can reach a speed of 15 miles per hour or more.

The bird's common name comes from its habit of running away rapidly when surprised. An extremely shy bird in the wild, it becomes tame in urban areas. The greater roadrunner is a member of the cuckoo family, and its voice reveals the affiliation. With its bill down, it starts with a high coo. With each coo, it raises its head and the pitch of the song becomes lower, until the bill points upward. It sings with a mournful tone, *coo-coo-coo-ohh-ohh*.

Habitat

Possibly the most distinctive and well-known bird throughout its range, the greater roadrunner is common in desert scrub, chaparral, and arid brush. It often inhabits farmlands and urban areas.

Migration and Winter Range

The bird is a year-round resident throughout its range.

Breeding Range

The roadrunner's range extends from north central California throughout the Southwest, east to eastern Oklahoma and northwestern Louisiana and south to central Mexico. It is the state bird of New Mexico and is resident in Nevada, Utah, Colorado, southwestern Kansas, and Texas. The bird is extending its range east.

Breeding Behavior

In spring the male bird goes to the eastern rim of a mesa or climbs to the top of a high cactus or dead tree to greet the rising sun with song. This love song may be preceded by much strutting, with the head held high and tail and wings drooping. During courtship, greater roadrunner may indulge in a sidestepping dance, raising and dropping their head and wings. Greater roadrunners mate for life and become year-round residents, developing a regular schedule in covering their area.

Nesting

The greater roadrunner places its 1-foot-diameter nest of coarse twigs lined with leaves, grass, feathers, rootlets, and snake skins in low, thorny growth such as cactus, mesquite, or palo verde trees. The female lays 3 to 6 white eggs at irregular intervals, usually between April and May. The female begins incubation after the first egg is laid, resulting in young birds in various stages of development in the same nest. Incubation takes about 20 days and the young birds fledge after 17 to 19 days.

Feeding Habits

The greater roadrunner's principal diet consists of lizards, grasshoppers, and crickets. The birds may also feed on insects, seeds, and fruit, including prickly pear. Roadrunners occasionally attack and eat mice, snakes (including rattlesnakes), and English sparrows, as well as other birds and their young. They have been recorded snatching swifts and sparrows out of the air. The roadrunner draws close to its prey, then with a quick dash and leap captures the airborne bird.

Plants *for* food *and* shelter include:

plains prickly pear (*Opuntia polyacantha*)

Greater roadrunner searching for insects.

ruby-throated hummingbird / *Archilochus colubris*

The ruby-throated hummingbird is the only hummingbird that regularly nests east of the Mississippi River. The birds are only 3 to 4 inches in length with a long, needlelike bill. Metallic green above and gray below, the male has a brilliant, iridescent, metallic red throat.

Constantly in motion, darting and hovering in flight, hummingbirds are the only birds that can fly backward. The birds' insectlike flight is accompanied by a characteristic humming sound made by their rapidly beating wings. Their call is a rapid, squeaky *chip-chip-chip* given in flight. In spite of their minute size, the birds' agility and speed of flight protects them from most enemies. In fact, they are extremely feisty and will drive away much larger birds.

Habitat
These hummingbirds prefer suburban gardens, parks, woodland clearings, and woods' edges, often near water. The birds may be found wherever nectar-bearing flowers are growing, especially if trees or thickets for shelter and perching or nesting are nearby.

Migration and Winter Range
The birds winter from northern Mexico and southern Texas south to Costa Rica. Some ruby-throated hummingbirds cross over 600 miles of ocean to reach Bermuda, or cross the Gulf of Mexico to Yucatan and farther south.

Breeding Range
Alberta eastward to Nova Scotia, south to the Gulf Coast and Florida, and west to North Dakota, and south Nebraska, Kansas, and central Texas.

Breeding Behavior
During courtship, the male performs display flights for the female. It loops backward and forward in a wide arc, as if hung from a pendulum, with a loud buzz from his wings at the bottom of the swing.

Ruby-throated hummingbird sipping nectar from the blooms of cardinal flower (*Lobelia cardinalis*).

Nesting

The female builds a neat little cup-shaped nest of soft plant down and spider webs, 1 to 1¼ inches in diameter. The nest is built on a limb and often covered with lichen. The female also incubates the eggs and raises the young alone. She lays 2 tiny white eggs and incubates them for 16 days. The young fledge when they are 20 to 22 days old. Per season, she raises 2 and sometimes 3 broods. The female apparently returns to the same nesting area each year.

Plants *for* food *and* shelter include:

See the Calendar for Hummingbird and Butterfly Flowers, the East Coast section (page 54).

Feeding Habits

Ruby-throated hummingbirds take nectar from flowering plants. They also feed on tiny insects.

Male ruby-throated hummingbird nectaring on jewelweed (*Impatiens pallida*).

Costa's hummingbird / *Calypte costae*

Costa's hummingbird has a green back and brilliant violet crown and throat. The throat has distinctive streamers down the side of the neck. The bird is distinguished by its slightly smaller, 3-inch size. The female Costa's hummingbird is smaller than the male and has a lighter gray underside than the female Anna's hummingbird. The call is a high-pitched metallic *tink*.

Male Costa's hummingbird sips nectar from the firecracker plant (*Penstemon eatonii*).

Habitat

A common bird of the southwestern deserts, preferring dry lands inhabited by yucca, ocotillo and cacti, and open chaparral in southern California. In the spring and fall, it often visits parks and gardens.

Migration and Winter Range

Males migrate through the desert areas in late February and March while the ocotillos are in flower. By the end of May, most birds have moved to coastal areas. The birds winter from southern California and southwestern Arizona south to Mexico.

Breeding Range

Central California, southern Nevada, southwestern Utah, southern Arizona, and southwestern New Mexico to northwest Mexico and Baja California.

Breeding Behavior

The male Costa's hummingbird performs amazing courtship display flights. Flying at speeds between 30 and 50 miles per hour, the bird climbs vertically to possibly 100 feet above the ground. The hummingbird turns and plummets toward the ground, turning at the last moment to climb again, tracing a U-shaped pattern. As the bird loops back and forth, its outer tail feathers produce a high-pitched whirring sound as it dives. The female watches from a nearby perch.

Nesting

Nesting between February and June, the female builds a relatively loosely made cup-shaped nest 1¼ to 2 inches wide. She weaves the nest from fine plant fiber bound with spiderwebs and decorates it with leaves or lichen fastened to the outside, and lines the nest with feathers.

The nest is usually built from 2 to 9 feet above the ground on a limb or twigs of oaks, alders, hackberry, willows or palo verde, or in sage branching cacti, or dead yuccas. The female continues to build up the sides of the nest during incubation until it is 1¼ to 1½ inches high. The female lays 2 white eggs, which she incubates for 15 to 18 days. The young leave the nest after about 3 weeks. It is believed that the female raises only 1 brood each year.

Feeding Habits

Like all hummingbirds, Costa's hummingbird feeds while hovering over flowers. Nectar, spiders, and insects make up its diet. While feeding, both sexes utter a light *chip* sound.

Plants *for* food *and* shelter include:

See the Calendar for Hummingbird and Butterfly Flowers, the Southwest section (page 50).

Male Costa's hummingbird taking nectar from the flowers of chuparosa (*Justicia californica*).

Anna's hummingbird / *Calypte anna*

The largest hummingbird in California and the only hummingbird that regularly winters in the United States. The 4-inch birds resemble living gems. Both sexes have a metallic green back and the male has a brilliant iridescent pink-red crown and throat; the female usually has a few red feathers on her throat.

Like all hummingbirds, the bird is a master of flight. It can fly backward or hover in place as it takes nectar, pollen, and insects from flowers. The wingbeats of hummingbirds are so rapid that they make a humming sound. The male's song is a repeated, squeaky *chee-chee-chee* sung while perched.

Habitat
A common garden bird, it is also found in coastal woods.

Migration and Winter Range
Some birds migrate north to British Columbia or south as far as Arizona and Texas in fall, returning to California in December.

Breeding Range
Resident bird within its breeding range, from northern Baja California and the coastal foothills of southern California north to southern Oregon. Summer pioneers reach British Columbia.

Breeding Behavior
The courtship flight consists of looping back and forth at high speed, climbing as high as 100 feet, tracing a towering U-pattern. The bird plummets to earth, keeping his eye on the female, and levels off at tremendous speed to pass over her, travelling into the sun so that his rose red throat glows in the sunlight. As he passes over her he produces an explosive *peek* sound by spreading out his specialized narrow tail feathers. This display flight is also used to discourage intruders from entering his territory.

Female Anna's hummingbird builds up the sides of her nest while incubating the eggs. The nest is in a desert willow (*Chilopsis linearis*).

Nesting

In California, Anna's hummingbird begins nesting as early as December, often while snow or frost is still on the ground. A tiny cup-shaped nest made of plant down and lichen, bound together with spiderweb, is fastened to a sheltered horizontal limb. The female often lays her 2 white eggs while the nest is only partially built, sometimes only a platform; she builds up the sides and completes the nest, decorating it with lichen while incubating the eggs.

Feeding Habits

Hummingbirds have evolved as efficient nectar feeders, with their long, thin, needlelike bills and extendable tongue. They prefer tubular flowers in open exposed groupings that allow the hummingbird to hover. As the bird feeds, pollen is deposited on its head and carried to the next plant. Hummingbirds also feed on small insects and spiders.

Plants *for* food *and* shelter include:

See the Calendar for Hummingbird and Butterfly Flowers, the Pacific Coast section (page 44).

Male Anna's hummingbird feeding on the flowers of Texas paintbrush (*Castilleja foliolosa*).

red-headed woodpecker / *Melanerpes erythrocephalus*

Usually very shy but amusing birds to watch, red-headed woodpeckers are often active and playful, chasing each other or drumming on dead limbs or tin roofs. When examining a tree for wood-boring insects, it will rap the timber sharply, then turn its head and listen carefully before deciding whether to continue drilling. With its red head, bluish black wings and tail, and its white underparts, it is a conspicuously handsome bird. The red-headed woodpecker's ranges in size from 8½ to 9½ inches long. Populations have declined through the clearing of dead trees required for nesting and the introduction of the European starling, which aggressively competes for nesting places. The call is a repeated, noisy, rattling *kwrrk.*

Habitat
Open deciduous woods, farmlands with scattered trees, and suburban areas. Uncommon in much of their range, populations are often very local.

Migration and Winter Range
In the extreme northern and western part of their range, the birds migrate south or southeast in autumn, wintering from the Great Lakes to the southern limits of the breeding range.

Breeding Range
Southern Saskatchewan east to New York and south to Texas, the Gulf Coast, and Florida.

Breeding Behavior
A noisy bird in the breeding season.

Two red-headed woodpeckers jostle playfully in the foliage and fruits of Allegheny serviceberry (*Amelanchier laevis*).

Nesting

A live tree, dead stub, utility pole, or fence post is selected for a nest site in May. Both sexes excavate the hole: one bird excavates, then calls the other, who returns before the first leaves. The nest is located from 8 to 80 feet above the ground. It has a 1¾-inch-diameter entrance and an 8- to 24-inch-deep cavity.

The female lays 4 to 6 round, glossy, white porcelainlike eggs. Both sexes share incubation for 2 weeks. In the southern parts of its range, it may raise 2 broods.

Feeding Habits

The red-headed woodpecker has evolved flycatcherlike traits, and spends much of its time darting out into the air to catch flying insects. In one record of an adult bird feeding young, insects were being consumed at the rate of 600 per hour.

The bird feeds on fewer larvae and grubs than other woodpeckers. Insects make up 50 percent of the bird's diet, and corn, fruits, and berries are also consumed.

Plants *for* food *and* shelter include:

serviceberries (*Amelanchier* spp.)

dogwoods (*Cornus* spp.)

wild strawberry (*Fragaria virginiana*)

red mulberry (*Morus rubra*)

wild cherries (*Prunus* spp.)

oaks (*Quercus* spp.)

blackberries (*Rubus* spp.)

elderberries (*Sambucus* spp.)

Red-headed woodpecker looks for wood-boring insects on the trunk of an American beech (*Fagus grandifolia*).

acorn woodpecker / *Melanerpes formicivorus*

With its harlequin face, white eyes and red crown, the boldly patterned, 9-inch acorn woodpecker is a handsome bird. These birds are especially noisy in spring. The birds drum against dead limbs and noisily chase each other through the treetops. Their call is a repeated high-pitched, sharp *waka-waka-waka*.

The common name, acorn woodpecker, refers to the bird's fondness for acorns, which are the most important item in its diet. The bird has a habit of riddling the trunks of communal "granary" trees and filling the holes with acorns. Sycamores, black oaks, yellow pines, and utility poles are usually selected. Also known as the California woodpecker because of its conspicuous presence in that state.

Acorn woodpecker at his acorn store in a California black oak (*Quercus kelloggii*).

Habitat
Valleys, foothills, and oak and pine-oak canyons.

Migration and Winter Range
Resident year-round throughout its range.

Breeding Range
Southwest Oregon south through California (west of the Sierra Nevada), throughout Arizona, New Mexico, and western Texas, south to Central America.

Breeding Behavior
Where food is plentiful the acorn woodpecker will live in loose colonies of 12 to 15 birds. The birds communally defend their territory. They also communally excavate the nest holes, incubate the eggs, and care for the young.

Nesting
Both sexes excavate the nest hollow. Oak trees, sycamores, cottonwoods, willows, and, more rarely, utility poles are excavated for nesting. The entrance hole is perfectly round, about 1¼ inches in diameter, with the chamber 8 to 24 inches deep. Usually nest holes are from 12 to 60 feet above the ground.

The female lays 3 to 4 white eggs between April and May, which are incubated communally for about 2 weeks. Possibly 2 and 3 broods may be raised in one season.

Feeding Habits

Acorn woodpeckers harvest and store acorns in autumn, when they are plentiful. Acorns are an important food source from fall into spring. The storage holes made by a colony are reused each year and are not deep enough to damage the tree.

During the summer months, insects make up 30 percent of the bird's diet. Fruits are also consumed and in June and July, the birds drill holes in the branches of oak trees and feed on the sap.

Plants *for* food *and* shelter include:

wild cherries (*Prunus* spp.)
oaks (*Quercus* spp.)
elderberries (*Sambucus* spp.)

Male acorn woodpecker.

red-bellied woodpecker / *Melanerpes carolinus*

The male red-bellied woodpecker is a handsome bird, with its black-and-white barred back and wings, and scarlet head and nape. The female has a scarlet nape only. This woodpecker is sometimes called zebra-back or zebra bird because of the pattern and coloration of its feathers.

A noisy and conspicuous bird that often visits parks and gardens. The birds have a repertoire of various churring, chattering calls, including a powerful and deliberate *chuck-chuck-chuck* descending in pitch.

Habitat
Farmland woodlots and hedgerows, bottomland, swamps, mixed coniferous-deciduous woods and shade trees in suburban yards.

Migration and Winter Range
Usually a nonmigratory permanent resident, the bird sometimes wanders outside its normal breeding range.

Breeding Range
Southeastern Minnesota to Connecticut and south to southern Florida and western Texas.

Breeding Behavior
The red-bellied woodpecker becomes especially noisy during the breeding season as it selects a suitable nesting site.

Male red-bellied woodpecker feeding on the small red berries of Fremont thornbush (*Lycium fremontii*).

Nesting

Dead trees or deciduous trees with softer wood, such as elm, maple, sycamore, poplar or willow are usually selected for nesting. They may also nest in utility poles and fence posts. A cavity 10 to 12 inches deep is excavated, usually less than 40 feet above ground. Both sexes assist in excavating the cavity and its 2-inch-diameter entrance hole. Man-made nest boxes may also be used.

The female lays 4 or 5 white eggs, which are incubated for 12 days by both sexes. Both sexes feed and care for the young, which leave the nest when 24 to 26 days old. The bird may raise 2 or 3 broods may be raised in the South, while 1 brood is usual in the northern limits of its range.

Feeding Habits

The red-bellied woodpecker feeds on wood-boring insect larvae as well as ants, beetles, grasshoppers, and other insects. It also feeds on corn, beech-nuts, pine seeds, acorns, and fruits.

Plants *for* food *and* shelter include:

dogwoods (*Cornus* spp.)

cedar (*Juniperus* spp.)

bayberries (*Myrica* spp.)

Virginia creeper (*Parthenocissus quinquefolia*)

pines (*Pinus* spp.)

wild cherries (*Prunus* spp.)

oaks (*Quercus* spp.)

common blackberry (*Rubus allegheniensis*)

elderberries (*Sambucus* spp.)

frost grape (*Vitis vulpina*)

Male red-bellied woodpecker.

northern flicker / *Colaptes auratus*

Northern flicker digging for ants. The wild strawberry (*Fragaria virginiana*) is another favorite source of food.

Northern (*red-shafted*) flicker.

Because of their amusing antics, noisiness, and abundance from Alaska to Mexico and coast to coast, the northern flicker is probably the best-known woodpecker in North America. In different parts of its range, two color variations are found. Both bear the signature white rump, which flashes when the bird flies up from the ground.

East of the Rocky Mountains and northwest into Alaska, the yellow-shafted flicker has a brilliant golden color on the underside of the wings and tail. The male has a black moustache and both sexes have a gray cap, a brown face and a red crescent on the nape of the neck.

The red-shafted flicker is the western equivalent of the yellow-shafted flicker. The male has a gray face, a brown cap and a red moustache. The wing and tail linings are a salmon or scarlet-orange color. Both sexes lack the red crescent on the nape.

The yellow-shafted and red-shafted variants commonly interbreed where their ranges overlap in the Great Plains, resulting in hybrids that may show a mix of characteristics. Because of this interbreeding, all flickers were collectively grouped as the common flicker by the American Ornithologists' Union in 1973, but since 1995 have been considered to be two separate species, the northern flicker and the gilded flicker found in southwestern Arizona and southeastern California.

Habitat

Common birds in deciduous or mixed woodlands, parks and gardens, orchards and desert areas.

Migration and Winter Range

The bird winters from near the northern limits to the southern limits of its breeding range. In the fall and winter, many northern flickers move southward from their summer territory, while others remain resident year-round.

The spring migration begins in late winter, with the northern movement beginning as early as February and continuing until April. The birds travel in loose flocks, with the males arriving in their breeding territory several days ahead of the females. The birds are noisy on arrival and seem to alert the woodlands to the coming of spring.

The male calls from a tall tree with a loud prolonged series of *wick-wick-wick-wick* or *yuck-yuck-yuck-yuck* and drums rapidly on a resonant limb, metal roof, utility pole, or house. The drumming is a continuous roll, often waking people in the early hours of the morning. These are challenge calls, establishing the bird's territorial boundaries, and are a preliminary to the courtship display.

Breeding Range
Alaska to Mexico and from coast to coast.

Breeding Behavior
Northern flickers usually mate for life. Both sexes return to the same breeding area each year. The drumming and calling brings the pair together and, when they greet each other, the birds indulge in head-bobbing displays as well as the frozen pose. During the head-bobbing display, wings may be lifted and the tail spread to reveal the underwing and undertail colors and a soft musical call may be made. A competing suitor commonly appears early in the breeding season. The males chase each other, with the intruder generally being driven away.

Nesting
When the pairs are united they begin nest building. Northern flickers have slightly curved bills and are relatively poor excavators among woodpeckers. They tend to select dead trees, limbs with rotted wood, or soft-timbered trees. Apple, sycamore, oak, cherry, elm, maple, beech, ash, and pine trees are favorite trees for nesting. In the Southwest, the saguaro cactus is most commonly used.

Both sexes work on the excavation, beginning at first light and sometimes working until late at night. A number of extra holes are bored high up in trees before the final home is completed. Old fence posts, utility poles, the sides of buildings, or a nest box may be selected from 2 to 60 feet above the ground. The birds will often make repairs to an old nest hole and reuse the nest.

The female usually lays 6 to 8 white eggs. Both birds share the incubation, each feeding the other while it is on the nest. The birds display affection toward each other throughout the breeding season. After 2 weeks of incubation, the young birds are fed by regurgitation and are ready to leave the nest, about 4 weeks after hatching.

Feeding Habits
The northern flicker commonly feeds on the ground, probing for ants with its long, barbed tongue. Ants are an important part of the diet. Native fruits make up about a quarter of their diet.

Plants *for* food *and* shelter include:

serviceberries (*Amelanchier* spp.)
hackberries (*Celtis* spp.)
dogwoods (*Cornus* spp.)
toyon (*Heteromeles arbutifolia*)
black tupelo (*Nyssa sylvatica*)
pines (*Pinus* spp.)
wild cherries (*Prunus* spp.)
oaks (*Quercus* spp.)
sumacs (*Rhus* spp.)
viburnums (*Viburnum* spp.)

Northern (yellow-shafted) flicker

downy woodpecker / *Picoides pubescens*

Downy woodpecker feeding on the berries of Virginia creeper (*Parthenocissus quinquefolia*).

The most familiar bird in the woodpecker family, the downy woodpecker is also the smallest and tamest eastern woodpecker. When European settlement spread across North America, the downy woodpecker adapted and is now commonly seen in settled areas. It is a small, black-and-white woodpecker with a broad white stripe that runs down the center of the back and a short, stubby bill. A distinguishing mark of the adult male downy woodpecker is a small, bright red patch on the back of his head. The call is a short, high-pitched *pik*.

Habitat

Downy woodpeckers are found in parks and gardens, farms, orchards, woodlots, and open mixed deciduous and coniferous woodland. Their preferred habitat contains deciduous trees with shrubs nearby, since downy woodpeckers forage lower to the ground than other woodpeckers and will often forage in shrubs.

Migration and Winter Range

Downy woodpeckers usually remain in their breeding grounds all year, though a few birds move south from the northern limit of their range in autumn or early winter. Birds also move from higher to lower altitudes.

Breeding Range

The downy woodpecker breeds across most of the United States, ranging from Southeast Alaska across southern Canada to Newfoundland, and south to southern California, central Arizona and central Texas, and along the Gulf Coast and Florida.

Breeding Behavior

In late winter, both sexes begin drumming, and males and females seek each other out for courtship. The male displays to the female by spreading his wings while facing the female on a limb. Another male may interrupt, courting the same female. Once the female has chosen the successful suitor, the search for a nest site begins. Some downy woodpeckers have remained paired for years.

Nesting

These woodpeckers nest in dead tree trunks or decaying branches. Nest boxes are also used. A gourd-shaped nesting cavity is chiseled out, and some wood chips are left on the floor.

The female lays 4 or 5 white eggs, which are incubated by both parents for 12 days. The young are fed insects and leave the nest when 21 to 24 days old. The young follow the parents around until they learn to find food for themselves. During the winter months, individual downy woodpeckers often join mixed flocks of chickadees, nuthatches, and titmice.

Feeding Habits

Wood-boring larvae of insects that damage trees are a favorite food. The bird taps at a branch and lays its head along the limb, apparently listening to the movement of borers under the bark. The birds quickly chisel the bark and extract the borer. Wild fruits and insects are also consumed.

Plants *for* food *and* shelter include:

serviceberries (*Amelanchier* spp.)

dogwoods (*Cornus* spp.)

wild strawberry (*Fragaria virginiana*)

Virginia creeper (*Parthenocissus quinquefolia*)

oaks (*Quercus* spp.)

mountain ashes (*Sorbus* spp.)

Female downy woodpecker.

Downy woodpecker feeding on a spruce cone (*Picea* sp.).

black phoebe / *Sayornis nigricans*

The black phoebe is the only black-breasted North American flycatcher. The color pattern of the bird is like a junco's, although its posture and behavior mark it as a flycatcher. This 6- to 7-inch bird is slate-black with a white belly and outer tail feathers. Characteristic of the black phoebe are its erect posture and its habit of moving its tail in spasmodic jerks when perched. It is unusually gentle and unobtrusive for a member of the tyrant flycatcher family.

Seemingly unperturbed by human activity, the black phoebe has become a common suburban garden bird. House-flies are a favorite food, making this bird a useful garden visitor. The black phoebe spends much of its time perched on low tree branches, stones, fence posts or other low vantage points from which it sallies forth like a large butterfly, sailing in eccentric arcs to snap at insects.

The black phoebe's song is a repetition of *fi-bee-fi-bee* with the first two notes rising and the last two dropping in pitch. This song gives the bird its common name. The bird's common call is a sharp *tsip* or *chee*, which it makes constantly in flight and whenever it alights.

Black phoebe feeding on the fruit of the blue elderberry (*Sambucus caerulea*).

Habitat

The black phoebe is partial to water and is usually found on the edge of mountain streams, irrigation ditches, ponds, and lake banks. A watering trough will also attract it, and the bird is common around barnyards. In winter months it is often seen in city parks and gardens throughout its range.

Migration and Winter Range

Resident throughout its range.

Breeding Range

California, southern Nevada, southwest Utah, Arizona, southern New Mexico, and central Texas, south to Baja California, through Mexico, and the Central and South American highlands to Argentina. The bird sometimes strays into Oregon and British Columbia, and it is a local resident in the bottom of the Grand Canyon in Arizona.

Breeding Behavior

A solitary species, and apart from mated pairs in the breeding season is always seen alone. The birds often remain in their territory throughout the year, and return to the same nest site year after year.

Nesting

For nesting, the birds require a sheltered rockface or timber wall in the vicinity of a ready supply of mud. Bridges are favorite nesting sites, as are niches in the rocks along mountain streams and the rafters of barns. The nest is built of mud pellets, which are plastered to the vertical surface and mixed with grass, forming a strongly built cup 4½ inches in diameter. The nest is lined with plant fiber and feathers.

The female lays 3 to 6 faintly speckled white eggs. She incubates the eggs for 15 to 17 days. The young leave the nest after about 3 weeks. She may raise 2 or 3 broods in one year.

Feeding Habits

Insects form the bulk of the black phoebe's diet. The bird usually flies down from its perch and often dives toward water, almost skimming the surface, its bill clicking as it snaps at insects. Occasionally the bird will dip its belly beneath the water to bathe in flight. Large insects are taken back and tapped against the perch until they die. The bird also sometimes feeds on elderberries and pepperberries.

Plants *for* food *and* shelter include:

elderberries (*Sambucus* spp.)

Black phoebe is often seen near water.

ash-throated flycatcher / *Myiarchus cinerascens*

The ash-throated flycatcher is a comparatively silent and shy flycatcher. The 8-inch bird has a pale sulphur-yellow belly, whitish throat, grayish brown back, cinnamon-rust primaries and tail feathers, and two wing bars. The bird's principal call notes include a clear *huit–huit* repeated several times, and low whistled notes of *hip* and *ha–whip*.

Ash-throated flycatcher at his nest hollow in a Fremont cottonwood (*Populus fremontii*).

Habitat

Western deciduous woods, mesquite, and saguaros. The bird's favorite haunts are apparently not affected by climatic conditions, since it summers from altitudes of 9,000 feet in the southern Sierra Nevada to below sea level in the broiling heat of Death Valley in California.

In Arizona, the bird favors dense mesquite thickets in creek bottoms, oak canyons, and dry brush. Along the Sacramento River in California, the flycatchers are found in sycamores, valley oaks, live oaks, and dead trees close to the river. Farther east, open woodland, piñon-juniper forests and sagebrush are favored.

Migration and Winter Range

The birds winter in southern Arizona, California, Mexico, and Central America. They move to their winter range from late September to mid-October, where they linger in dense thickets of vegetation along streams or desert washes.

Breeding Range

Southwestern Oregon and eastern Washington to southern Idaho, southwestern Wyoming, Colorado, New Mexico, and north and central Texas to Baja California and Mexico.

Breeding Behavior

The birds arrive in their breeding grounds from mid-March in southern Texas to early May in Washington.

Nesting

Because of the shortage of protective concealing foliage in much of the bird's range, the ash-throated flycatcher has become a cavity nester, but still builds an elaborate nest inside the cavity. The bird usually selects a natural cavity in a mesquite, ash, oak, cottonwood, or sycamore tree. Holes left by broken branches of Mojave yuccas and Joshua trees are frequently used. Old woodpecker holes are also used, and the flycatchers sometimes evict woodpeckers from their newly constructed cavity or often nest near human habitation, using nest boxes or other containers.

If the cavity is too large, the birds fill the extra space with grasses and dried animal dung. The cup-shaped nest is made of animal fur on a foundation of grass, usually 20 feet or less above the ground.

The eggs are not the normal white eggs of a cavity-nester, but have the camouflage markings of a foliage-nesting bird, indicating that the species has adopted cavity-nesting comparatively recently. The female lays 4 or 5 eggs and incubates them for 15 days, often leaving the nest for several hours in the warmer parts of the day but remaining close by. Both parents feed the young with insects, often preparing the softer portions of large insects by removing the wings and legs before feeding.

The young leave the nest after 16 or 17 days and follow the parents around for some time, begging for food with quivering wings until they can care for themselves.

Feeding Habits

Unlike most flycatchers, the ash-throated flycatcher does not usually return to the same perch after sallying forth to capture insects on the wing. The bird also forages among low shrubs feeding on insects; some berries are also included in the diet.

> Plants *for* food *and* shelter include:
>
> elderberries (*Sambucus* spp.)

Ash-throated flycatcher forages for insects in a blue palo verde (*Cercidium microphyllum*).

blue jay / *Cyanocitta cristata*

Blue jay alights on a red oak
(*Quercus rubra*).

The blue jay is a strikingly beautiful, 11- to 12½-inch bird, among the most familiar birds of North America. The bird's call is a defiant *jay-jay*, often sounded in a discordant chorus with other jays, setting up a commotion if an enemy is spotted. Blue jays also mimic other birdcalls.

Habitat
Originally a cautious bird of the oak forests, blue jays have become common in city parks and suburban yards, preferring areas with oak trees.

Migration and Winter Range
Although seen throughout the year, local populations seem to move south during winter and are replaced by birds from farther north, traveling in large, loose flocks in spring and fall.

Breeding Range
East of the Rocky Mountains from southern Canada to Mexico.

Breeding Behavior
During the breeding period, blue jays are uncharacteristically quiet until the young birds have fledged. During courtship and at the nest, the male feeds the female selected morels.

Nesting

Both sexes help to construct the nest. The birds break twigs and small branches from trees to build a bulky untidy structure lined with grasses in the crotch of a tree or on a limb. Usually nests are 10 to 15 feet from the ground, although they can be placed as high as 50 feet.

Females lay 4 to 6 brown, spotted eggs and incubate them for 16 to 18 days. The devoted male feeds the female at the nest, approaching it quietly at a lower level and warily hopping in a spiral up to the nest. The young leave the nest when they are 17 to 21 days old. The adults fearlessly defend their nest and young by dive-bombing and pecking intruders.

Feeding Habits

The blue jay is omnivorous. Acorns and beechnuts are favorite foods when in season.

Plants *for* food *and* shelter include:

sunflowers (*Helianthus* spp.)

hollies (*Ilex* spp.)

red mulberry (*Morus rubra*)

wild cherries (*Prunus* spp.)

oaks (*Quercus* spp.)

sumacs (*Rhus* spp.)

blackberries (*Rubus* spp.)

blueberries (*Vaccinium* spp.)

viburnums (*Viburnum* spp.)

wild grapes (*Vitis* spp.)

Blue jay foraging in mulch.

Steller's jay / *Cyanocitta stelleri*

Steller's jay often nests in fir trees, including the grand fir (*Abies grandis*), and feeds on seeds from the cones.

The Steller's jay is unmistakable with its large size (11½ inches), handsome blue to blue-black coat, and prominent crest. It is the only crested jay in the West. Usually an extremely shy bird, it adapts to humans around picnic areas or at feeding stations. Birds often roam together in small flocks.

Intelligent, cunning, alert, and inquisitive, the Steller's jay is also a noisy, boisterous bird. Its low-pitched raucous screams and calls echo through the woodlands warning of an approaching intruder. It may imitate the screams of the golden eagle or red-tailed hawk, or call with a harsh rasping *shack-shack-shack-shack* or a mellow *klook-klook-klook*.

Habitat
Coniferous and mixed forests, picnic grounds, orchards, and gardens.

Migration and Winter Range
Resident throughout its range. In fall and winter, small numbers of the birds often descend to the lowlands.

Breeding Range
Rocky Mountains west to the Pacific Coast, from coastal Alaska south through California and Mexico to El Salvador and the highlands of Nicaragua, and east to southwestern Texas.

Breeding Behavior
Secretive during the breeding season. While nest building or attending the nest, they become silent and slip through the foliage, vanishing from sight.

Nesting
Both sexes share in nest-building. They construct a large, well-made structure from twigs, cemented with mud and lined with rootlets and pine needles. The nest is commonly built in a spruce or fir tree (often a Douglas fir), usually 8 to 40 feet above the ground, but also as high as 100 feet or more. The nests are usually well concealed. The female lays 3 to 5 greenish, spotted eggs and incubates them, mostly herself, for about 18 days. The full-grown young join their parents in family groups for some time after leaving the nest, breaking up in early fall and scattering through the forest.

Feeding Habits

Plant food makes up over 70 percent of the Steller's jay's natural diet. Acorns and pine seeds are their main food source, and they sometimes raid the acorn woodpecker's stored supply.

Steller's jay also feeds on insects and sometimes snakes, and has a reputation for raiding other birds' nests and consuming the chicks and eggs. Native fruits and some cultivated fruits are also consumed, but the bird is too shy to visit the more established orchard areas.

Plants *for* food *and* shelter include:

dogwoods (*Cornus* spp.)

wild strawberry (*Fragaria virginiana*)

pines (*Pinus* spp.)

wild cherries (*Prunus* spp.)

oaks (*Quercus* spp.)

western raspberry (*Rubus leucodermis*)

elderberries (*Sambucus* spp.)

Steller's jay.

Mexican jay / *Aphelocoma wollweberi*

Mexican jay feeding on fallen acorns from Gambel oak (*Quercus gambelii*).

Also called the gray-breasted jay and Arizona jay, this large, 11- to 13-inch blue-gray jay without a crest is possibly the most interesting bird of the crow family. Mexican jays usually live in flocks of from 6 to 20 birds throughout the year and are semicommunal in the breeding season. If an intruder comes near the nest, the whole colony will join in the defense, noisily screaming at the enemy while twitching their tails and bobbing their heads; 30 or 40 birds from the surrounding area may bond together to loudly scold the intruder. The bird's alarm call is a loud *wheat-wheat-wack, wack-wack*. Call notes include a high-pitched *werk-werk-werk*.

Habitat

Mexican jays live in oak and oak-pine forests from 2,000 to 9,000 feet elevation, only occasionally descending to the lower zones.

Migration and Winter Range

The Mexican jay is a resident bird year-round within its range.

Breeding Range

The bird's breeding range is southern Arizona, southwestern New Mexico, western Texas (Chisos Mountains), and south to central Mexico.

Breeding Behavior

Two adult pairs of the flock construct separate nests while the rest of the flock maintains a communal interest, bringing nesting material and helping to build and defend the nests. The nonbreeding birds in the flock also later assist in feeding the young.

Nesting

The nests are usually built 15 to 25 feet above the ground in oaks or occasionally pine trees. The birds construct a bulky, conspicuous basket of coarse sticks and leafy oak twigs that is held in place by the branches' crooked shapes. The jays break twigs from trees rather than picking them up from the ground. The basketlike nest is lined with a closely woven cup of rootlets, animal hair, and fine grasses.

The female lays 4 or 5 green eggs between March and July and incubates them for 18 days. Young leave the nest 24 to 25 days after hatching.

Feeding Habits

Acorns provide the bulk of the Mexican jay's diet, and they are often seen hopping around under oak trees searching for food. When a jay finds an acorn, he holds it between his two feet and raps it with his bill to open the shell. If there is an abundance of acorns, the birds hide them under rocks or ledges for future food. Wild fruits, grasshoppers, and other insects are also in their the diet, as are small birds' eggs and chicks. In many picnic areas, the gray-breasted jay becomes tame, and readily accepts handouts of food.

Plants *for* food *and* shelter include:

oaks (*Quercus* spp.)

Mexican jay foraging on an oak tree (*Quercus sp.*).

purple martin / *progne subis*

Purple martin perched near big bluestem (*Andropogon gerardii*), a useful plant for nesting material.

The purple martin is the largest swallow in North America. The male is a glossy blue-black and the females and immature males are gray to white below and duller above. The bird's voice consists of loud and cheerful chirping notes and gurgles. It is noted for its apartment-style nesting in man-made community houses in the eastern region. American Indians traditionally hung hollow gourds for them to use as nesting sites. East of the Rocky Mountains, purple martins now breed almost exclusively in man-made martin houses, but in western North America where they are less common, they usually nest in natural hollows or abandoned woodpecker holes, often in solitary pairs. If martins breed successfully, they will return every year.

Habitat

Purple martins prefer open woodland, agricultural land, towns, and lawns near lakes or ponds.

Migration and Winter Range

A summer resident, the purple martin arrives in North America from late January through April. In late August it begins the southward migration to winter in South America.

Breeding Range

Purple martins range across the United States, from southern Canada south to central Mexico, the West Indies, and southern Florida.

Breeding Behavior

Males are usually the first to arrive at nesting sites, and begin chirping loudly, a liquid, low-pitched, twittering song, and defending a tree hollow or a room in a martin house. The female arrives and chooses a nesting site. The birds may nest alone, but usually in the east they nest communally.

Nesting

Both sexes gather material including grass, leaves, twigs, feathers, and mud to construct the nest. The female lays 3 to 8 white eggs between March and July and incubates them for 15 or 16 days. The male guards the nest when the female is absent. When 28 days old, the young leave the nest. Both parents assist in feeding the young. In August or September when the young can fly, the martins abandon their nest and prepare for the southward migration. They gather in huge flocks in the evening, with as many as 100,000 birds in a roosting flock.

Feeding Habits

The purple martin takes almost all its food on the wing, consuming flying insects including flies, mosquitoes, and dragonflies. Enormous quantities of insects are fed to the young at the nest; parents may return to the nest as often as 205 times in a 4-hour period. Because of their huge appetite for insects, purple martins are very beneficial to home gardeners and farmers.

Plants *for* food *and* shelter include:

big bluestem (*Andropogon gerardii*) grasses, for nest-building material

Male and female purple martins at their nest hollow in an abandoned woodpecker hole in the trunk of a birch tree (*Betula sp.*).

Perching on its nest box, a purple martin displays its wide gape used to catch insects.

wrentit / *Chamaea fasciata*

Wrentit feeding on the fruits of the snowberry (*Symphoricarpos albus*).

The wrentit is not closely related to any other North American bird species and its placement in the classification of bird families has periodically changed. Currently, it is a member of the family Sylviidae.

The wrentit is 6½ inches long, with a dark gray-brown back and cinnamon-brown belly. It has a streaked breast and a very noticeable white eye. It has a small, thick bill similar to that of a chickadee; it resembles a wren in coloration, scolding behavior, and long tail.

Elusive birds seldom showing themselves in the open, wrentits keep to the security of low, dense cover. The wrentit is a weak flier and usually chooses to hop through the vegetation rather than navigate the air. Mature birds establish their territories of about 2½ acres and maintain them for most of their lives.

The bird's call consists of 6 or more loud ringing whistles that are delivered in the same tone. Beginning slowly, the notes of this call speed up and finally run together in a trill. When angry, the bird makes a distinctive low-pitched chatter.

Habitat
Wrentits are found in chaparral and other brushy growth and in suburban gardens and parks.

Migration and Winter Range
Wrentits are resident year-round within their established territory.

Breeding Range
The bird's breeding range is from western Oregon to northern Baja California.

Breeding Behavior
Defense of the territory is more vigorous during the breeding season. Pairs mate for life and live together all year long. The couple feed together, roost together, and often preen each other. Their interest in each other is heightened as nest-building begins, when the male chases the female in rapid flight.

Nesting

A compact cup of course bark, grasses, and plant fibers, bound with spiderweb, is built in a low, dense shrubbery by both sexes. The female lays 3 to 5 greenish blue eggs and incubates them for 15 to 16 days, and the young leave the nest when they are 15 to 16 days old.

Feeding Habits

The wrentit feeds on insects, as well as fruits, especially from low-growing bushes.

Plants *for* food *and* shelter include:

toyon (*Heteromeles arbutifolia*)

twinberry honeysuckle (*Lonicera involucrata*)

bayberries (*Myrica* spp.)

sumacs (*Rhus* spp.)

common blackberry (*Rubus allegheniensis*), for nesting

elderberries (*Sambucus* spp.)

grasses (*Andropogon* spp.), for nesting

Wrentit feeding in the foliage of a birchleaf mountain mahogany (*Cercocarpus montanus* var. *glaber*, formerly *Cercocarpus betuloides*).

bridled titmouse / *Baeolophus wollweberi*

Named for the black-and-white stripes on the head that resemble a horse's bridle, the bridled titmouse is the most beautiful of the crested titmice. This 5¼-inch bird has a small black bib, setting off its whitish belly and gray back. Sexes have the same markings. The bird is often confused with the mountain chickadee, which is a similar size and color but lacks the titmouse's distinctive crest.

The call of the bridled titmouse is a rapid, squealing *chick-a-dee-dee-dee* or high-pitched, repeated, quick *fee-bee* whistles.

Bridled titmouse in the branches of one of its favorite trees, silverleaf oak (*Quercus hypoleucoides*).

Habitat

The bridled titmouse inhabits the evergreen-oak or pine-oak woodlands in mountain foothills up to 6,000 feet elevation.

Migration and Winter Range

A resident bird throughout its range, the bridled titmouse roams in small flocks except during the breeding season. In winter, the bird may move down to wooded valleys and streamsides where cottonwoods occur.

Breeding Range

The bridled titmouse breeds from central and southeastern Arizona and southwestern New Mexico mostly in oak or mixed oak-pine-juniper woodland and south to the highlands of western Mexico.

Breeding Behavior

Pairs form in nonbreeding season while in mixed-species flocks, and will usually remain together for life. Breeding occurs between March and May.

Nesting

These birds nest in natural tree cavities, preferring live or dead oaks, but will also use nest hollows in cottonwoods or mesquite. Similar to the tufted titmouse, it will also nest in bird boxes or old woodpecker holes. The nest is lined with soft material including plant down and animal hair, and is usually about 4 to 28 feet above the ground. The female lays 5 to 7 white eggs and incubation is usually 14 days. Family groups are formed in late August after the young have fledged. The young birds are taught to forage in oak trees before joining larger flocks in the fall.

Feeding Habits

Bridled titmice search out insects, insect eggs, and larvae on oak branches and bark crevices and often forage on the ground. They are fond of caterpillars, acorns, and pine seeds and also feed on other seeds, nuts, and berries. They do not store food for future use as other titmice species commonly do.

> **Plants *for* food *and* shelter include:**
>
> pines (*Pinus* spp.)
> cottonwoods (*Populus* spp.)
> oaks (*Quercus* spp.)

Bridled titmouse foraging for insects in an Emory oak (*Quercus emoryi*).

tufted titmouse / *Baeolophus bicolor*

The largest of the titmice, the 6-inch tufted titmouse is a plainly colored bird with a gray back and whitish belly. The flanks beneath each wing are tinged with a rusty brown. The bird has a prominent pointed crest that is raised when it becomes excited. When the bird feels aggressive, the crest is flattened against its head.

The tufted titmouse flits through the foliage searching for insects, always alert and inquisitive. In spring and early summer, the call is incessant, a loud whistled series of 4 to 8 notes, *peto–peto–peto–peto*.

Tufted titmice feeding on fruits of common hackberry (*Celtis occidentalis*).

Habitat
Common in woodlands and clumps of large shade trees in suburban parks and gardens.

Migration and Winter Range
The tufted titmouse is resident year-round.

Breeding Range
Southeastern Nebraska (Missouri River), southern Wisconsin, central New York, southern Ontario, and southwestern Connecticut south through the Mississippi River Valley to the Gulf Coast, southeastern Texas, and central Florida.

Breeding Behavior
In early spring, the birds separate into breeding pairs. The birds mate for life.

Nesting
The birds nest in cavities in trees, nest boxes, or abandoned woodpecker holes 3 to 90 feet above the ground. They show a preference for hollows in dogwood and chinquapin oak trees. The cavity space is filled with bark strips, grass, and leaves before the cup-shaped nest of animal fur, moss, and fibrous bark is built. The female lays 4 to 8 brown-dotted white eggs. The male feeds the incubating female away from the nest after calling her, and she covers the eggs before leaving the nest hollow.

The female sits closely on the eggs for about 2 weeks, fearlessly guarding her clutch, and the young leave the nest hollow when about 18 days old. Both parents feed the young long after they leave the nest. The birds travel around as a family group in early summer before joining mixed flocks for fall and winter.

Feeding Habits

Caterpillars form half the bird's diet and insects make up another 17 percent. Titmice also feed on wild fruits and nuts. Acorns are a favorite food. The titmouse carries the acorn to a suitable limb; then holding it with both feet, cracks the nut with a fast hammering of its bill.

Plants *for* food *and* shelter include:

serviceberries (*Amelanchier* spp.)

hackberries (*Celtis* spp.)

sunflowers (*Helianthus* spp.)

red mulberry (*Morus rubra*)

bayberries (*Myrica* spp.)

pines (*Pinus* spp.)

oaks (*Quercus* spp.)

common blackberry (*Rubus allegheniensis*)

elderberries (*Sambucus* spp.)

wild grapes (*Vitis* spp.)

Pair of tufted titmice engage in courtship feeding.

black-capped chickadee / *Poecile atricapillus*

Because of its friendliness, fearlessness, and cheerful song, the black-capped chickadee is one of America's best-known and best-loved birds. Chickadees are small birds, 4¾ to 5¾ inches long, with gray backs, white underparts, and a black bib and cap. This good-natured bird with its cheery *chick-a-dee-dee-dee* call brings joy to the spirit. The bird obtains its common name from its coloration and its *chick-a-dee* call.

Black-capped chickadee favors the fruits of California wax myrtle (*Myrica californica*).

Habitat

Mixed hardwood-coniferous forests, woodlots, and suburban gardens are preferred habitats.

Migration and Winter Range

The bird is mostly a year-round resident in its range, its winter range extending slightly southward. In the winter months, chickadees rove the woods in small, loose flocks in defined territories. The flock of 6 to 10 birds is formed in late summer after the young have dispersed. A hierarchical pecking order may develop, with a pair that nested successfully in the territory outranking the fall arrivals. That pair may dominate all others of their own sex within the flock and take precedence when food is found or a roosting place is decided. The pair establishes a feeding territory and defends it against adjacent flocks of the same species. At the end of winter, the dominant pair remains in the breeding territory, while the other birds disperse.

Breeding Range

The breeding range extends from central Alaska and southern Canada south to northwestern California, northeastern Nevada, central Utah, northern New Mexico, northeastern Oklahoma, central Missouri, southern Ohio, eastern Tennessee, western North Carolina, western Maryland, and northern New Jersey.

Breeding Behavior

In late winter, the male chickadee begins to give his *fee-bee* song, which is heard more often as the males define their breeding territory and the winter flocks break up. The birds form breeding pairs and become more shy as they establish a nesting site.

Nesting

Normally the birds excavate a nest cavity in partially rotten wood. Old woodpecker holes, natural cavities, or bird boxes are sometimes used. Birch or pine trees are commonly selected, and the birds often use a woodpecker hole made from drilling the tree for insects. The hole is enlarged, with the birds scattering the excavated wood chips away from the nest site. The female lines the nest chamber with plant fiber, insect cocoons, and animal fur. She then lays 5 to 10 lightly spotted white eggs. Both parents incubate the eggs and feed the nestlings. The young leave the nest after 14 to 18 days and are fed by the parents for another 10 days. They disperse after a few weeks.

Feeding Habits

The chickadee feeds on enormous quantities of insect pests. About 30 percent of its diet is from plants, including the seeds of conifers and wild fruits.

Plants *for* food *and* shelter include:

serviceberries (*Amelanchier* spp.)

birches (*Betula* spp.)

sunflowers (*Helianthus* spp.)

winterberry (*Ilex verticillata*)

bayberries (*Myrica* spp.)

pines (*Pinus* spp.)

hemlocks (*Tsuga* spp.)

viburnums (*Viburnum* spp.)

Black-capped chickadee feeding on the fruit of staghorn sumac (*Rhus typhina*).

mountain chickadee / *Poecile gambeli*

Mountain chickadee feeding on insects from the foliage of Arizona mountain ash (*Sorbus dumosa*).

The 5- to 5¾-inch mountain chickadee resembles the black-capped chickadee except for its white eye stripe, which is missing during summer molt. The mountain chickadee's call is *chick-a-dee-a-dee-a-dee*. The bird also has a soft whistled call, the tune resembling the first three notes of "Three Blind Mice."

Habitat
During the breeding season and for much of the year, the bird's favorite habitat is coniferous mountain forest up to 10,000 feet elevation.

Migration and Winter Range
The bird is resident year-round throughout its range. In fall and winter, loose flocks venture down to the valleys and foothills to forage in oaks, cedars, and pines.

Breeding Range
The mountain chickadee breeds at higher altitudes from Southeast Alaska, British Columbia, and southwestern Alberta south to northern Baja California, Arizona, New Mexico, and southwestern Texas.

Breeding Behavior
The birds move in spring to the coniferous forests of the mountains and the males establish breeding territories with their distinctive call. Breeding pairs are formed and a nest site is selected.

Nesting
The mountain chickadee is similar to the black-capped chickadee in nesting habits. Like the black-capped chickadee, the mountain chickadee builds its nest in a hole it excavates in rotten wood, or uses a natural cavity or abandoned woodpecker hole. The nest is lined with fur or hair. The female lays 7 to 9 plain white or spotted eggs. Both parents incubate the eggs and feed the nestlings. The young leave the nest after 14 to 18 days and are fed by the parents for another 10 days. After a few weeks, the young leave the breeding territory.

Feeding Habits

Like all chickadees, the mountain chickadee is an arboreal acrobat, hanging head-down as he investigates foliage for scale insects. The bird also feeds on insect larvae, caterpillars, aphids, spiders, beetles, and seeds and nuts when available. In fall and winter, pine seeds are an important food source.

Plants *for* food *and* shelter include:

sunflowers (*Helianthus* spp.)

pines (*Pinus* spp.)

lodgepole pine (*Pinus contorta*)

piñon pine (*Pinus edulis*)

ponderosa pine (*Pinus ponderosa*)

Colorado spruce (*Picea pungens*)

oaks (*Quercus* spp.)

Mountain chickadee feeding on the tasty seeds of the piñon pine (*Pinus edulis*).

verdin / *Auriparus flaviceps*

Verdins at their nest in a western hackberry (*Celtis reticulata*).

The verdin is a small bird, 4½ inches long, with a yellow head and bright reddish chestnut shoulder epaulettes. This bird has a very distinctive voice, calling in a loud, piping whistle, which is quite out of proportion to its size. The common call is heard as a staccato *tsit–tsit–tsit*.

Habitat

The verdin is a conspicuous resident of low brushy desert scrub and mesquite thickets.

Migration and Winter Range

The bird is a year-round resident in its range.

Breeding Range

Southeastern California, southern Nevada, southwestern Utah, Arizona, New Mexico, and Texas south to southern Baja California and central Mexico.

Breeding Behavior

Verdins are sociable during the winter months, roaming the desert in small family groups, but become secretive during the breeding season, hiding in dense thickets.

Nesting

During courtship, the male begins building a large, round nest 3 to 10 feet above the ground in a desert shrub or cactus. Both birds complete the nest. The ball-shaped nest, measuring about 8 inches across, is usually constructed at the end of a low limb in a conspicuous position; it is possibly the most labor-intensive nest of all North American birds. Thorny twigs are interlaced so that the free ends stick out from the nest, quill-like, protecting it from intruders. Coarse grass, leaves, and plant stems are also used in the construction, and spiderweb is used to help bind the nest together. Spiderweb and plant fibers are used to block up holes. The nest is lined with grass, leaves, and feathers, which are also bound together with spiderweb.

The resulting nest is a strong, compact structure able to withstand the fiercest sandstorms. The nest is well insulated and able to protect the young from desert heat, wind, and sandstorms. Verdins build additional nests throughout the year, including thickly insulated nests for winter roosting with soft, silky lining, as well as more open, "air-conditioned" nests for summer. One pair of verdins in Arizona was recorded as having built 11 nests in one year.

The nests last for many years after use and, along with the birds' habit of also building roosting or winter nests, may give a false impression of the verdin population in an area. The female lays 3 to 6 spotted, greenish eggs between March and June and incubates them for about 10 days. The young leave the nest at 21 days, returning to sleep.

Feeding Habits

Hanging upside down from a twig, the bird seeks out insects, inspecting under leaves and in bark crevices. It feeds on insects and their larvae, as well as wild fruits and berries, including hackberries. Verdins sometimes nest 10 miles away from a water supply.

Plants *for* food *and* shelter include:

hackberries (*Celtis* spp.)
desert willow (*Chilopsis linearis*)
ocotillo (*Fouquieria splendens*)
Fremont thornbush (*Lycium fremontii*)
opuntia cacti (*Opuntia* spp.)

Verdin feeding on the berries of Fremont thornbush (*Lycium fremontii*), an important food source for desert birds.

white-breasted nuthatch / *Sitta carolinensis*

The white-breasted nuthatch is the common nuthatch of deciduous trees in the east and oaks and conifers in the western portions of the United States. It is 5¾ inches long with a black cap and rusty brown under the tail. The common names nuthatch and nuthacker refer to the way the bird takes a nut in its claws and hacks at it with its bill or wedges it in the bark of a tree and hacks it with hard strokes to break it open.

The nuthatch is a relative of the chickadee and titmouse. It has adapted to a life on tree trunks. The bird usually feeds head-down, moving down tree trunks, a position that may help it find food overlooked by creepers and woodpeckers that forage upright on the trunk. It will also climb upward or sideways in its search for insects and nuts. In spring, the bird's distinctive call is most noticeable, a nasal *yank-yank-yank*. This is supplemented with various other calls, including a soft *hit-hit* and the bird's song, a hollow whistled *tew-tew-tew-tew*.

Pair of white-breasted nuthatches at their nest hollow in sugar maple (*Acer saccharum*).

Habitat
A common bird of mature deciduous woodlands, woodlots, mixed forests, and large shade trees in residential areas.

Migration and Winter Range
The bird is resident year-round throughout its range.

Breeding Range
Southern Canada (British Columbia, Ontario, and Nova Scotia) south to Florida, the Gulf Coast, and southern Mexico. Not present in most of the Great Plains of the United States.

Breeding Behavior
The birds mate for life and travel singly or in pairs throughout the winter. As spring approaches, the male becomes more attentive to the female, often shelling seeds and tenderly feeding her or chasing her with short careening flights.

Nesting

Favorite nesting trees are native oaks, chestnuts, and maple trees. A natural cavity, old woodpecker hole, or nest box is selected 15 to 50 feet above the ground. The birds sometimes excavate a hollow in a decaying limb. The cavity is lined with shreds of bark, rootlets, animal fur, grasses, and feathers.

The female lays 5 to 10 (usually 8) spotted, white eggs. Both parents incubate the eggs for 12 days and tend the young, which leave the nest in about 2 weeks. The birds stay together as a family group until winter, when they scatter to roam the woods, often in mixed flocks with chickadees, woodpeckers, and an occasional brown creeper.

Feeding Habits

Insects form the bulk of their diet in spring and summer. They devour enormous quantities of caterpillars (including codling moth larvae), woodborers, aphids, and other pests, making these valuable birds for the garden. They are quite tame and are regular visitors at bird feeders.

The white-breasted nuthatch also feeds on acorns, beechnuts, hickory nuts, sunflower seeds, and corn. If food is plentiful, the nuthatch will store supplies in crevices in the bark of trees and, when icestorms freeze over its normal supply of seeds and acorns, it will raid its larder.

Plants *for* food *and* shelter include:

maples (*Acer* spp.)

sunflowers (*Helianthus* spp.)

pines (*Pinus* spp.)

oaks (*Quercus* spp.)

elderberries (*Sambucus* spp.)

White-breasted nuthatch foraging for insects in rough bark.

red-breasted nuthatch / *Sitta canadensis*

The red-breasted nuthatch is an extremely active little bird that spends most of its life in the northern coniferous forests. It differs from the white-breasted nuthatch by its small size, 4½ inches, is chunkier in appearance, and has red-brown underparts. This nuthatch is the only North American nuthatch with a broad black line through the eye and a white line above it.

The red-breasted nuthatch has a high-pitched, nasal, slightly drawled call, *yna-yna*. It also makes a high-pitched *ank-ank-ank*.

Habitat
The bird's preferred habitats are the coniferous forests of balsam and spruce in the north and the fir forests of the Pacific Coast. They often use conifers in suburban gardens for nesting.

Migration and Winter Range
A resident bird, it usually winters in coniferous forests. The bird is thought to make irregular migrations about every 2 years when northern cone-bearing trees fail to produce a crop of seeds. They then travel south, where they winter from southern Canada to northern Mexico and the Gulf Coast.

Red-breasted nuthatch leaving his favorite food tree, black spruce (*Picea mariana*).

Breeding Range
Upper Yukon River Valley, northern Manitoba, southern Quebec, and Newfoundland south to northern Minnesota, Michigan, Indiana, the mountains of New York and Massachusetts through the Allegheny Mountains to east Tennessee and western North Carolina in the east. Pacific Coast and south in the mountains of California, Arizona, and New Mexico in the west. The bird in recent years has begun extending its breeding range into eastern New York and Pennsylvania.

Breeding Behavior

Red-breasted nuthatches mate for life.

Nesting

In the breeding season, both sexes excavate a nesting hole, usually in a dead coniferous tree, a stump, or the dead wood of a living cottonwood or oak. The nest hollow has an entrance diameter of 1½ inches, slants for 3 to 4 inches, and then goes down vertically for about 4 inches. It is built 5 to 40 feet above ground level. The birds begin building by marking out the entrance hole with a series of small holes to form a circle before excavating. Deserted woodpecker holes and nest boxes are also used. A nest of grasses, rootlets, mosses, and shreds of bark is built inside the excavated cavity, and pitch is smeared around the entrance hole. Pitch from balsam fir and spruce is preferred in the north, while farther south pitch is gathered from pine trees. The pitch is carried on the tip of the bird's bill in little globules and tapped in place around the entrance. It is thought that the pitch may help keep insects, other birds, and small predators from entering the hole. On entering the cavity, the bird usually flies straight in to avoid the pitch.

The female lays 4 to 7 spotted white eggs, which are incubated by both sexes for 12 days. The young leave the nest after about 3 weeks.

> **Plants *for* food *and* shelter include:**
>
> firs (*Abies* spp.)
> spruces (*Picea* spp.)
> pines (*Pinus* spp.)

Feeding Habits

When feeding, the red-breasted nuthatch seems to prefer smaller outer branches rather than the tree trunk, hunting insects including beetles, woodborers, wood lice, caterpillars, spiders, and scales. It often spirals around branch tips or darts out into the air and captures flying insects like a flycatcher.

Seeds of pines, spruces, firs, and other conifers are the nuthatches' favorite food and, in parts of their range (such as the north Adirondack Mountains), the seeds of the black spruce make up almost the total diet. The bird often clings upside down to the extreme tips of branches while feeding, and may often be seen hovering around cones searching for a convenient foothold from which to reach the food source within. When food is plentiful, the birds store seeds in larders that are occasionally some distance from the food source.

Red-breasted nuthatch feeding on the seeds of pitch pine (*Pinus rigida*).

pygmy nuthatch / *Sitta pygmaea*

Pygmy nuthatch feeding on insects in the bark of a ponderosa pine (*Pinus ponderosa*).

A noisy, gregarious little bird, it is most abundant in stands of ponderosa pines from 3,500 to 10,000 feet elevation. This nuthatch is the smallest of the North American nuthatches, only 3½ inches long and the western counterpart of the brown-headed nuthatch, which it resembles in habits and appearance. The birds are most conspicuous in fall and winter, traveling through the woods in flocks of up to 100 birds.

As they drift through the tops of the pine trees, the birds keep in contact through their ceaseless chatter. They call each other with a high staccato *ti-di ti-di ti-di* and while in flight utter a soft *kit-kit-kit*. The flock is often joined by other species of native birds including chickadees, titmice, warblers and an occasional smaller woodpecker or white-breasted nuthatch.

Habitat
Ponderosa pines in the Rocky Mountains, also in the juniper-piñon belt in Arizona, and ponderosa and other pines of the Pacific Coast.

Migration and Winter Range
The bird is a year-round resident in mountainous areas. During winter, the pygmy nuthatch may drift to lower elevations and forage among oaks and in the juniper-piñon belt, returning to the pines in early spring.

Breeding Range
Mountains in the southern interior of British Columbia, western Montana, and southwestern South Dakota south to northern Baja California, Arizona, and the central plateau of Mexico to Morelos and Puebla.

Breeding Behavior
In spring, the nuthatches pair off from the winter flock.

Nesting
Both sexes help excavate a nest hollow, usually high up in a dead pine. Deserted woodpecker holes and nest boxes are also used. The birds dig with their bills and carry the wood chips and dust to the entrance, then shake their bill, flinging the contents to the wind. The nest cavity is 8 to 10 inches deep and is lined with shreds of bark, fur, feathers, and bits of cocoons.

The female lays 4 to 9 speckled white eggs. The eggs are incubated mostly by the female, for 14 days. Both parents feed the young, who leave the nest after 22 days. The young travel with their parents as a family group, later joining other families to form the large flocks of fall and winter. They roost communally at night in cavities in trees or nest boxes.

Feeding Habits

Moving with short hops, exploring branches, cones, and outermost twigs for insects, it also prizes insects from the bark, moving head-down as it descends the trunk in true nuthatch fashion or, on occasion, head-up. Insects account for over 80 percent of the diet. The pygmy nuthatch also feeds on pine seeds, cracking the nut with its powerful little bill to release the seed.

Plants *for* food *and* shelter include:

firs (*Abies* spp.)
pines (*Pinus* spp.)

Pygmy nuthatch at its nest hollow in a ponderosa pine (*Pinus ponderosa*).

house wren / *Troglodytes aedon*

The house wren is the most common wren in the eastern states. Aggressive, with boundless energy, it bustles around the garden examining each twig and leaf for insects. It is possibly best known for its bubbling joyous song. House wrens are 4¾-inch brownish birds with barred wing and tail feathers.

Habitat

Woodland edges, city parks, and residential areas.

Migration and Winter Range

Although the birds do not travel in large flocks, their scolding chirrs announce their presence. The birds return to the previous year's breeding territory, an area usually between ¼ and ¾ acre in size. In summer after breeding, the house wren leaves the vicinity of houses and becomes a shy, secretive bird, frequenting low bushy areas of woodlands. On migrating south, the birds become forest birds, rarely singing or coming near human habitation.

The bird winters from southern California east across the United States to Georgia, Virginia, southern Florida, the Gulf Coast and into Mexico.

Breeding Range

Southern Canada south to northern Baja California, southeastern Arizona, northern Texas, northern Arkansas, Tennessee, and northern Georgia.

Breeding Behavior

The male birds arrive before the females and almost immediately begin to sing, The song is repeated constantly as part of territory formation.

Other acts of territory formation include claiming all available nest sites. The nest hollows are cleaned of the previous year's nesting material and then refilled with twigs to form a foundation for new nests. The house wren empties all nesting cavities in his territory and, if the contents include other birds and their eggs or young, these may be evicted. Birds as large as a flicker may be driven away by a wren dropping twigs into its cavity nest and covering its eggs.

The male wren patrols his territory, flying at any intruder with tail

House wren feeds on insects attracted to a twinberry honeysuckle (*Lonicera involucrata*).

lowered and spread out. Finally the female arrives and the male's song changes its tone to a harsher sound with high-pitched squeaks added, accompanied by wing and tail quivering; as the male becomes increasingly excited, his tail becomes more erect.

Nesting

Wrens are well known for their odd nesting sites. They also favor nesting boxes.

The female begins inspecting the partially built nests and, once she has decided on a site, she lines the rough twigs with a soft lining of grass, fur, and feathers. She lays 6 to 8 pinkish white eggs, which she incubates for about 2 weeks. Both parents feed the young, which leave the nest when about 17 days old. After leaving the nest, the young stay with the parents for up to 2 weeks, when the female leaves to start a second brood. If house wrens fail to raise a brood of their own or fail to obtain a mate, they may care for the young of other species.

Feeding Habits

Insects, spiders, caterpillars, flies, plant lice, beetles, and grasshoppers make up 97 percent of the house wren's diet. The remaining 3 percent is made up of vegetable matter accidently consumed while gathering insects, and very occasionally the bird takes seeds, including sunflower seeds.

Plants *for* food *and* shelter include:

poplars (*Populus* spp.)
oaks (*Quercus* spp.)
grasses (*Andropogon* spp.), for nesting

House wren taking nesting material to a rustic garden nest box.

cactus wren / *Campylorhynchus brunneicapillus*

The cactus wren is the largest wren in the United States, at 8½ inches. The brown-backed bird has a conspicuous long, white eye stripe and a heavily spotted breast. It is a common bird among thorny shrubs and cholla cactus in deserts and arid hillsides in the Southwest. This bird is also found in shade trees and open mesquite close to human habitation.

Habitat
The bird favors deserts and arid hillsides where thorny shrubs and trees offer secure nesting sites.

Migration and Winter Range
It is resident year-round within its range.

Breeding Range
Southern California south to southern Baja California, southern Nevada, southwestern Utah, central and southern Arizona, southern New Mexico, and central Texas to central Mexico.

Breeding Behavior
The male bird sings throughout the year from a prominent perch to advertise his territory. The voice is a deep, throaty, prolonged, churring *cha-cha-cha-cha-cha*, which is a familiar, evocative call of the desert.

Nesting
Nests are usually in the tops of cholla cacti or other prickly shrubs. The nest is a football-shaped mass of coarse grass stems and fine plant fiber lined with feathers and soft plant fiber with an inside diameter of about 6 inches and an overall length of about 12 inches. It is placed horizontally with access via a long passageway up to 14 inches long, built of grass stems usually supported by a horizontal branch.

Nests are used throughout the year for weather protection and evening roosting and are kept in a state of good repair, with rebuilding when necessary. Before the onset of cold weather, they reline their nests and replenish the straw entrance passageway. Each pair of wrens has several roosting nests, and new nests are built in spring and summer for breeding purposes. The female lays 3 or 4 dotted pinkish eggs, which

Cactus wren peering from an old woodpecker hole in a saguaro (*Carnegiea gigantea*).

are incubated for 16 days. Both parents share the nesting duties, bringing worms and insects to the young, which fledge after about 3 weeks. The parents remain together all the year.

On leaving the nest, the young birds soon begin making their own individual roosting nests. In an area that provides nesting opportunities, many nests may be seen in close proximity. If the first brood is successful, the cactus wren will build a new nest and raise a second brood.

Feeding Habits

The cactus wren usually searches for food on the ground, carefully inserting its bill under an object and lifting one side as it peers for insects, then quickly snatching its prey. Insects make up over 80 percent of the diet. Fruits are also fed on, and occasionally a small lizard or tree frog.

Plants *for* food *and* shelter include:

hackberries (*Celtis* spp.)
opuntia cacti, including cholla (*Opuntia* spp.)
sumacs (*Rhus* spp.)
elderberries (*Sambucus* spp.)
soaptree yucca (*Yucca elata*)

Cactus wren at its nest in cane cholla (*Cylindropuntia spinosior*).

blue-gray gnatcatcher / *Polioptila caerulea*

Gnatcatchers are small active birds with thin bills, members of the old-world warbler family. The blue-gray gnatcatcher is often described as a tiny, 4½-inch mockingbird, with its blue-gray back and wings, white breast and belly, and long tail, which is often cocked like a wren's. A fidgeting midget, it is constantly flicking its tail upward or jerking it from side to side as it forages for insects in the upper branches of tall trees. The bird's common call, which is heard constantly as it forages for food and tends the nest, is a thin *ting* like the twang of a banjo string. The habit of constantly calling as it works through the trees makes it easy for you to spot these birds.

Habitat

Prefer deciduous woodland, chaparral, piñon-juniper chaparral, and live oaks.

Migration and Winter Range

The birds winter from Virginia along the Atlantic Coast south into Mexico, Cuba, and Guatemala.

Breeding Range

Northern California, Utah, eastern Nebraska, southern Wisconsin, southern Ontario, and New York south to central Mexico.

Breeding Behavior

In common with many of the smaller bird species there seems to be no definable courtship ritual. The male birds defend a territory with extremely active fidgeting, bloodless combat, and constant chattering and singing. A mate is selected in a short time and breeding commenced.

Nesting

The mated pair construct their beautiful nest together. They usually build the nest on a horizontal branch, often in an oak. In South Carolina, the gnatcatchers prefer live oaks, while in Florida and Alabama, they favor scrub oaks. A cup-shaped nest of plant fibers bound together with spiderweb is lined with bark strips, fine grass, and feathers. Lichen is fastened to the outside of the nest with spiderweb or caterpillar silk, giving the nest the appearance of a lichen-covered knot on a limb. Because the

Pair of blue-gray gnatcatchers at their nest in live oak (*Quercus virginiana*). The male assists the female (below) in feeding the nestlings.

birds are so active and noisy, even during nest building, it is often easy to find the location of a nest.

The female lays 4 to 5 pale blue eggs, most of them spotted with red-brown, and both sexes share the incubation for about 13 days. The nestlings are fed small insects, and fledge after 10 or 12 days.

Feeding Habits

The diet consists of insects and spiders. The birds gather the insects from leaves and outer twigs, but may also flit from the foliage like a fly-catcher for flying insects or hover like a hummingbird to catch insects.

Plants *for* food *and* shelter include:

maples (*Acer* spp.)
pines (*Pinus* spp.)
oaks (*Quercus* spp.)

The tiny, fidgeting blue-gray gnatcatcher foraging for insects and spiders.

black-tailed gnatcatcher / *Polioptila melanura*

Black-tailed gnatcatcher feeding in the foliage of a red-osier dogwood (*Cornus sericea*).

In the Southwest, the ranges of the blue-gray gnatcatcher and the black-tailed gnatcatcher overlap, making identification difficult. The tail of the blue-gray gnatcatcher, however, is mainly white when viewed from below, while that of the black-tailed gnatcatcher is black underneath with white only on the outer web and tip. The male black-tailed gnatcatcher has a glossy black cap from late February to August, while the male blue-gray gnatcatcher has only a black forehead stripe and a black stripe over the eyes. Black-tailed gnatcatchers are 4½ to 5 inches long. The call of the black-tailed gnatcatcher is less plaintive and more wrenlike than the blue-gray's. It is a repeated *pee-ee-ee*, whereas the blue-gray gnatcatcher usually gives a single note.

Habitat
Mesquite thickets in desert country.

Migration and Winter Range
Resident year-round throughout its range.

Breeding Range
Southern California, Nevada, Arizona, New Mexico, and Texas south into Mexico and Baja California.

Breeding Behavior
The birds are considered to be monogamous and may begin nest building long before the breeding season, often building several nests that are later deserted or destroyed before the final nest is constructed.

Nesting
For nesting, the black-tailed gnatcatcher prefers medium-size shrubs such as buckthorn and laurel, sumac, sagebrush, or cactus. The nest is a small, deep cup of plant fiber, sage leaves, plant down, and spiderweb, and is usually built low: only 2 to 4 feet above the ground. The female lays 3 or 4 spotted, pale blue eggs, and both sexes incubate for 14 days. The young leave the nest after 9 or 10 days.

Feeding Habits

Insects make up the bulk of the black-tailed gnatcatcher's diet. Small amounts of seeds are also consumed.

Plants *for* food *and* shelter include:

palo verdes (*Cercidium* spp.)
creosote bush (*Larrea tridentata*)
mesquites (*Prosopis* spp.)
sumacs (*Rhus* spp.)

Black-tailed gnatcatcher feeding on insects that are attracted to the flowers of creosote bush (*Larrea tridentata*).

eastern bluebird / *Sialia sialis*

Eastern bluebirds at their nest hollow in an abandoned woodpecker hole in a western sycamore (*Platanus racemosa*).

western bluebird range

Henry David Thoreau described the bluebird as the bird of heaven and earth because of its sky-blue and earth-red coloration. A member of the thrush family, this beautiful bird with its musical song is generally regarded as the beloved herald of spring.

The eastern bluebird has an intensely blue head, back, wings, and tail, a reddish brown breast, and a white belly. It is very similar to its western counterpart, the western bluebird.

Bluebirds are cavity nesters. The practice of removing dead wood in orchards and other woodlots, the use of metal fence posts rather than wood, the use of pesticides, and the introduction of English sparrows and European starlings, which aggressively compete for available hollows, have all contributed to the decline of the bluebird population. Bluebird Trails and backyard birdwatchers who add nest boxes to their yards have done a lot to increase the bluebird population. Eastern bluebirds are also susceptible to the vagaries of climate: many adults are killed during harsh late winter weather, and early spring nests may not survive.

Habitat
Open woodlands, old orchards, parks, gardens, and around farms where old trees, fence posts, or nest boxes provide nesting sites.

Migration and Winter Range
The birds winter from south of the Ohio Valley and the Midwestern states south into Mexico, the Gulf Coast, and southern Florida. Some northern birds remain in their nesting grounds all winter. During fall and winter, the birds form loose flocks of 6 to 25 birds.

Breeding Range
Atlantic Coast to the Rocky Mountains and from southern Canada south through Mexico to Nicaragua, the Gulf Coast, and southern Florida.

Breeding Behavior
The male birds usually arrive first, but sometimes pairs arrive together. Some pairs remain year-round in the breeding territory. Courtship may

involve a display flight by the male, fluttering high above his treetop perch and sailing back to the perch, singing his soft, warbled call while in flight.

Nesting

Eastern bluebirds prefer nesting sites adjacent to open grassy areas. Old woodpecker holes and natural cavities in old trees, stumps, or fence posts are selected. Bluebird nest boxes are welcomed. The female builds a nest of grasses, fine twigs, and weed stems, lined with fine grasses, hair, or feathers. Between March and July, she lays 4 to 6 pale blue eggs. The female incubates for 13 to 16 days, and the young leave the nest when they are 15 to 20 days old. Both parents feed the young and keep the nest clean. They usually raise 2 broods.

Feeding Habits

Bluebirds feed on insects, waiting on a low perch, then flying to the ground after their prey. The bird also flies out from a high perch to snatch flying insects or hovers above foliage to catch disturbed insects. Grasshoppers, caterpillars, beetles, ants, spiders, earthworms, and snails make up over 70 percent of the bird's diet; the rest is mostly native fruits.

Plants *for* food *and* shelter include:

serviceberries (*Amelanchier* spp.)
hackberries (*Celtis* spp.)
dogwoods (*Cornus* spp.)
hollies (*Ilex* spp.)
red cedar (*Juniperus virginiana*)
Virginia creeper (*Parthenocissus quinquefolia*)
sumacs (*Rhus* spp.)
elderberries (*Sambucus* spp.)
frost grape (*Vitis vulpina*)

Male eastern bluebird.

wood thrush / *Hylocichla mustelina*

The wood thrush favors the fruits of the pin cherry (*Prunus pensylvanica*).

Possibly the best known of the North American spotted brown thrushes and the only one that commonly nests in parks and gardens, the 8-inch-long wood thrush is noted for its incredibly musical song, a flutelike *ee-oh-lay*. The wood thrush is known by several other names, including bellbird, in reference to its clarionlike song.

Habitat

Cool, moist, deciduous woodlands with tangled undergrowth and sapling growth, parks, and gardens.

Migration and Winter Range

Spring migration begins in March, and by mid-May they have progressed to the northern limit of their range. The birds winter from southern Texas and southern Florida south to Panama.

Breeding Range

Southern Ontario, southwestern Quebec, southwestern New Brunswick, and Nova Scotia in Canada, south to Florida and the Gulf of Mexico.

Breeding Behavior

The male bird arrives in its breeding territory before the female. The breeding territory may be from $\frac{1}{8}$ acre to 2 acres. The first evidence of the bird's arrival is its song, which it uses to challenge a territory intruder. The females arrive 2 or 3 days after the males. Courtship displays include the male chasing the female in 6 or 7 circular flights; then the birds feed together. The male also sings to impress his mate.

Nesting

A nest is built in a sapling or bush, usually 5 to 15 feet above the ground. Nests are similar to robins' nests, with the addition of dead leaves and mosses, and are lined with rootlets. Maple, witch hazel, hawthorn, elm, and birch trees are among the trees selected for nest sites. The female lays 3 or 4 pale blue or blue-green eggs and incubates them for about 2 weeks. The nestlings are fed by both parents. Berries, caterpillars, and small insects are fed to the young, which leave the nest when 12 or 13 days old. Usually, 2 broods are raised.

Feeding Habits

The wood thrush finds a large part of its food by scratching around the roots of shrubs. Insects make up about 60 percent of the bird's diet and the balance is fruit.

Plants *for* food *and* shelter include:

serviceberries (*Amelanchier* spp.)

dogwoods (*Cornus* spp.)

hollies (*Ilex* spp.)

honeysuckles (*Lonicera* spp.)

red mulberry (*Morus rubra*)

black tupelo (*Nyssa sylvatica*)

wild cherries (*Prunus* spp.)

common blackberry (*Rubus allegheniensis*)

elderberries (*Sambucus* spp.)

highbush blueberry (*Vaccinium corymbosum*)

viburnums (*Viburnum* spp.)

wild grapes (*Vitis* spp.)

The wood thrush prefers to forage in a cool and moist, overgrown corner of the garden.

American robin / *Turdus migratorius*

American robin at its nest in a lodgepole pine (*Pinus contorta*).

The familiar adult American robin is 9 to 11 inches long, with a gray back and brick-red breast. Males have a black head and tail, while females, which are generally paler in color overall, have a gray head and tail. The song is the first heard in the morning and the last in the evening; it has a joyous liquid quality. Although it is looked for as the harbinger of spring, many American robins spend the entire winter in the northern latitudes (which is not widely known), frequenting cedar bogs and swamps away from civilization.

Habitat

Parks and gardens, open woodlands, and orchards.

Migration and Winter Range

Flocks form in fall. Robins winter from southern Canada and the northern United States south to Baja California, the Gulf Coast, and Florida, and as far south as Guatemala.

Breeding Range

Breeding from the tree line in Alaska and across Canada south to southern Mexico and the Gulf Coast.

Breeding Behavior

Robins remain in flocks throughout winter and disperse in spring, signaling the beginning of the breeding season. The male bird becomes less tolerant of other males and generally restricts his own movements to within an area of about 1 acre. They return to the same breeding area each year and begin their familiar caroling when the females arrive.

Nesting

The American robin is one of the earliest birds to nest, often selecting evergreen trees for protection of early nests. The female constructs a deep, cup-shaped nest of mud and grasses, lined with fine grasses. The female may carry mud in her bill for a quarter of a mile from the nest site, and molds the nest shape by sitting inside and pushing against the edges with her breast.

The female usually lays 3 or 4 blue eggs and incubates them for about 2 weeks. Both parents feed the nestlings vast quantities of insects and worms. Young robins have speckled breasts, indicating their family relationship to thrushes. The female often leaves the nest to begin nest building and to raise another brood, leaving the male to feed the fledglings.

Feeding Habits

A familiar sight on suburban lawns in spring, feeding on earthworms and insect pests. In winter, they also feed on fruit.

Plants *for* food *and* shelter include:

serviceberries (*Amelanchier* spp.)

hackberries (*Celtis* spp.)

dogwoods (*Cornus* spp.)

hawthorns (*Crataegus* spp.)

toyon (*Heteromeles arbutifolia*)

hollies (*Ilex* spp.)

eastern red cedar (*Juniperus virginiana*)

red mulberry (*Morus rubra*)

bayberries (*Myrica* spp.)

wild cherries (*Prunus* spp.)

sumacs (*Rhus* spp.)

common blackberry (*Rubus allegheniensis*)

elderberries (*Sambucus* spp.)

mountain ashes (*Sorbus* spp.)

viburnums (*Viburnum* spp.)

grasses (*Andropogon* spp.), for nesting

American robin.

gray catbird / Dumetella carolinensis

Gray catbird favors the fruits of frost grape (*Vitis vulpina*).

The gray catbird is a bird of shady thickets. It may sing its varied and delightful song from an open perch but, when disturbed, will dart into a thicket and remain hidden from view. Male and female are similar in appearance: 9-inch-long slate-gray birds with a black cap and chestnut undertail coverts.

The catbird's song is a melody of various phrases, some musical, others discordant, punctuated by short pauses, and often containing some mimicry of other bird songs. A complaining call note, a nasal catlike *mew*, which gives the bird its name, is usually included in the complete song. The catbird also often sings at night.

Habitat

Catbirds can be found in low, dense, deciduous thickets preferably by streams and in damp forest edges. They are also often found in bushes and hedges in gardens, sometimes close to houses.

Migration and Winter Range

Catbirds migrate at night. Most catbirds winter in the southern United States and Central America.

Breeding Range

Catbirds breed from southern British Columbia to Nova Scotia, south to eastern Oregon, central Arizona, Texas, and central parts of the Gulf states.

Breeding Behavior

The females appear at the breeding ground just after the males, and courtship antics begin. The male sings, pausing to dash off in pursuit of the female. The male struts with lowered wings and erect tail, wheeling around and exhibiting the chestnut patch on his undertail coverts.

Nesting

The nest is a coarse, bulky structure of sticks and twigs, neatly lined with fine rootlets and bark shreds. The female lays an average of 4 blue-green eggs and incubates them for 12 to 13 days. The young leave the nest when 10 to 15 days old. They often raise 2 broods. The male feeds the female at the nest and guards the nest when the female leaves to feed herself.

Feeding Habits

The catbird's diet is about half insects, and it also feeds on many kinds of fleshy fruits.

Plants *for* food *and* shelter include:

serviceberries (*Amelanchier* spp.)

hackberries (*Celtis* spp.)

dogwoods (*Cornus* spp.)

hollies (*Ilex* spp.)

red mulberry (*Morus rubra*)

bayberries (*Myrica* spp.)

wild cherries (*Prunus* spp.)

sumacs (*Rhus* spp.)

common blackberry (*Rubus allegheniensis*)

elderberries (*Sambucus* spp.)

mountain ashes (*Sorbus* spp.)

highbush blueberry (*Vaccinium corymbosum*)

viburnums (*Viburnum* spp.)

wild grapes (*Vitis* spp.)

Gray catbird feeding on the fruits of American beautyberry (*Callicarpa americana*).

northern mockingbird / *Mimus polyglottos*

Northern mockingbird feeding on
the fruits of saskatoon serviceberry
(*Amelanchier alnifolia*).

The northern mockingbird is a slender, long-tailed, 10-inch gray bird with white patches on the tail and wings. Once considered a southern bird at home among the moss-covered live oaks and flowering magnolia trees, the mockingbird has adapted very well to civilization and has increased its range northward and westward.

The bird's call consists of stanzas of repeated phrases, a loud, melodious, and impassioned song often poured out on a warm spring moonlit night from a conspicuous perch. It is noted for its ability to repeat the songs of other bird species. The birds are never still when singing, raising a foot or changing perches or singing a rapturous flight song continuously.

Habitat
The birds are frequently seen in shrubbery tangles, hedges, city parks, and gardens. Suburban gardens provide ideal habitat.

Migration and Winter Range
Usually year-round residents within their range.

Breeding Range
Southern Canada south to the Caribbean.

Breeding Behavior
The northern mockingbird's courtship performance is unique. As spring approaches, the male pauses from his song and, raising his wings above his head, exposes his large white wing markings. This is repeated several times. The courtship antics include a nuptial dance. A pair of birds may face each other a foot apart, hopping up and down and moving from side to side, with their heads and tails held high and feathers depressed.

Nesting

Both birds share in nest building. The completed nest is a coarse, bulky structure usually built of small, dead twigs and lined with grass and rootlets. The nest is usually 3 to 10 feet above the ground in a bush or low tree, but may be as high as 50 feet.

The female lays 3 to 5 green eggs with brown spots and incubates them for 12 days. Young birds leave the nest when 10 to 12 days old. They may raise 2 or 3 broods in one season. After breeding, the parents establish and defend their winter territories.

Feeding Habits

Mainly insectivorous during spring and early summer. As wild fruits ripen, they feed on them with relish, for nearly half of their diet.

Plants *for* food *and* shelter include:

serviceberries (*Amelanchier* spp.)
hackberries (*Celtis* spp.)
dogwoods (*Cornus* spp.)
toyon (*Heteromeles arbutifolia*)
hollies (*Ilex* spp.)
eastern red cedar (*Juniperus virginiana*)
red mulberry (*Morus rubra*)
bayberries (*Myrica* spp.)
wild cherries (*Prunus* spp.)
sumacs (*Rhus* spp.)
blackberries (*Rubus* spp.)
elderberries (*Sambucus* spp.)
viburnums (*Viburnum* spp.)
wild grapes (*Vitis* spp.)

Northern mockingbird, a common garden visitor.

brown thrasher / *Toxostoma rufum*

The brown thrasher gets its name from its brown color and its habit of thrashing in leaf litter with its long, curved bill as it searches for insects. The bird has a long, graceful tail, and is bright reddish brown above, with white or pale buff, heavily streaked underparts and 2 white wing bars.

Adult birds have yellow eyes. A member of the mockingbird family, the spring song is a loud, melodious carol, often with phrases repeated in pairs. A shy and elusive bird, when approached it will retreat into dense shrubbery.

Brown thrasher driving a snake away near a stand of Indian rice grass (*Oryzopsis hymenoides*).

Habitat
Deciduous thickets, woodland edges, and bushy fields.

Migration and Winter Range
Eastern Oklahoma east to North Carolina and south to southern Florida. Some birds remain in the northern parts of the breeding range over winter.

Breeding Range
Rocky Mountains, although it may occasionally wander west of the mountains. It nests from Alberta to Québec and south to Texas and Florida.

Breeding Behavior
In early spring, the male sings from a perch in the top of a tree or large bush to attract the female. Courtship occurs near the ground in dense shrubbery and is not easily observed. The male often struts gracefully around the female with his lowered tail touching the ground. The male's song becomes subdued and soft. After the nest is completed, the male's full voice returns and he sings loudly once again.

Nesting
Both sexes of brown thrasher share nest building, constructing a large, bulky, loosely built nest of twigs, leaves, and grass. The nest is lined with a cup made of rootlets. It is built in thickets or a garden shrub or small tree, usually within 10 feet of the ground, but occasionally on the ground.

The female lays 4 or 5 pale blue to white, brown dotted eggs, incubated by both sexes for 12 to 14 days. When 9 to 13 days old, the young leave the nest. Each season, they raise 2 broods.

Feeding Habits

Brown thrashers spend most of their time on the ground. They run or hop, foraging for insects. In spring, spiders and insects, especially caterpillars, make up most of the bird's diet. In summer and autumn, the main food is wild fruit. They also include small snakes, lizards, cicadas, and tree frogs in their diet.

Plants *for* food *and* shelter include:

serviceberries (*Amelanchier* spp.)

dogwoods (*Cornus* spp.)

wild strawberry (*Fragaria virginiana*)

hollies (*Ilex* spp.)

eastern red cedar (*Juniperus virginiana*)

red mulberry (*Morus rubra*)

bayberries (*Myrica* spp.)

Virginia creeper (*Parthenocissus quinquefolia*)

wild cherries (*Prunus* spp.)

oaks (*Quercus* spp.)

sumacs (*Rhus* spp.)

common blackberry (*Rubus allegheniensis*)

elderberries (*Sambucus* spp.)

blueberries (*Vaccinium* spp.)

viburnums (*Viburnum* spp.)

frost grape (*Vitis vulpina*)

Brown thrasher singing from a chokecherry (*Prunus virginiana*).

cedar waxwing / *Bombycilla cedrorum*

Cedar waxwing feeding on the berries of Rocky Mountain juniper (*Juniperus scopulorum*).

Waxwings get their name from the red, waxy droplets on the tips of their secondary wing feathers. The 7-inch bird is robed in soft, silky, harmoniously colored plumage. With its slim appearance, conspicuous crest, rich grayish brown upper parts, black mask and chin, greenish yellow belly, and yellow-tipped tail, it often sits motionless with an erect bearing.

The waxwing's crest is used to express emotion. When pointing backward, it signifies that the bird is unperturbed. If the bird is disturbed, the crest is erect; if it's frightened, the crest is pulled flat. Cedar waxwings may suddenly appear in an area where their favorite wild fruits are abundant and then just as quickly disappear. They travel in groups of up to 20 birds. The birds fly in close ranks at treetop level and suddenly, when in full flight, may wheel around and dive to a tree to feed. On alighting, the birds remain perfectly still and are often very difficult to detect.

Habitat
Open and sparse woodlands, orchards, second-growth stands on the edges of rivers, swamps, or dams, parks, and gardens with berry-producing trees and shrubs.

Migration and Winter Range
Highland birds winter in southern parts of the breeding range south to Mexico and the northern regions of South America. Migration is often erratic, depending on availability of fruiting trees.

Breeding Range
The bird's breeding range extends from Southeast Alaska, northcentral British Columbia, and northern Alberta east across Canada to Newfoundland, and south to northern California, northern Utah, northwestern Oklahoma, southern Illinois, northern Alabama, and northern Georgia.

Breeding Behavior
During courtship, the male may approach the female, carrying a flower petal or berry in his bill, hopping sideways along the branch. A responsive female may take the offering and hop once to the side, standing erect. After a short pause, she returns to the male, who takes the offering and

hops away with one hop, pauses, and hops back. The dance is repeated several times, with a dignified rhythm and precision.

Nesting

The birds are late nesters, usually beginning nest building in June or as late as September. Since the young are fed on fruit, the birds may time their nesting to coincide with a plentiful supply of ripe fruits. The birds nest in deciduous or coniferous trees or shrubs, usually at the extreme end of a horizontal branch 6 to 40 feet above ground. They build a cup of bulky, loosely woven twigs, dry grasses, rootlets, bark strips, mosses, pine needles, and lichens.

The female lays 3 to 6 pale gray or blue-gray eggs marked with black dots. She incubates them for 12 to 16 days. The young are fed small fruits and insects. The parents often return to the nest with their gullets bulging with food.

Feeding Habits

Adult birds feed on mostly fruit and berries. They are fond of mountain ash berries and cherries. When eating, the birds may gorge themselves until they are unable to fly. They are fond of cankerworms and are a major foe of the elm leaf beetle and other insect pests. In late summer and early fall, the cedar waxwing becomes an adroit flycatcher, sallying from a high perch to catch insects in midair.

Plants *for* food *and* shelter include:

serviceberries (*Amelanchier* spp.)
hackberry (*Celtis* spp.)
dogwoods (*Cornus* spp.)
hawthorns (*Crataegus* spp.)
black crowberry (*Empetrum nigrum*)
toyon (*Heteromeles arbutifolia*)
hollies (*Ilex* spp.)
cedars (*Juniperus* spp.)
crabapples (*Malus* spp.)
bayberries (*Myrica* spp.)
black tupelo (*Nyssa sylvatica*)
wild cherries (*Prunus* spp.)
wild roses (*Rosa* spp.)
mountain ashes (*Sorbus* spp.)
viburnums (*Viburnum* spp.)

Cedar waxwing feeding on the berries of eastern red cedar (*Juniperus virginiana*).

Cape May warbler / *Setophaga tigrina*

Cape May warbler often nests in the foliage of red spruce (*Picea rubens*).

One of the most beautiful of the warblers, the Cape May warbler is uncommon, although often seen in migration. The male bird in breeding plumage has chestnut cheeks and a white wing patch, and is yellow below with heavy black streaks. The female has a duller coloration but retains a suggestion of the cheek patch. Both sexes are 5 inches long.

Like most wood warblers, the Cape May warbler occupies its own ecological niche in the forest so that feeding habits and nesting sites don't compete with other wood warblers in the same area. The male's song, often heard while it is feeding in the tops of trees, is a high-pitched, monotone *zee-zee-zee-zee*.

Habitat

During migration, the Cape May warbler may be seen passing through coniferous or deciduous woods or suburban parks and gardens. On its breeding grounds, it prefers open, parklike stands of large mature spruce and fir trees, or the edge of forests or forest openings with a mixture of tall birch and hemlock trees.

Migration and Winter Range

The main fall migration flight is east of the Mississippi River, and the birds winter in Mexico and in the West Indies.

Breeding Range

Alberta east to Nova Scotia and south to northeastern North Dakota, Minnesota, northern Wisconsin, northern Michigan, southern Ontario, northeastern New York, central and eastern Vermont, and southern Maine.

Breeding Behavior

Little is known of the Cape May warbler's courtship behavior. Observers have noted that the male chases the female and, by the following day, the female has apparently completed the nest building.

Nesting

They prefer nesting in black spruce, red spruce, and fir trees. The female builds a compact, cup-shaped nest of moss, grass, and twigs near the top of the tree, 30 to 60 feet above the ground. She lays 6 to 7 heavily spotted cream-white eggs. Nesting information is limited because of the birds' habit of nesting high in treetops and the fact that much of their breeding range is beyond settled areas.

Feeding Habits

The birds feed on insects in the tops of trees, often darting into the air to catch them. They will puncture grapes to drink the juice and take sap from holes drilled by sapsuckers.

Plants *for* food *and* shelter include:

firs (*Abies* spp.)
spruces (*Picea* spp.)
wild cherry (*Prunus pensylvanica*)
goldenrods (*Solidago* spp.)
wild grapes (*Vitis* spp.)

Cape May warbler feeds on insects and juices from small fruits including pin cherry (*Prunus pensylvanica*).

yellow-rumped warbler / *Setophaga coronata*

The yellow-rumped warbler favors fruits of the wax myrtle (*Myrica cerifera*).

The yellow-rumped warbler has two distinct forms: the myrtle race of the northeast and the western Audubon's race. The myrtle warbler was named for its fondness for fruits of bayberry, or wax myrtle. It is the most numerous of all the American wood warblers. The 5- to 6-inch bird is easily identified by its 4 distinct patches of yellow, which are found on the crown, rump, and each side of the breast.

The bird has a distinctive song, a trill, something like the tinkling rattle of a small chain. The ordinary call note is a sharp *chek*.

Habitat

Coniferous and mixed forests. Widespread during migration.

Migration and Winter Range

In spring, the birds pass over the Rio Grande into Texas and move up the coast, with waves of birds drifting through the tall deciduous woods of Massachusetts by about mid-April. It is one of the last of the warblers to begin the fall migration, drifting south from September. With numbers now swelled by the young birds, they may stop off where food supplies are abundant and spend the winter. Many birds remain in coastal areas where bayberries provide winter food. The birds apparently return to winter in the same place each year.

Breeding Range

Northcentral Alaska and across Canada throughout much of the forested areas to Labrador and Newfoundland, and south to northern British Columbia, central Alberta, northern Minnesota, central Michigan, eastern New York, eastern Pennsylvania, and Massachusetts.

Breeding Behavior

As summer approaches, the males begin to court the females, following them and displaying their beauty spots by fluffing out their side feathers, erecting their crown feathers, and raising their wings.

Nesting

The birds build a relatively (for warblers) bulky and loose nest. The female does most of the building, with the male occasionally bringing nesting material to the site but mostly encouraging her with singing and companionship. The nest is built of twigs, rootlets, and grass interwoven with animal hair, and is usually 5 to 50 feet up on a horizontal branch of a spruce, red cedar, or pine tree.

Between May and June, the female lays 3 to 5 brown-spotted white eggs and incubates them for 12 to 13 days. The young fledge 12 to 14 days after hatching. The juvenile plumage is kept for only a short period, and by August the young birds have acquired their first winter plumage.

Feeding Habits

The warbler's favorite food is bayberry. It also feeds on the berries of dogwood, red cedar, viburnum, honeysuckle, mountain ash, and Virginia creeper. In the South Atlantic states, it feeds on the berries of the native tree palms or palmettos. During the winter, it favors poison ivy berries.

During spring and summer, it prefers insects, and the bird flits around bushes, taking them from the foliage and bark. It often flutters above the foliage to catch mosquitoes, gnats, or flies. It also feeds on the seeds of grasses, sunflowers, and goldenrods.

Plants *for* food *and* shelter include:

dogwoods (*Cornus* spp.)
sunflowers (*Helianthus* spp.)
eastern red cedar (*Juniperus virginiana*)
honeysuckles (*Lonicera* spp.)
bayberries (*Myrica* spp.)
Virginia creeper (*Parthenocissus quinquefolia*)
pines (*Pinus* spp.)
sumacs (*Rhus* spp.)
mountain ashes (*Sorbus* spp.)
viburnums (*Viburnum* spp.)
grasses (*Andropogon* spp.), for nesting

Yellow-rumped warbler feeding on the waxy fruits of bayberry (*Myrica pensylvanica*).

black-and-white warbler / *Mniotilta varia*

Black-and-white warblers probe for insects in the bark of white ash (*Fraxinus americana*).

The black-and-white warbler is one of the 56 species of the American wood warbler family found in North America. They are second only to the finch family in number of species among North American songbirds. This handsome 4½ to 5½-inch bird has black stripes running horizontally along its head, back, and wings, with a white breast and belly.

Once called the black-and-white creeper, the black-and-white warbler displays even more agility than the brown creeper when feeding. The warbler creeps over the trunks and larger branches of trees and shrubs, gathering insects from crevices in the bark. As it feeds, it flits from tree to tree, creeping around the trunk. It may move up the trunk like a creeper, vertically down like a nuthatch, or spiral around the trunk, pursuing an insect and catching it in flight like a flycatcher.

Although called a warbler, unlike other warblers the black-and-white warbler is not particularly noted for its song. The song is an attenuated, high-pitched, squeaky *weesy–weesy–weesy–weesy*, sung as it searches the bark for insects and occasionally during flight.

Habitat

Usually common in deciduous and mixed woodlands, preferring damper areas. During migration, it is common in parks and gardens throughout its range.

Migration and Winter Range

One of the earliest warblers to arrive in spring, it is most conspicuous when most deciduous trees are just beginning to sprout the first light green leaflets. The fall migration is a slow drift to the south. The birds often remain in New England until mid-October, long after the frosts have arrived in that area.

The bird winters from southern Baja California, Mexico, southern Texas, central Florida, and the Bahamas south to the West Indies and central America to Ecuador, Columbia, and northern Venezuela.

Breeding Range

Northeastern British Columbia across central and southern Canada to Newfoundland and south to eastern Montana, central Texas, southeastern Louisiana, central Alabama, central Georgia, and southeastern North Carolina.

Breeding Behavior

After the arrival of the females, the males often flutter their black-and-white plumage, indulge in frequent song, periodically chase the female, and warn off other males before settling down with their partners.

Nesting

The female builds a cup-shaped nest of dry leaves, rootlets, bark strips, and pine needles on the ground, usually hidden from the top under a log or against a tree or shrub. The birds sometimes nest in a low stump or under the roots of a fallen tree. She lines the nest with fine grass, then incubates her 4 or 5 purple-spotted white eggs for 11 or 12 days. The young leave the nest 8 to 12 days after hatching, and soon ascend a nearby tree, where they are fed by the parents.

Feeding Habits

The black-and-white warbler mainly eats insects that are harmful to trees, as well as spiders and daddy longlegs. They are attracted to rough-barked trees where insects are likely to be found.

Plants *for* food *and* shelter include:

maples (*Acer* spp.)
pines (*Pinus* spp.)
oaks (*Quercus* spp.)

Black-and-white warbler probes for insects in crevices in the bark.

Blackburnian warbler / *Setophaga fusca*

Blackburnian warbler usually nests in hemlocks, such as the Canada hemlock (*Tsuga canadensis*).

The Blackburnian warbler is considered to be the most brilliant of all the wood warblers, with the bright plumage of a tropical bird. This 5-inch bird's beauty is best appreciated seen in its forest home against a backdrop of dark conifers. The male in breeding plumage has a vivid orange throat, a large white wing patch, and distinctive black head markings. The female and young have similar but paler markings.

The song is a thin, very high-pitched *zip-zip-zip-zip-zeeeeee*. The Blackburnian warbler is one of the first birds to stop singing in summer.

Habitat

An arboreal bird, usually keeping well concealed in the foliage of the tall spruce, pine, and hemlock trees it prefers. The bird's high-pitched song is usually the only indication of its presence. It often uses the tip of a tall tree for a singing perch.

Migration and Winter Range

The Blackburnian warbler is known only as a migrant throughout most of the eastern United States. By late summer, most of the birds have left their breeding grounds and, throughout August and September, are seen drifting through deciduous woods in mixed flocks with other warblers. By early October, most have left the United States en route to their winter range from Guatemala south to central Peru and Venezuela.

Breeding Range

The bird's breeding range covers the mature and well-developed second-growth coniferous and mixed woodland forests of the lower Canadian and upper transition zones from central Saskatchewan east to the Gaspe Peninsula and Nova Scotia, and south to central Minnesota, central Wisconsin, central Michigan, northeastern Ohio, southeastern New York, Massachusetts, and the Appalachian Mountains, to northern Georgia and South Carolina.

Breeding Behavior

The male bird characteristically frequents the tops of tall trees in his breeding area, facing his colorful breast into the sunlight. A glimpse of the vivid orange shows why this bird is also called firethroat.

Nesting

The birds nest in coniferous trees, including hemlocks, spruces, firs, pines, and cedars, and tamaracks. Its fondness for hemlocks has earned it the name hemlock warbler. They build a nest of small twigs, dry grasses, and soft plant down or lichen, lined with lichens, mosses, rootlets, and hair, on a horizontal branch well out from the trunk and 5 to 85 feet above the ground. The female lays 4 or 5 brown-spotted white eggs. The male may occasionally share the incubation duties, which last for 11 or 12 days. Both parents feed the young.

Feeding Habits

The Blackburnian warbler is mainly insectivorous like other wood warblers. It feeds on beetles, crane flies, ants, and small caterpillars, and also will consume some berries.

Plants *for* food *and* shelter include:

elderberries (*Sambucus* spp.)
hemlocks (*Tsuga* spp.)

Blackburnian warbler in his breeding plumage foraging for insects.

yellow warbler / *Setophaga petechia*

The most widespread of the wood warblers, the 5-inch yellow warbler is also the easiest to recognize, with its seemingly all-yellow plumage. At closer range, the male bird's reddish streaked breast can be seen. This little ray of sunshine is represented by 7 distinct subspecies in North America, with each subspecies varying in intensity of color from orange-yellow to pale yellow. During courtship, the male sings every minute or two with a high-pitched melodious *sweet-sweet-sweet-sweeter-than-sweet*. One male has been recorded as having sung 3,240 times in one day at the peak of the mating season.

Habitat

Shrubby areas in open country or roadside thickets, the edges of streams and ponds, hedges, parks, and gardens. They are often found wherever patches of trees and shrubs grow.

Migration and Winter Range

The yellow warbler begins its southern migration early, with some birds crossing the Gulf of Mexico in mid-July. By mid-August, most of the breeding birds have left the northern states. The bird winters from southern Baja California, central Mexico, and the Bahamas, south to Peru and Brazil.

Breeding Range

Alaska near the tree line across Canada to Newfoundland, and south to southern Baja California, central Peru, coastal Venezuela, Trinidad, the Antilles, Bahamas, Galapagos Islands, and Florida Keys.

Breeding Behavior

Soon after their arrival to their breeding grounds, the male bird selects a territory and defends it against other males. The territory may be about 150 feet in diameter. The male courts the female with singing and persistent chasing.

On finding a cowbird egg in its nest, the yellow warbler will often build another layer on the nest and lay more eggs. The nest is in common blackberry (*Rubus allegheniensis*).

Nesting

The female does most of the nest building, though she is helped by the male. The bird's favorite nesting sites are moist thickets, along small streams and brooks, and on the edge of swamps among alders, willows, and blueberry and elderberry bushes. It also selects overgrown fences and cutover areas with regrowth of wild raspberry, blackberry, or low shrubs.

In Iowa, it is reported that the bird most frequently nests in the snowberry bush, a prairie shrub with leathery leaves and pale pink flowers. It builds a strong, compact, cup-shaped nest of plant fibers, grasses, and plant down, fastened to a fork of a sapling branch, shrub, or bramble from 7 to 12 feet above the ground. The birds are fairly tame and don't mind a human audience, even when building their nest, so you can often get a close look at the process. The female lays 3 to 6 brown-spotted pale blue eggs and incubates them for 11 to 12 days. The young leave the nest after 9 to 12 days.

The yellow warbler is one of the most frequent hosts of cowbirds. These parasitic birds will visit at least once a large majority of nests in areas where cowbirds are common, and lay their eggs in the warbler's nest. Many yellow warblers have learned to circumvent the cowbird by building another nest on top of the first. The cowbird's egg is left to cool off in the basement. This process may be repeated several times if the cowbird persists, and in one record a six-storied nest was constructed, each story containing a cowbird's egg. When yellow warblers nest in swampy areas inhabited by colonies of red-winged blackbirds, they may be protected from the cowbirds since the blackbirds won't tolerate cowbirds in their territory.

> **Plants *for* food *and* shelter include:**
>
> elderberries (*Sambucus* spp.)

Male yellow warbler singing in the spring foliage of red-osier dogwood (*Cornus sericea*).

Feeding Habits

The yellow warbler is a very beneficial bird, whose diet consists almost entirely of insect pests, including caterpillars, which make up 67 percent of the diet when plentiful.

American redstart / *Setophaga ruticilla*

With its fluttering motions and bright patches of orange on the wings and tail, the American redstart is commonly referred to as the butterfly of the bird world. The male is unmistakable, with the orange patches contrasting with the black body and white belly. Females and young are olive-gray above, with yellow tail and wing patches.

The American redstart can also be recognized by its habit of spreading its tail and drooping its wings. The song is high-pitched and varies in its pattern; one sounds like *tseet-tseet-tseet*.

Habitat
The redstart's preferred habitat includes open deciduous and mixed woodlands, tall shrubbery, and woodlots. During migration, the birds may be found in almost every habitat.

Migration and Winter Range
The American redstart can be found from Mexico to South America during winter.

Breeding Range
It breeds from Southeast Alaska east to Newfoundland and south to eastern Oregon, northern Utah, northern Colorado, southeastern Louisiana, and central Georgia.

Breeding Behavior
The males arrive before the females and defend a chosen territory, advertising their presence by singing. The males aggressively defend their territories. When the females arrive, the males posture for them and flash their colors.

Nesting
The female bird builds a neat, cup-shaped nest from grass, rootlets, and bark fiber bound with spiderweb and ornamented with lichens. She builds the nest in the crotch of a deciduous tree or shrub, usually 10 to 20 feet above ground. She lays 4 whitish eggs speckled with gray and brown and incubates them for 12 days. Both parents feed the young, who leave the nest after 8 or 9 days.

Male American redstart feeding on insects attracted to the red flowers of the Arizona honeysuckle (*Lonicera arizonica*).

Feeding Habits

The American redstart feeds on forest insects, including beetles, borers, and caterpillars, as well as flies, aphids, spiders, and moths. This bird is attracted to insects that live in most garden trees and shrubs, and is easily identified by its flashy colors and its habit of darting into midair after flying insects. Berries and seeds may supplement the diet in late summer.

Plants *for* food *and* shelter include:

maples (*Acer* spp.)
alders (*Alnus* spp.)
serviceberries (*Amelanchier* spp.)
birches (*Betula* spp.)
elderberries (*Sambucus* spp.)

Female American redstart.

Male American redstart.

California towhee / *Melozone crissalis*

California towhee favors the fruits of the western raspberry (*Rubus leucodermis*).

Towhees are found across North America. Geographical races or sub-species are differentiated by markings or eye color. In the Northeast, towhees are red-eyed; in the Southeast, they are white-eyed; in the West, white dots mark the backs and shoulders. The reddish brown, or rufous sides, is common to all rufous-sided towhee subspecies. The California towhee is one of the most common garden birds in California, where it dominates smaller birds. An 8- to 10-inch gray-brown bird, it has cinnamon or rusty undertail coverts, buff throat, and upper breast, and sometimes with a rufous cap. Hopping and scratching for food on the ground, it usually appears as a drab bird, but when seen in the proper light, the plumage is a subtle blending of earthy ochres and umbers.

At times, the male bird may utter a soft, finchlike warbled *chink-chink-ink-ink-ink-ink*. The California towhee's call note is a repeated metallic sounding *chink*.

Habitat

Naturally a bird of coastal and foothill chaparral, foothill canyons, open woods, and piñon-juniper woodlands, the California towhee is one of the wariest of all birds. Unobtrusive and shy, it is rarely seen as it constantly moves under shrubs and through undergrowth. The bird's short, rounded wings do not allow for effective flight, so it depends on its strong legs for locomotion. Where it inhabits suburban areas, it loses its shyness. It is highly territorial and may spend most of its life within an area as small as ½ to 1 acre, if conditions are suitable. Suburban gardens with open lawns, dense plantings with low-growing limbs for cover, and permanent water provide ideal environments.

Migration and Winter Range

A permanent resident throughout its range.

Breeding Range

The bird is widely distributed from southwestern Oregon, along the coast, south to Baja California.

Breeding Behavior

The birds are seen in pairs throughout the year and they probably mate for life. The male bird is a dedicated partner, standing lookout while the female feeds, or staying close to her while foraging on the ground. During the breeding season, the male becomes aggressive toward other males and patrols the limits of his territory from dawn until sunset, calling his repeated metallic *chink* note to announce his possession of the area.

Nesting

Popular nesting shrubs are California buckwheat (*Eriogonum fasciculatum* var. *filiolosum*) and common buckbrush (*Ceanothus cuneatus*), both attractive garden shrubs. The nest is a bulky, well-made deep cup of twigs, grasses, and plant stems, lined with finer grasses, bark strips, and rootlets, 3 to 12 feet above the ground. The female lays 3 or 4 lightly spotted, bluish green eggs and incubates them for 11 days. The young leave the nest after 8 days, and may remain with the parents for an additional 4 to 6 weeks. If the parents lay a second brood, the young are driven out of the territory after the next clutch hatches.

Feeding Habits

The California towhee forages on the ground for insects and seeds. Weed seeds are the favorite food, making up over 50 percent of the total diet. Grains make up about 30 percent; insects and fruits make up the balance. The birds are particularly attracted to blackberry and raspberry tangles.

Plants **for** food **and** shelter include:

sumacs (*Rhus* supp.)
common blackberry (*Rubus allegheniensis*)
western raspberry (*Rubus leucodermis*)
elderberries (*Sambucus* spp.)
California buckwheat (*Eriogonum fasciculatum* var. *filiolosum*) and common buckbrush (*Ceanothus cuneatus*), for nesting

California towhee attracted to a garden pond.

eastern towhee / *Pipilo erythrophthalmus*

Eastern towhee favors the fruits of American holly (*Ilex opaca*).

The male eastern towhee has a black head and upperparts, rufous sides, and white underparts. The female is similar but duller, with the male's black replaced by brown.

The common name, towhee, is from an imitation of the bird's call note, given by the naturalist Mark Catesby in 1731 as *to-whee*. Towhees spend most of their time on the ground, so they are easier to find and recognize than many backyard birds. Their distinctive backward hop, repeated often as they search for food, makes them unmistakable.

spotted towhee range

Habitat

The eastern towhee is a bird of dense brush, tangles, and thickets with leaf litter cover on the ground. It is also found in woodland edges and openings.

Migration and Winter Range

The bird lives year-round within most of its breeding range. In the northern limits of the range, it moves slightly south, but often winters as far north as southern New England and southeast Ontario. The species is in decline in the northeastern part of its range.

Breeding Range

The eastern towhee's breeding range extends from southeastern Manitoba, North Dakota, the Great Lakes, and Massachusetts, south to the central Gulf states and Florida.

Breeding Behavior

The male arrives at the breeding ground before the female. He soon flies to a perch in a bush or tree and begins singing. When the female arrives, the male follows her, with his wings and tail opening and closing rapidly as he chases her through the undergrowth.

Nesting

The female builds a well-concealed, loose nest of bark strips, twigs, rootlets, and grasses, on or near the ground, carefully concealed under a shrub or bush, and she lines the nest with hair and fine grass. She lays 4 to 6 white, gray or greenish eggs, speckled with red-brown, and incubates them for 12 to 13 days. The young leave the nest when they are 10 to 12 days old. They normally raise 2 broods. The well-camouflaged female will sit tight on the nest until almost stepped on by an intruder.

Feeding Habits

The eastern towhee feeds on seeds, insects, and wild fruits. It finds weed and grass seeds and unearths insects while scratching in leaf litter.

Plants *for* food *and* shelter include:

serviceberries (*Amelanchier* spp.)
wild strawberry (*Fragaria virginiana*)
hollies (*Ilex* spp.)
crabapples (*Malus* spp.)
bayberries (*Myrica* spp.)
pines (*Pinus* spp.)
cherries (*Prunus* spp.)
oaks (*Quercus* spp.)
common blackberry (*Rubus allegheniensis*)
blueberries (*Vaccinium* spp.)
frost grape (*Vitis vulpina*)

Male eastern towhee.

Female eastern towhee.

lark bunting / *Calamospiza melanocorys*

Male lark bunting at his nest on the ground under common sagebrush (*Artemisia tridentata*).

A characteristic bird of the open prairie grasslands and weed-filled pastures of southern Canada and the west-central United States, the lark bunting is a stocky, thick-billed finch. The male in breeding plumage is a black bird with conspicuous white wing patches, which are most noticeable in flight. The male in winter and the female all year are dull brown, 7-inch birds, striped with darker brown above and white with brown streaking on the undersides.

Because of the lack of trees and elevated song perches on the prairies, the lark bunting indulges in spectacular song flights over the breeding grounds that have given it the name of lark. Its song is a flutelike series of whistles, trills, and slurs. The call note is a soft, whistled *hoo-ee*.

Habitat

Dry, treeless plains and prairies where the grasses contain clumps of sagebrush.

Migration and Winter Range

The lark bunting begins its northern migration in early March, drifting into southwestern Kansas from late March on, and reaching central Nebraska in the first week of May. The birds continue their journey, slowly reaching the northern limits of their breeding range in southern Canada by early June. They travel in flocks sometimes numbering several hundred.

The southward migration begins in late July or early August. The bird winters from southern California, central Arizona, and northcentral Texas, south to central Mexico.

Breeding Range

East of the Rocky Mountains, its breeding range extends from southern Alberta, southern Saskatchewan, southwestern Manitoba, southeastern North Dakota, southwestern Minnesota, and west-central Montana, to southeastern New Mexico, northern Texas, western Oklahoma, and southcentral and eastern Kansas.

Breeding Behavior

Courtship takes place during pauses in the northward migration. The male birds sing to their chosen mates, leave a perch near ground level, and, with a conspicuous fluttering of the wings, rise above the prairie. They hover about 15 feet up, then descend, all the while pouring out their rich, modulated warbling that is like a canary singing. Sometimes up to 100 males may be airborne at the same time, filling the air with their music.

On arrival at their breeding grounds, the flocks disperse into mated pairs, but remain sociable during the breeding season, often nesting in small colonies.

Nesting

Both birds build a nest of grasses, rootlets, and weed stems, lined with plant down, in a depression in the ground, with the rim level with or slightly raised above the ground. The female lays 3 to 6 light blue eggs and incubates them for about 12 days. The male sings to his mate constantly throughout the incubation period and may sometimes share the incubating duties with her. Both parents care for the nestlings.

Feeding Habits

The lark bunting's diet consists of 79 percent insects, and 21 percent seeds, which are mainly weed seeds.

Plants *for* food *and* shelter include:

grasses (*Andropogon* spp.), for nesting

Small flock of lark buntings on their northern migration.

song sparrow / *Melospiza melodia*

Song sparrow feeds on the fruits of hollyleaf cherry (*Prunus ilicifolia*).

The song sparrow is brown-backed, with its whitish underparts heavily streaked with brown and a large brown central spot on the breast. Male and females are 5 to 7 inches long and are similar. In flight the bird pumps its longish tail. It sings throughout spring and summer. A sweet, variable song, it was rendered by Thoreau as *"Maids! Maids! Maids, hang up your teakettle-ettle-ettle,"* which expresses the swing and tempo.

Possibly the most common of the native sparrows, the song sparrow is also the most variable bird in North America, with 31 different subspecies recognized in the most recent American Ornithologists' Union (AOU) Check-list of North American birds. The development of subspecies with different plumage variations illustrates the bird's response to varying environmental and climatic conditions, but they are always various shades of streaky brown and commonly found in open, shrubby areas.

Habitat

The birds prefer bushy shrubbery in the vicinity of water and undergrowth, in gardens and city parks.

Migration and Winter Range

Absent from parts of its northern range in winter, the song sparrow is one of the first birds to return in spring. The bird winters from Southeast Alaska and southern Canada south into Mexico.

Breeding Range

Aleutians, Alaska, and Newfoundland, south to North Dakota, the Carolinas, and Mexico.

Breeding Behavior

Song sparrows spend a great deal of time in courtship. A warm spell in winter or spring causes a display of territorial possessiveness. The male defends an area of about an acre. Considerable rivalry between the males occurs, with competitions in song and flight.

Nesting

When a pair has mated, the male song sparrow devotes himself to song while the female builds the nest. She lays 3 to 5 pale green, brown-spotted eggs in a cup-shaped nest of grass and leaves lined with finer grasses, roots, and hair. The nest is concealed in grasses on the ground or in a bush or small tree. The female incubates the eggs over 12 or 13 days. She may hatch 2, 3, or 4 broods in a season, depending on conditions.

Feeding Habits

In summer, half the bird's diet consists of insects, including beetles, grasshoppers, cutworms, and flies. Weed seeds account for about 67 percent of the yearly diet. The bird also feeds on wild fruits and spilled grain.

Plants *for* food *and* shelter include:

sunflowers (*Helianthus* spp.)

Virginia creeper (*Parthenocissus quinquefolia*)

wild cherries (*Prunus* spp.)

common blackberry (*Rubus allegheniensis*)

elderberries (*Sambucus* spp.)

highbush blueberry (*Vaccinium corymbosum*)

Song sparrow feeding on the seeds of western red cedar (*Thuja plicata*).

white-throated sparrow / *Zonotrichia albicollis*

The white-throated sparrow is attracted to the small black fruits of black crowberry (*Empetrum nigrum*).

The sweet song of the white-throated sparrow is a series of whistled notes, which change pitch during the song, and is traditionally interpreted as *"Old Sam Peabody, Peabody, Peabody."* This gives the bird its other common name, Peabody bird. In Canada, the song is interpreted as *"Sweet, Sweet, Canada, Canada, Canada."* The white-throated sparrow sings this beautiful song often, and it can be heard at dusk as well as throughout the day. The sparrow has a brown back, gray breast, pale belly, and a distinctive white throat patch. Head stripes may vary from black and bright white to brown with tan. Between the eye and bill, this bird has a distinctive yellow spot.

Habitat

White-throated sparrows prefer thickets, coniferous and mixed woodlands, weedy roadsides, and woods' edges. They are also found in dense patches of shrubbery alongside lawns in gardens.

Migration and Winter Range

White-throated sparrows winter from northern California, Kansas, Ohio, and Massachusetts to Texas, Florida, and the Gulf Coast.

Breeding Range

The bird breeds from the northern wooded parts of Canada south to British Columbia, northern North Dakota, and Wisconsin, and in the mountains as far south as West Virginia.

Breeding Behavior

The male birds arrive at the nesting grounds and begin singing, usually from a coniferous tree.

Nesting

The female constructs the cup-shaped nest of grasses, twigs, and pine needles, lined with rootlets, grasses, and deer hair. She usually builds the nest on the ground under a shrub. She lays 4 or 5 pale green, blue, or white eggs, heavily marked with brown, and incubates them for 12 to 14 days. The young leave the nest when they are about 7 to 12 days old.

Feeding Habits

The white-throated sparrow mainly feeds on the ground, hopping and scratching in the soil. Its favorite food is weed seeds, but it also consumes ants, beetles, flies, and other insects, as well as wild fruits and buds.

Plants *for* food *and* shelter include:

maples (*Acer* spp.)

dogwoods (*Cornus* spp.)

hollies (*Ilex* spp.)

eastern red cedar (*Juniperus virginiana*)

honeysuckles (*Lonicera* spp.)

oaks (*Quercus* spp.)

elderberries (*Sambucus* spp.)

frost grape (*Vitis vulpina*)

White-throated sparrow showing its distinctive white throat patch and black and white head stripes, singing in spring from the shelter of a red spruce (*Picea rubens*).

dark-eyed junco / *Junco hyemalis*

In 1973, the American Ornithologists' Union determined that several geographical forms of junco should be considered one species, the dark-eyed junco. All forms have dark eyes and both sexes are 5½ to 6¾ inches long. The slate-colored race is the most widespread. Common in winter in the east and across most of the United States, the male slate-colored junco has slate-gray upper parts and breast, which are sharply defined against the white underparts and white outer tail feathers that are usually shown in flight. The female is similar but a paler gray.

The Oregon race is the western subspecies, abundant in suburbs, fields, and gardens in winter. It has a black hood and chestnut mantle with white underparts, buff sides, and white outer tail feathers. Females have a gray hood and are less colorful. The white-winged race is an isolated population confined to the Black Hills of South Dakota and eastern Montana. It is similar to the slate-colored junco, but is distinguished by its 2 white wing bars and extensive white outer tail feathers.

The male dark-eyed junco sings with a ringing metallic trill. The call note is a constant *chip*.

Dark-eyed juncos favor the fruits of the sweet birch (*Betula lenta*). The slate-colored junco is shown at top and the Oregon junco is shown below.

Dark-eyed Oregon junco.

Habitat

Subspecies vary slightly in their habitat, with most preferring openings and edges of coniferous and mixed woodlands in the nesting season. They are often found in weedy patches in fields, along roadsides, and in gardens in winter and during migration.

Migration and Winter Range

Slate-colored juncos winter from southern Canada to the southern limits of the United States; Oregon juncos winter in the western half of the country, south to Mexico; and white-winged juncos winter in the Southwest and south into Mexico.

Breeding Range

The slate-colored junco's breeding range extends from the wooded areas of Alaska to Newfoundland and across the northern United States. The Oregon junco's breeding range extends along the Northwest Coast south to Baja California. The white-winged junco's breeding range is confined to the Black Hills of South Dakota and eastern Montana.

Breeding Behavior

The male dark-eyed junco proclaims his breeding territory by singing from the treetops, and may continue singing for several days before a female arrives. The birds' courtship display involves hopping around each other with wings dropped and the tail fanned, showing the white outer feathers. The pair stays close to each other throughout the day.

Nesting

The female constructs a deep, well-concealed, cup-shaped nest of mosses, twigs, rootlets, and grasses, usually on the ground, under tree roots, overhanging vegetation, or ledges. She lays 3 to 6 (usually 4 or 5) bluish white blotched eggs and incubates them for 11 or 12 days.

Both parents care for the young, feeding them regurgitated food for the first few days; later, green caterpillars form the main course. The birds fledge when 12 or 13 days old, but remain partially dependent on the parents for 3 more weeks.

Feeding Habits

Juncos are mainly ground-feeding seed eaters, preferring grass and weed seeds and the seeds of conifers. Seed-bearing annuals provide food in the garden. In summer, various insects make up about half of the diet.

Plants *for* food *and* shelter include:

firs (*Abies* spp.)

birches (*Betula* spp.)

tamarack (*Larix laricina*)

honeysuckles (*Lonicera* spp.)

pines (*Pinus* spp.)

sumacs (*Rhus* spp.)

hemlocks (*Tsuga* spp.)

Dark-eyed, slate-colored junco. Birds fluff out their feathers in cold weather for added insulation and to conserve energy.

rose-breasted grosbeak / *Pheucticus ludovicianus*

The rose-breasted grosbeak is one of the most beautiful North American birds, an accomplished songster and one of our most useful birds that feed on insect pests. The male is unmistakable with his black and white plumage, large triangle of rose-red on the breast, and pink wing linings, which are shown in flight.

The female is more modest, with heavily streaked grayish brown plumage and a prominent white eyebrow. Both sexes have the large, thick, powerful bill adapted for cracking tough seeds, which form an important part of their diet. The bird is long-lived, surviving up to 24 years in captivity. The male sings a sweet mellow song, a long, continuous robinlike warble. The call note is a high-pitched metallic *clink*. The female has a similar, softer voice.

Female rose-breasted grosbeak at her nest in a flame azalea (*Rhododendron calendulaceum*).

Male rose-breasted grosbeak in breeding plumage feeding on the fruits of red mulberry (*Morus rubra*).

Habitat

This bird prefers moist deciduous and mixed woodlands where tall trees are adjacent to tall shrubs, such as borders of streams, lakes, ponds, or swamps.

Migration and Winter Range

Keeping to the treetops, the rose-breasted grosbeak drifts south, reaching Central America in mid-October. It winters from southeastern and southern Mexico south to Ecuador, Colombia, and Venezuela.

Breeding Range

Extends from northeastern British Columbia east across Canada to Nova Scotia; south to southcentral Alberta, northern North Dakota, eastern Kansas, southwestern Missouri, eastern Tennessee, northern Georgia, and western North Carolina (in the mountains); and north through sections of the Atlantic states to southeastern Pennsylvania, southeastern New York, and central New Jersey.

Breeding Behavior

Arriving at his breeding grounds, the male grosbeak begins to sing. As a prelude to courtship, males often indulge in combat, which is more visual display than physical contact. Males may be seen dashing through the woods in pursuit of a female, pouring out their sweetest music while fighting with each other. The female accompanies the victor, and the two become constant companions for the breeding season.

Nesting

The male often selects the nest site, usually 10 to 15 feet above the ground in a fork of a deciduous tree. Both birds may share in the nest building, constructing a loosely built structure of small sticks, fine twigs, and grass, lined with rootlets and fine grasses. The female lays 3 to 5 purple-spotted, whitish eggs. Both sexes share the incubation for 12 or 13 days. The male bird often sings while on the nest. While the female incubates, he often feeds her and stands guard nearby, singing sweetly. The young birds are cared for by both parents and fledge when 9 to 12 days old.

Feeding Habits

It is known as the potato-bug bird from its habit of feeding on potato beetle larvae. Other insect pests make up 52 percent of the diet. The remainder is wild fruit and small quantities of seeds and grain.

Plants *for* food *and* shelter include:

maples (*Acer* spp.)
dogwoods (*Cornus* spp.)
hawthorns (*Crataegus* spp.)
red mulberry (*Morus rubra*)
black tupelo (*Nyssa sylvatica*)
Virginia creeper (*Parthenocissus quinquefolia*)
sumacs (*Rhus* spp.)
elderberries (*Sambucus* spp.)
wild grapes (*Vitis* spp.)

Female rose-breasted grosbeak.

northern cardinal / *Cardinalis cardinalis*

The male northern cardinal has true red plumage, with a black bib and black narrow area surrounding its bill. The female is olive-gray or brownish, with a touch of red on the crest, wings, and tail. Both sexes are 8 to 9 inches long. The birds have a prominently crested head and use their crests to indicate annoyance. They have a heavy grosbeaklike red or orange bill.

The northern cardinal is one of the rare songbirds that sing throughout the year. The male sings with a loud, clear, whistle. If disturbed at night, it will often erupt into song, and there are at least 28 songs in his repertoire. Both sexes sing, sometimes together, the female slightly more softly than the male. The common call is a sharp metallic *tsip*.

Habitat
Dense thickets, tangled shrubby growth, woodland edges, and bushy swamps. A common resident in parks, and gardens where bushy shrubs are grown.

Migration and Winter Range
Year-round residents in their range. In winter, in the more sheltered areas of their range, they often gather in flocks of up to 70 birds. The bird is extending its range north and breeding in areas where it was once a casual visitor.

Breeding Range
The northern cardinal is a permanent resident from southeastern South Dakota, southern Ontario, and Nova Scotia, south to the Gulf of Mexico and southeastern Florida, and west to southeastern California, central Arizona, southern New Mexico, and Belize.

Breeding Behavior
In spring, the male accompanies the female more often, and singing by both sexes increases. The male defends his breeding territory, flying at other intruding males. He often feeds the female as part of courtship.

Male northern cardinal (top) helping the female care for their young in nannyberry (*Viburnum lentago*).

Nesting

The male follows the female, often singing to her while she constructs a loose, bulky, bowl-shaped nest in a tall shrub or small tree usually from 2 to 8 feet above the ground. Dense thickets are preferred, including blackberry or gooseberry bushes, rose canes, or honeysuckle vines.

The female lays 2 to 5 red-brown spotted, pale green eggs and incubates them for 12 or 13 days. During incubation, the male feeds the female. Both parents care for the young, who fledge when 10 to 11 days old. When the young birds can fly, the female leaves them in the care of the male while she attends to a second brood. The male becomes a restless and anxious guardian for 3 weeks or more. The pair usually raises 2 or 3 broods in a single year.

Feeding Habits

The bird's diet consists of about 30 percent insects and 70 percent vegetable matter. The bird feeds while hopping on the ground or moving through the trees and shrubs, feeding on many of the worst agricultural pests. At least 33 species of wild fruit are consumed.

Plants *for* food *and* shelter include:

hackberries (*Celtis* spp.)
dogwoods (*Cornus* spp.)
hollies (*Ilex* spp.)
red mulberry (*Morus rubra*)
wild cherries (*Prunus* spp.)
sumacs (*Rhus* spp.)
elderberries (*Sambucus* spp.)
viburnums (*Viburnum* spp.)

Male northern cardinal.

Female northern cardinal.

indigo bunting / *Passerina cyanea*

Indigo buntings feeding on the seeds of New England aster (*Symphyotrichum novae-angliae*).

The adult male indigo bunting in full breeding plumage is the only small North American finch that appears blue all over. In fact, the bird has no blue pigment at all; light refraction gives the feathers a blue coloration. The bird is usually seen singing from a high perch and in poor light and appears as a black silhouette, relying on perfect lighting conditions to reveal his bright turquoise-blue color. The female is a drab brown with indistinct streaking. Both sexes are 5½ inches long. The bird sings throughout the day from his arrival in spring until mid-August and sometimes later. The song is a fast, excited warble. The bird also has a flight song that may last for 8 seconds or more and is usually sung at dawn and twilight. The call note is a *tsick*.

Habitat
Dense, concealing cover for nesting and moderately high perches for singing. Among its preferred habitats, it likes woodland edges and openings, abandoned farmland, cornfields, shrubby roadsides, open brushy fields, and hedgerows. The birds avoid mature forests.

Migration and Winter Range
When the young have grown strong and the male is dressed in his brown fall plumage, the birds leave for central Mexico and the West Indies and head south to central Panama.

Breeding Range
Southwestern South Dakota and southern Manitoba east to Maine and south to southwestern Oklahoma, southeastern Texas, the Gulf states, and northern Florida.

Breeding Behavior
The males appear in their nesting areas several days before the female birds. The male soon begins singing in defense of his territory, warning other males to keep away. When the females arrive, pairing begins, and the male follows his mate around, singing constantly.

Nesting
The indigo bunting accepts a wide choice for nest sites, including thorny bushes, barberry or witch hazel thickets, hackberry, elm, maple, or

ironwood saplings. The female selects the site and constructs the nest, generally in the crotch of a shrub or sapling 2 to 12 feet above the ground. The nest is a well-woven cup of dried grass, bark strips, twigs, and weed stems, lined with fine grasses, hair, or feathers. The female lays 3 or 4 pale blue eggs and quietly incubates them while the male, resplendent in his brilliant plumage, climbs the highest tree and pours out his song. The eggs are incubated for 12 or 13 days, the male sometimes relieving the female on the nest.

The young leave the nest 8 to 10 days after hatching. They normally raise 2 broods each year.

Feeding Habits

The birds have a diversified diet, including cankerworms, which may make up 78 percent of their total food during an infestation. Other insect pests are consumed. Seeds constitute a large proportion of the diet.

Plants *for* food *and* shelter include:

elderberries (*Sambucus* spp.)
asters (*Symphyotrichum* spp.)
grasses (*Andropogon* spp.), for nesting

Male indigo bunting feeding on green foxtail grass (*Setaria viridis*).

lazuli bunting / *Passerina amoena*

The western counterpart of the indigo bunting, the lazuli bunting has similar habits. It has increased its range with the clearing of forests for agriculture, and on the Great Plains its range now overlaps that of the indigo bunting.

The male lazuli bunting is a living gem, with its brilliant, contrasting coloration seeming to glow in the sunshine. His distinctive markings include a light cerulean blue back with a light cinnamon chest, a whitish belly, and 2 white wing bars. The female is a dull brown above and unstreaked buff below, much like the female indigo bunting. Both sexes are 5 to 5½ inches long. The song is usually delivered from a high, open perch and is a variable, loud, strident series of warbled phrases sounding like *see-see-see-sweert-sweert-zee-see-sweet-zeer-see-see*. They sing at all hours. The call note is a soft *chip*.

Lazuli bunting at his nest in Nootka rose (*Rosa nutkana*).

Habitat
The lazuli bunting's ideal environment includes low hillside vegetation, wild rose thickets along mountain streams, open scrublands, weedy thickets, and pastures. This bird prefers a diversity of plant types, including dense thickets for nesting, interspersed with open areas. In breeding season, the birds prefer areas near streams, but avoid damp or boggy areas. They are found from sea level on the Pacific Coast to elevations of 10,000 feet in the Sierra Nevada.

Migration and Winter Range
The bird winters from southern Baja California, southern Arizona, and southwestern New Mexico, south to southcentral Mexico. The birds begin their northern movement out of Mexico in late March and reach the United States in early April. They reach the San Francisco Bay Area in the last week of April and extend into the northern limits of their range in early May.

Breeding Range
Southern British Columbia east to southern Saskatchewan, northeastern and central North Dakota, and northeastern South Dakota south to southeastern California, northwestern Baja California, southern Nevada, central Arizona, western Oklahoma, and eastern Nebraska.

Breeding Behavior

The male birds usually arrive before the females and claim suitable breeding areas. The male defends the territory by singing from elevated perches within the territory. The female arrives and helps in the defense of the territory. The male courts the female with much singing, displaying his brilliant plumage and extending his trembling wings.

Nesting

The birds' nest is a coarsely woven cup-shaped nest of dried grasses lined with finer grasses, lashed to a supporting branch or the crotch of a wild rose, gooseberry, currant, willow, or manzanita shrub, usually 2 to 4 feet above the ground.

The female lays 3 to 5 (usually 4) pale blue eggs and incubates them for 12 days. The female feeds the young, shades them when necessary during the day, and broods them at night, apparently with little or no help from the male. The male usually stays around the nest area and sometimes accompanies the female on her foraging trips. The young fledge after 10 to 15 days. After nesting, the birds roam the countryside, congregating where food is abundant.

Feeding Habits

Their diet is made up of 64 percent insects in the spring and 53 percent in the summer. They also feed on seeds of grass and wild lettuce (*Lactuca* spp.).

Plants *for* food *and* shelter include:

grasses (*Andropogon* spp.), for nesting

Male lazuli bunting in breeding plumage.

summer tanager / *Piranga rubra*

The male summer tanager retains his bright rose-red color and brown flight feathers throughout the year, while the female is olive-green above and a deep yellow below. Both sexes are 7 to 8 inches long. The summer tanager has a long yellowish brown bill in the breeding season, which changes to a darker color in the fall and is a dusky color in young birds. The bird's common call is a distinctive rattling *chicky-tucky-tuck*.

Though the plumage of the male summer tanager is unmistakable, like the scarlet tanager it is difficult to detect the bird in the dense concealing foliage of the woodland trees that he inhabits. The bird is solitary in its habits and deliberate in its movements.

Flowering dogwood (*Cornus florida*) is a common nesting tree of the summer tanager.

Habitat

Summer tanagers prefer mature trees in the dry oak and mixed forests in the South, and the cottonwood and willow thickets along streams in the Southwest.

Migration and Winter Range

The summer tanager is one of the many North American species that migrate across the Gulf of Mexico from Central America to the Gulf states. A common summer resident of the southern states, the birds arrive in Florida as early as late March. The main northern migration occurs throughout April, with the birds reaching the northern limit of their breeding range by early May.

The migration south begins as early as late August and continues until mid-October, as the birds return to their Central and South American winter haunts. The bird winters from northern Mexico south to Bolivia and Brazil.

Breeding Range

The bird's breeding range extends from southeastern California, New Mexico, Nebraska, Iowa, central Ohio, Maryland, and Delaware south to southern Florida, the Gulf Coast, and northern Mexico.

Breeding Behavior

The male proclaims his territory with a rich, varied musical song similar to the scarlet tanager's, but sweeter and less harsh. The female is attracted to the song, and the male spreads his wings and tail with his bill pointed vertically as part of a courtship display.

Nesting

The female constructs a flimsy, shallow, cup-shaped nest from stems, grasses, bark and leaves. Nests are usually near the tip of a limb 10 to 35 feet above the ground. In northwestern Florida, the flowering dogwood is a common nesting tree. Turkey oak and Jack oak as well as other oaks are also favored trees, since the nests become very difficult to spot among the large leaves. Pine trees are sometimes also used for nesting.

The female lays 3 or 4 brown-spotted blue-green eggs and incubates them for 11 or 12 days. Both sexes feed the young.

Feeding Habits

Insects, beetles, wasps, spiders, and worms are included in the summer tanager's diet. The birds often catch insects on the wing, like a flycatcher. Their habit of catching bees and feeding on soft larvae of wasps out of their nests has earned them the common name of beebird in some southern parts of its range. Wild fruits such as blackberry are also consumed.

Plants *for* food *and* shelter include:

dogwoods (*Cornus* spp.)
wild strawberries (*Fragaria* spp.)
pines (*Pinus* spp.)
wild cherries (*Prunus* spp.)
oaks (*Quercus* spp.)
western raspberries (*Rubus* spp.)
elderberries (*Sambucus* spp.)

Male summer tanager showing his yellow-brown bill, which will darken after the breeding season.

scarlet tanager / *Piranga olivacea*

Male scarlet tanager displaying his scarlet plumage while courting a female in staghorn sumac (*Rhus typhina*).

Seen in sunlight, the male in breeding plumage is a brilliant scarlet with black wings and tail. The female has an olive-green back, brown wings, and yellow breast and belly; both birds are 7½ inches long. Between July and August, the male scarlet tanager adopts a winter plumage that is similar to the female, dull green above and yellowish below, but he retains his black wings and tail.

An arboreal bird, it tends to remain hidden in the trees. The song is a husky, repetitive caroling sounding like *querit-queer-queery-querit-queer*. The call note is a nasal *chick-kurr*.

Habitat

It prefers mature deciduous woods of oak, tulip tree, hickory, and ash, but it often frequents mixed woods of pine and hemlock, wooded parks, and large trees in suburban areas.

Migration and Winter Range

Arriving in the United States in April, it drifts into the northern parts of its range in early to mid-May. It has usually left the United States by mid-October for its winter haunts in South America from Colombia to Bolivia.

Breeding Range

Southeastern Manitoba, east to New Brunswick, and the east central United States, and south to eastern Oklahoma, central Alabama, and northern Georgia.

Breeding Behavior

The male bird arrives several days before the female and claims his territory, warning off other males with frequent singing from tall trees. The female is attracted to the song, and the male courts her by positioning himself on a lower branch and spreading his wings to display the scarlet plumage of his back, which is hidden when his wings are folded.

Nesting

The female constructs a small, flat, cup-shaped nest from twigs, rootlets, and grass lined with finer grasses or pine needles, usually far out on the limb of a large tree. The nest is usually 8 to 75 feet above the ground. She lays 3 to 5 brown-spotted greenish eggs and incubates them for 13 or 14 days. Both parents help to feed the young, who leave the nest about 9 to 11 days after hatching.

Feeding Habits

Insects make up over 80 percent of the bird's diet and they are drawn to oaks because of their many insect pests. They can control outbreaks of the small caterpillars of the gypsy moth. They also feed on fruits.

Plants *for* food *and* shelter include:

serviceberries (*Amelanchier* spp.)

dogwoods (*Cornus* spp.)

red mulberry (*Morus rubra*)

bayberries (*Myrica* spp.)

black tupelo (*Nyssa sylvatica*)

wild cherries (*Prunus* spp.)

sumacs (*Rhus* spp.)

common blackberry (*Rubus alleghraiensis*)

elderberries (*Sambucus* spp.)

highbush blueberry (*Vaccinium corymbosum*)

Male scarlet tanager foraging for insects in the foliage of chokecherry (*Prunus virginiana*).

eastern meadowlark / *Sturnella magna*

Western meadowlark probing the ground for insects.

western meadowlark range

This beautiful grassland bird has a bright yellow breast with a striking black V-shaped mark. Its back is mottled brown, and its tail shows distinctive white outer feathers in flight. Despite its name, the eastern meadowlark is not a lark but a member of the blackbird family, related to the European starling, which it resembles in its swaggering gait, and in flight it has the same flapping, then gliding action.

The eastern meadowlark is almost identical in appearance to the western meadowlark. The mottled back of the eastern species is darker than the back of its western cousin. The two birds are similar in appearance, habits, and haunts, but when the two sing, the difference is apparent.

The western meadowlark is by far the better musician, possibly unequalled in quality of song among North American birds. The song of the eastern meadowlark is a plaintive, slurred whistle usually rendered as *spring-o-the-year*. The song is one of the earliest heard in spring. The bird also has a harsh, chattering, guttural alarm call, and male birds perform a bubbling, tinkling flight song.

Habitat

The eastern meadowlark is found in open grasslands, prairies, and fields with shrubby borders.

Migration and Winter Range

In fall, the birds leave the northern limits of their range, though some winter as far north as southern Ontario and part of New England. In winter, they roam in loose flocks of several families.

Breeding Range

The bird breeds from southeastern Ontario and Nova Scotia through the prairie country of Canada, and south through the central and eastern United States to Arizona, New Mexico, Texas, and the Gulf states to northern South America. The birds are early spring migrants, with the males arriving first at the breeding territory.

Breeding Behavior

Nesting begins early. The male bird defends his breeding territory with song, advertising to other males that the area is occupied. Males may have more than one mate. The territory is usually about 7 acres, and intruding meadowlarks are chased to the borders.

Nesting

The female builds a beautiful nest in a 1- to 3-inch-deep depression in the ground in meadows, pastures, the edges of a marsh or any open grassy area. Damp or wet ground is often preferred. She lines the depression with coarse, dry grass, then with fine grasses, forming a grassy saucer. The nest is often given a dome-shaped roof made of grass interwoven with surrounding vegetation, with the entrance on the side. The nest is well concealed and very hard to detect. The bird's coloration helps it blend with its surroundings.

The female lays 3 to 7 (usually 5) whitish pink eggs, speckled with brown and lavender, and incubates them for 13 to 15 days. The young leave the nest when they are 11 or 12 days old and wander around in the grass with their parents until they are able to fly. The birds then roam the countryside in small family groups.

Feeding Habits

Apart from all their other attributes, meadowlarks are very beneficial birds to farmers, with insect pests making up 70 percent of their diet. They feed on beetles, weevils, cutworms, crickets and their eggs, caterpillars, and snails in great quantities. They also consume spilled grain, weed seeds, and grass seeds, as well as some wild fruits.

Plants *for* food *and* shelter include:

big bluestem (*Andropogon gerardii*)
wild strawberry (*Fragaria virginiana*)
sunflowers (*Helianthus* spp.)
common blackberry (*Rubus allegheniensis*)

Eastern meadowlark foraging for insects among prairie flowers, including the bright yellow sneezeweed (*Helenium autumnale*).

Brewer's blackbird / *Euphagus cyanocephalus*

Male Brewer's blackbird courts
a female among bunchberry
(*Cornus canadensis*).

In spring, the male Brewer's blackbird is dressed in glossy greenish black plumage with a purplish black head and neck and yellow eyes. The female has a subdued brownish gray plumage and dark eyes. The bird has a peculiar gait, walking with short forward jerks of the head or running with its head held quite still as it forages on the ground for insects. It commonly flocks with red-winged blackbirds, tricolored blackbirds, or brown-headed cowbirds. In summer, fall, and winter, these flocks may contain 40 to 100 Brewer's blackbirds plus the other species. The flocks roost communally in groves of trees and in marshes. The common call note is a harsh *check*.

Habitat

Frequents ranches, prairies, roadside shrubbery, golf courses, parks, and lawns.

Migration and Winter Range

Southwestern Canada, Montana, Kansas, Arkansas, Tennessee, Mississippi, and Alabama to southern Baja California, central Mexico, the Gulf Coast, and east to western Florida.

Breeding Range

Extending from British Columbia east to southern Manitoba, northern Minnesota, western Ontario, and northern Wisconsin south to Baja California, central California, southern Nevada, southwestern and central Utah, central Arizona, western and south central New Mexico, northern Texas, Oklahoma, northern Iowa, southern Wisconsin, northeastern Illinois, northwestern Indiana, and southwestern Michigan.

The bird first appeared in Washington state at the turn of the century, and is also a recent arrival in Ontario. It is extending its range east.

Breeding Behavior

In spring, the flocking behavior is modified as the birds begin to associate in pairs within the flock. The birds indulge in an elaborate display during the breeding season, with both sexes fluffing out their feathers while spreading the tail and wings and cocking the tail with the bill held upward and the wings quivering. The courting male's song is a creaky, wheezing *que-ee*. The pair remains together as they walk or perch. The male becomes very protective of the female, driving away an intruder by flying directly at him or blocking his path.

The female selects a nest site, and aggressive behavior may result from competition with other pairs for possession of the site. The birds may nest in loose colonies of from 6 to 30 or more pairs.

Nesting
Accompanied by the male, the female alone constructs the sturdy nest of interlaced twigs and coarse grass reinforced with mud or dried cow dung and lined with rootlets and fine grass and hair. The nest may be on the ground (common in the East) in thick weedy vegetation, in marshes, in wind-breaks or in tall conifers up to 150 feet above the ground, but usually between 20 and 40 feet above ground.

The female lays 3 to 7 blotched, light gray eggs and incubates them for 12 to 14 days. While the female is incubating, the male spends less time guarding her, and if an unmated female is present, he may mate with her also. The male in this case guards both nests and later helps feed both sets of nestlings. The young birds fly 13 or 14 days after hatching, and juveniles have plumage similar to the female.

Feeding Habits
Their diet consists of 32 percent insects and 68 percent fruits and vegetable matter. Fruit and weed seeds, which are mainly fed on in winter, are also consumed.

Plants *for* food *and* shelter include:

sunflowers (*Helianthus* spp.)
wild cherries (*Prunus* spp.)
grasses (*Andropogon* spp.), for nesting

Brewer's blackbird, in glossy spring plumage.

orchard oriole / *Icterus spurius*

Male orchard oriole (top) and a female orchard oriole favor the fruits of the red mulberry (*Morus rubra*).

The 6- to 7-inch orchard oriole spends much of its time out of sight in the dense foliage of shade trees as it flits around searching for insects. The adult male is the only brick-red oriole and the only eastern oriole with a solid black tail. The head, back, and wings (with a single white bar) are black. The female is the only eastern oriole with a greenish yellow breast. The spring song is a rapid musical warble with piping whistles interspersed and ending in a loud, slurred *where*. It is delivered from a perch or on the wing and can be heard from the bird's arrival through to early summer.

Habitat

Orchards, roadside shade trees, and scattered garden trees are also suitable. The bird avoids densely wooded areas.

Migration and Winter Range

The orchard oriole reaches the United States in March or early April, mainly moving up the Mississippi Valley where it remains common. The birds reach the northern limits of their range in early May. It is one of the first birds to return south to its winter range, leaving in mid-July for southern Mexico, Colombia, and Venezuela.

Breeding Range

Most of the eastern United States, from southern Manitoba to Massachusetts south to southern Texas, northern Mexico, the Gulf Coast, and northern Florida, and west to central Nebraska and northeastern Colorado.

Breeding Behavior

During courtship, the male bird often flies high above the foliage and sings as he descends to his sheltered perch.

Nesting

Orchard orioles often nest in loose colonies. They prefer oak trees for nesting. The nest is a beautifully woven basket of grasses suspended from a horizontal fork in a branch of a tree or shrub, usually 10 to 20 feet above the ground. The female constructs the nest and lines it with fine grasses and a thick padding of plant down. She lays 3 to 6 whitish eggs with purple marks and incubates them for 11 to 14 days. The male feeds the female while she is on the nest, and both sexes tend the young, which fly after 11 to 14 days.

Feeding Habits
The orchard oriole's diet is about 90 percent insects. The bird also feeds on fruit, especially red mulberries.

Plants *for* food *and* shelter include:

wild strawberry (*Fragaria virginiana*)
red mulberry (*Morus rubra*)
wild cherries (*Prunus* spp.)
common blackberry (*Rubus alleghceniensis*)
viburnums (*Viburnum* spp.)
wild grapes (*Vitis* spp.)

Male orchard oriole.

Female orchard oriole in a meadow garden feeding on insects attracted to the bright yellow flowers of Small's ragwort (*Packera anonyma*).

hooded oriole / *Icterus cucullatus*

One of the brightest colored birds in the Southwest, the hooded oriole's yellow or orange "hood" and black throat seem emphasized by desert sunshine. The hooded oriole is more slender than other orioles and is the only oriole in the United States with an orange crown. Both sexes are 7 to 7¾ inches long with a thin, black, slightly downcurved bill. They sing in a warbling, throaty whistle, interspersed with chatter. The call note is a liquid, whistled *wheet*.

Habitat

A hooded oriole is a common bird in suburban parks and gardens with suitable shade trees and open woodlands, especially near streams. Although regarded as a shy bird, it is well known because it has found congenial surroundings in palm plantations and ornamental shrubs of suburban areas and ranches.

Migration and Winter Range

The hooded oriole arrives in California and Texas in March and in Arizona in April. The bird has usually left its summer range by late August, with some immature birds remaining until early September before moving into Mexico. It sometimes winters in southern Texas and southern California as far north as Los Angeles.

Breeding Range

Central California, southern Nevada, central and southeastern Arizona, southern New Mexico, and western and southern Texas south to southern Mexico, Baja California, Guatemala, and Belize. The most common breeding oriole in southern Texas. The bird is extending its range north.

Breeding Behavior

In late April the male begins courting, chasing the female and advancing toward her with exaggerated bows.

Nesting

The female constructs a well-built, basket-shaped nest from shredded palm or yucca fibers, suspended from the underside of a palm leaf or in a bunch of Spanish moss or mistletoe. The palm leaf provides shelter

Male hooded oriole feeding on nectar and insects in the blossoms of soaptree yucca (*Yucca elata*).

from rain and sun as well as concealment. This nesting habit has earned the bird its other common name, palm-leaf oriole. Hackberry, mesquite, sycamore trees, and yuccas are also used for nesting.

The female lays 3 to 5 spotted blue-white or gray-white eggs and incubates them for 12 to 14 days. The young leave the nest about 14 days after hatching, but are fed and cared for by the parents for some days after that. The young birds resemble the female, and the young males have a black throat. The birds may have 2 or 3 broods a year.

Feeding Habits

The bird spends most of its time restlessly foraging for insects on the foliage of large trees, often hanging upside down and rarely descending to the ground. The diet includes insect larvae and grasshoppers. Hooded orioles enjoy nectar, and they often puncture large flowers at the base to rob them of nectar. They also feed on berries and fruits.

Plants *for* food *and* shelter include:

wild cherries (*Prunus* spp.)
elderberries (*Sambucus* spp.)
soaptree yucca (*Yucca elata*)

Male hooded oriole foraging in mesquite flowers (*Prosopis* spp.). Birds east of Big Bend, Texas, are more orange.

Baltimore oriole / *Icterus galbula*

Female Baltimore oriole leaving her nest in slippery elm (*Ulmus rubra*), the oriole's favorite nesting tree. The buds and fruits of this tree are fed on by many birds.

The Baltimore oriole is a brilliantly colored, melodious oriole. The male is black above and orange below, while the female is olive above and yellow-orange below. Both birds have white wing bars and are 7 to 8½ inches long. The song is flutelike, a low *hew-li*. With the planting of trees across the Great Plains, the Baltimore oriole has extended its range west to meet the western Bullock's oriole, and some interbreeding occurs.

Habitat
Prefers places where large trees are present in relatively open areas, such as shade trees along country roads, in city parks, and in suburban areas.

Migration and Winter Range
Winters from southern Mexico to Colombia and Venezuela, though it is sometimes found in southeastern Canada and the eastern United States. In mid-August, about 2 weeks before it migrates south, the bird's song is often heard.

Breeding Range
Central Alberta east to central Nova Scotia and south to west-central Oklahoma, northeastern Texas, southeastern Louisiana, northcentral Georgia, western South Carolina, central Virginia, and Delaware.

Breeding Behavior
The males arrive at the breeding grounds several days before the females. On the female's arrival, the male begins a series of displays of his brilliant plumage. First he raises his wings and spreads his tail as he shows off his orange breast, then in bright sunlight he shows off his brilliant black, orange, and white upperparts, all the while uttering low, sweet, seductive whistling notes. Breeding pairs are formed each year and the pair remains constantly together until their young are independent.

Nesting
The female builds a nest that is a well-woven, deep, silvery pouch suspended by the rim from the end of a long, drooping tree branch: elms, poplars, maples, birches, and oaks are favored. The nest is often placed 25 to 30 feet above the ground, where it tosses in the wind. The nest is woven from plant fibers, string, cloth, and hair. Many people enjoy supplying the birds with short lengths of string or yarn. The nest is lined with

wool, hair, and fine grasses. The female lays 4 (sometimes 5 or 6) dark brown- and black-marked grayish eggs that she incubates for 12 to 14 days. The young fly 12 to 14 days after hatching. They join their parents and wander in family groups, feeding on wild fruits and berries, and soon become independent. The birds seem to return to the same nesting site year after year.

Feeding Habits

The birds spend much of their time in the dense foliage of shade trees, gathering insects from the leaves and twigs. Caterpillars are an important food source, usually making up over 33 percent of the total diet. The birds have been known to eradicate local infestations of orchard tent caterpillars. The diet also includes wild fruits and nectar.

Plants *for* food *and* shelter include:

serviceberries (*Amelanchier* spp.)
red mulberry (*Morus rubra*)
wild cherries (*Prunus* spp.)
highbush blueberry (*Vaccinium corymbosum*)

Male Baltimore oriole.

house finch / *Haemorhous mexicanus*

The house finch is attracted to the fruits of wild sweet crabapple (*Malus coronaria*).

As with other red finches, the intensity of color varies considerably in this bird. The head, chest, and rump of the male house finch can be bright red, orange-red, dull orange, or even dull yellow. The rest of the plumage is streaked grayish brown. The female house finch is streaked with gray-brown all over.

Both the male and the female birds measure 5 to 5¾ inches long. The male house finch is a tireless singer, his song a joyous, spirited warble. The female bird also sings, even when on the nest. The call note is a *queet*. A native of the west, the house finch has benefitted from the clearing of land for agriculture, extending its range and increasing in numbers. In 1940, California cage-bird dealers shipped numbers of house finches to New York for illegal sale as Hollywood finches. Escaped birds were recorded nesting on Long Island in 1943, and by 1971 the bird was established in urban New York City.

Habitat

Open woods, around farms, towns, and cities, and in coastal valleys, chaparral, deserts, and orchards.

Migration and Winter Range

The bird is a permanent resident within its range. In late summer, the birds gather in flocks and roam the countryside seeking more open feeding areas.

Breeding Range

In very recent years, the house finch has expanded its breeding range so that it is now found across the continent. Its successful spread across the barrier of the Great Plains is a result of ornamental plantings of blue spruce, which are ideal for nesting and shelter.

Breeding Behavior

In March and April, flocks of house finches break up into pairs, and the male may be seen following the female around while singing and fluttering his wings.

Nesting

The female builds the nest, which is a well-made, compact, cup-shaped structure of twigs, grass, and rootlets, in a shrub, cactus, vines, or shrubbery around houses, in a natural cavity or bird box, almost anywhere.

The female lays 4 or 5 lightly spotted, pale blue eggs and incubates them for about 13 days. The male feeds the incubating female by regurgitation. The young birds fledge 11 to 19 days after hatching. The birds are sociable while nesting and appear to return to the same nest for a second brood and also in subsequent years.

Feeding Habits

The house finch feeds on mainly weed seeds and fruit, which make up 86 percent of its diet.

Plants *for* food *and* shelter include:

honeysuckles (*Lonicera* spp.)

pines (*Pinus* spp.)

western sycamore (*Platanus racemosa*)

sumacs (*Rhus* spp.)

elderberries (*Sambucus* spp.)

grasses (*Andropogon* spp.), for nesting

House finch feeding on the seeds of brittlebush (*Encelia farinosa*).

red crossbill / *Loxia curvirostra*

The red crossbill is known for its distinctive crossed bill—the bill tips are elongated and cross each other like shears—and parrotlike behavior. A member of the finch family, the male of the species has brick-red plumage that is brighter on the rump, and a dusky brown back, wings, and tail. The female is a dull olive-gray, yellowish on the rump and breast, with dusky brown wings and tail. Both male and female measure 5¼ to 6½ inches long. Immature birds resemble the female in coloration. The usual call of the red crossbill is a sharp *jip-jip*.

Habitat
Coniferous forests and suburban areas with conifers.

Migration and Winter Range
Crossbills wander erratically in winter, drawn to an area because of food availability. Winter flocks visiting New England may have traveled from as far away as the Rocky Mountains.

Breeding Range
Southeastern Alaska east to Newfoundland, and south through the Sierra Nevada to northern Baja California and northern Nicaragua. In the east, the range extends to northern Wisconsin and the Appalachian Mountains to Tennessee and North Carolina.

Breeding Behavior
The red crossbill has an erratic breeding period, from as early as January to August, apparently determined by the pine cone crop. If the cone crop fails, the birds may breed later in the year in the sunny, warmer southern regions where food is abundant. In northern areas, pairs may form in mid-January and perform a brief courtship, which includes much singing and a courtship flight. The female may sit in the top of a tree while the male circles her constantly with vibrating wings, singing his melodious song. The male then swoops across to the top of an adjacent tree and the female follows him.

Red crossbill feeding on seeds from the cones of a tamarack tree (*Larix laricina*).

Nesting

The male may contribute nest-building material, but the female builds the loosely constructed, bulky, shallow, saucer-shaped nest from twigs, rootlets, bark strips, lichens, and grass and lined with moss and plant down. The nest is placed far out on a horizontal limb 10 to 40 feet above the ground in a pine, cedar, or spruce tree.

The female lays 3 to 5 (usually 4) lightly spotted, pale blue-green eggs and incubates them for 12 to 14 days. The female may be fed on the nest by the male. Both parents feed the young. The young leave the nest when they are about 17 days old, though their bills do not cross until some time later. The pair raises 1 brood each season.

Feeding Habits

The bird prefers conifer seeds for food. It uses its specialized bill to force and hold the pine cone scales apart while it extracts the seeds with its tongue. It also feeds on seeds of birch, alder, willow, and other trees. In late spring and summer, it consumes some insects. During winter, the birds frequently visit gardens with fruiting larches or spruce, and will remain until they empty cones of their seed.

Plants *for* food *and* shelter include:

firs (*Abies* spp.)
maples (*Acer* spp.)
alders (*Alnus* spp.)
birches (*Betula* spp.)
tamarack (*Larix laricina*)
spruces (*Picea* spp.)
pines (*Pinus* spp.)
hemlocks (*Tsuga* spp.)

Male and juvenile red crossbill feeding on the seeds of piñon pine (*Pinus edulis*).

pine siskin / *Spinus pinus*

The pine siskin is a brown, dark-streaked finch with a sharply pointed bill, a notched tail, and yellow on the wings and tail. On female siskins, the yellow color is not as evident. Both sexes are 4½ to 5 inches long. The call is a loud *clee-ip*, *bzzzt*, or *shree*.

This bird is noted for its erratic wanderings, governed by the abundance of food. A sociable bird, from late summer to late winter it forms mixed flocks with redpolls, goldfinches, crossbills, purple finches, cedar waxwings, and juncos in flocks of 50 and 200 birds.

Habitat

The pine siskin prefers coniferous and mixed woods, ornamental groves, and shade trees in towns, alder thickets, and bushy pastures.

Migration and Winter Range

The pine siskin appears to migrate to the southern areas of its range in autumn and to move north in spring. Winter wanderings are erratic and unpredictable. The usual winter range is from Southeast Alaska and southern Canada, south to the mountains to Baja California and the Gulf Coast, but the bird can turn up practically anywhere in its range.

Breeding Range

The bird's breeding range extends from Alaska, to the Mackenzie Mountains and central Saskatchewan and to central Quebec, south through the higher mountains of the western United States to southern California, southeastern Nebraska, and the mountains of North Carolina.

Breeding Behavior

Larger flocks break up by late January into social groups. A pair bond forms within the social group, with symbolic feeding and flight song displays before breeding.

Pine siskin feeding on the seeds of white alder (*Alnus rhombifolia*).

Nesting

The birds often nest in loose colonies. The female builds a nest of twigs, moss, and bark strips lined with down, fur, hair, and feathers in a conifer 6 to 40 feet above the ground. She lays 3 or 4 lightly speckled, pale green eggs. The male feeds the female during the 13-day incubation period and for about 10 days thereafter. The young leave the nest when they are 15 days old. The birds sometimes raise 2 broods a season.

Feeding Habits

The bird's diet largely consists of pine and alder seeds, along with other tree seeds, insects, and weed seeds. It also favors sunflower seeds.

Plants *for* food *and* shelter include:

maples (*Acer* spp.)

alders (*Alnus* spp.)

birches (*Betula* spp.)

sunflowers (*Helianthus* spp.)

eastern red cedar (*Juniperus virginiana*)

honeysuckles (*Lonicera* spp.)

spruces (*Picea* spp.)

pines (*Pinus* spp.)

Pine siskin feeding on the seeds of Canada hemlock (*Tsuga canadensis*) cones.

American goldfinch / *Spinus tristis*

Male American goldfinch perched on common sunflower (*Helianthus annuus*), a favorite food source.

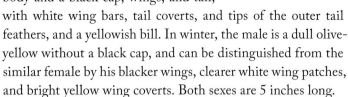

The familiar "wild canary" seems like the happiest of all birds. It seems to celebrate life through its bouncy, undulating flight in flocks, its lively effervescent song, and its amiable nature.

The male in summer has a yellow body and a black cap, wings, and tail, with white wing bars, tail coverts, and tips of the outer tail feathers, and a yellowish bill. In winter, the male is a dull olive-yellow without a black cap, and can be distinguished from the similar female by his blacker wings, clearer white wing patches, and bright yellow wing coverts. Both sexes are 5 inches long.

The goldfinch song is a sweet, high-pitched warble similar to a canary's song, and is sung by males from an exposed perch. A light, gentle twittering can be heard throughout the year as the birds fly overhead, heard on the upswing of their bouncy flight.

Habitat

The birds prefer weedy grasslands and brushy thickets not far from the edge of woods or patches of woods. When nesting, they are found around open, deciduous shrubs.

Migration and Winter Range

Goldfinches are believed to be year-round residents, but there is seasonal movement in spring and fall in flocks of between ten and several hundred birds. Their winter range is from southern Canada and the northern United States to Mexico and the Gulf Coast.

Breeding Range

The bird's breeding range is from central Canada south to southern California, Utah, Colorado, northeast Texas, and the Midwest east to South Carolina.

Breeding Behavior

In spring, the males burst into warbling songs and begin to chase the females. Short fights may break out between males. During the summer, goldfinches break up into smaller groups and become less conspicuous, with pairs forming long before nest building begins.

Nesting

The goldfinch is one of the latest birds to nest, usually at the end of July through September, which coincides with the ripening of thistledown, which is used to line the nest. The female constructs a well-made, delicate, cup-shaped nest of grasses and plant down, usually placed only a few feet off the ground in the forked stem of a shrub. She lays 4 or 5 pale blue eggs and incubates them for 12 to 14 days. The male feeds the female at the nest. The young leave the nest when 12 to 16 days old.

Feeding Habits

The bird feeds on a small quantity of aphids and caterpillars, but they are primarily seed-eaters. Goldfinches commonly feed in flocks. They consume weed seeds consumed in vast quantities. The goldfinch hulls the seeds before consuming them. It favors seeds of sunflowers, alders, and thistles. In spring, the birds feed on birch and alder catkins.

Plants *for* food *and* shelter include:

maples (*Acer* spp.)

alders (*Alnus* spp.)

birches (*Betula* spp.)

sunflowers (*Helianthus* spp.)

tamarack (*Larix laricina*)

honeysuckles (*Lonicera* spp.)

spruces (*Picea* spp.)

pines (*Pinus* spp.)

asters (*Symphyotrichum* spp.)

grass and weed seeds

Male American goldfinch attracted to the flowers of purple coneflower (*Echinacea purpurea*) growing with black-eyed Susan (*Rudbeckia hirta*). Goldfinches feed on the seeds of both plants.

METRIC CONVERSIONS

⅛ inch = 3 millimeters

¼ inch = 6 millimeters

½ inch = 12 millimeters

¾ inch = 2 centimeters

1 inch = 2.5 centimeters

12 inches/1 foot = 30.5 centimeters

2 feet = 61 cm

36 inches/1 yard = 0. 9 meter

4 feet = 122 cm

6 feet = 183 cm

15 feet = 4.6 meters

1 acre = 0.4 hectare

1 mile = 1.6 kilometers

15 miles = 24 kilometers

100 miles = 161 kilometers

2,000 miles = 3,219 kilometers

8 fluid oz/1 cup = 240 milliliters

4 fluid cups/1 quart = 0.94 liter

4 quarts/1 gallon = 3.8 liters

RESOURCES

Internet

American Birding Association
www.aba.org

American Ornithologists' Union
www.aou.org

Bird Studies Canada
www.bsc-eoc.org

Canadian Wildlife Federation
www.cwf-fcf.org

Cornell Lab of Ornithology
www.birds.cornell.edu

Cornell Lab of Ornithology
The Birds of North America Online
bna.birds.cornell.edu/bna

Ladybird Johnson Wildflower Center
The University of Texas, Austin
www.wildflower.org

National Audubon Society
www.audubon.org

National Wildlife Federation
www.nwf.org

Protecting Wild Birds From Cats
www.abc.birds.org/cats

U.S. Fish and Wildlife Service
www.fws.gov

Associations, Societies, and Publications

American Nature Study Society
5881 Cold Brook Road
Homer, NY 13077

American Ornithologists' Union
National Museum of Natural History
Smithsonian Institution
Washington, DC 20560

Backyard Wildlife Association
4920 Liberty Lane
Allentown, PA 18106

Bird Feeders Society
PO Box 225
Mystic, CT 06335
(*Around the Bird Feeder* quarterly magazine)

Bird Friends Society
Essex, CT 06462
(*Wild Bird Guide* quarterly magazine)

Bird Watcher's Digest
Box 110, Dept AJ3
Marietta, OH 45750

Brooks Bird Club, Inc.
707 Warwood Avenue
Wheeling, WV 26003

Canadian Nature Federation
453 Sussex Drive
Ottawa, Ontario
Canada K1N 6Z4

Canadian Wildlife Federation
1673 Carling Avenue
Ottawa, Ontario
Canada K2A 3Z1

Cooper Ornithological Society
Department of Biology
University of California
Los Angeles, CA 90024-1606

Laboratory of Ornithology
Cornell University
159 Sapsucker Woods Road
Ithaca, NY 14850

National Audubon Society
950 Third Avenue
New York, NY 10022
(*Audubon* magazine)

National Institute for Urban Wildlife
10921 Trotting Ridge Way
Columbia, MD 21044-2831

National Wildlife Federation
1412 Sixteenth Street NW
Washington, DC 20036
(*National Wildlife* magazine)

North American Bluebird Society
PO Box 6295
Silver Spring, MD 20906
(*Sialia* quarterly journal)

Superintendent of Documents
US Government Printing Office
Washington, DC 20402
(booklets and bulletins on backyard birds;
write for price list)

US Fish and Wildlife Service
Washington, DC 20240

Wildlife Habitat Canada
1704 Carling Avenue, Suite 301
Ottawa, Ontario
Canada K2A 1C7

Wildlife Management Institute
1101 14th Street NW, Suite 725
Washington, DC 20005

Wildlife Society
5410 Grosvenor Lane
Bethesda, MD 20814

Wilson Ornithological Society
c/o Josselyn Van Tyne Memorial Library
Museum of Zoology
University of Michigan
Ann Arbor, MI 48104

RECOMMENDED READING

Armitage, Allan. *Allan M. Armitage's Native Plants*. Portland, OR: Timber Press, 2006.

Audubon Society Field Guide to North American Trees: Western Region. New York: Alfred A. Knopf, 1980.

Bull, John, and John Farrand, Jr. *The Audubon Society Field Guide to North American Birds: Eastern Region*. New York: Alfred A. Knopf, 1977.

Cox, Jeff. *Landscaping with Nature*. Emmaus, PA: Rodale Press, 1991.

Cullina, William. *Native Trees, Shrubs, and Vines: A Guide to Using, Growing, and Propagating North American Woody Plants*. New York: Houghton Mifflin Harcourt, 2002.

Cullina, William. *Wildflowers: A Guide to Growing and Propagating Native Flowers of North America*. New York: Houghton Mifflin Harcourt, 2000.

Dirr, Michael A. *Dirr's Encyclopedia of Trees and Shrubs*. Portland, OR: Timber Press, 2011

Dirr, Michael A. *Manual of Woody Landscape Plants. 5th ed*. Champaign, IL: Stipes Publishing, 2009.

Field Guide to the Birds of North America. 5th ed. Washington, DC.: National Geographic, 2006.

Field Guide to Western Birds. Boston: Houghton Mifflin, 1972.

Greenlee, John. *The Encyclopedia of Ornamental Grasses*. Emmaus, PA: Rodale Press, 1992.

Greenlee, John, and Saxon Holt. *The American Meadow Garden*. Portland, OR: Timber Press, 2009.

Kress, Stephen W. *The Audubon Society Guide to Attracting Birds*. Ithaca, NY: Cornell University Press, 2006.

Little, Elbert L. *The Audubon Society Field Guide to North American Trees*: Eastern Region. New York: Alfred A. Knopf, 1980.

Leopold. Donald J. *Native Plants of the Northeast*. Portland, OR.: Timber Press, 2005.

Niering, William A. *The Audubon Society Field Guide to North American Wildflowers: Eastern Region*. New York: Alfred A. Knopf, 1979.

Peterson, Roger Tory. *A Field Guide to the Birds of Eastern and Central North America*. 4th ed. Boston: Houghton Mifflin, 1980.

Spellenberg, Richard. *The Audubon Society Field Guide to North American Wildflowers: Western Region*. New York: Alfred A. Knopf, 2001.

Tallamy, Douglas W. *Bringing Nature Home*. Portland, OR: Timber Press, 2007.

Udvardy, Miklos D. F. *The Audubon Society Field Guide to North American Birds: Western Region*. New York: Alfred A. Knopf, 1977.

Wells, Jeffrey. *Birder's Conservation Handbook*. Princeton, NJ: Princeton University Press, 2012.

ACKNOWLEDGMENTS

I would like to thank the following people, staff, and institutions for their generous assistance: individuals Dianne Adams, Corinne Mansell, Ellen Wheat and the team at Timber Press, Minette Layne, Bryan Matthew and Jessica Lee, Kelly Colgan Azar, Linda Tanner, John Beetham, Michael J. Pazzani, Ken Thomas, Steve Berardi, John Brew, Avis Boutell, Joe Decruyenaere, James Ellison, Mike Gifford, Shane Hesson, Jason Hollinger, Amanda Lahale, Matt Lavin, Tim Lenz, Rachel Kramer, Deb Merritt, Will Stuart, Bill Schmoker, Will Cook, and Mr. and Mrs. Philips; the staff at Tyler Arboretum, Cape May State Park, Point Pelee National Park, Rancho Santa Ana Botanic Gardens, Lady Bird Johnson Wildflower Centre, University of California Botanical Gardens at Berkeley, Van Dusen Botanical Gardens of British Columbia, Arizona-Sonora Desert Museum, Boyce Thompson Arboretum in Arizona, and the North Carolina Botanical Garden of University of North Carolina at Chapel Hill; and the University of Texas-Austin Native Plant Data Base, U.S. Department of Agriculture, and the Cornell Lab of Ornithology.

INDEX

PHOTO CREDITS

Deborah Allen, 19 top, 236 top

Kelly Colgan Azar, 19 below, 20 below left, 96 top, 212 below, 244 top, 253 below, 267 top, 363, 369, 389 right, 397

Corrie Barklimore, 237 top

Thomas G. Barnes/USFWS, 41, 97 top right, 228 top

Simon Pierre Barrette, 153

Mike T. Barry, 42

John Beetham, 76 top left, 76 below left, 99 top left, 223 center left, 224 below, 224 center, 251 top, 251 below, 279 center right, 280 center, 281 top, 288 center, 288 below, 321 left

John Benson, 29 below, 161 below, 213 top, 223 top, 222 below right, 289 center, 361, 371

Steve Berardi, 37, 36, 41 below, 246 below

Shanthanu Bhardwaj, 333 right

Ken Bosma, 210

Bill Boulton, 36 top, 292 below

Avis Boutell, 104 below, 280 below

Tom Brandt, 215 below left, 233 top, 233 below, 235 below

John Brew, 202 top, 245 top

Bill Buchanan/USFWS, 232 below

Arthur Chapman, 289 top

Kevin Cole, 223 center right, 259 below

Susan Kelly Cole, 152

Patrick Connally, 151, 375, 425

Will Cook, 40 below, 63 below right, 77 top right, 66 top, 171, 197 top, 206, 207 top, 208 below, 265 top, 266 top

Wendy Cutler, 267 below

Dennis Dahn, 101 below

Mark K. Daly, 276 below

Joe Decruyenaerem, 74 top right, 203 below, 229

Donna Dewhurst/USFWS, 205, 284 below

J. Dexter, 270 below

Giles Douglas, 160

Maja Dumat, 272 below, 293 below

Barbara Eisenstein, 62 below, 230, 290 top, 290 below

James Ellison, 192 top, 211 top, 249 top, 265 below, 283 top, 284 top, 284 center, 285 top, 285 below

Dawn Endico, 292 top

Mimi & Jorg Fleige Wildflower Trails of the San Fransicso Bay Area, 201 top

Brian Gautreau, 216 center

George Gentry/USFWS, 100 below, 101 top

Mike Gifford, 31 top, 231 below, 248

Raymond Gobis, 238 below

Becky Gregory, 222 below left

Christine Haines, 31 below, 212 top

Marlin Harms, 240 below

Shane Hesson, 269 center

Steve Hillebrand/USFWS, 65 below

Jason Hollinger, 75 top right, 97 top left, 99 top right, 104 top, 211 below, 232 top, 250 below

Harry P. Hunt, 231 top

Richard Ingram/Hawkman, 38 top

J. Jebousek/USFWS, 156 below

Steve Jones, 280 top

Manjith Kainickara, 67, 317, 401 left

Keith Kanoti/Maine Forest Service, 288 top

David Kinneer, 65 top

Michael W. Klein Sr/USFWS, 202 below

Sharon Komarow, 204, 62 top

Rachel Kramer, 327

Paul Kusmin, 276 top

Amanda Lahale, 294–295

Matt Lavin, 75 top left, 76 top right, 104 center left, 200 below, 203 center right, 258 top, 269 top, 274 top

Minette Layne, 24, 100 left, 235 centre, 268 top, 272 top, 283 bottom, 318, 396

Jessica Lee, 399

Tim Lenz, 207 below, 227 top 286 below

Carl E. Lewis, 275 below right

Scott Loarie, 238 top, 279 center left

Matt MacGillivray, 193 center, 347, 401 right

Steve Maslowski/USFWS, 25, 194 top, 271 below

Maslowski Wildlife Productions, 154 below, 307, 321 right

Bryan Matthew, 39, 197 below, 225 top, 271 top, 323, 405, 419

Joshua Mayer, 59 below left, 60 top right, 77 top left, 97 below left, 219, 238 top, 269 below

Raphael D. Mazor, 256 top

Michael McCarthy/MSMcCarthy Photography, 155 below

Jim McCullock, 74 below left

Jeff McMillan/USDA-NRCS, 224 below

Charles Melton, 38 below, 246 top, 309, 311

John Menard, Phoenix AZ, 68 top

Dave Menke/USFWS, 234

Deb Merritt, 18, 99 below, 103, 148–149, 159

Brent Meyers, 20 below right, 216 top, 305

Daryl Mitchell, 278 top

Chris M. Morris, 155 top

Oldmantravelling flickr, 277 top

ABOUT THE AUTHOR

George Adams is a writer, landscape designer, wildlife artist, photographer, and traveler. Drawing on a lifelong interest in natural science and concern for the damage inflicted by the built environment on the natural world, he developed a concept for landscaping in which birds and other wildlife are a vital part of the garden's design.

MARY ADAMS